BATTLEGROUND

RELIGION

VOLUME 2 (H–Z)

Edited by Daniel L. Smith-Christopher

GREENWOOD PRESS
Westport, Connecticut • London

Library of Congress Cataloging-in-Publication Data

Battleground religion / edited by Daniel L. Smith-Christopher.
    p. cm.
  Includes bibliographical references and index.
  ISBN 978–0–313–34098–7 (set: alk. paper)
  ISBN 978–0–313–34099–4 (vol. 1: alk. paper)
  ISBN 978–0–313–34100–7 (vol. 2: alk. paper)
  1. Religion and sociology.   I. Smith-Christopher, Daniel L.
  BL60.B315   2009
  200—dc22   2008038760

British Library Cataloguing in Publication Data is available.

Library of Congress Catalog Card Number: 2008038760
ISBN: 978-0-313-34098-7 (set)
    978-0-313-34099-4 (vol. 1)
    978-0-313-34100-7 (vol. 2)

First published in 2009

Greenwood Press, 88 Post Road West, Westport, CT 06881
An imprint of Greenwood Publishing Group, Inc.
www.greenwood.com

Printed in the United States of America

The paper used in this book complies with the
Permanent Paper Standard issued by the National
Information Standards Organization (Z39.48–1984).

10   9   8   7   6   5   4   3   2   1

CONTENTS

GUIDE TO RELATED TOPICS

ART
Animation as a New Medium
Graphic Arts
Prime Time Religion
Science Fiction
Western Cinema
World Religion Aesthetics

CULTURE
Animal Sacrifice
Muslim Minorities in the West
Prime Time Religion
Western Cinema

ECONOMICS AND BUSINESS
Bible and Poverty
Capitalism and Socialism
Gambling and the Religious Conscience
Immigration
Marketing Religion
Prime Time Religion
Religious Publishing
Rock Music and Christian Ethics
Sanctuary Movement

EXTREMISM
Apocalypticism and Nuclear War
"Deep Ecology" and Radical Environmentalism
Female Subordination in Christian Thought
Gospel of Prosperity
Hucksterism and Religious Scandals
Nation of Islam
New Religions as Growth Industry
Right-Wing Extremism

PERSONAL BEHAVIOR
Abortion
Addiction and Recovery
AIDS
Animal Sacrifice
Birth Control and Family Planning
Clergy Sex Abuse Scandal in America
Divorce
Euthanasia and Physician-Assisted Suicide
Gambling and the Religious Conscience
Homosexuality
Jailhouse Conversions
Marriage, Sexuality, and Celibacy
Same-Sex Marriage
Vegetarianism as Religious Witness

POLITICS AND POLITICAL IDEAS
Bible and Poverty
Capitalism and Socialism
Christian Zionism
Genocide
Islamic Nationalism
Just War
Liberation Theology
Nationalism, Militarism, and Religion
Personal Pacifism versus Political Nonviolence
Religious Conversion
Religious Diplomacy
Separation of Church and State
Terrorism

RELIGIOUS IMPACT ON SOCIETY
Anti-Catholicism and American Politics
Apocalypticism and Nuclear War
Christian Zionism
Civil Disobedience

HEALTH REFORM MOVEMENTS

Since time immemorial, religion and medicine have been interrelated, religion often setting the parameters for what was considered to be appropriate in the treatment of illnesses of the human body and mind. In Western medicine, two trends emerged: the professional practice of medicine, generally supported by the affluent classes, and folk medicine, most commonly practiced among the peasant populations. Over the years these two trends have existed in tension and, at times, have drawn on each other. The numerous health reform movements that have arisen in Europe and the United States have been influenced by Chinese, ayurvedic, as well as Christian philosophies and theological positions, often in conflict with mainstream medical practice, which in the United States has found itself in tension with alternative medical approaches that are growing in popularity as "regular" medicine becomes more focused on symptoms with more sophisticated and expensive healing procedures.

ROOTS OF THE JUDEO-CHRISTIAN HEALTH
AND RELIGION CONNECTION

The Jewish Tradition

Although the Torah is the basic religious document of Judaism, most of its directives regarding medical ethics and practice come from rabbinic literature. The principal source of rabbinic discussion on medical matters is the Mishnah (220 c.e.) and the Palestinian and Babylonian Talmuds (400 and 500 c.e., respectively). In the Jewish tradition, since God created the body, the body is not only good, but it displays God's power and infinite goodness. Unlike other religious traditions, the body was not a *prison house* for the soul, but the means by which God's will could be fulfilled, if the body was treated correctly.

The human body is *loaned* to each human being and, therefore, they are required to care for it. Hygiene, diet, exercise, and sleep were matters of legal obligation, not just suggestions for better living. Such notable rabbis as Hillel and Maimonides laid out the theological undergirdings of the body's care, and Jews were to observe the dietary restrictions indicated in the biblical books of Leviticus and Deuteronomy. Nor was care for the body necessarily related to its contribution to good health.

Causes of disease, according to the Talmud, were blood, bile, air, contaminated food, bodily discharges, and insects (particularly worms and flies). Excessive eating, drinking, fasting, and sexual activity were also seen as disease producing. Psychological causes of disease were also taken into account—fear and changes in routine, for example.

Before the Greek introduction of a kind of secular medicine, Jewish rabbis forbade treatments used by pagan practitioners whose use of magic were seen as inconsistent with a belief in God. Treatments approved by rabbis included bloodletting, warm and cold compresses, sweating, sunbaths, hydrotherapy, psychotherapy, massages, and exercises. Wine was considered to be the most healing of medicines, but herbs were widely used in the form of powders and liquids. Clean air and sunlight were also considered among the best cures.

By the seventeenth and eighteenth centuries, Jewish doctors were guided by the practices of the time, and not by Talmudic instructions, now seen as outdated and even dangerous.

Christian Era

The core of New Testament theology was that God had given salvation to the human race through Jesus Christ who, in turn, had restored the broken fellowship with God. It was revolutionary as a religious tradition in that it presented itself as a religion of healing. It was the religion of the sick and afflicted, promising them physical and spiritual restoration. Caring for the sick was a Christian imperative. For the afflicted, though sickness and suffering were to be the lot of the Christian, God's grace would sustain them through it all. Such suffering was, after all, only temporary and inconsequential when compared with the joys of heaven awaiting them.

The Gospels' treatment of illness revolves around Jesus's miraculous healings. The Acts and Epistles again underscore examples of miraculous interventions (the blind man at the Gate Beautiful, the resurrection of Dorcas, and others). The writings of St. Paul suggest that more importance is to be given to the cultivation of godliness than physical training (I Timothy 4:7–8), but I Corinthians 3:16 makes it clear the our bodies are sacred ("God's temple"), and in II Cor. 6:16 the concept is underscored once again: "For we are the temple of the living God."

The New Testament carries over from the Old Testament the notion that illness derives from sin, or that it is a punishment for sin. Jesus seemed to suggest that illness also came from demon possession (Luke 13:11,16). Far from disparaging the body, as did some Greek modes of thinking, New Testament Christianity honored the body as God's creation that would one day inherit eternal life. But care for one's own body was to be subsumed to care for the suffering of others. Jesus was the supreme example of selfless charity in the care of the hungry, thirsty, sick, and imprisoned (Matthew 25:35–40).

Taking up this Christian imperative, Christian hospitals began to appear soon after Christianity was legalized in Rome. Another outgrowth of the Christian's view of the human body as God's creation was the notion of inherent human worth, demanding that human dignity be protected. Therefore, abortion, infanticide, euthanasia, suicide, and murder were strongly opposed.

During the post-Apostolic period, Christians rejected some forms of secular medicine and sought healing principally through prayer, the laying on of hands, and exorcism. Nevertheless, early Christian fathers such as Origen, Clement of Alexandria, and John Chrysostom saw physicians and medicine as gifts of God.

THE MIDDLE AGES AND THE COUNTERREFORMATION

The Middle Ages were dominated by the Christian Catholic church, increasingly influenced by pagan asceticism, magic and superstition, the veneration of relics, and the growing influence of holy men. Dualism—whereby the body came to be disdained in preference for the spirit—was an outgrowth of the new asceticism that encouraged celibacy, virginity, and contempt for the material world. The idea that disease is caused by demons and the use of magic in healing persisted throughout the Middle Ages as did healings based on miraculous intervention by holy men and women called *saints*.

The Church's stance in the face of the Black Death (1348–1349) was a temporary concession to physicians as a response to an urgent need, but the plague was still seen as a God's punishment for sin. Special indulgences were conceded to clergy ministering to the sick.

Meanwhile, the widespread Church corruption that was already being addressed in Italy and the Netherlands, for example, resulted in the Protestant Reformation led by Martin Luther and a cry for reform of abuses. As for its position on medicine, the Church walked a fine line at the ensuing Council of Trent (1545–1563) between secular medicine and miracles, even superstition, preserving in this way its traditions.

HEALTHFUL LIVING: THE NINETEENTH AND TWENTIETH CENTURIES

The nineteenth and early twentieth centuries in the United States were characterized by four Protestant Christian revivals called *Great Awakenings*. The First Great Awakening ran roughly from the 1730s to the 1740s, the second from around 1820 to 1830, the third from 1880 to 1900 and the fourth, from the 1960s to the 1970s. The last three have had the most impact on health issues in American life.

Some scholars explain these revival phenomena as cultural revitalizations that arise at the end of one cycle of beliefs and values, to be replaced or enriched by those of a new generation. Traditional family values are challenged by new opportunities, usually available to youth. These cultural revolutions are generally marked by the rise of numerous new denominations, sects, and religions.

Generally speaking, "awakenings" look back to an idealized time of peace free from "evil" manifestations. Some themes of such movements have been women's rights, sexual purity, the environment, physical exercise, diet, or a return to nature. Health reform has often accompanied these times of awakening that attempt to change the "bad habits" of previous generations, having to do with the abuse of alcohol, tobacco, sexuality, food, and physical fitness.

Health reform, or what Prof. Ruth Engs calls clean living movements can be divided into four phases: (1) moral persuasion, setting out arguments in favor of the change; (2) coercion, through which attempts are made to legislate the new behaviors in some way; (3) a backlash to strategies of coercion; and (4) complacency after failure to impose the reforms (Engs 2000).

JACKSONIAN ERA HEALTH REFORM (1830–1860)

This movement coincided with a wave of Protestant revivalism and aimed its darts at the ills of drinking rum and other strong drink. Most active in the New England states and western New York, the movement created two new religions: the Church of Jesus Christ of Latter-day Saints and the Seventh-day Adventists. Both religions incorporated healthful living as part of their religious creed.

Together with a perfectionist tendency deriving from a millennialist mentality that gave urgency to preparedness for the Second Coming of Christ, these religions believed that illness was neither a punishment from God, nor an ill to be born stoically. Disease is avoidable by humans taking positive action to prevent it. Health and salvation soon became one and the same in importance.

In general, the attitudes of Mormons and Adventists toward illness arose from their mistrust of orthodox physicians. In *Word of Wisdom*, Smith's treatise on health and the fundamental health document of the Mormon church, he advances the virtues of hygiene and domestic health, as well as abstinence from the use of tobacco and liquor. The *Word of Wisdom* advised moderation in the use of meat and wine, but by the early twentieth century, advice became mandate for regular membership in the church.

Health reform in the Adventist church came chiefly through visions given to Ellen White, with subjects ranging from abstinence from liquor and tobacco and stimulants, such as coffee and tea, to vegetarianism. Sickness was to be addressed exclusively with natural remedies such as sunlight, fresh air, exercise, water, and proper diet. Like the Mormons, Adventists disdained the fashionable corsets of the day in favor of more practical dress, and spoke in favor of hygiene as a means to safeguard health. In hundreds of articles, and in a book titled *The Ministry of Healing,* Ellen White championed all the health reform issues of the day.

Under the influence and guidance of White, the Western Health Reform Institute opened in 1866. A decade later, under the able leadership of Adventist-raised

John Harvey Kellogg, the institute was renamed Battle Creek Sanitarium, and soon became the center of the second wave of health reform. Of the new "health foods" served at the sanitarium to such dignitaries as presidents Taft and Rockefeller and business tycoons, J.C. Penney and Montgomery Ward, granola and other precooked cereals, peanut butter, and other nut-based meat substitutes emerged, and have ever since formed part of the American diet along with the name "*Kellogg*."

Both Mormon and Adventist health reform was set against the Temperance Movement that arose from an American cultural clash between Northern and Southern European attitudes toward drinking. Drinking habits of Roman Catholic immigrants coming into the country during the nineteenth century clashed with those of the native-born Protestant mainstream. The two most influential Christian physiologists, William Andrus Alcott (1798–1859), and Sylvester Graham (1794–1851), went beyond the drinking problem to promote exercise, cleanliness, fresh air, and proper diet as means to health.

Likewise, an antitobacco movement developed between 1830 and 1860 as a result of the Second Great Awakening. Tobacco was seen as a "gateway" drug to other more harmful substances. Stimulants such as tea and coffee were denounced, because they increased sexual appetites, interfered with digestion, and drained the body of vital energy. And spices such as cinnamon, mustard, vinegar, ginger, and salt were thought to overstimulate the appetite.

Another outgrowth of the Second Great Awakening was the women's rights movement, initially linked to health reform. Victorian mores that denied women proper medical care attracted women to the health movement. The dress reform also grew out of concerns for women's health, with Amelia Jenks Bloomer creating the famous *bloomer* associated with the women's rights movement. Bloomers, the combination pant-skirt named after its inventor, Amelia Bloomer, grew out of the women-led abolitionist, suffrage, and temperance reform movements of the nineteenth century and was meant to address the unhealthful skirts that dragged on the filthy streets of Victorian America, perpetuating the common illness of the time. Other issues addressed during this reform period were human sexuality (birth control, abortion, masturbation, and homosexuality), phrenology (eugenics, or the role of inheritance on health), and the role of immigration on American public health (with the outbreaks of cholera in the middle to end of the nineteenth century).

THE THIRD CLEAN LIVING MOVEMENT (1880–1920)

This movement grew out of the religious revival called the Third Great Awakening that responded to the need for a spirituality to address the changing life of American society with its rapid urbanization, immigration, and industrialization.

To this period belongs the Social Gospel Movement out of which arose the Young Men's Christian Association (YMCA) in response to the perceived "feminization" of Protestantism during the Victorian era. Church brotherhoods came into being to cultivate the manly physical virtues in the Christian man. Sports and physical fitness became central.

The period between 1890 and 1930 was one of the most experimental spiritual periods, including sects based on Eastern philosophies and mental healing. Theosophy, Baha'i, the Vedanta Society, hypnotism, and Spiritualism begin to gain followers. Out of the New-Thought movement emerged Mary Baker Eddy and the Christian Science religion, with its emphasis on mental healing. On the other hand, the poorer and immigrant classes were developing their own religious response to the rapid social and theological changes. The fundamentalist revivalist movement consisted of three factions: (1) the *holiness revivals* within the Methodist tradition that created the Salvation Army and the Nazarenes, (2) Pentecostalism with its speaking in tongues and faith healing, and (3) Baptist *dispensationalism* that encouraged resisting *secular humanism*.

Other outgrowths of this period were the Physical Culture Movement (gymnastics and physical education), the Anti-Saloon Movement that resulted in Prohibition, the Eighteenth Amendment, the creation of the Women's Christian Temperance Union, the Anti-Tobacco Crusade, the *Purity* or antiprostitution movement (to prevent sexually transmitted diseases), eugenic sterilization (to prevent passing on severe mental and physical health problems, including alcoholism), and the Birth Control Movement with Margaret Sanger. The Pure-Food and Anti-Drug movements had their beginnings during this time, and contributed to the passage of various acts controlling the adulteration of food and the use of narcotics. In June of 1906, Congress passed the Pure Food and Drug Act, and a law requiring the inspection of animals in meat-packing plants. A call for honest labeling and patenting of medicines were other strategies that were meant to ensure public health.

The leading cause of death during this period was chronic disease, chiefly tuberculosis and influenza. A Tuberculosis movement began with Edward Trudeau (1847–1915) who, stricken with the disease, went to upstate New York's Adirondack region to spend his last days. Rather than die, he recovered, and began to treat others at a sanatorium he set up there. Public health measures increased during the first decade of the twentieth century to protect the public from the spread of the disease, and national associations and societies were established to monitor these laws.

The term *preventive medicine* arose around the 1890s. It was linked to immunization and sanitation gains made during the second half of the nineteenth century.

THE FOURTH CLEAN LIVING MOVEMENT (1970–PRESENT)

This religious revival that began toward the end of the 1950s and early 1960s drew on widely diverse spiritual traditions, including occultism, paganism, and Eastern mystical religions. By the 1980s this movement had the name of *New Age* and included concerns about diet and alternative and holistic health. The health reform crusades that began in the 1970s and 1980s continue having their effects today.

The Christian Right grew out of the charismatic churches that sprouted all over the country, attracting those seeking a more personal and passionate religion. These churches advocated a return to a more traditional morality. Many of the advocates of grassroots health and moral reform were associated with these religious groups. This conservative tendency found its expression in the 1970s with the Moral Majority and, in the 1980s, with the Christian Coalition, among others, who were less interested in health and healing than promoting their religio-political agenda against abortion, pornography, illicit drugs, and homosexuality.

Together with this wave of conservatism, an eclectic wave of spirituality, inspired by Eastern spiritual traditions, occultism, and neo-spiritualism was gaining strength with its agenda to recreate a new society. Transcendental meditation, tarot cards and astrology, and practices based on Celtic, Greek, and Norse mythology, sustained a kind of neo-paganism. Adherents of these religions embraced alternative healing, Eastern-inspired exercise, and vegetarian diets.

The last two decades of the twentieth century saw the rise of the alternative medicine and holistic health movements. After World War II, conventional medicine became increasingly technological, raising health care costs and ignoring the needs and rights of patients. In response, many Americans began to seek alternative treatments. By the 1970s, these alternative and unorthodox modes of healing gave rise to the holistic health and wellness movement, concerned chiefly with the prevention of disease.

The 1970s saw the appearance of antibiotic-resistant diseases, the HIV/AIDs epidemic, and the lack of cures for chronic conditions, including the "new" autoimmune diseases, all of which further whittled away at confidence in mainstream medicine. Eventually, physicians such as Herbert Benson, Dean Ornish, and Andrew Weil began to incorporate alternative healing techniques into their practices, and the federal government established the Office of Alternative Medicine (OAM) within the National Institutes of Health (NIH) in order to explore what they called "unconventional" medical practices.

Alternative medicine has been divided into six categories by the OAM: (1) mind-body interventions (meditation, imagery, hypnosis, yoga, prayer, etc.), (2) bioelectromagnetic (laser and radio-frequency hyperthermia), (3) alternative systems of medical practice (acupuncture, homeopathy), (4) manual healing (massage therapy, chiropractic), (5) pharmacological and biological treatments (alternative drugs and vaccines), and (6) diet and nutrition medicine (herbs, vegetarian or vegan diets).

See also Faith-Based Health Care, Religious Morality, and Institutional Policies; Universal Health Care as a Religious Ethical Issue.

Further Reading: Buettner, Dan. "The Secrets of Long Life." *National Geographic* (November 2005): 2–26; Engs, Ruth Clifford. *Clean Living Movements: American Cycles of Health Reform.* Westport, CT: Praeger, 2000; Gevitz, Norman, ed. *Other Healers: Unorthodox Medicine in America.* Washington, D.C.: Johns Hopkins University Press, 1988; Harakas, Stanley S. *Health and Medicine in the Eastern Orthodox Tradition.* New

York: Crossroads, 1990; Hubbard, Reuben A. *Historical Perspectives of Religion and Health.* Berrien Springs, MI: Andrews University Press, 1986; Koenig, Harold George, Michael E. McCullough, and David B. Larson. *Handbook of Religion and Health.* New York: Oxford University Press, 2001; Koenig, Harold George, Michael E. McCullough, and David B. Larson. *The Healing Connection: The Story of a Physician's Search for the Link Between Faith and Science.* Philadelphia: Templeton Foundation, 2000; Marty, Martin E. *Health and Medicine in the Lutheran Tradition.* New York: Crossroads, 1983; Marty, Martin E. and Kenneth L. Vaux. *Health /Medicine and the Faith Traditions: An Inquiry into Religion and Medicine.* Philadelphia: Fortress Press, 1982; Numbers, Ronald L. and Darrel W. Amundsen, eds. *Caring and Curing: Health and Medicine in the Western Religious Traditions.* New York: MacMillan, 1986; Plante, Thomas G. and Allen C. Sherman. *Faith and Health: Psychological Perspectives.* New York: Guilford Press, 2001; Reid, George W. *A Sound of Trumpets: Americans, Adventists, and Health Reform.* Washington, D.C.: Review and Herald Publishing Association, 1982; Spencer, Colin. *Vegetarianism: A History.* New York: Four Walls Eight Windows, 1993, 2000.

Lourdes E. Morales-Gudmundsson

HIGHER INTELLIGENCE ANIMALS

Do unique religious ethics apply to the treatment of some animals in a unique way? What about those animals that are proven to have a capacity for higher intellectual ability? As we learn more about the mental capabilities of higher intelligence animals such as the great apes (gorillas, chimpanzees, and bonobos) and cetaceans (dolphins)—some have argued that humans have greater ethical responsibilities toward such *sentient species* (that is *thinking species*), while others argue that *species loyalty*—or showing a preference for human beings over all animals—remains an acceptable religious value.

RESEARCH ON ANIMAL INTELLIGENCE

In 1661, Samuel Pepys, a member of Parliament at the time, happened to see what he called a "baboon" (probably a chimpanzee) on the London docks. In his famous diaries, he speculated that such great apes may be able to develop the ability to communicate with human beings. He would hardly guess how far this modest suggestion would be taken in the late twentieth century, and the issues that this would raise.

Scientists who work with chimpanzees (*Pan troglodyte*) frequently point out that humans and chimpanzees share 98.5 percent of the same genetic patterns (some estimates are higher, some lower). Indeed, the genetic "gap" between humans and chimpanzees is closer than the genetic similarities between, for example, Asian and African elephants. In the case of dolphins, the comparison with human species on the genetic level are obviously quite divergent, but here the relevant comparison is the ratio of *brain size to body size*—almost identical between humans and dolphins, with brain sizes and weights also almost identical. Do such comparisons mean that these particular species of animals are in a unique moral category apart from other animals in the world?

ANCIENT JEWISH AND CHRISTIAN TRADITIONS AND ANIMALS

According to the famous *Creation story* of Genesis, the sea and air animals were created on the fifth day, and land animals were created with human beings on the sixth day. But humans received a particular distinction in this ancient account, and theologians of both the Jewish and Christian tradition have debated about the precise meaning of humans being created in the "image of God" (Genesis 1:27). While the precise meaning of this "image" is debated, the Jewish and Christian traditions agree that at the very least, it means that humans were intended to occupy a unique and special place in the creation.

One of the religious and philosophical storms of debate between materialist evolution (all is merely chance based on the behavior of atoms and cells) and religious-based ideas of "creation" (without defining the means of creation), is that evolutionary theory tends to reduce the differences between humans and other living species, and question the privileged position of humans in the general scheme of nature. Some forms of evolutionary theory suggest that humans are simply one among many species, and although presently dominant, are no more "deserving" of life than any other species. Western religious traditions, however, have always maintained that humans have a special status, but then debate whether this special status allows humans to treat everything else in creation as "raw materials," or whether there are responsibilities that are connected to that unique status as created in the "image" of God. The Genesis accounts, after all, also suggest that humans are dominant:

> God blessed them, and God said to them, "Be fruitful and multiply, and fill the earth and subdue it; and have dominion over the fish of the sea and over the birds of the air and over every living thing that moves upon the earth." God said, "See, I have given you every plant yielding seed that is upon the face of all the earth, and every tree with seed in its fruit; you shall have them for food. And to every beast of the earth, and to every bird of the air, and to everything that creeps on the earth, everything that has the breath of life, I have given every green plant for food." And it was so. (Genesis 1:28–30)

Jewish and Christian theologians debate, however, whether this passage is a *blank check* or *license* to use the physical world and exploit animals in any way that humans may wish. Some religious scholars have argued that there is an ethic of responsibility implied in this passage by arguing that the meaning of having *dominion* suggests rule, as in the rule of a king or political leader. The importance of this interpretation is simply to point to the biblical tradition that strongly suggests that all rulers must not ever be cruel or despotic, and that they must take just and compassionate care of those over whom they have "dominion" (1 Kings 10:9; Psalms 72, etc.), in short, dominion can imply compassion, not cruelty.

The biblical tradition is also well aware of cruelty to animals: in the charming story of Numbers Chapter 22, Balaam's donkey is allowed to "speak" to Balaam while he is riding it, and the donkey complains about mistreatment! Animals were allowed to have a "Sabbath rest" (Leviticus 25). The twentieth century Jewish philosopher and rabbi, Abraham Kook, believed that many of the biblical dietary constraints are designed to keep alive a sense of reverence for life so that people would eventually return to vegetarian diets. He also believed that the future "Messianic age" will be vegetarian. He based this on the words of Isaiah (11:69): " . . . the wolf will dwell with the lamb . . . the lion will eat straw like the ox . . . and no one shall hurt or destroy in all of God's holy mountain."

In the Christian tradition, even though there is very little in the New Testament about animals specifically, in early Christian folklore outside of the Bible, there is a charming story of St. Paul converting a lion, and when the same animal later turns up in a Roman coliseum where Christians are being fed to lions, the animal astonishes the Roman audience by refusing to eat Paul (*The Martyrdom of St. Pelagia*, second century?).

WERE THERE "HIGHER ANIMALS" IN THE BIBLE?

Despite these and other passages often cited as a religious basis for compassion toward animals, it is also observed by those biblical scholars interested in these issues (e.g., Linzey and Regan 1988; Waldau 2002) that there does not seem to be much evidence in the biblical tradition of a special awareness of uniquely intelligent animals, and thus any basis for *particular responsibilities* unique to those species such as the great apes or dolphins. In the case of the apes, however, this is likely to be from simple lack of contact with these species of higher apes, whose habitats in central Africa were far from the Mediterranean lands of the Bible, both Old and New Testaments. Some biblical scholars have tentatively suggested that cetaceans like dolphins might be implied in at least one use of the generic term for large sea-creatures, usually translated in English as *Leviathan*. This famous example is Psalm 104:26, because of its reference to obvious behavior of dolphins near sailors:

> Yonder is the sea, great and wide, creeping things innumerable are there, living things both small and great. There go the ships, *and Leviathan that you formed to sport in it.* (Psalm 104:25–26)

In general, however, the Christian tradition seems to have accepted the general Greek philosophical view that argued for a clear division between humans capable of "reason," rational thought, and communication, and all the other "beasts" who are not (Aristotle). It is precisely this radical separation between humanity and *all* other species that is now under serious question, as a direct result of research on the intelligence of "higher animals"—and most particularly great apes and dolphins.

EXAMPLES OF LEARNING IN GREAT APES

There are three species of apes that have received the most laboratory work related to teaching communication and language skills. Chimpanzees (*Pan troglodytes*) and bonobos (*Pan paniscus*) have received the most training, but the famous Koko is a mountain gorilla. The accomplishments of much of this research is impressive, and at times, controversial. To date, the most common forms of communication experiments have used three methods of communication: (1) American sign language, (2) lexigrams (signs on a keyboard the animal selects, and must select in proper order), and (3) plastic magnetized symbols that can be arranged on a board.

There are four particularly important examples of primate research noted here. In 1966, Beatrix and Allen Gardner begin to teach Washoe, a chimpanzee born in West Africa in 1965. By 1969, the Gardners reported in *Science* that Washoe recognized 85 signs resembling those of the American sign language. Further, Washoe could identify objects based on pictures correctly 86 to 96 percent of the time—pure guessing would be 4 to 15 percent. Washoe learned to apply the term *open* to anything he wanted opened, including cans, boxes, and even items whose names he was not taught. Perhaps even more impressive, Washoe taught another chimpanzee, Loulis, over 40 signs in addition to the seven Loulis was taught by human trainers.

By 1968, Ann and David Premack begin to teach Sarah, a chimpanzee, to communicate with plastic symbols lined up on a magnetic board. Similarly, Duane and Sue Savage-Rumbaugh began to teach a bonobo, Lana, to use a lexigram board. Lana was able to arrange signs in proper order, correct mistakes, and even ask for names of specific objects. In 1986, Sue Savage-Rumbaugh published on her earlier work with chimpanzees Sherman and Austin, who were able to communicate with each other through a keyboard, and correctly instruct each other on methods of retrieving food that they then shared between themselves. The most famous bonobo subject, however, was Kanzi, whom Dr. Savage-Rumbaugh worked with in the 1980s. Kanzi, at age 8, could correctly respond to verbal instructions without seeing the trainer 74 percent of the time—compared to a three-year-old child who responded to the same instructions correctly 65 percent of the time.

Perhaps the most celebrated case of all, however, began in 1972, when Dr. Francine Patterson began to work with Koko, an African mountain gorilla born on July 4, 1971. Very early in the process, it was noted that Koko was able to apply lipstick using a mirror, and was aware of herself in a mirror sufficient to touch ink spots on her face when they applied without her prior knowledge. Dr. Patterson claimed that Koko was proficient with over 200 signs in American sign language at 5 years of age, and even made up names for objects shown her for the first time, such as "elephant baby" for a Pinocchio doll, and "eye-hat" for a mask. School children across North America and in Asia know her name, and know the famous story of Koko's attachment to a kitten. Koko is now using over 700 signs.

While it is overly-sentimental to compare these apes closely to humans, or even to suggest that they actually understand human language, these are points that are never argued by the researchers themselves. What is beyond dispute is that the level of communication and interaction with humans has achieved an astonishing level of sophistication unimaginable as late as the mid-twentieth century. That such a realization ought to place these species in a unique category of animals in relation to humans seems almost impossible to dispute, at least

THE DECLARATION ON GREAT APES

In 1993, a group of scientists, ethicists, and philosophers who formed The Great Ape Project issued the following *Declaration on Great Apes*. The Great Ape Project is hoping to encourage the UN to adopt the provisions of this statement:

1. The Right to Life

The lives of members of the community of equals are to be protected. Members of the community of equals may not be killed except in very strictly defined circumstances, for example, self-defense.

2. The Protection of Individual Liberty

Members of the community of equals are not to be arbitrarily deprived of their liberty; if they should be imprisoned without due legal process, they have the right to immediate release. The detention of those who have not been convicted of any crime, or of those who are not criminally liable, should be allowed only where it can be shown to be for their own good, or necessary to protect the public from a member of the community who would clearly be a danger to others if at liberty. In such cases, members of the community of equals must have the right to appeal, either directly or, if they lack the relevant capacity, through an advocate, to a judicial tribunal.

3. The Prohibition of Torture

The deliberate infliction of severe pain on a member of the community of equals, either wantonly, or for an alleged benefit to others, is regarded as torture, and is wrong.

Source: www.greatapeproject.org/declaration.php

among the popular and scholarly supporters of human-nonhuman communication research. Why would religious persons object? The debate seems to be complicated on three levels: (1) scholarly skepticism; (2) economic and political implications; and (3) philosophical debates, sometimes associated with evolution on the one hand, or vegetarianism on the other.

SCHOLARLY SKEPTICAL RESPONSE TO ANIMAL COMMUNICATION EXPERIMENTS

There have been scholarly skeptics of the claims that apes understand language. In 1979, for example, David Terrace reported largely negative results with his chimpanzee, Nim Chimsky, and his writings had a devastating impact on subsequent funding for, and interest in, communication with primates, until more recently. However, at least one major "skeptic," Dr. Thomas Soebeck, reportedly reversed his initial opposition in 2002, and stated that Savage-Rumbaugh's work, in particular, deserves recognition. Joel Wallman's work, *Aping Language* (1992), remains the most widely cited critical study that challenges the notion that apes, specifically, are actually learning language in any meaningful sense. The skeptical response is largely based on the idea that apes are simply learning to respond to positive feedback that results in their being fed, and furthermore, they are responding in ways that are only occasionally more interesting than similar behaviors in other "lower" animals.

Furthermore, the notion that animals are "thinking" is considered pure sentimental attachment by "animal lovers," and not true and careful science. It should be clearly stated, however, that serious researchers, such as Savage-Rumbaugh, the Gardners, and Peterson, have all vigorously responded to these criticisms in academic literature, and have insisted on maintaining careful laboratory standards in their research to resist precisely these accusations. But laboratory methods are not the only grounds for objecting to many of the more positive interpretations of primate-human communication studies.

ECONOMIC AND POLITICAL IMPLICATIONS

If it is accepted that dolphins and great apes do indeed deserve a unique moral category of animals in relation to humans, and even are deserving of certain "rights," the economic results of these "rights" become controversial. Many companies involved in the tuna fishing industry, in particular, have already been forced to make costly adjustments to large-scale net-fishing methods in the open seas in order to minimize killing dolphins. Further, some cultures are resistant to giving up eating habits that have a long history (e.g., dolphin meat is served in Japan, along with whale meat, etc.). Are dolphins, then, worth the foreign policy problems and economic difficulties that would be created if, for example, the United States adopted a stronger pro-Dolphin stand that began to alienate Asian business partners? It is also argued that a strong education campaign to discourage certain eating practices would be costly, and might even be misconstrued as interfering in the *cultural rights* of some Asian nations.

Similarly, African nations often demand increased foreign aid from Western nations in exchange for the costs of policing the habitats of great apes in central African states against poaching. Part of the problem is the cost of setting aside vast tracts of forest land as preserves, rather than opening up these tracts to forestry and mining, as well as urban development. While the tourist industry may have the economic benefits to eventually provide steady streams of income for African nations who are willing to set aside large wildlife reserves, in the short term there is too little political stability in these regions to build the financial and physical foundations (hotels, restaurants, etc.) for a thriving tourist trade.

Even more immediately serious, however, is the illegal trade in *bushmeat*. The term *bushmeat* refers to all forms of African wildlife caught and eaten for food, and the practice is especially prominent in towns, villages, and major poverty-stricken areas of Central Africa. It is estimated that 30 million people live within the forested regions of Central Africa, and of these, 30 to 40 percent of these peoples rely on the meat of wildlife as a primary source of animal protein (Bushmeat Crisis Task Force, http://www.bushmeat.org/portal/server.pt).

The bushmeat trade includes all kinds of forest and jungle animals, but hunting monkeys and apes is also a prominent part of the legal, and illegal, trade in bushmeat generated by increasing human population growth. Changes in these economic practices would require economic and political cooperation among forestry industries, mining industries, and the introduction and maintenance of alternative forms of protein in either vegetable/fruit production, or raising farming animals for consumption, as opposed to rare and wild species. The potential financial beneficiaries of these new policies may not always be the same companies and businesses that now benefit from the present market in bushmeat, and should the resistance to the continued market in bushmeat gain momentum as an African, or even international issue, there is likely to be a period of serious struggle between the interests of established cultural practices (again, including a matter of *cultural tastes* as well as traditions) and established businesses (those making money under the present practices), against the newer businesses that would seek to build on more conservation-minded principles, often by marketing other kinds of products. Finally, there is often an issue that indigenous peoples feel *violated* by outside interests that appear to be "interfering" with the traditional life and practices of those who have lived on bushmeat for generations. Again, the economics of mounting major re-education campaigns have both political and economic implications.

RELIGIOUS AND PHILOSOPHICAL ISSUES

The final issue that complicates specifically religious involvement in efforts to consider *higher animals* in a separate moral category is *guilt by association* with evolutionary debates on the one side, and more extreme advocates for animal rights that insist on full commitment to vegetarianism, on the other side.

It is largely the case that research dedicated to communication with higher intelligence animals is often championed by biological and philosophical Evolutionists. In the minds of these advocates, to establish the intelligence of apes (even more than dolphins) is considered to be evidence to further establish the arguments for human evolution from earlier primate species in history—so that human-primate communication is almost seen as "communicating with our past." Clearly, some religious inspired resistance to the implications of animal intelligence, are influenced more by the potential *use and interpretation* of this research, rather than the research itself.

If Christians, for example, believe that humanity was made in the *image of God*, and that this "image" is mainly concerned with the ability to have a "consciousness" or engage in rational thought, then research on communication with higher animals threatens a clear, and age-old separation, between humans and animals. It would suggest a third category—something like *near humans*, at least near *enough* to be in a special moral category that confers certain rights to preservation and existence, and certainly rights against being the subjects of painful or lethal medical research for the benefit of the human species alone. The celebrated primatologist, Dr. Jane Goodal, has raised questions about any confinement of great apes under any circumstances. It seems difficult to argue that biblical writers would never have allowed such a *third category* if, as seems conclusively to be the case, they had no experience of these species of creatures in any sustained or regular manner. This does not mean, however, that such an additional *third* category between "animal" and "human" could not be determined based on biblical and religious inspired principles.

ANIMALS' RIGHTS AND THE PROBLEMS OF THE "THIRD CATEGORY"

The reason that such a *third category* would seem necessary to some religious thinkers would be the need to preserve the argument in favor of these *higher animals* so that the unique issues are not *swallowed up* by the more general ethical arguments for animal rights for all species. Such generalized arguments, for example, would be typically used by those arguing for a full endorsement of vegetarianism by granting *all* animals equal rights to life in the world alongside human beings. Such is the position taken by the Jain religion, for example, and certain forms of Hinduism. But a rejection of this *extreme case* does not thereby remove the potential need for a newly articulated "religious responsibility toward Koko" (to put it in somewhat emotional terms). Furthermore, increasing numbers of Christians and Jews are making a case for vegetarian eating—but this debate is clearly not directly concerned with higher intelligence species.

The wider debates about animal rights in general, however, tend to avoid the special case of the higher animals. Those who argue for full equality of animal rights as against human rights, do not wish to give up some of their strongest examples—namely the higher animals—who help make their case more effectively than, say, arguing for compassion for rabbits. Those who argue against such full animal rights advocates, also avoid the separate case of the higher animals, and argue in general for an acceptable loyalty to the human species over all others. The general issue of animal versus human rights, however, is a different debate.

Is it possible to argue for the unique rights of *higher animals* without advocating similar rights for all animals? While it may be difficult to establish set criteria for making such a difference between the rights of rats and the rights of mountain gorillas, it would seem that contemporary research on mental capacities of higher animals are forcing the issue. The present very elementary understanding of *precisely* the differences between the mental capacities of housecats, as opposed to dolphins, is simply too meager to begin to establish clear and widely accepted criteria—but this does not mean that such criteria will not eventually become clear and possible to articulate in public debate.

It should be theoretically possible to ground such a third category of higher animals by pooling what we know about the biological, neurological, and psychological differences between species in order to inform a theologically significant difference between acceptably herding cows for food, and unacceptably killing chimpanzees for bushmeat.

It is furthermore not necessarily the case that Christian, or other religious acceptance of such a proposed *third category* of unique rights granted to higher animals, would mean that all the other ethical, nonethical, or other philosophical conclusions advocated by materialist evolutionists must also be accepted.

In religious debates in the West, there is definitely the fear of an ethical domino effect connected to animal rights' debates. This fear seems to be directed at arguments that would seem to lead toward either evolutionary materialism, or full vegetarianism. It is clear, however, from the growing literature surrounding both human-primate, and human-cetacean communication, and the growing literature around religious conservationism, and animal rights, that this issue will become increasingly urgent in the twenty-first century.

See also Evolution versus Creationism in Public Schools.

Further Reading: Bushmeat Crisis Task Force. http://www.bushmeat.org/portal/server.pt; Chapple, Christopher. *Nonviolence to Animals, Earth, and Self in Asian Traditions.* New York: State University of New York Press, 1993; Corbey, Raymond. *The Metaphysics of Apes.* Cambridge: Cambridge University Press, 2005; Gould, James L., and Carol Grant Gould. *The Animal Mind.* New York: W.H. Freeman [Scientific American Library], 1994; Griffin, Donald R. *Animal Minds.* Chicago: University of Chicago Press, 1992; Hauser, Marc D. *Wild Minds: What Animals Really Think.* New York: Henry Holt, 2000; Hillix, W.A., and Duane Rumbaugh, eds. "Animal Bodies, Human Minds: Ape, Dolphin, and Parrott Language Skills." In *Developments in Primatology: Progress and Prospects,* vol. 3. London: Kluwer Academic/Plenum Publishers, 2004; Linzey, Andrew. *Animal Gospel.* Westminster: John Knox, 1998; Linzey, Andrew, and Tom Regan, eds. *Animals and Christianity: A Book of Readings.* New York: Crossroad, 1988; Linzey, Andrew, and Dorothy Yamamoto, eds. *Animals on the Agenda.* Chicago: University of Illinois Press, 1998; Pinches, Charles, and Jay McDaniel, eds. *Good News for Animals?: Christian Approaches to Animal Well-Being.* New York: Orbis Books, 1993; Waldau, Paul. *The Specter of Speciesism.* Oxford: Oxford University Press, 2002; Wallman, Joel. *Aping Language (Themes in the Social Sciences).* Cambridge: Cambridge University Press, 1992.

Daniel L. Smith-Christopher

HOMESCHOOLING

Homeschooling has risen as an alternate to public education in the United States. Originally confined to fringe religious groups like the Amish, it has turned into a social phenomenon in America, including middle-class suburbanites and urban elites. Additionally, it has become a large commercial market that provides everything from school supplies tailored to the homeschool market to conferences for homeschool teachers.

HOMESCHOOLING STATISTICS

In 1999, and again in 2003, the National Center for Educational Statistics (NCES) did a nationwide study of homeschooling in the United States. In the latter study, the NCES estimated that there are more than one million home-schooled students. Approximately 2.2 percent of all students are homeschooled. That percentage had risen by almost one-third since the 1999 study. The study showed that the vast majority of home-schooled students are white, urban, and from the South. Additionally, the majority of students come from traditional two-parent homes where one parent works and the other stays home. While middle-class parents predominate (defined as household incomes between $25,000 and $75,000), lower-class families make up more than one-quarter of homeschooled-students, while just over one-fifth of home-schooled students come from upper-class parents. Likewise, home-schooled parents are fairly well educated, with the majority having a degree or some college level education, though graduate/professional school parents make up the smallest percentage (NCES 2006).

The NCES study also measured not just raw numbers, but included a multivariate approach that showed the likelihood of a given group to homeschool given all other variables being held equal. Here the results were somewhat different. This study showed that lower-class parents were significantly more likely to homeschool their children than either middle- or upper-class parents. Likewise, families with three or more children were more than twice as likely to homeschool as those with fewer children. Also, in a multivariate analysis, rural families were significantly more likely to homeschool than urban families (NCES 2006).

However, it is important to note that homeschooling need not be an all or nothing proposition. Eric Isenberg notes that 21 percent of home-schooled students attend public school part-time, usually going a few hours a week. He also shows that parents who have multiple children may choose not to homeschool all their children, but select one or more to homeschool, sending the others to public school. This percentage is higher than might be imagined; Isenberg states that 55 percent of parents that homeschool with multiple children "sent at least one other child to school" (Isenberg, 2007). Additionally, students may be homeschooled in some grades, but not in others. However, families that homeschool their children for religious reasons are more likely to homeschool all of their children.

What is clear from this statistical analysis, is while the likelihood of homeschooling is higher for certain groups, there are larger numbers of homeschooling children, a variety of social and ethnic classes, and homeschooling may not be as exclusively relegated to evangelical Christians as is generally believed, particularly if there are private school alternatives available. Thus, homeschooling is not limited to a particular subgroup, but is a widespread phenomenon in the United States.

THE LEGAL ASPECTS OF HOMESCHOOLING

There is no federal law that regulates homeschooling. Section 9506 of the *No Child Left Behind Act* of 2001 specifically forbids federal control of homeschooling. Thus, currently all law related to home schools is state based, and therefore laws regarding home school vary greatly from state to state. States are able then to regulate home schooling as they see fit, theoretically even to ban it. However, at this point, all states recognize homeschooling as an educational option.

The most significant legal barrier to home schooling has been compulsory attendance laws. Homeschooling, by definition, demands exemption from compulsory education attendance requirements. States thus must legislate specific exemption for home schooled children. Likewise, states may determine to what degree a home-schooled student may participate in extra-curricular activities like sports, or band, or classes the parents feel inadequately prepared to teach, like foreign language, chemistry or music. In *Swanson v. Guthrie,* the tenth circuit appeals court held that a homeschooled child may be denied access to selected classes if there is a board policy denying all part-time students such access. Additionally, the courts have held that there is no constitutional right to extracurricular activities even for public school students, and therefore may correspondingly exclude home school students as well.

On the other hand, states may exercise their rights to determine the qualifications of homeschool teachers. However, this must also be consistent. If private schools are allowed to employ noncredentialed teachers, then there can be no requirement that homeschool teachers be credentialed. But if a parent does not fulfill the uniform standard of teacher qualifications for a state, then the homeschooling request may be denied. North Dakota has some of the most stringent requirements for homeschool teachers, requiring either a teaching certificate or a bachelor's degree. If the parent has neither of those, but they have a General Educational Development test (GED) or equivalent, they may still teach, but are supervised by a credentialed teacher. They may also qualify by passing the teacher exam. North Dakota, however, is an exception. The majority of states have no qualification requirements for homeschool teachers.

In general, states have been quite accommodating of homeschool students. The Home School Legal Defense Association (HSLDA) rates 25 out of 50 states as having either no regulation or low regulation (meaning parents only have to notify the state that they intend to homeschool). Another 19 states are rated as having moderate regulation (parents are required to indicate student progress to the state through grades, test scores, portfolios, etc.). Only 6 out of 50 states are considered by the HSLDA as having high regulations. Generally these states require more documentation in terms of attendance and student progress.

REASONS FOR HOMESCHOOLING

Homeschooling started in the 1950s as a liberal rebellion against an educational system that was perceived as too institutional and rigid. Parents eager to try more cutting edge educational methods took their children out of the public schools and began educating them at home. Starting in the 1970s through the 1980s with Supreme Court decisions banning school prayer and mandatory bible reading, the homeschooled student body shifted to a more conservative group. It was now religious conservatives who made up the bulk of homeschooling families. While this group still comprises the majority of homeschoolers, homeschooling advocates claim that homeschoolers come from across the political spectrum (though a 2002 study indicated that 75 percent of homeschooling families are conservative Christians).

Homeschool families have been divided into two different categories: Ideological and pedagogical. Ideological homeschool families do so because they believe that public schools do not support their beliefs and values. Often these are conservative Christians who feel the absence of prayer and bible reading, and the teaching of evolution, sex education, and "moral relativism," makes the public schools hostile to their core beliefs. On the other side are pedagogical home-schooling families. These are families, sometimes with special needs' students, who feel that public schools are not teaching their children appropriately. The problem here is not with content, as it is with ideological homeschoolers, but rather with method. Pedagogical homeschooling families believe they can meet the educational needs of their children more effectively than the public schools. In contrast to the ideological homeschoolers who often follow textbooks quite rigidly, pedagogical homeschool parents will adapt and selectively use material developed by homeschool publishers. These parents often focus on experiential learning, and pedagogical methods can vary daily. It appears that these (peda-gogical) parents are growing in number. Studies have suggested that ideological reasons for homeschooling appear to be subsiding in importance for this general population, whereas pedagogical and special needs' reasons are becoming in-creasingly important motivators for parents' decisions to home school.

Another study on homeschooling divides parental reasons for homeschool-ing differently. For this study, the reasons of homeschool parents can be mapped between *parent-focused* homeschooling and *partnership-focused* homeschooling. Parent-focused homeschool parents are those who feel an enormous responsi-bility for their children's education, and thus take the responsibility for them-selves. These parents may *go it alone* without getting involved in homeschooling groups. Likewise, these parents are not necessarily negative in regards to public schools; they have a different priority. Partnership-focused homeschool parents are actually in flight from the public school system. They seek another organiza-tion to work with, and have found the public schools wanting. As a result, they have rejected the public school as their partner, and have turned to homeschool-ing groups for partnerships.

Still, this study does not dispute a religious or value-based motivation for homeschooling. In fact, their study confirms such a belief, though it warns against a single-designation of homeschool families as ideologues. While values do inform parents' decisions to homeschool, the argument is that, just as impor-tant, is the parents' conception of their role in their children's education. They hold that religious belief structures are in the end only a part of the explanation, rather than the entirety of it.

The National Household Education Surveys Program (NHES) also mea-sured reasons for homeschooling. Isenberg (2007) compiled a number of studies of homeschooling families. The data with regards to religion was somewhat ambiguous. When asked why they homeschooled, 30 percent of parents who homeschool their children reported religious reasons as the primary cause. On the other hand 48 percent of parents listed educational reasons as their primary impetus to homeschool. Moreover, the number of homeschooled students taking the SAT who report having a religious faith (41.8%), is lower than those in public schools (52.5%). Though the number of homeschool students who report being Baptist is higher (17.7%) then those in public school (10.3%). However, the competition may actually not be from the public school sector as much as from the private school sector. Isenberg concludes: "In small towns, however, private school enrollment does depend on the percentage evangelical Protestant, showing that they substitute private schooling for homeschooling when economies of scale for private schooling can be obtained" (Isenberg 2007). It has also been pointed out that many parents homeschool because of behavioral or special needs issues, particularly with older children. Isenberg notes that those parents who give the reason for homeschooling more than doubles from students age 13 and younger to students age 14 and older. Additionally, when one examines the number of parents who include this reason as significant (though not primary), the number of students who are homeschooled for behavioral and special needs concerns age 14 and above is 48 percent as opposed to younger children, whose parents cite this reason at a level of less than half as often (22%).

Thus, the contrary to popular conception of homeschooling as a fundamentalist or evangelical exodus from the public school system to defend a rightfully imperiled premodern world view is not proven. The data shows that the reasons for homeschooling are far more complex. Certainly, religion is an important factor in a family's choice to homeschool their children, yet there are often other reasons that are more important from the parents' point of view. As public education is increasingly denounced as "a failure," one of the beneficiaries of this is the homeschooling movement, as parents try to find alternatives to improve their children's education.

HOMESCHOOL OUTCOMES

Studies that follow homeschooling outcomes are methodologically difficult to undertake due to the lack of consistent requirements by the state to track homeschooled students.

The question that is often asked is how successful is homeschooling as compared to conventional schooling in terms of student achievement? Brian Ray's study of homeschool outcomes tried systematically to examine the test data on homeschool students (Ray 2004). Several states require homeschool students to participate in state standardized tests. Ray's examination of the data showed that homeschooled students generally scored as well, or better than their conventionally schooled counterparts. Ray is quick to point out, however, that one cannot draw conclusions about homeschooling per se, but rather that a number of factors, including low teacher to student ratios, teaching to the test, and high levels of parental involvement, may be significant factors as well. Controlling for these factors, homeschool students may not perform significantly better than conventionally schooled students.

In terms of social effects, homeschool students appear not to lag behind their conventional peers. Psychological testing of homeschooled children shows a self-concept generally at, or above the norm. While homeschool students appear less peer-focused than non–homeschool students, a study of their level of socialization showed that they had a great deal of peer interaction through homeschooling organizations, community groups, and churches. Studies of homeschooled children found no negative psychological indications that can be directly traced to the homeschooling environment.

THE HOMESCHOOL MARKET

Homeschooling is not a task that can be taken on without preparation. The homeschooling parent knows that they need resources and materials in order to teach the variety of topics that are a part of a well-rounded education. To this end there has arisen an entire new market to provide these materials to willing and wanting parents. Broadly, two curriculum options are available for parents who homeschool: Complete curriculum and learning resources.

There are complete curricula that start at over $500 but provide lessons in math, reading, history, and so forth. Companies market these is a variety of ways. From A Beka Home School, which offers a choice of traditional and accredited programs "designed to provide an excellent Christian education for those who teach their child at home," to Clonlara School, with its holistic emphasis on the child and its affirmation that "Clonlara School is welcoming: We do not discriminate on the basis of race, religion, color, gender, nationality or ethnic origin in administration of our educational and/or admissions policies." Clonlara likewise touts accreditation for homeschoolers who sign-up with them. For those looking for accreditation, and thus an easier entry for their children into college, the costs of programs like these can run upwards of $1000 per year, including materials.

There are also resource vendors who are willing to sell workbooks, hands-on supplies, games, and other teaching materials. Many of these books are the same products that regular classroom teachers use to supplement their district curriculum from publishers well known to public school teachers like Teacher Created Resources, and Frank Schaffer Publications. Other texts are more specifically designed for those attempting to integrate religious instruction into their material, with books and materials from publishers like Alpha Omega Publication, and Bob Jones University Press. What is perhaps most interesting is the cost of these products. Individual workbooks often cost around $20 and *subject packs* like those offered by Bob Jones University Press can cost in the hundreds of dollars.

Thus, the homeschool market is a growing and profitable industry, which is buoyed by local conferences where vendors are able to display their wares, and online communities in which home school parents are able to share their insights and recommendations regarding different curriculum choices. In fact, some homeschool organizations have turned to on-line tutoring and communication as a way of supporting homeschool teachers, as well as providing avenues for students to discuss educational topics with one another. Web sites like Jubilee Academy offer an on-line educational experience where students can take courses over the internet. As on-line education becomes more feasible at the adult level, homeschool organizations are likewise seeing their value as a way of creating more value in the homeschool market. This has particular appeal to those parents who wish to homeschool their children in the higher grades, but do not have the specialized knowledge to teach subjects like World History or Calculus.

CONCLUSION

The homeschool world is still very small. Estimates put homeschooling at two to three percent of the education populace. Still, in the United States this translates to over a million homeschool students. As we have seen, those who homeschool do so from a variety of social and economic backgrounds, and do so for a variety of reasons. There is not doubt that fundamentalists and evangelicals make up a large percentage of those who homeschool, but increasingly homeschooling is seen as a viable option by those who are not necessarily inclined towards a more conservative religious ideology. The percentage of homeschool parents who listed religion as their primary reason actually declined from 1999 to 2003. As the public school system is increasingly under attack as ineffective or worse, parents from a variety of backgrounds are seeing homeschooling as a workable alternative. The homeschool market is addressing the needs of these parents, and with the increasing power of the Internet, on-line courses may soon become a staple of homeschooling life.

See also Separation of Church and State.

Further Reading: Bielick Stacey, Kathryn Chandler, and Stephen P. Broughman. "Homeschooling in the United States: 1999." *Education Statistics Quarterly* 3, no. 3 (Fall 2001): 25–32; Collom, E. "The Ins and Outs of Homeschooling: The Determinants of Parental Motivations and Student Achievement." *Education and Urban Society* 37, no. 3 (May 2005): 307–35; Green, Christa, Joan M. T. Walker, and Kathleen Hoover-Dempsey, V. "Parents' Motivations for Involvement in Children's Education: An Empirical Test of a Theoretical Model of Parental Involvement." *Journal of Educational Psychology* 99, no. 3 (August 2007): 532–544; Green, Christa L. and Kathleen Hoover-Dempsey, V. "Why Do Parents Homeschool? A Systematic Examination of Parental Involvement." *Education and Urban Society* 39, no. 2 (2007): 264–287; Home School Legal Defense Association. http://www.hslda.org; Isenberg, Eric J. "What Have We Learned About Homeschooling?" *Peabody Journal of Education* 82, nos. 2–3 (2007): 387–409; Kern, Alexander, and David M. Alexander. *American Public School Law.* 6th ed. Belmont, CA: Wadsworth Publishing, 2004; Mur, Cindy, ed. *At Issue: Home Schooling.* San Diego, CA: Greenhaven Press, 2003; National Center for Education Statistics. "Trends in the Use of School Choice: 1993 to 2003." http://nces.ed.gov/pubs2007/2007045.pdf (accessed November 2006); Ray, B. D. "Homeschoolers on to College: What Research Shows Us." *Journal of College Admission* 185 (Fall 2004): 5–11; Ray, B. D. "Home Schools: A Synthesis of Research on Characteristics and Learner Outcomes." *Education and Urban Society* 21, no. 1 (November 1988): 16–31; Romanowski, Michael H. "Revisiting the Common Myths about Homeschooling." *Clearing House* 79, no. 3 (Jan/Feb 2006): 125–129; Van Galen, J. A. "Ideology, Curriculum and Pedagogy in Home Education." *Education and Urban Society* 21, no. 1 (1988): 52–68.

Randall Reed

HOMOSEXUALITY

With the possible exception of the fight over abortion, no topic has been the focus of more heated debate in the battleground of religion than homosexuality, and its related issues of sexual orientation, same-sex marriage, the ordination of homosexual clergy, biblical interpretation, and gay/lesbian/bisexual/transgender identity in relation to religious traditions.

BIBLICAL INTERPRETATION

The interpretation of the few biblical passages that deal in some way with same-sex relations has been an important battleground in the fight over homosexuality, even though the topic of homosexuality occasions very little attention from the biblical writers. Indeed, whereas the status of same-sex relations is one of the most divisive ethical issues in the modern religious debate, it is barely of passing interest to the ancient biblical authors. There are basically six passages in the Bible that refer directly to homoerotic relations, three in the Old Testament/Jewish Scriptures (Genesis 19:1–11; Leviticus 18:22 and 20:13), and three in the New Testament (Romans 1:26–27; 1 Corinthians 6:9; and 1 Timothy 1:10).

The famous story of the destruction of Sodom and Gomorrah in Genesis 19 includes a passage stating that the men of the city wanted "to know" (*yadah*) Lot's guests. Lot calls their desire "wicked" and offers his daughters for them "to know," indicating that the term *to know* here connotes sexual relations (similar to Adam *knowing* his wife Eve). The men apparently want to rape Lot's foreign guests by way of demeaning them. Little do the men of the city realize, of course, that their evil desire only confirms God's judgment against the city, a judgment the visiting angelic guests soon carry out. Some scholars point to the violation of hospitality as the primary issue in the passage, but Lot's offer of his daughters suggests overtones of sexual violence as well (a similar passage is found in Judges 19:14–29).

The two passages from Leviticus 18:22 and 20:13 occur within the context of the Holiness Code (Leviticus 17–26), where the Israelites receive instructions on how they shall conduct themselves upon entering the Holy Land. Both passages give clear prohibitions against same-sex relations between men, though no reason for the proscription is given. The second prohibition in 20:13 adds the punishment of death to men engaged in same-sex relations. There are many other prohibitions in the Holiness Code (e.g., crossbreeding of animals, sowing two kinds of seed in one field, wearing garments made of two different fabrics, rounding off the hair of one's temples, receiving a tattoo; cf. Leviticus 19:19, 27–28; 21:5). It appears that these various practices were perhaps markers for the previous idolatrous inhabitants of the land. In modern discussions, the rationales for these various prohibitions, including same-sex relations, forms a significant issue of debate.

All of the New Testament passages come from the Pauline letters. The Romans 1:26–27 passage is the most important, as here Paul clearly views homoerotic behavior (male or female) as a consequence of idolatry, unnatural, and an expression of excessive lust. The modern interpreter must ask, of course, about Paul's understanding of homoeroticism in the first century Greco-Roman world. Most scholars acknowledge that Paul knew of homoeroticism indirectly and in stereotypically Jewish terms, which means that Paul was referring to the Gentile practices of pederasty and male prostitution. This becomes somewhat clearer in the reference from 1 Corinthians 6:9, where homoeroticism finds inclusion in a typical vice-list of prohibited behaviors. Issues of translation are particularly important here, as there was no word in ancient Greek corresponding to our modern term *homosexuality* (which was coined at the end of the nineteenth century). Literally translated, the terms in question, *malakoi* and *arsenokoitai,* mean *soft people,* and something like *men who go to bed,* respectively. These terms may be euphemisms for the passive and active partners in same-sex activity, whether in relation to pederasty or male prostitution, but the exact meanings of the terms are disputed. Modern translations, however, often mislead the reader by rendering these terms as *sodomites* (reading the Sodom and Gomorrah story into the text; e.g., New Revised Standard Version [NRSV], New King James Version [NKJV], New American Bible [NAB]) or as *homosexuals* (anachronistically reading modern understandings of sexual orientation into the text; e.g., New International Version [NIV], NKJV). It may well be that Paul derives the term *arsenokoitai* from the Septuagint version of Leviticus 20:13 (*meta arsenos koiten*). The passage in 1 Timothy 1:10 also refers to *arsenokoitai* in the context of a vice list, with the same unclear, but apparently sexual, meaning as in 1 Corinthians 6.

The relative lack of attention to homosexuality in the biblical writings means that the few passages where it does arise have attained an exaggerated importance in the modern debates. The difficulties of using the Bible to address homosexuality in the modern era are further complicated by: (1) issues of translation, (2) differing contextual understandings of same-sex relations in antiquity, and (3) placing homosexuality within the larger frameworks of biblical approaches to human sexuality. As seen above, how best to translate both the terms, and the understanding of homoerotic sexuality in the biblical texts into modern English (or any other language), is a significant issue, especially in relation to 1 Corinthians 6:9. This difficulty is directly related to changing understandings of same-sex relations over time. Whereas in antiquity, same-sex relations were typically understood as exploitive and a perversion of the natural order, modern understandings of homosexuality differ significantly—particularly in terms of mutuality rather than exploitation, and in terms of people having different naturally occurring sexual orientations. Here it is important to note that the concepts of heterosexuality and homosexuality as sexual orientations is a modern construct not found in antiquity (the term *homosexuality* was coined in late nineteenth-century German psychological literature). Further, another issue is how the biblical materials should be understood in light of the modern psycho-social and biological sciences regarding human sexuality. The larger frameworks of human sexuality from biblical perspectives also come into view. The Bible includes various sanctioned sexual relationships that in the modern world are generally viewed as unethical (e.g., polygamy, and levirate marriage). Thus there has been significant and ongoing religious debate across the ages over what counts as appropriate and inappropriate expressions of human sexuality. At present, many religious traditions are deeply divided regarding the full inclusion of gay, lesbian, bisexual, and transgender believers within their faith communities.

BUDDHIST VIEWS OF HOMOSEXUALITY

In Buddhist thought, the core philosophy of renunciation has directly affected Buddhist approaches to the topic of homosexuality. Sexual desire in general (heterosexual or homosexual) has been judged in negative terms within Buddhist tradition (which originated in the sixth and fifth centuries B.C.E). Engaging in sexual relations was generally viewed as giving in to physical bondage and sensual pleasure, which would impede the achievement of spiritual enlightenment. The spiritual value of renunciation and asceticism, then, has long been a key value within Buddhist thought and practice. The body is viewed as a kind of prison for the human spirit, and all love should be universal and nonsexual in expression. These values are important especially for Buddhist monks. For committed lay Buddhists, it was understood that they would have families, but still the goal was to imitate the ideals lived out by Buddhist monks. Lay Buddhists typically take vows of temporary celibacy in order to devote themselves to achieving enlightenment and wisdom. Because the general attitude of Buddhism towards human sexuality is one of renunciation, there has not been any particularly negative view of homosexuality as opposed to heterosexuality. Finally, within some forms of Buddhist tradition the notion of a third sex, the *napuusaka* (literally, *non-male*) exists, alongside the male and female genders. Still other Buddhist traditions have a more positive view of homoeroticism, and sexual activity in general, though the Dalai Lama has reasserted traditional Buddhist views of sexual renunciation.

ROMAN CATHOLIC CHRISTIAN TRADITION

In the Roman Catholic tradition, the most recent official statement on homosexuality is Cardinal Joseph Ratzinger's 1986 *Letter to the Bishops of the Catholic Church on the Pastoral Care of Homosexual Persons.* This letter was written when Cardinal Ratzinger was the head of the Congregation for the Doctrine of the Faith of the Roman Catholic Church, the organization within the Church that maintains oversight over matters of doctrine and official teaching. This document has taken on all the more weight in light of Cardinal Ratzinger's election as Pope Benedict XVI in 2005. In this letter, Cardinal Ratzinger appealed primarily to scripture, church tradition, and a certain understanding of the complementarity of the sexes. In appealing to scripture, Ratzinger simply repeats the admonitions of the Bible without any real attention to the historical contexts of the passages in question. More significant is the testimony of church tradition. In keeping with the official teaching of the Church, Ratzinger maintains that the only appropriate expression of human sexuality is within a monogamous heterosexual marriage that is open to the possibility of procreation in every sexual encounter. Since same-sex relations cannot, by definition, result in a procreative act, Ratzinger argues that all such relations go against nature, and against the teachings of the Church. Further, for Ratzinger, the biology of physical complementarity between the sexes that can result in the transmission of new life demonstrates that only such heterosexual relations (in marriage) are valid expressions of human sexuality. According to Ratzinger, this is simply how the natural order works (Ratzinger 1986).

What, then, of homosexuality from this view? Ratzinger declares that homosexuality is "a disordered sexual inclination which is essentially self-indulgent" (Ratzinger 1986, 7). Indeed, "although the particular inclination of the homosexual person is not a sin, it is a more or less strong tendency ordered toward an intrinsic moral evil; and thus the inclination itself must be seen as an objective disorder" (Ratzinger 1986, 3). Thus, having a homosexual orientation is not in and of itself sinful, but acting on this orientation in any way is sinful. The only faithful course of action, from this perspective, is for gay and lesbian people to abstain from all same-sex relations as disordered. Though there have been strong reactions against this official teaching of the Church (see, e.g., J. McNeill 1993), the Church has not changed its stance over the years.

PROTESTANT CHRISTIAN TRADITION

The Protestant Christian tradition has had a different approach to the topic of homosexuality from the Roman Catholic Church, but with much the same results. Taking its lead from the plain sense of scripture, Protestant tradition in the late 20th century was extremely cautious in changing its approach towards homosexuality. Conscious of the task of being a church *semper reformans* (always reforming), the leadership of most Protestant denominations took seriously the call by many to reconsider its traditional teachings on homosexuality. In the United States, for example, the United Methodist Church, the Presbyterian Church U.S.A., the United Church of Christ, the Evangelical Lutheran Church in America, and the Episcopal Church, all engaged in multi-year studies of how to respond to the presence of gay and lesbian Christians in their congregations and in their church leadership. Such deliberations led to deep divisions in each of these denominations, as year after year some church leaders called for the church to change with the times and be more inclusive of gay and lesbian Christians, while others called just as strongly for the church to take a firm stand against endorsing any form of homosexual expression, especially by ordained clergy.

Those seeking inclusion of gay and lesbian Christians in the church have emphasized sexual *orientation* as a natural God-given predisposition that individuals discover as they mature. Those seeking to uphold traditional sanctions against homosexuality have emphasized centuries of church teachings against same-sex *practices* and, though not seeing homosexual orientation itself as a matter of personal sin, have argued that such an orientation is a distortion of God's creative purposes. From this perspective, homosexual persons can be welcomed into the church, but are called to abstain from same-sex relations. Most Protestant churches in recent years have issued official pronouncements ruling against the ordination of noncelibate homosexual Christians, as well as against the blessing or recognition of same-sex unions. Still, significant and vocal movements within the various Protestant denominations have continued to call for full acceptance of openly gay and lesbian clergy, and for recognition of gay/lesbian unions and committed relationships. The United Church of Christ and the United Church of Canada have not prohibited the ordination of gay/lesbian clergy. And in a celebrated case, the Episcopal Church (the U.S. branch of the Anglican Church of England) ordained Rev. Gene Robinson, an openly gay man, as a Bishop of the church.

Protestant churches have also sought to incorporate into their reasoning about homosexuality, some of the more significant findings from the psychological and biological sciences, though these findings continue to be the subject of tremendous debate. In particular, churches have paid attention to the 1973 decision of the American Psychiatric Association to stop treating homosexuality as a pathology or disordered condition in need of treatment. Some controversial biological research has also suggested various genetic factors contributing to homosexual orientation. These developments have encouraged many to rethink the Natural Law tradition, and the degrees to which the formation of gender identity is a function of essential sexual identity and/or of changing social constructions. The significant debate that has ensued in the church has basically been between two camps. On the one hand, the majority position advocates that heterosexual marriage has always been God's intended and exclusive norm for the expression of human sexuality (emphasizing the unitive and procreative functions of sex in marriage). On the other hand, the minority position advocates that changing notions of gender roles are crucial in shaping all sexual identities, ancient and modern, and that there have always been various notions of sexual identity attributed to divine sanction: for example, polygamy, celibacy, eunuchs, levirate and monogamous marriages. Though homosexuality has been increasingly accepted as a normal and natural way to live in American and European societies at large, more traditional Protestant churches have called into question both the psychological and physical health of homosexual expression. A number of para-church and controversial change ministries have arisen that seek to heal people of their homosexuality (e.g., Exodus International Ministries), with the understanding that people can shift from homosexuality to heterosexuality. Such claims have been hotly debated within the church, and have been largely dismissed by the psychological community.

Perhaps the most important and difficult component to factor into Protestant attitudes towards homosexuality, involves the ways people have experienced the presence of gay and lesbian Christians in the various denominations. The "coming out" of many prominent Protestant church leaders as gay/lesbian/bisexual persons has forced churches to respond to the tension created by their effective ministries in light of traditional church teaching against homosexuality. The personal witness of successful and capable gay/lesbian Christian leaders has been a powerful presence that has convinced many to push churches to be more accepting of these leaders in particular, and to encourage the larger society to be more accepting of homosexual persons in general. At the same time, the traditional Protestant rejection of homosexuality has led many gay and lesbian Christians to leave the church completely, or to find local congregations that have publicly embraced an inclusive attitude towards homosexual persons. The rejection of gay/lesbian Christians in several Protestant denominations also led to the formation of the Universal Fellowship of Metropolitan Community Churches, a denomination dedicated to the full inclusion of gay/lesbian/bisexual/transgendered Christians. In sum, Protestant churches have often been of two minds in their approach to homosexuality. On the one hand, many denominations have passed binding resolutions ruling against the ordination of noncelibate gay and lesbian Christians and against same-sex unions. On the other hand, most denominations have also passed resolutions calling on elected government officials to pass legislation that makes discrimination against homosexual people illegal.

TRANSGENDER AND TRANSSEXUAL

Significant confusion revolves around the realities of transgendered and transsexual persons. The term *transgender* refers in a general way to people whose behavior and identity differs from traditional and stereotypical gender and sex norms. Transgendered people typically identify in some way with the opposite biological sex, whether through cross-dressing, being a drag queen/king, or even going through sexual reassignment treatment. The term *gender variant* is also often used to describe transgender. The term *transsexual* refers more specifically to individuals who feel strongly that their spiritual gender identity does not match their biological gender identity, namely that they were born into the wrong biologically gendered body. Transsexual persons have an overwhelming desire to transform their physical identity to match the personal gender identity they feel within themselves, and so to live as members of the opposite biological gender. For transsexual persons the most significant issues are typically related to cross-living and to gender reassignment surgery that begins with hormonal therapy. *Intersexed* individuals are persons born with physical genitalia and/or chromosomes that are biologically both male and female.

Like the development of the understanding of homosexuality in the psychological community, transgender and transsexuality are no longer viewed as psychological disorders, but as naturally occurring orientations that cause individuals to experience significant *gender dysphoria*, the term used to describe this experience. Further, while transgendered and transsexual persons are often grouped together with gay and lesbian persons (e.g., in the acronym GLBTQ [gay, lesbian, bisexual, transgender, queer]), many transgendered and transsexual persons do not identify with gay or lesbian communities. The reason for this is that sexual orientation (e.g., heterosexual, bisexual, or homosexual) is not at all the same as gender identity (the rubric for transgender). But in popular culture, these different groups are often viewed together because they all are at variance with the dominant heterosexual cultural and sexual norms. The situation gets even more confusing when it becomes clear that many transgender people are homosexual or bisexual. For example, a man who is transgendered may dress as a woman and be sexually attracted to men, but this attraction derives from a female gender identity that the man expresses. For gay men, by contrast, the sexual orientation to men comes from a male gender identity that is simply different from that of the male gender identity that leads other men to have a heterosexual orientation.

When it comes to religion and transgendered and transsexual persons, these individuals regularly experience the same kind of rejection that gay and lesbian persons have long received, especially in western religious traditions, and particularly within Christianity. A biblical passage from Deuteronomy 22:5 is often cited against transgendered practice: "A woman shall not wear a man's apparel, nor shall a man put on a woman's garment; for whoever does such things is abhorrent to the Lord your God." Historically this passage most likely was an ancient Israelite prohibition against Canaanite worship practices that simulated change of sex. Thus, the prohibition was less against what we would call cross-dressing, and targeted at practices that could lead to the worship of false idols in violation of God's law.

Within the Christian community, the question about same-sex relations remains much the same, whether one is discussing a man whose transgendered identity is female, and so is attracted to men (thus technically a heterosexual orientation from a gendered female within a biologically male body), or whether one is discussing a gay man whose sexual orientation is homosexual. In either case, most Christian traditions prohibit any form of same-sex relations regardless of gender identity or sexual orientation. For this reason it is not uncommon for transgendered individuals to live in denial or to be closeted, even more so than for gay or lesbian persons. While there is growing acceptance of gay and lesbian persons in popular culture, transgendered persons still face significant social stigmas. Ironically, these social constraints come not only from the traditional heterosexual population, but can also come from gay and lesbian individuals who do not understand the gender dysphoria that a transgendered person experiences. By the same token, gay and lesbian persons can experience similar criticism from transgendered persons who do not believe that a homosexual orientation comes from God. Still, transgendered and homosexual persons are typically viewed by the heterosexual mainstream as belonging to the same group of nonnormative sexuality, and therefore suspect.

CHANGING VIEWS OF HOMOSEXUALITY

A significant factor in twentieth-century debates over homosexuality in Catholic and Protestant churches can be traced in changing views about homosexuality in the larger society. Three general overlapping stages can be seen in popular attitudes towards homosexuality. At the beginning of the twentieth century, homosexuality was widely viewed as a perversion of God's natural order, and was punishable as a crime against God and society. As the century progressed, and as general attitudes towards sexual behavior became more relaxed, a more accepting attitude began to develop towards homosexuality (especially in the aftermath of the Kinsey report of the 1950s, which suggested that people fell on a sliding scale between absolute heterosexuality and absolute homosexuality). The language associating homosexuality with "perversion" started to be seen as harsh and judgmental. In the latter half of the twentieth century the language of *sexual preference* began to be employed. This term still suggested personal choice in the realm of sexual activity, but same-sex *sexual preference* increasingly came to be seen as a relatively benign departure from societal norms. Toward the end of the twentieth century, in addition to the language of *sexual preference*, the term *sexual orientation* gained prominence, which suggested that an individual had no real choice about gender identity and sexual attraction, and that such identity was more of a given. Since homosexuals were not personally responsible for choosing their sexuality, a movement developed, that encouraged healthy and self-affirming homosexuals not to be ashamed of their identity, but to accept their homosexuality as a natural predisposition and orientation. This acceptance led, in the last decades of the twentieth century, to "gay pride" and to a sense of belonging to a gay community seeking and gaining acceptance from larger society. Such acceptance has led to the tacit nonenforcement of most laws against homosexuality, to the de-criminalization of many older laws against homosexual behavior, to the recognition of same-sex domestic partners by many businesses and some states, and to the wide depiction of gay and lesbian people as normal individuals through the vehicle of popular entertainment. These developments and changes in societal attitudes towards homosexuality have had a significant effect on mostly the Christian and Jewish traditions in particular, with the result that at the beginning of the twenty-first century, many churches and synagogues are more open than ever towards gay and lesbian adherents, while at the same time most official denominational pronouncements have ruled against the full inclusion of noncelibate gay and lesbian couples. This tension has led to serious debate in various faith communities about whether believing communities are behind the times and failing to follow the lead of God's reforming Spirit by including gay/lesbian believers, or whether churches/synagogues are most faithful in holding firm against recognizing any homosexual relationship as legitimate.

The Roman Catholic Church has also faced significant debate and discussion about homosexuality, though on somewhat different terms than the Protestant tradition. First, whereas Protestant churches have spent a great deal of energy addressing the issue of whether or not to allow the *ordination* of noncelibate gays and lesbians, this has not really been an issue for the Roman Catholic Church, since all priests are by definition celibate, be they homosexual or heterosexual. In the Protestant tradition clergy are typically married, and this automatically raises the question of how gay or lesbian couples serve as models for Christian marriage, which has traditionally been envisioned in heterosexual terms. Second, as mentioned above, in the Roman Catholic tradition, the role of *procreation* in marriage has been central, though the unitive function of sexuality has also gained in importance. This has meant that, since homosexual unions cannot by themselves procreate children, homosexual unions cannot receive the blessing of the church. By contrast, in the Protestant tradition, the *unitive* function of sexuality has typically held slightly greater importance than procreation (hence the common use of birth control in the Protestant tradition and not in official Roman Catholic teaching). While critics of homosexual relationships have raised questions about the biological complementarity of same-sex couples, those advocating the appropriateness of blessing same-sex relationships in the church argue that it is wrong to define sexual complementarity in exclusively heterosexual terms.

See also Same-Sex Marriage.

Further Reading: Brawley, Robert. *Biblical Ethics and Homosexuality: Listening to Scripture.* Louisville: Westminster/John Knox Press, 1996; Brooten, Bernadette. *Love Between Women: Early Christian Responses to Female Homoeroticism.* Chicago: University of Chicago Press, 1996; Dover, Kenneth. *Greek Homosexuality.* Cambridge: Harvard University Press, 1978; Gagnon, Robert. *The Bible and Homosexual Practice: Texts and Hermeneutics.* Nashville: Abingdon Press, 2001; McNeil, John J. *The Church and the Homosexual.* Boston: Beacon, 1993; Nissinen, M. *Homoeroticism in the Biblical World: A Historical Perspective.* Minneapolis: Fortress Press, 1998; Ratzinger, Cardinal, and Archbishop Borone. "Congregation for the Doctrine of Faith," October 1986. Rogers, Jack. *Jesus, The Bible, and Homosexuality.* Louisville: Westminster John Knox Press, 2006; Seow, Choon Leong. *Homosexuality and Christian Community.* Louisville: Westminster/John Knox Press, 1996; Siker, Jeffrey S., ed. *Homosexuality in the Church: Both Sides of the Debate.* Louisville: Westminster/John Knox Press, 1994; Siker, Jeffrey S., ed. *The Encyclopedia of Religion and Homosexuality.* Westport, CT: Greenwood Press, 2006; Via, Dan and Gagnon, Robert. *Homosexuality and the Bible: Two Views.* Minneapolis: Fortress Press, 2003.

Jeffrey S. Siker

HUCKSTERISM AND RELIGIOUS SCANDALS

In 2007, Alexandra Pelosi made a documentary about evangelical Christians, *Friends of God: A Road Trip with Alexandra Pelosi that* featured Ted Haggard making a speech about his purity, honesty, and integrity as a mainstream, politically powerful evangelical. This documentary was released scant weeks before the scandal of Haggard's homosexual liaisons and crystal methamphetamine use became public knowledge. Haggard's ministry collapsed in the wake of the scandal, and it appeared to some that the old equation of two-faced licentious preachers and huckster religious leaders deceiving their congregations while getting rich and having illicit sex is still as much as part of America today as it was when Sinclair Lewis penned his satirical antihero pastor Elmer Gantry. Yet this age-old problem of ministerial sexual and financial misconduct has not destroyed the credibility of religious leaders, and in fact, televangelists continue the American tradition of incorporating theatrical methods and business models in their sermons and "performances". The long-awaited secularist victory is still frustrated, as Americans continue to attend church in roughly the same numbers as 200 years ago. In the ever-competitive marketplace of American religion, sincere preachers, huckster ministers, and televangelists continue to compete for the hearts, souls, and dollars of America's Christians, and the secular revolution seems to be even farther away than when Max Weber suggested it in the 1920s. To paraphrase Ronald Reagan, a man who never hesitated to use religious language, and regularly gave carefully crafted extemporaneous political sermons, one person's religious huckster is another person's charismatic leader.

AWAKENINGS AND REVIVALS

Elmer Gantry, the fictitious antihero of Sinclair Lewis's 1927 novel of the same name, is a caricature of a charismatic religious leader. He embodies all that

Lewis found objectionable in "enthusiastic" religion. Gantry betrays his followers, who are true believers, through personal failures, hypocrisy, and dishonesty about his use and abuse of alcohol and sex. Gantry is able to avoid prosecution and, despite personal tragedy and loss, alcoholism and voracious sexuality, he remains a minister. While he lusts for money, booze, and women, he preaches hellfire and brimstone, frugality, abstinence, and temperance. His congregation is devoted to him without question. Gantry is a consummate performer: he is able to sway and hold his followers through his persuasive rhetorical style. This has been called Lewis's most satirical novel, and certainly provoked a great deal of controversy. The novel was banned in several cities, and denounced by ministers and lay-Christians alike. The fallen (and redeemed) leaders that Gantry reflects are often more complicated in the real world but have similarly very strong relationships with their faith communities. Many use the performance techniques that Lewis's character embodies, and face similar personal foibles: passionately preaching against specific sins, and all the while engaging in those very sins in secret.

Gantry's image is not pure fiction, it is based on a number of preachers, and a kind of preaching that is a unique product of the American religious experience. In the mid-eighteenth century, George Whitefield (1714–1770), an Anglican minister, preached throughout England and the American colonies. He is considered one of the leading ministers of the First Great Awakening, a religious revival that swept through England and across the Atlantic to the English colonies. Whitefield offered his sermons outside to very large crowds. While Whitefield's theological method followed standard Calvinist lines regarding sin, salvation, and redemption, he added a bit of panache to his sermons. Gesticulating dramatically, shouting about hellfire and brimstone, weeping and wailing openly, Whitefield's vibrant extemporaneous preaching style captivated his audiences. His innovation was pure theater, but also pure genius, as many preachers embraced the new style of dramatic, extemporaneous preaching. Old style preachers, such as Jonathan Edwards, read their carefully crafted sermons in an even, sonorous voice; Whitefield and his followers hollered and cajoled, and paraded their emotions throughout their sermons. Converts expressed their religious experience emotionally as well, weeping and wailing in response to Whitefield's preaching. While giving the appearance of preaching without any preparation, Whitefield's sermons were as carefully constructed as Edwards's more staid and traditional sermons. But that spur-of-the-moment quality distinguished Whitefield, and introduced a new kind of preaching to a new kind of church: the revival circuit. Evangelical preachers and converts rejected the older forms of preaching as lacking in piety, inspiration, and grace, and embraced the newer emotionally-laden style of religion. As Whitefield and his followers were itinerant ministers, traveling from town to town and delivering their dramatic rendition of the gospel message, hometown pastors often found their authority in jeopardy, and had to change in order to keep their congregations content.

After the American war for independence, Charles Grandison Finney (1792–1875) continued this pattern of emotional, extemporaneous preaching to large crowds outside, known as tent meetings, throughout the antebellum period.

There were a few significant changes though, in the new nation's religious fervor. First, while Finney and his itinerant colleagues continued to preach with an emphasis on human sin, an emerging sense of human action, in combination with religious experience, began to emerge. This emerging pattern of the experience of conversion developed into clear steps: terror of eternal damnation, a strong sense of release found in redemption, and the ecstatic promise of achieving heaven. Second, it was not only faith or belief that these itinerant ministers were inciting in their listeners; conversion was a life-changing experience that happened to those who attended the tent meeting. Continuing the tradition of weeping and wailing openly at the thought of eternal damnation, many of those attending camp meetings underwent a profound experience of God's love and grace, causing them to flail on the ground, weep and sing with joy at the relief they experienced with God's forgiveness. This intensely emotional series of events gave antebellum Christians a new sense of self, profoundly changing individuals and their relationship with, and to the world. Third, Finney and many like him, took their religious revival into the south, preaching to slaves as well as white Christians. Those who attended the meetings reflected the growing population of the United States; immigrants, factory workers, women, and slaves. Many greeted these ministers and their tent meetings with suspicion, not only because of the rampant emotionality and high spirits that dominated the service, but because of the people who were experiencing this emotional Christianity. As the population of the United States continued to grow, larger urban settlements required a change in revival and tent meeting style. Dwight Moody (1837–1899) was a lay minister who spearheaded the urban revival front. Possibly the most well-known urban evangelical preacher was William A. (Billy) Sunday (1862–1935). The challenge for these urban ministers was to bring the energy of the tent meeting to a more confined space. Billy Sunday continued to preach along a circuit, just as the itinerant ministers of the past had. But rather than meeting in a big field outside a town or village, Sunday held his meetings indoors, often with other classes offered during weekdays. By the 1920s, Sunday had an entourage of traveling musicians, bible school teachers of both sexes, and custodians to set up and break down the performance areas. Revival style religion, with its flamboyant preaching and high-emotion experiences, had become an institutionalized facet of the American urban landscape.

While many of these groups and leaders were scandal free, the strong emotional content of the emerging holiness movement continued to be controversial. The scandals that were reported were, and continue to be, big news—drawing national attention from supporters and detractors. For example, in the 1840s an Episcopalian minister, Benjamin Onderdonk, was accused of seducing his female parishioners while intoxicated. For many flourishing Holiness-Pentecostal movement preachers during the late nineteenth and early twentieth centuries, the intense emotional and physical aspects of the revival tradition became a regular part of weekly worship, such that even regular worship services became revivals. The specter of licentious preachers hovered over the heads of many holiness preachers, who were regarded as suspicious characters by many. And the intense emotionality of the service, coupled with the intimate relationship between the minister and his parishioners, especially female parishioners, was ripe for scandal, real or imagined. Historian of Christianity, Ann Taves, has traced this experiential trend, noting the ways Christians and secularists who did not participate in the religious fervor of the Holiness movement tended to treat those religious experiences as pathological—inauthentic religion, inspired by theatrical preachers to excite and provoke the masses. Class and race contributed to these assessments of authentic versus inauthentic religious experience (Taves 1999).

Adding to the mix of emotionally laden religious experiences were several new religious movements that erupted in the United States during the nineteenth and twentieth centuries. Mormonism and its early emphasis on a tradition of plural wives, led to controversy over sex and marriage. At the same time, the Oneida Community, with their beliefs in the importance of sexual relations as a way of creating more spiritually perfect individuals, gave Americans a counter example to debate. Both these groups combined sex and religion in innovative ways, and challenged the expectations of mainstream Christians. While Mormonism officially removed plural marriage from its religious practice in the early 1900s, some groups of Mormons continue to practice polygamy. Most recently, Warren Jeff's Fundamentalist Church of Jesus Christ of the Latter Day Saints (FLDS) at Zion Ranch in Texas has come under scrutiny for polygamy and under-age marriage. While considered a "breakaway" sect of Mormonism, the scandal of the FLDS reveals the fascination America has with sex in general, and Mormon sexual practices in particular. Scholar R. Laurence Moore argues that the power of these scandals is, in part, that the scandals themselves provide a forum for Americans to discuss issues that are generally considered taboo (Moore 1995). In the case of Mormonism, issues of marriage and sexual satisfaction within marriage were a prominent part of the public debate about the legitimacy of Mormonism and the practice of polygamy.

CONTEMPORARY CHURCH LEADERS AND SCANDALS

The twentieth century saw many different religious scandals that gave support to the enduring stereotype of the two-faced preacher and her or his gullible congregation. In the early part of the twentieth century Four Square church founder Aimee Semple McPherson preached Pentecostal revivals to standing-room only crowds. It was alleged that she had an extramarital affair and, when faced with being caught, faked her own death. She later claimed that she had been kidnapped. Thorough investigation could neither prove she had been kidnapped, nor find evidence that she had faked the kidnapping. McPherson was one of the first evangelists to use media, in her case the radio, to spread her religious message and gain financial support from listeners. During the 1980s, the trend of incorporating technology to spread Christianity reached its peak: Peter Popoff stated the home addresses and specific illnesses from his large audience attending his revival style ministry with eerie accuracy. He claimed this was his "God given ability" and shrugged off nay-sayers as tools of the devil. In reality, Popoff was using an earpiece, and being fed information via walkie-talkie by his wife. She and her assistants talked to members of the audience as they came into the service area, and then passed the information on to Popoff. Popoff's ministry went bankrupt in 1987, after James Randi and Steve Shaw revealed his method. Much like Elmer Gantry reflected methods and styles of ministers from the early twentieth century, the fictionalized account of Popoff's scandal was told in Richard Pearce's 1992 film *Leap of Faith*. The minister in that film, Jonas Nightengale, uses technology to fool his audience before taking their offering and leaving town.

Televangelists in the 1980s and 1990s raised a great deal of money through their ministries by utilizing technology. Robert Schuller's Crystal Cathedral was funded by donations collected in church and via television ministry. His particular blend of religion and business models have made the Crystal Cathedral one of the most successful churches and businesses in the United States today. Schuller preaches a gospel of success and values that equates spiritual success with financial success. The Crystal Cathedral is a site of pilgrimage for many Protestants, and promises to be a place where success is generated and Jesus is Lord. A radically individualistic message of salvation and success, Schuller offers his followers, viewers, listeners to his radio show, and pilgrims, an opportunity to be part of the cathedral itself through donations that contribute to the walk, the cathedral's signature tower, or Schuller's worldwide ministry. While many are skeptical of Schuller's combination of the gospel and large donations from his flock, his ministry has remained untouched by major scandals.

The same cannot be said of Oral Roberts. There are two financial scandals that rocked Roberts' religious empire. In the late 1970s, Roberts, ordained by the Pentecostal Holiness Church, claimed that Jesus told him in a vision to build a medical center that would be a successful blend of modern medicine and faith-based healing. The center opened in 1981, and at that time it was one of the largest health campuses of its kind. Shortly after the opening, Roberts claimed that Jesus had commissioned him in person to find a cure for cancer. The City of Faith Medical and Research Center operated for merely eight years before closing. In a unique twist that some considered spiritual blackmail, Roberts told his television audience in 1986 that God told him if he did not raise eight million dollars in a matter of a few months, God would "call him home" to heaven. He raised 9.1 million dollars.

Though Oral Roberts has since left the public scene, his lasting impact is seen in Oral Roberts University (ORU). Yet even ORU has had its share of scandal, most of which has been the result of allegations of fiscal improprieties by Roberts's son and university president, Richard Roberts. Richard Roberts has been accused of misusing university funds, and using the university to further conservative political purposes, which would threaten the tax-exempt status of the university. In addition to the allegations of financial impropriety, were allegations that family cell-phones were used to send suggestive text messages to under-age boys in the middle of the night. Though Oral Roberts returned to the public spotlight to defend his son, eventually Richard Roberts was forced to resign as president of the university, and the university board of regents formally broke all ties to Oral Roberts Ministry, which Richard Roberts was president of as well.

Perhaps the most notorious evangelical Christian scandal of the late twenti-eth century involved Jim Bakker, his wife Tammy Faye, a woman named Jessica Hahn, and Jimmy Swaggart. In the 1970s, the Bakkers founded Praise The Lord ministries. PTL grew into a multi-million dollar organization, reporting $129 million in revenue in 1986, and operated a worldwide television ministry by satellite. PTL also owned and operated the now defunct 2,000+ acre Heritage USA Christian amusement park in Fort Mill, South Carolina. In the late 1980s, PTL was rocked by several scandals. First, the acclaimed and very successful Jim Bakker was accused not only of committing adultery and using PTL funds to pay off the woman in question, Jessica Hahn, but also of defrauding his view-ers and supporters. The scandal was brought to light by Jimmy Swaggart, who Bakker and his lawyers feared was attempting a hostile takeover of PTL. Called The First Felon of TV Evangelists by the *New York Times,* Bakker was charged with, and convicted of 24 counts of fraud and conspiracy. He was sentenced to 45 years in prison, and served four years in a minimum security prison. His followers were deeply horrified at the charges, and shocked by the conviction. Despite promising life-time vacations at Heritage USA in exchange for financial support of his ministry, and then diverting millions of dollars to his own opu-lent home and fleet of expensive automobiles, Bakker's followers maintained his innocence. However, in 1996, a few of the Bakkers' more disgruntled followers brought a class action suit against him, but a North Carolina court dismissed the suit. In 2003 Bakker returned to TV ministry and currently appears on his own show *The Jim Bakker Show* with his second wife, Lori Bakker, broadcast from Branson, Missouri.

Jimmy Swaggart himself was caught in a similar scandal involving prostitutes, though the financial improprieties were not as extensive as those that plagued PTL. In an attempt to save his ministry, Swaggart went on television and pub-licly repented. Tears flowed down his cheeks as he wailed "I have sinned!" He apologized to God, his wife, and his audience. Swaggart was suspended from his ministry for three months for his behavior. However, shortly afterwards a prostitute came forward stating that Swaggart had paid her to pose nude for him in a New Orleans hotel, and the denomination increased his suspension to one year. Swaggart rejected the harsher punishment and was defrocked by the Assemblies of God denomination for his lack of compliance. Nonetheless, he returned to the pulpit after three months. Yet in 1991, Swaggart was again found with a prostitute at a traffic stop in California. At that point he resigned as head of Swaggart ministries, and turned over the reins to his son.

The television ministry business is a cutthroat endeavor. Jim Bakker accused Jimmy Swaggart of being behind his undoing and then claimed Jerry Falwell, who had been given custodianship of PTL during Bakker's absence, was trying to hijack the ministry. Both Swaggart and Falwell denied the claims, and Fal-well eventually removed himself from PTL's helm. But an even more interesting component of the Swaggart saga is the intrigue between Swaggart and another pastor, Marvin Gorman, who headed a small television ministry in New Or-leans. Swaggart published accusations that Gorman had committed numerous adulteries. Gorman admitted to a single affair in the late 1970s, claiming that he had repented and filed suit against Swaggart for libel. Gorman, however, was instrumental in Swaggart's own subsequent downfall, when he provided pictures to the police of Swaggart and a prostitute in a New Orleans hotel. Eventually the court ruled in favor of Gorman, and awarded him $10 million (though considerably less than the $90 million he sued for), and the two settled out of court before the appeal was heard. By that time, both ministries were in bankruptcy.

In 2005, Ted Haggard, founder of the 14,000-member New Life megachurch in Colorado Springs, Colorado, and leader of the National Association of Evangelicals, resigned under suspicion of "immoral sexual conduct." Male escort Michael Jones came forward and alleged that he and Rev. Haggard had been involved in a three-year homosexual affair. Initially, Haggard denied the affair, but admitted to buying methamphetamine from Jones. Jones denied selling drugs, but maintained his allegation of the affair. Utilizing rules that Haggard himself had developed, the New Life church board of overseers removed Haggard from his ministerial position. New Life church is not a member of any denomination, and answers only to Haggard's handpicked board of overseers. While shocked by how rapidly Haggard was removed from his position, the New Life church congregation rallied around Haggard, offering support, forgiveness, and a generous severance package of $138,000 (one year's salary). Haggard admitted to committing "sexual misconduct" and agreed that the overseers had done the right thing by removing him from the pulpit. He agreed to undergo intensive counseling, and after three weeks declared himself "completely heterosexual." Regardless, he did not return to his congregation. In 2007, Haggard and his wife sent a message to their former New Life congregation asking for money to help them pursue degrees in psychology and counseling as full-time students at the University of Phoenix. Haggard's former board of overseers chastised him for asking for financial support, saying that Haggard should have consulted with the church board first. Haggard and his wife would like to go back to serving Christians in the Phoenix Dream Center, a faith-based half-way house, after they complete their degrees.

CONCLUSION

In the 1997 film *The Apostle,* staring Robert Duvall, the issues of hucksterism and religion are presented in a brilliant way. Sonny, the pastor of a large Pentecostal church, finds his wife in bed with his youth minister, who then orchestrates a leadership coup of Sonny's megachurch in Texas. While admitting to his own infidelities, Sonny goes too far in revenge for his wife's unfaithfulness and the loss of his church and beats his rival to death. He then flees the state and begins again, once more as a Pentecostal pastor. Sonny's charismatic preaching coupled with the scandal that eventually ends with him in prison, still preaching, highlights the attractiveness of these pastors, and the humanness that is so often their downfall. Religious parishioners look on first in denial, and then despair, as their beloved pastor's transgressions are revealed. Yet the American religious penchant for faith in those who in the end show themselves unworthy, often after fleecing their flocks for thousands or millions of dollars, continues to fascinate historians, sociologists, novelists, filmmakers, and psychologists of religion. Perhaps the aphorism, "there's a sucker born every minute" is never truer than in the realm of religion.

See also Apocalypticism and Nuclear War; Prime Time Religion.

Further Reading: Butler, Jon. *Awash in a Sea of Faith: Christianizing the American People.* Cambridge, MA: Harvard University Press, 1992; Chidester, David. *Authentic Fakes: Religion and American Popular Culture.* 1st ed. California: University of California Press, 2005; Finke, Roger and Rodney Stark. *The Churching Of America, 1776–2005: Winners And Losers In Our Religious Economy.* Revised ed. New Jersey: Rutgers University Press, 2005; Holman, Hugh, C. "Sinclair Lewis: Overview." In *Reference Guide to American Literature,* ed. Jim Kamp. 3rd ed. Detroit: St. James Press, 1994; Moore, R. Laurence. *Selling God: American Religion in the Marketplace of Culture.* USA: Oxford University Press, 1995; Price, Joe. "Salvation as Success: The Charisma of the Crystal Cathedral." Unpublished; Randi, James. *The Faith Healers.* New York: Prometheus Books, 1989; Stout, Harry S. *The Divine Dramatist: George Whitefield and the Rise of Modern Evangelicalism.* Grand Rapids, MI: Wm. B. Eerdmans Publishing Company, 1991; Taves, Ann. *Fits, Trances, and Visions.* Princeton, NJ: Princeton University Press, 1999.

Laura Ammon

HUTTERITES: COMMUNAL LIVING VERSUS INDIVIDUAL FREEDOM

Hutterites are the oldest continually existing society practicing community of goods in North America. Since their beginnings in Moravia (1529) during the Protestant Reformation, and following their migration to North America starting in 1874, the Hutterites have sustained their commitment to the rule of economic sharing practiced by the apostolic communities described in Acts 2 and 4. The thriving of such communities in which private property has been abolished, relies to a significant extent on the voluntary subjugation of individuals and families to the authority of the church community. Because such a privileging of the community over the individual challenges basic premises of modern liberal societies, the Hutterites have experienced numerous controversies, both between their communities and the host cultures, as well as among different factions and applications of the communal principle within their society. These controversies have included differences of view about the proper location of the nuclear family within the community, the relationship of personal spirituality to communal authority, the exercise of legal rights versus submission to the church, the application of church discipline to members who dissent or leave, and the integration of communal economics with the surrounding capitalist economy.

ANABAPTIST ORIGINS AND SCHISMS

Anabaptist communities first emerged in Europe during the early part of the sixteenth century. Dissenters unsatisfied with the scope and intensity of reforms initiated by leaders like Martin Luther and Ulrich Zwingli established "free churches" that were neither supported nor protected by established political authorities. These church communities were often called *Anabaptist* (rebaptizer) because they rejected infant baptism, and insisted on voluntary and uncoerced decisions to join their churches. Two additional significant teachings of some of these communities were a rejection of the sword, including military service, and an affirmation of communal economics—the sharing of all resources in common among believers. But not all Anabaptist communities rejected military service or private property. One such "sword-bearing" Anabaptist community was at the city of Nikolsburg in Moravia, where its pastor, Balthasar Hubmaier, had established a city-wide Anabaptist reformation protected by magisterial authority. A pacifist group influenced by Anabaptist missionary Hans Hut and led by Jacob Wiedemann, living in and around the city, challenged Hubmaier's sword-bearing version of Anabaptism, and eventually divested themselves of their property before leaving the city. This peaceful and communal-minded group of Anabaptists eventually settled at Austerlitz, and became a destination for numerous Anabaptist refugees seeking a stable practice of pacifist and communalistic Christianity. As refugees poured into their community, the Austerlitz Brethren struggled to routinize alternative forms of economic distribution, eventually dividing over differences concerning the economic privileges of their leaders. A vocal leader by the name of Jacob Hutter led a faction that separated from the Austerlitz Brethren. This group also opposed several other communally-minded Moravian Anabaptist groups that became aligned with Austerlitz. Partly because of its strong group discipline and missionary zeal, the Hutterite group flourished and established multiple colonies throughout Moravia.

The pattern of community established by Jacob Hutter and his associates, included the gathering of all members of a colony into a *bruderhof:* a concentration of large houses where members of the community lived and worked together under the joint leadership of spiritual leaders called *servants of the word* and managers of the communal economy called *stewards*. In the *bruderhof,* individual families maintained their identities, but collectivized the rearing and education of their children, pioneering the first nursery schools called *kindergartens*, and preparing youth for their roles in the craft production that sustained their communities financially.

Although many Hutterite leaders, including Jacob Hutter, were brutally executed by authorities carrying out the Hapsburg monarchy's policy of intolerance toward Anabaptists, the Moravian Hutterite colonies survived, and throughout the latter half of the sixteenth century experienced a golden age where their population swelled to nearly 30,000, living in *bruderhofs* throughout the Moravian lands. However, by the middle of the seventeenth century, most of these *bruderhofs* had been brutally destroyed, victims of the Catholic counterreformation and religious strife during the Thirty Years War. Some Hutterites managed to reestablish their communal life in Hungary and Transylvania, but in Hungary, tolerance eventually was replaced by a policy of Catholicization, leading to the dissolving of the few remaining *bruderhofs*. In Transylvania, which was tolerant of religious diversity until the Hapsburg monarchy took over, Hutterite *bruderhofs* managed to hang on until 1695. However, Hutterite beliefs and practices were discovered by a group of Lutheran refugees from Carinthia, who settled in Transylvania in 1755. The Lutherans reestablished community of goods and revitalized Hutterian teachings, eventually leaving the region to settle in Russia in 1770 near the Mennonite colonies of the Ukraine.

In Russia, the Hutterite communities flourished once again, yet with disagreement over when and how to reestablish the *bruderhof* pattern of community of goods. These disagreements led eventually to the three different varieties of Hutterite communities that persist to the present, named after their original leaders or that leader's occupation: the *Dariusleut*, the *Schmiedeleut*, and the *Lehreleut*. The Hutterites began migrating to America in the latter part of the nineteenth century in response to the introduction of compulsory military service by the Russian government, and the refusal of the government to confirm their privileges as conscientious objectors.

The first North American Hutterite communities were established in 1874, starting with the Bon Homme colony in present-day South Dakota. While the American Hutterite communities have generally grown and prospered, there are no longer any Hutterite communities in Europe. The European descendants of Hutterites, called *Habaner*, continue to live in parts of the present-day Czech Republic and Romania. Although the Hutterites settled originally in the United States, beginning with their first colony in South Dakota, significant numbers fled to Canada in the aftermath of persecution of Hutterite conscientious objectors during World War I. The Hutterite colonies in Canada now outnumber those in the United States.

Not all Hutterites who came to North America adopted the model of communally owned property. Those who did not came to be known as *Prairieleut*. Most of the *Prairieleut* ended up joining Mennonite churches and leaving behind their Hutterite roots.

In the twentieth century, following the aftermath of World War II, a communal society of German origin called the *Bruderhof*, migrated to the United States (after a brief sojourn in Paraguay). This community, led by Eberhard Arnold, had been influenced by sixteenth-century Hutterite writings, and eventually joined themselves formally to Hutterites. However, differences in habit and piety, as well as disagreements between the leaders of the two groups, led ultimately to the *Bruderhof* going its separate way in 1991.

THE FAMILY AND COMMUNAL LIFE

In today's Hutterite colonies, communal life is given priority over the autonomy of families. The colonies are organized around three significant centers of activity: the meetinghouse, the schoolhouse, and the dining hall. In the meetinghouse, daily evening services are held, in addition to the Sunday morning worship service. In the schoolhouse, children are gathered for instruction in both Hutterite religious principles and in secular practical knowledge. And in the dining hall, the community gathers three times each day for a communal meal. Each day's routines are established by the community's leaders, and by the seasonal requirements for attending to a large agricultural cooperative—a kind of mega-farm—that provides sustenance and income for the colony.

A patriarchal authority structure provides for an orderly way of life in the various spheres of colony activity. A colony boss manages the colony's financial enterprises, and establishes the work responsibilities of the able-bodied men and women of the community. He is subject, along with the rest of the community, to the minister or elder, who oversees the spiritual life of the community and leads the worship services. Other subsidiary positions of authority for men may include an assistant minister, a field boss who focuses on supervising farm work, and other areas of leadership responsibility related to specific enterprises of the community, such as plumber or dairyman. Women serve in such positions as head cook, head of the kindergarten, and gardener.

Children begin the process of induction into communal life and identity at the age of three, at which age they begin spending much of the day in the colony nursery under the supervision of a kindergarten teacher. At the age of six, children graduate to the colony school, where time is divided between the "German school," which focuses on passing on the Hutterite faith and the German language, and the "English school," which is oriented around practical subjects taught by an employee of the public schooling system.

As teenagers, the youth of the colony are encouraged to consider carefully the step of being baptized in the faith community of the Hutterite brotherhood. Baptism marks a decision to be subject to spiritual authority of the church, to give up all ownership of personal property, and to devote one's life to the well-being of the community. But most importantly, baptism marks a decision to enter the spiritual "ark" of salvation, the church, where one is safe from the judgment of God, as well as from the corruptions of the surrounding society. Those who are baptized are assumed to have received the Holy Spirit, and are therefore entrusted with greater responsibility.

The next step for a younger person after baptism is typically marriage, a decision that is initiated through a process of courtship—typically between young people from different colonies. This decision must be approved by the parents of both partners, and by the elders of both communities.

These priorities and routines of colony life circumscribe the privacy and autonomy of Hutterite families, who are maintained as distinct units on the one hand, and are subject to the authority of the community on the other hand. Nuclear families, especially when extended by marriage into networks of influence, pose a constant threat to the ultimate authority of the colony. The tension between communal and family authority is managed through habits of communication that rely on directness rather than subtlety. Such cooperation—based on habits of command and obedience—is cultivated by encouraging a discipline of yieldedness, or acceptance of one's place in the colony structure throughout childhood. Nevertheless, sociologists have noted that expressions of dissent or resistance are given voice within certain contexts. For example, although women occupy a secondary location to men in the authority structure (they are unable to vote in colony decision-making), it is not uncommon for wives to express discontent about a social arrangement to their husbands, who have the status to voice such concerns in more public assemblies.

SPIRITUAL FREEDOM VERSUS COMMUNAL IDENTITY

For Hutterites, spiritual life is experienced communally, defined to a very significant extent by the expectation of surrender to God and to the church. As Jakob Hutter put it in his *eighth letter* (1535): "Let us not waste the time we still have on earth, doing only what our flesh desires, but let us serve and obey God and His children as long as we live." Early Hutterite teaching made surrender of life and property to the community an article of faith on par with other essential doctrines of Christian faith. In Peter Walpot's article book of 1577, for example, article three, titled *True Surrender and Christian Community of Goods* insists that "all lie who say 'community is not necessary and is no basis of doctrine,' for it is an article of the faith, yea an institution of Christ and of the Holy Spirit and His teaching. Therefore, just as it is necessary for us to hold to the doctrine of the apostles, to prayer and to the breaking of bread, even so it is necessary for us to hold to community of goods" (Walpot 1577).

Such teachings make the spiritual discipline of yieldedness to communal authority a central tenet of Hutterite piety. However, Hutterites are not immune from influence by outside forms of spirituality with the capacity to undermine the communal life. A BBC film of 1992 directed by Jane Treays documents the strife that takes place in one Hutterite commune in Montana, when some of its members are converted to evangelical Christianity and consider themselves "born again." The film deals with the effects of such "conversions" on extended family relationships, and on life within a colony fractured by differences in piety. Evangelical piety, which emphasizes a personal relationship with Jesus Christ, contradicts the Hutterite emphasis on attachment to Christ through the church.

Another example of the tension between personal religious curiosity and Hutterite communal authority is the argument that ensued in the 1960s within a Manitoba *Schmiedeleut* colony over the teachings associated with Herbert W. Armstrong and the Worldwide Church of God. Several members had been listening to the Armstrong radio broadcasts, which featured apocalyptical teachings regarding the end of the age, along with sabbatarian views advocating for Saturday observance of the Sabbath and the return to Jewish kosher food laws and religious holidays. Those influenced by Armstrong's teachings broke colony rules against listening to the radio, and began to adopt the practices and beliefs of the Worldwide Church of God, thereby dividing the colony. After the colony elders expelled them from the community, the dissident group refused to leave, drawing on the resources of the Worldwide Church of God to bring a lawsuit against the colony, demanding that the resources of the colony be distributed fairly among all the members, including the dissidents. This demand challenged the longstanding Hutterite rule that anyone leaving the community forfeits all rights to communal property. The court battle was carried out amidst considerable publicity, and eventually ended up before the Canadian Supreme Court in

1966, which ruled on behalf of the colony, thereby forcing the dissident group to leave the community.

LEGAL RIGHTS AND COMMUNITY AUTHORITY

The issue of the rights that ex-Hutterite individuals have to communal property they have participated in accumulating has been an ongoing controversy. Historically, court litigation around this question has been initiated by aggrieved former colony members, not by colony leaders, who have adhered to the Anabaptist conviction against using the coercive power of the secular legal system to settle disputes within the church. However, in 1987, the leaders of a *Schmiedeleut* colony in Manitoba brought a lawsuit against dissidents who had been expelled but who had refused to leave. The leaders were apparently influenced by their association at that time with the *Bruderhof*—the communal societies originating in twentieth-century Germany under Eberhard Arnold's leadership and focused mostly on the eastern seaboard of the United States. The *Bruderhof* had a long tradition of using the court system to enforce expulsions and to defend themselves against what they perceived to be slander.

The lawsuit came about because of a long-simmering dispute that threatened the unity of the entire *Schmiedeleut* brotherhood in both Canada and the United States. This conflict arose when the patent rights to a new hog feeder design that had been obtained by one colony, Crystal Spring, were disputed by Daniel Hofer, a member of the Lakeside colony, on whose behalf Hofer claimed to have actually submitted the patent claim earlier. The leader of the Crystal Spring colony, Jacob Kleinsasser, also happened to be senior elder of the *Schmiedeleut*. Through its official distributor, Crystal Spring had been active in enforcing its patent rights to the point of sharing infringement claim proceeds won by the distributor from fellow Hutterite colonies. When ordered by the distributor for Crystal Springs, through the distributor's lawyers, to stop manufacturing hog feeders, Hofer—who was head of the Lakeside stainless steel shop—refused to submit, claiming that Crystal Spring colony had stolen the patent from him. When the colony's leaders, backed by *Schmiedeleut* overseers, ordered him to stop, and negotiated a settlement with the Crystal Spring distributor, instead of submitting, Hofer actively sought to nullify the settlement. Threatened with excommunication, Hofer demanded adjudication by the broader *Schmiedeleut* leadership. However, partly because of the influence of the *Schmiedeleut* elder, Jacob Kleinsasser, Hofer and other dissidents from Lakeside who supported him were expelled from the colony, an action to which Hofer and his associates responded by refusing to leave. The decision by colony leaders and *Schmiedeleut* overseers to force the dissidents to leave through the intervention of the court was met by a countersuit filed by Hofer and his friends that argued their expulsion did not follow correct procedure and was therefore nulled.

Meanwhile, the extended family networks reaching beyond the Lakeside colony, expanded the local division throughout the *Schmiedeleut* brotherhood, with colonies in both the United States and Canada dividing according to whether or not to support the Daniel Hofer faction or the Hutterite leadership. More lawsuits ensued, and the obvious significance of the question at hand helped to bring the Hofer suit before the Supreme Court of Canada, which agreed with Hofer that the Hutterite leaders had not followed their own rules in the process of expelling Hofer and his associates, and that, therefore, the dissidents were still legally members of the Lakeside colony. This decision exacerbated rather than resolved the intensity and scope of the conflict among *Schmiedeleut* colonies, which experienced a proliferation of lawsuits and countersuits by factions and colony leaders. At the same time, the credibility of Jacob Kleinsasser's leadership of the *Schmiedeleut* increasingly became a question of dispute, leading ultimately to a church-wide division and the establishment of two separate Hutterite conferences of *Schmiedeleut*. Colonies now were forced to decide which of the conferences to align with, a question that typically led to division, and then to the question of how to dispose of colony resources in the wake of a church-wide schism. Did the leadership of the colony have the authority to constitute the legal affiliation of the colony and thereby to deprive those in their community who sided with the rival group of any claim to resources? In Canada, through a series of interventions by Canadian judges, dividing colonies were encouraged to distribute the resources proportionately. In the United States, the courts typically refused to become involved in the disputes, citing separation of church and state precedents; as a result, the U.S. colonies tended to follow a winner-take-all approach to division, with minority dissidents being forced to leave without any claim to colony resources.

These lawsuits and their outcomes illustrate the complexity of interaction between liberal societies based on individual rights, and communal societies based on social authority. Hutterite communities toward the end of the twentieth century were increasingly engaged in competitive market practices that compromised their long tradition of mutual support and sharing. As a result, they became involved in court disputes that also undermined the authority of church leaders to manage conflicts according to Hutterian traditions and processes, granting instead to secular courts increasing power to determine how the Hutterite community conducted its affairs.

TRADITIONAL FARMING COMMUNITIES VERSUS COMMUNAL LAND OWNERSHIP

Hutterite communities have, in recent decades, become fairly wealthy communities, owning multi-million dollar agribusiness and manufacturing enterprises, demonstrating that communal surrender carries with it the potential for a good life full of considerable security. Such wealth has sometimes presented obstacles to neighborly relationships, with families and individuals playing the capitalist game without the resources of communal life.

Already in 1942, the state of Alberta forbade the sale of land to "enemy aliens, Hutterites, and Doukhobours," a law modified later to permit the sale of land as long as Hutterite colonies did not form within 40 miles of one another. Later, that law was amended in 1960 to provide for even greater flexibility, yet requiring all land sales to Hutterites to be approved by a government agency. Manitoba

Hutterites at one point were required to restrict their colonies to one or two per municipality, and to separate them by at least ten miles.

The branching of Hutterite colonies into new areas often produced protest that provincial governments in Canada sought to address, typically by creating liaison offices that managed public relations aspects of Hutterite branching, in order to reassure local farm populations that their communities would not be outnumbered by Hutterites. The efforts by Canadian provinces to restrict the density of colony locations, resulted in the dispersion of the Hutterites geographically, and forced them to locate colonies in less than optimal settings for farming. These colonies have nevertheless thrived because of the efficiencies of communal farming, and through innovations in agricultural methods. At the same time, colonies have increasingly moved beyond farming to the manufacture of agricultural products, with considerable success and profit. The economic success of well-established Hutterite colonies has led to an era of security and well-being, perhaps unmatched since the Golden Age in Moravia.

See also Amish; Personal Pacifism versus Political Nonviolence.

Further Reading: Esau, Alvin J. *The Courts and the Colonies: The Litigation of Hutterite Church Disputes.* Vancouver: UBC Press, 2004; Gross, Leonard. *The Golden Years of the Hutterites.* Scottdale, Pa.: Herald Press, 1980; Gross, Paul S. *The Hutterite Way.* Saskatoon: Freeman Publishing Company Limited, 1965; Hassenberg, Kathleen, trans. "A Notable Hutterite Document Concerning True Surrender and Christian Community of Goods." *Mennonite Quarterly Review* 31, no. 1 (January 1957): 22–62; Hostetler, John A. *Hutterite Society.* Baltimore: Johns Hopkins University Press, 1997; Hutter, Jakob. *Brotherly Faithfulness: Epistles from a Time of Persecution.* Rifton, New York: Plough Publishing House, 1979; Janzen, William. *Limits on Liberty: The Experience of Mennonite, Hutterite, and Doukhobor Communities in Canada.* Toronto: University of Toronto Press, 1990; Kraybill, Donald and Carl Bowman. *On the Back Road to Heaven: Old Order Hutterites, Mennonites, Amish, and Brethren.* Baltimore: Johns Hopkins University Press, 2001; Packull, Werner. *Hutterite Beginnings: Communitarian Experiments during the Reformation.* Baltimore: Johns Hopkins University Press, 1995; Peter, Karl. *The Dynamics of Hutterite Society: An Analytical Approach.* Edmonton: The University of Alberta Press, 1987.

Gerald Biesecker-Mast

IMMIGRATION

Immigration is the historical process of peoples crossing into new regions. As opposed to migration, immigration denotes a certain degree of permanence in the change of location of the migrating persons. Immigration is often caused by economic and political push-and-pull factors between nations. It is also a form of escape for peoples suffering from religious, political, or cultural persecution. A process carrying vast numbers of persons, immigration has profound effects on both the region left, and the region ventured into by immigrants. As a result, immigrants are often received with hostility and conflict in the new land. The phenomenon of immigration has continued into the twenty-first century and still greatly affects modern culture. For religious Americans, the effects of immigration have continued to be debated as individuals try to balance religious encouragements to "welcome the stranger" (a high value in the Jewish, Christian, and Islamic traditions especially), and yet also respect for laws regarding border passage.

ANCIENT IMMIGRATION IN THE BIBLE: EGYPT AND THE EXODUS

Modern immigration is not a new phenomenon, and the Judeo-Christian scriptures feature many cases of crossing borders, such as the famous population movements depicted in the book of Exodus. The *beginning* of Exodus describes Jacob and his 12 sons as immigrants seeking refuge in the land of Egypt from famine. Fearing the large amount of Israelites entering their nation, affluent Egyptian leadership created an oppressed work force out of these sojourners. The economic and political suppression of the Israelites led to their desire to once again migrate to another land. While the Hebrew Exodus from Egypt is an event that is very telling of why people choose to immigrate, the period of exile that followed gives much insight into the struggles of immigrants following the physical movement of immigration. The cultural struggle of the Israelites proved to be difficult as they attempted to adjust in a new land while maintaining their distinct identity—a struggle that often led to violence between resident groups in their "promised land". These opposing desires illustrate the struggles of all immigrants as they balance the traditions of the past, and the hopes of the future. The cultural shock of living in a Diaspora is present in all stories of immigration as the questioning of national identity and self-identity forges beyond mere lines and borders.

MODERN IMMIGRATION: THE GLOBAL EFFECTS

Immigration is a fluid and dynamic attribute of humanity that is constantly occurring between nations. Throughout the twentieth and early twenty-first centuries, there are examples of especially active borders and issues of immigration, including the borders separating the United States and Mexico, separating Mexico and Guatemala, and separating Morocco and Spain, as well as Sudanese refugee immigration to many neighboring nations. Each of these distinct movements is characterized by deep historical, economic, and political influences. While Moroccan immigrants seek economic opportunities, Sudanese immigrants seek refuge from their authoritarian government. Furthermore, each case of immigration is the story of an individual seeking the opportunity for a better life.

THE HISTORY OF IMMIGRATION
TO THE UNITED STATES

The United States was founded as a land of immigrants when European immigrants from Britain sought religious freedom in the West. Beginning on the East Coast, the nation has been filled by centuries of global immigration. The only citizens of the United States who cannot attribute their past to another land are Native Americans who, because of immigration to the United States, have nonetheless been consistently *internally displaced* persons. The Statue of Liberty sends forth the message: "Give me your tired, your poor, your huddled masses yearning to breathe free, the wretched refuse of your teeming shore. Send these, the homeless, tempest-tost to me, I lift my lamp beside the golden door." Ironically, the history of immigration in the United States has been far less pleasant than this famous monument suggests. The original flow of immigration from Europe (in waves that often reflected population movements from different parts of Europe) has been followed by an influx of Asian immigration in the early 1900s, and Latin American immigration in the late twentieth and early twenty-first centuries.

A HISTORY OF REJECTION

Mass famines in Ireland and a failed revolution in Germany created an influx of European immigration to the United States in the mid-1800s. This impulse was ill-received by nativists—as evident in opposition groups such as the Know-Nothings who feared the spread of Catholicism. Asian immigration in the late nineteenth century was referred to as the yellow peril, and was restricted legislatively through the Chinese Exclusion Act in 1882. Until 1982, several other legislative endeavors continued to limit immigration by targeting specific groups through health tests and other tactics. The Immigration Act of 1942 created a quota system that allowed for only certain amounts of immigrants from individual nations. None of these legislative attempts to bar immigration included exclusion of Latin American immigrants.

HISTORY OF UNITED STATES-MEXICO RELATIONS

Conflicting interests between the United States and Mexico began early while the United States expanded in the name of Manifest Destiny, that is, a sense of God-given privilege to expand and gain power. This period of rapid territorial growth included encroachment of Mexican territory in what today is referred to as the Southwest of the United States. In 1846, the United States declared war on Mexico over this territory, and in 1848 acquired half of Mexico's territory through the Treaty of Guadalupe Hidalgo. Although part of the settlement included a payment to Mexico of $15 million, the United States acquired an immense amount of property, as well as the superior role within the relationship of these two nations.

Following the United States' military domination, the United States acted on its' economic supremacy as well. As U.S. investment began to supersede the agricultural endeavors of Mexico, 96 percent of Mexican families were left landless by 1910. This disparity between Mexican and United States prosperity was heightened with the passing of the North American Free Trade Agreement (NAFTA) in 1994. NAFTA created the opening of U.S. fruit and vegetable markets to Mexico, and the Mexican grain market to the United States. This policy has resulted in the dependency of the Mexican economy on the United States, who now absorbs 88 percent of Mexican exports. The production of corn, Mexico's main crop, was devastated by the importing of cheap U.S. corn (whose price was subsidized by U.S. government assistance to farmers) resulting in the bankruptcy of Mexican farmers.

THE CONTEXT OF MEXICAN IMMIGRATION
INTO THE UNITED STATES

Once U.S. citizens began moving toward urbanized and industrialized workforce options, the U.S. agricultural sector was in need of cheap labor. Between 1942 and 1964, 4.8 million Mexicans were used as seasonal workers under a system called the Bracero Program. Under the program, Mexican farm workers were contracted to live in the United States during crop seasons, and then move back to Mexico once the crop was harvested. Since this movement between the United States and Mexico was advantageous for American agriculture, the immigration of Mexicans was not affected by the legislative restrictions put in place throughout the first half of the twentieth century. The program did, however, safeguard any hopes of permanent residence for the seasonal workers.

Family members were not allowed to travel with the workers during the crop season in hopes that the fathers and husbands would yearn to go home at the end of the crop. Secondly, a portion of the bracero's wages were not paid until arrival back home in Mexico.

The success of the Bracero Program created the first instances of "illegal immigration". The popularity of the program led to the exclusiveness of becoming a bracero worker. As a result, many men chose to travel north without the papers, and still received work alongside the chosen braceros. Growers began enticing these undocumented workers, which was unsupported yet permitted by the U.S. government. By 1949, there were 74,600 braceros and 142,000 undocumented workers in the fields of the southern United States.

Mexican immigration was originally sought by the United States in its time of economic need; however, the influx of workers also stirred another round of xenophobic fears, which led to further pressure for immigration restrictions similar to those enacted earlier in the century and directed to Asians and other potential immigrants. During the period of McCarthyism (1940s–early 1950s), racism and fear of communism caused tighter control on all American borders, which created the first series of legislative restrictions on Mexican immigration. In 1954, Operation Wetback called for the deportation of between one and two million undocumented Mexicans. This change in perspective towards the Mexican immigrant from "agricultural aide" to "illegal alien" is a change that continues to permeate much of the general American reaction to Mexican immigration as portrayed in the media.

MODERN ENDEAVORS TO HALT
MEXICAN IMMIGRATION

The escalating conflict of Mexican immigration into the United States has increased attention given to the physical border between the two nations. In 1994, Operation Gatekeeper enhanced the effectiveness of government enforcement along the U.S.-Mexico border. The increased funding was allocated towards additional border patrol agents, more technology and security measures, as well as the building of the physical border. This financial increase toward border security illustrated the change in paradigm, that immigration was no longer a concept to be struggled with, but instead it had become a physical battle between these two nations.

HR 4437, the proposed Sensenbrenner-King Bill in 2005, sought to take matters further by criminalizing the act of associating with an undocumented immigrant. In this sense, not only were immigrants targeted, but so too were United States' citizens who contributed to the livelihood of an undocumented immigrant. Highly controversial, HR 4437 did not pass. However, it did illustrate the highly political debate that was erupting over immigration reform.

THE PUSHES AND PULLS OF IMMIGRATION

Despite the countless legislative attempts to restrict immigration, it has been a continued reality across the deserts of the U.S.-Mexico border. Though the act of illegally entering the United States has become increasingly more difficult, the immense pressure from economic pushes and pulls still drives immigration. The disparity of wealth within Mexico leaves 18 percent of the nation living under the poverty line (compare 12.3% in the United States for 2006, where poverty is measured at a higher economic level), while the national GDP continues to grow steadily. This growing gap causes the immigration of the country's poorest out of simple economic necessity. Even college-educated individuals in Mexico have extreme difficulty finding a sustainable income within the Mexican job market. Immigrants in this context, and across the world, are pushed by the desires to escape poverty, to provide better education to their children, to find more job opportunities, and to find hope for a better life. While Mexican immigrants are pushed by these desires, they are equally pulled by forces from within the United States. While the United States sends a message that illegal immigration is a criminal act, the job market suggests otherwise. Immigrants fill what are referred to as the 3-D jobs: the dangerous, difficult, and dirty jobs such as agriculture and construction. Many complain that undocumented immigrants filling these jobs hinder our economic growth. Economists argue, however, that our economy has benefited from the labor of undocumented workers. This truth is what allows corporations and businesses to act as the pull factor as they invite undocumented laborers to fill their job openings.

THE POLITICS OF THE IMMIGRATION DEBATE

The complexity of these economic pushes and pulls has resulted in a highly contentious political debate. While many speak of whether we should have an open or closed border, the most pressing issue is how the United States will create a path towards legalization. Beyond the issue of continued immigration into the United States, the government is working to detail an approach toward addressing the undocumented immigrants already within the borders of the United States. Deadlocked congressional legislation in the summer of 2007 presented many different formulas to tackle this dilemma. A point system was proposed that would determine which types of peoples amongst the immigrants would first be granted citizenship. Many supported family reunification efforts by providing more points towards relatives. Others argued that more points should go towards those who will contribute most to the United States, such as scientists and highly skilled workers. While this debate continues, most undocumented immigrants have no hope of being granted citizenship, since the system is now backlogged for years to come.

THE DESERT BORDER CROSSING

While debate over legislative reform discusses necessary institutional changes, Mexican immigrants continually risk their lives crossing the U.S.-Mexico border. Project Gatekeeper provided funding to build up the physical border between the two nations. Established in the original location of mass immigration, Tijuana, Mexico, illegal border crossings have moved farther East in the past decade. As a result, many immigrants cross through the deserts of Arizona and

New Mexico where the border is less regulated. This dangerous trek has caused 238 immigrant deaths since 2006 in Arizona alone. In addition to the heat of the desert, immigrants are faced with extreme blisters from their long journey, abuse from coyotes, dehydration, and other daunting factors.

Additionally, increased military technology has made an illegal entrance an even harder task. As a result, immigrants are very cautious of Border Patrol agents and tend to travel only at night. When caught by the Border Patrol, immigrants are then taken to Wackenhut in vans. Wackenhut is a private security company paid by the U.S. government to deliver undocumented border crossers back into Mexico. Ironically, the company is known world-wide for its countless human rights violations. As a result, much discontent has arisen from this additional component to the already contentious debate on immigration. A frightening truth is that many of the undocumented immigrants placed back in Mexico are not Mexican. Many immigrants travel from the extreme distances of Central America. The simple immigrant drop offs into Mexican border towns hold even further disappointment for these individuals.

IMMIGRATION INTEREST GROUPS

Immigration from Mexico to the United States does not only affect the immigrant; instead, its repercussions are felt by many groups within the United States. Of special interest are the corporations who benefit from the labor of these undocumented workers. Many of these companies and businesses have become dependent on this exploitable labor, so legislative changes that would further enforce documentation of all workers would severely alter the nature of their work force. Other people highly involved in the immigration debate include vigilante groups. Highly patriotic, these people volunteer to physically help the border patrol in preventing illegal immigration. The aid of minutemen to the border patrol has been highly opposed due to instances of extreme violence and even murder between themselves and immigrants. There are other groups that side on the interest of the immigrant. Many nonprofit groups defend the rights of the immigrants, and work against the xenophobia and racism that escalate the immigration debate.

THE FIGHT AGAINST IMMIGRATION

Beyond mere racist or xenophobic disdain for immigrants themselves, there are many other reasons why United States citizens oppose Mexican immigration. Many citizens fear the economic ramifications of immigration, and are disgruntled in particular by issues such as taxation and health care. Others are opposed to immigration due to the connections between drug cartels and illegal immigration. Immigration has also been highly resisted following September 11. Terminating illegal immigration from Mexico has been included as an effort to prevent future terrorist attacks on the United States.

THE RELIGIOUS RESPONSE TO IMMIGRATION:
OLD TESTAMENT TEACHING

Despite the complexity of immigration, most religious traditions have a sound response: compassion toward the immigrant. This message is depicted in biblical sojourners throughout the Old Testament. The exploitation of immigrants is shown as a contradiction to the desire of God as depicted in Deuteronomy: "[God] executes justice for the orphan and the widow, and. . . loves the strangers, providing them food and clothing" (10:18). Following the book of Exodus, the Old Testament describes the compassion of God towards the exiled Israelites. A message of hope is revealed in Isaiah 40:3–5: "In the wilderness prepare the way of the Lord, make straight in the desert a highway for our God. Every valley shall be lifted up, and every mountain and hill will be made low. . . Then the glory of the Lord shall be revealed."

JESUS CROSSING BORDERS

The Gospels continue a message of hope for the immigrant through the life of Jesus. Jesus consistently sided with the marginalized while breaking political, religious, and cultural borders. In John 4:9, Jesus speaks with a Samaritan woman who bewilderingly asks him: "You are a Jew and I am a Samaritan woman. How can you ask me for a drink?" Jesus breaks this border based on nationality and embraces the foreigner as a neighbor. Similarly, when Jesus was asked "who is my neighbor?", he replied with the Parable of the Good Samaritan (Luke 10). In this example, Jesus explains that a neighbor is not one of physical proximity or political alliance, but one who rightfully shows mercy. He calls others to break boundaries and to show mercy to all.

Hispanic Theology in the United States, derived from Liberation Theology, also places emphasis on the life of Jesus as a call for compassion toward the immigrant. Virgil Elizondo illustrates the fact that Jesus was a Galilean Jew, as opposed to the culturally superior Jews of Judea. Drawing a correlation between Mexican Americans caught between two cultural identities, Jesus is seen as a mestizo between Judea and Galilee. This portrayal of Jesus is especially meaningful for immigrants who are caught between two conflicting societies. The depiction of Jesus as a mestizo is also very pertinent to immigration, in that it illustrates God's becoming human in the severely marginalized and rejected of the world. This creates a call for the Christian community to continue to meet Jesus in the marginalized, to find Jesus in the immigrant. This call has been heard by countless Christian groups who work to better the plight of the immigrant.

CHRISTIAN ACTION IN RESPONSE TO
U.S.-MEXICAN IMMIGRATION

Since the majority of Mexican immigrants come from Catholic backgrounds, the Catholic Church on both sides of the border plays a significant role in U.S.-Mexican immigration. For instance, Cardinal Mahoney of Los Angeles pledged to defy HR 4437 if it were enacted, for he argued that it defied Catholic Social Teaching. Catholic Social Teaching upholds the principles of the dignity of the human person, the preferential option for the poor, and the dignity of work, all of which promote empathy for the immigrant. Cardinal Mahoney's rejection of HR 4437 and his Justice for Immigrants Campaign have enhanced Catholic support for the dignity of the immigrant. Catholic Relief Services has created a program called Diocese Without Borders, which works to connect the efforts of Catholic churches on both sides of the U.S.-Mexico border. The goal of this program is to create greater solidarity within this universal church, while acknowledging that the kingdom of God has no borders.

Another attempt to create solidarity between people of faith on both sides of the border is through the religious celebration of Las Posadas. This annual re-enactment of Mary and Joseph's struggle to find shelter in Bethlehem currently takes place on the U.S.-Mexico Border. In this way, the reenactment presents a parallel between the refusal of the holy family, and the refusal of Mexican immigrants. The fact that Mary and Joseph eventually received shelter in time for the birth of Christ acts as a symbol of hope for greater hospitality and empathy between the two communities.

THE JEWISH AND ISLAMIC RESPONSES TO IMMIGRATION

The narratives of Moses and the Exodus in the Torah are especially meaningful within the Jewish tradition. Breaking their exploitation, God liberated the Hebrew people from Egypt and delivered them to a "land flowing with milk and honey" (Deuteronomy 26:8). Some believe that modern Jews are still in exile until they return home to Israel. Because of this exilic identity, the Jewish tradition has a long history of aiding the refugee and the migrant. Many efforts to create a more empathetic approach towards U.S.-Mexican immigration include interfaith organizations combining the efforts of the Christian, Jewish, and Islamic communities.

See also Sanctuary Movement; Separation of Church and State.

Further Reading: Brewer, Stewart. *Borders and Boundaries: A History of U.S.-Latin American Relations.* London: Praeger Security International, 2006; Chacon, Justin Akers and Mike Davis. *No One is Illegal: Fighting Racism and State Violence on the U.S.-Mexico Border.* Chicago: Haymarket Books, 2006; Dawson, Alexander S. *First World Dreams: Mexico since 1989.* London: Fernwood Publishing, 2006; Deck, Allan Figueroa, ed. *Frontiers of Hispanic Theology in the United States.* New York: Orbis Books, 1992; Ekblad, Bob. *Reading the Bible With the Damned.* Louisville: Westminster John Knox Press, 2005; *Hill Notes, February 2007: Comprehensive Immigration Reform.* United States Conference of Catholic Bishops: Migration and Refugee Services. http://www.usccb.org/sdwp/projects/200702immhn.pdf; Hoppe, Leslie J. *There Shall Be No Poor Among You.* Nashville: Abingdon Press, 2004; Koenig, John. *New Testament Hospitality: Partnership with Strangers as Promise and Mission.* Philadelphia: Fortress Press, 1985; Laufer, Peter. *Wetback Nation: The Case for Opening the Mexican-American Border.* Chicago: Ivan R. Dee, 2004; Nevins, Joseph. *Operation Gatekeeper: The Rise of the "Illegal Alien" and the*

Making of the U.S.-Mexico Boundary. New York: Routledge Taylor ad Francis Group, 2002; Smith-Christopher, Daniel L. *Jonah, Jesus, and Other Good Coyotes.* Nashville: Abingdon Press, 2007; Stalker, Peter. *The No-Nonsense Guide to International Migration.* London: New Internationalist, 2001; *Strangers No Longer: Together on the Journey of Hope: A Pastoral Letter Concerning Migration From the Catholic Bishops of Mexico and the United States.* Washington D.C.: United States Conference of Catholic Bishops, 2003.

Elizabeth Shaw

ISLAMIC NATIONALISM

According to the teachings of the Prophet Muhammad, the Muslim community (*ummah*) is one that transcends territorial, ethnic, and racial boundaries. The concept of nationalism, which implies fidelity to a nation (according to *Webster's,* a group of people associated with a particular territory possessing its own government), stands contradictory to the teachings of the Prophet. National loyalty, in the modern sense, was introduced to Muslims through European colonization in the eighteenth century. As a result of European domination and the arbitrary division of the Islamic world into nation-states, Muslim leaders inherited a Westernized geographical reality. While there were some in the Islamic community who embraced traditional Western nationalism, there were others who rejected it, warning of the consequences. Today, throughout parts of the Muslim world, nationalism has evolved from the concept of nation-states to a nationalist movement, which supports a religious foundation.

HISTORICAL ISLAMIC COMMUNITY

The violent and unjust society of seventh-century pre-Islamic Arabia provided the setting for the emergence of a monotheistic religious tradition, eventually referred to as Islam. In a cave outside Mecca, Muhammad ibn Abdallah is said to have received revelations from God, in the form of a new scripture, the Qur'an. The Qur'an instructed believers (Muslims) to submit wholly to God and behave in an ethical manner toward one another. In response to tribal conflicts, vendettas, and immoral behavior, which pervaded the region of western Arabia, the first duty Muhammad assigned to his followers was to create a just society. This new society took the form of a community called an *ummah*. Living according to the Will of God was essential to the prosperity of the *ummah*, and consequently, if the Muslim community suffered misfortune of any kind, Muslims could deduce that they were not practicing authentic Islam. Critical to the teachings concerning the *ummah*, was the instruction from Muhammad that Muslims identify themselves through membership in the spiritual community rather than through their individual ethnicity, language, or geography. Ideally, the Islamic world was to operate as a single political unit, governed by a caliph, who would, under the tenets of Islam, preserve the integrity of the *ummah*. However, Caesar E. Farah, in his book, *Islam,* writes, "As early as the second century of Islam, the conquered Iranians resented the refusal of the conquering Arabs to accord them the full social equality ordained by Islam. The challenge to caliphal authority equated with Arab hegemony resulted frequently from such resentment. The nature of the challenge often took on the form of 'ethnicism.'" (Farah 2003). The persistent problem of ethnic sentiment resulted in the discontented local groups being given the authority to rule their immediate areas under the guidance of the caliph. Muslims became accustomed to ethnic loyalty, regional differences, and kinship ties, however, not disregarding the "universality of the *ummah* and Islam" (Farah 2003). It was within this diverse cultural setting that an unsuspecting Muslim population encountered a menace from the West.

EUROPEAN COLONIALISM AND NATIONALISM

By the mid-eighteenth century a newly industrialized European society emerged. Having cast off the religious restraints of the pre-Reformation period, and embracing rational and scientific principles, the West was free to advance economically within its new secular, democratic society. Efficiency and productivity epitomized the modern nations. As a result of a growing economy, British traders, looking to expand their markets, advanced on India. Flush with a sense of superiority, the European countries expressed a national pride that disregarded the welfare of not only India, but that of other Muslim nations. By the mid-nineteenth century, with the forced expulsion of the last Mughal emperor, British rule was established throughout India. Russia sought to take control of Central Asia, the French annexed Tunisia, Italy occupied Libya, and the British advanced into Egypt. Muslim lands were devastated politically, economically, and culturally due to colonization. In response to the loss of political and social positions in India, the majority of Muslims rejected anything associated with the British. However, some Muslims, such as educator and reformer Sir Sayyid Ahmad Khan (1817–1898), refused to retreat from the influence of the British, and encouraged Muslims to study Western arts and sciences. As this attitude influenced young Muslim men, some of them began using their European educations to voice their grievances. Known as Modernists, they sought solutions to the problems of modernity, while keeping their religious ideals. One such man was Jamal ad-Din al-Afghani (1838–1897), known as "the Awakener of the East."

THE MODERNISTS

Al-Afghani, an Iranian schooled in the Shiite tradition, traveled to India in 1856 with the goal of furthering his education. Witnessing the cruelty of the British during the Indian rebellion of 1857, he devoted his life to the cause of Muslim freedom from European domination. Convinced that Islam provided the answers to the desperate situation in which the Muslims found themselves, al-Afghani encouraged the return to *ijtihad* (independent reasoning). He promoted the implementation of rational thinking as put forth by the Prophet and the Qur'an, to propel Muslims into the modern world. Instead of embracing the European system, he rejected their secular politics and insisted on an Islamic approach to modernization. Al-Afghani allied himself with a group of Turkish academics who believed that Western democracy could be presented in an Islamic context. It is within this atmosphere of Islamic self-determination and reformation that Pan-Islamism became popular. Pan-Islamism is, in essence, a return to Muhammad's original concept of an Islamic community—the *ummah*. Colonialism had torn the Islamic world into separate states, but the hope was that the ideology of Pan-Islamism could unite all Muslims, and rid themselves of the European imperialists. Al-Afghani united with a young Egyptian scholar, Muhammad Abduh (1849–1905), and founded the Salafiyyah reformist movement, which viewed "Islam as civilization."

Muhammad Abduh believed that in order to address the needs of a modern Islamic world, the Sharia (Islamic law) needed to be reformed, and the educational system updated. He felt that the average Muslim could not understand the principles of modern law and politics unless they were presented in an Islamic context. After the death of al-Afghani, Abduh and the journalist, Rashid Rida (1865–1935), tried to advance Pan-Islamism as the ideology of Egyptian politics. They were successfully opposed by secular nationalists who believed that Islam itself was holding Muslims back. Rida, sensing that secularism was a threat to the ideals of the *ummah*, responded by putting forth the notion of a modern Islamic state based on an updated Sharia. The Indian poet and philosopher, Muhammad Iqbal (1876–1938), may have been influenced by Rida's call for a complete update of Islamic law. Living in India under British rule, Iqbal was exposed to the realities of colonialism, but it took a journey to England in order to evoke his fierce repudiation of European nationalism.

Muhammad Iqbal, born in the Punjab province of Pakistan and educated in Quranic studies, traveled to England in 1905 to continue his education. There he received a view of nationalism that would determine the course of his life. Iqbal had long been in favor of Indian nationalism and had shown support for a Hindu-Muslim state. He had believed that an individual could be loyal to his country and retain his own religious beliefs without serious conflict. While in England, Iqbal observed a growing tension between the European powers due to aggressive nationalistic policies. Judging against the selfishness of Western nationalism, he began to favor the promise of a just and compassionate society that could be achieved through the universalism of the *ummah*. Recognizing the pitfalls of nationalism, Iqbal rejected the idea of a Hindu-Muslim state and began to call for a separate Muslim nation, eventually earning the title, "spiritual father of Pakistan." By the commencement of World War I, the Muslim world was in a state of despair, and Iqbal responded to the situation by focusing on the worldwide Muslim community—the *ummah*. He wrote, "The essential difference between the Muslim Community and other Communities of the world consists in our peculiar conception of nationality. It is because we all believe in a certain view of the universe, and participate in the same historical tradition that we are members of the society founded by the Prophet of Islam. Islam abhors all material limitations, and bases its nationality on a purely abstract idea, objectifies in a potentially expansive group of concrete personalities. It is not dependent for its life-principle on the character and genius of a particular people; in its essence it is non-temporal, non-spatial" (Mir 2006). Iqbal, as a proponent of an Islamic religious concept of nationality, saw no conflict between the formation of separate Muslim states and the unification of Muslims on a spiritual rather than a geographical basis. Rather, he put forward the idea of a Muslim League of Nations that would recognize the existence of multiple Muslim states, while promoting common goals. Iqbal embraced a humanitarian ideal of Pan-Islamism, rather than the political concept of one Muslim nation under a single caliph. Secular nationalism, however, was on the rise in the Middle East.

ARAB NATIONALISM

A group of Arabs throughout the Middle East were employing secular nationalism as a means to fight European colonialism. They believed that the only way to defeat the imperialists was through racial unity (Pan-Arabism), not religious solidarity (Pan-Islamism). Sati-al-Husri (1880–1968), a leading promoter of Pan-Arabism, in order to rally support, argued that Arab nationalism was not incongruous with Islam, as Islam had its roots in Arab history. Arab nationalists agreed with the Pan-Islamists that Muslims must return to the ideal of the Medinan *ummah*, but emphasized that since the original community was Arab, Arab unity was essential to Muslim unity. However, by the twentieth century the Arabs were a small fraction of the Muslim community—approximately 20 percent. Nevertheless, secular nationalism triumphed after the First World War with the collapse of the Ottoman Empire, and consequently, the Caliphate. The Turkish Nationalist movement under the leadership of Ataturk, defeated their European occupiers and established the secular, ultranationalist Turkish republic (1922–1924). Their success motivated much of the Muslim world. Conversely, there were some who became alarmed at the specter of secular rule.

MUSLIM BROTHERS AND SOCIAL CHANGE

Hasan al-Banna (1906–1949), a member of the Hasafiyyah Sufi Order, arrived in Egypt in 1923 seeking a higher education. While in Cairo, he became appalled by the squalid conditions of the people, as well as the widespread secularism established by the British and Egyptian elite. Influenced by al-Afghani and Muhammad Abduh, al-Banna believed that a return to the Islamic ideals of equality and social justice would be the only way to change the plight of the people. He rejected nationalism, and therefore Pan-Arabism, as a solution, declaring that nationalism was actually responsible for the ills of Muslim society. Al-Banna founded a movement in 1928 called the Society of the Muslim Brothers. His organization, engaged in religious, social, educational, and charitable activities, asserted that modern life must be met with Islamic values. Extending their movement to other Arab countries—Syria, Jordan, Algeria, Tunisia, Palestine, Sudan, Iran, and Yemen, the Brothers were becoming politically active. However, frustrated in their efforts to enact change in Egypt, a small minority engaged in terrorist activities. This resulted in the 1948 assassination of the Egyptian Prime Minister, subsequently followed by the assassination of al-Banna.

By the end of World War II, the Egyptians had turned toward Arab nationalism with little improvement in the impoverished conditions of its people. In 1952, a group of discontented military leaders, called the *Free Officers*, seized power. The Muslim Brothers, who had aided in putting an end to British domination, were promised the implementation of social reforms. However, it soon became clear that the authoritarian rule set up by Jamal Abd al-Nasser (1918–70) conflicted with the Islamic ideals promoted by the Brothers. This sense of betrayal eventually led to an assassination attempt on Nasser by one of the Brothers. In response, thousands were rounded up and thrown into prison, some tortured and executed. The Brotherhood, now outlawed, went underground and continued its activities, which included attempts to overthrow the regime. One of its ideologues, Egyptian-born Sayyid Qutb (1906–1966) would come to be known as the founder of Islamic radicalism.

Sayyid Qutb, influenced by liberal nationalism, had at one time embraced Western ideas and secular politics. Influenced by the writings of the ideologist, Mawdudi, from the Indian subcontinent, he became disillusioned with secular ideas and turned down an offer from Nasser to join his government. Qutb joined the Muslim Brothers and became one of many thrown in jail after the attempt on Nasser's life. Experiencing the inhumane conditions of prison, and witnessing the brutal torture and executions of his friends, Qutb became hardened in the belief that secularists could not live in peaceful coexistence with people of religion. He wrote,

> The homeland (watan) a Muslim should cherish and defend is not a mere piece of land; the collective identity he is known by is not that of a regime . . . Neither is the banner he should glory in and die for that of a nation (qwan) . . . His jihad is solely geared to protect the religion of Allah and His Shari'a and to save the Abode of Islam and no other territory . . . Any land that combats the Faith, hampers Muslims from practicing their religion, or does not apply the Shari'a, becomes ipso facto part of the Abode of War (Dar al-Harb). It should be combated even if one's own kith and kin, national group, capital and commerce are to be found there . . . A Muslim's homeland is any land governed by the laws of Islam. Islam is the only identity worthy of man . . . Any other group identity . . . is jahili identity of the type humanity has known during its periods of spiritual decadence. (Moaddel 2005)

Jahiliyyah, *the Time of Ignorance*, had been the term used to describe the pre-Islamic period in Arabia. Qutb's declaration, that non-Muslims should be fought to the death, is in direct opposition to Islam, which upholds a doctrine of tolerance, nonviolence, and inclusiveness. Quranic belief holds that God granted people with freedom to choose, therefore, to implement forceful conversion is to disobey God's command. Qutb distorted the message of the Qur'an and the teachings of the Prophet, however, the concept of his new ideology, Islamism, would come to impact every Sunni fundamentalist group. In 1966 Qutb was hung for treason after the publication of his manifesto, *Milestones*, in which he called for the removal of all secular governments.

The remaining Muslim Brothers sought refuge in Saudi Arabia—the only country that would accept them—where ultraconservative Wahhabism was the official Islamic law of the land. Incredibly wealthy due to the discovery of vast oil reserves, the Saudi royal family created the Muslim World League in 1962 in order to spread Wahhabi Islamic doctrine to the entire Muslim world. Reza Aslan writes, "Since the creation of the Muslim World League, the simplicity, certainty, and unconditional morality of Wahhabism have infiltrated every corner of the Muslim world. Thanks to Saudi evangelism, Wahhabi doctrine has dramatically affected the religio-political ideologies of the Muslim Brothers, Mawdudi's Islamic Association, the Palestinian Hamas, and Islamic Jihad, to name only a few groups. The Saudis have become the patrons of a new kind of Pan-Islamism: one based on the austere, uncompromising, and extremist ideology of Islamic fundamentalism, which has become a powerful voice in deciding the future of the Islamic state" (Aslan 2006). In a bizarre turn of events, the Saudi royal family has itself become the target of a Wahhabi indoctrinated group called al-Qaeda. Any Muslim who does not observe the Sharia, and interpret the Qur'an according to this puritanical form of Islam, is considered an infidel. It is in this fundamentalist context that an extreme form of Islamic nationalism, in its intolerant and militant form, is displayed.

CONCLUSION

Nationalism, secular and religious, has taken on a central role in modern Islamic history. Although nation-states were unheard of in the precolonial Muslim world, ethnic inequality under a central Caliphate had surfaced early. By the advent of European occupation, the caliph was a mere figurehead, and the state of Islam had become stagnant due to the rigidity of the religious scholars who had "closed the gates of ijtihad." The devastation brought on by occupation prompted an elite group of intellectuals to try and rebuild Islamic identity through education and religio-political reform. After the First World War, the Muslim countries were ripe for reformists dedicated to improving the conditions of the *ummah*. Citing nationalism as the cause for society's ills, they called for a return to Islamic social justice and equality. Ultimately, this led to a clash with the nationalist governments and the dispersion of socialist groups throughout the Muslim world. The ideals of the reformers inspired later generations in various ways. A small minority took the call to return to Islamic values as a directive to use whatever means necessary, including violence, to implement change. In recent decades, the Islamic nationalist movement has become an intense topic of controversy, with its share of opponents and proponents within the Muslim world and beyond.

See also Nation of Islam; Separation of Church and State.

Further Reading: Armstrong, Karen. *Islam: A Short History.* New York: The Modern Library, 2002; Aslan, Reza. *No god but God: The Origins, Evolution, and Future of Islam.* New York: Random House, 2006; Coury, Ralph M. "Nationalism and Culture in the Arab and Islamic Worlds: A Critique of Modern Scholarship." In *Islamic Thought in the Twentieth Century*, eds. Suha Taji-Farouki and Basheer M. Nafi. New York and London: I. B. Tauris,

2004: 128–171; Esposito, John L. *What Everyone Needs to Know about Islam: Answers to Frequently Asked Questions, from One of America's Leading Experts.* Oxford: Oxford University Press, 2002; Farah, Caesar E. *Islam.* 7th ed. Hauppage, N.Y.: Barron's, 2003; Joffé, E.G.H. "Arab Nationalism and Palestine." *Journal of Peace* 20, no. 2 (June 1983): 157–170; Lewis, Bernard. *Islam and the West.* New York and Oxford: Oxford University Press, 1993; Mir, Mustansir. *Iqbal.* New York and London: I. B. Tauris and Oxford University Press India, 2006; Mir, Mustansir. *Understanding the Islamic Scripture: A Study of Selected Passages from the Qur'ān.* New York: Pearson Longman, 2008; Moaddel, Mansoor. *Islamic Modernism, Nationalism, and Fundamentalism.* Chicago and London: The University of Chicago Press, 2005; Saeed, Abdullah. *Islamic Thought: An Introduction.* New York and London: Routledge, 2006.

Candace Lev

JAILHOUSE CONVERSIONS

Over two million people are imprisoned in the United States. More prisons and jails were constructed in the United States between 1980 and 2000 than had been built in the previous 200 years. The American prison system costs well over $60 billion dollars per year. In Michigan, the workings of the prison system takes up 20 percent of the state budget, while in the 1980s, it was only seven percent. Housing a prisoner for one year costs a national average of $25,000 a year.

THE HISTORY OF RELIGION AND PRISONS

Religious organizations have always been involved in prisons, and in fact, religious organizations inspired the very concept of prison. It is often pointed out among ancient historians that prisons simply did not exist in the ancient world—either in Greece, Rome, or biblical Israel. In Greece and Rome, there were places where debtors were held until payment arrangements could be made, but there was apparently no concept of a long-term incarceration as a form of punishment.

There are references in the Bible to "prisons" (Genesis 39:20, 22), such as the holding place for Samson (Judges 16:21, 25), but there are no laws in the Bible discussing prison as a legal institution or punishment. It is clear that there were no long-term incarcerations in ancient Israel, either, and the mentions of "prisons" were merely as holding places until judgment had occurred, or payments made, as in classical Greece or Rome.

Skotnicki (2006) suggests that Christians were drawn to the idea of "encouraging penitence" because they were skeptical about making use of the Roman legal system during the long centuries when Christianity itself was illegal or publically persecuted (St. Paul asks, in 1 Corinthians 6:1: "When any of you has a grievance against another, do you dare to take it to court before the unrighteous, instead of taking it before the saints?"). The presumption of an antagonistic relationship with the state is also perhaps the theme in the teachings of Jesus, suggesting the importance of visiting those in prison (Matthew 25), and an early Christian writer writes:

> Remember those who are in prison, as though you were in prison with them; those who are being tortured, as though you yourselves were being tortured. (Hebrews 13:3)

In Western Christian society, however, the institution of the monastery inspired the idea of *cells* for those who need to be removed from wider society and allowed to reflect and pray about their lives, and hopefully then to be *penitent*. However, secularized prisons—apparently developing from the treatment of errant monks within the monastery—was a slow development, and only began to emerge in the twelfth and thirteenth centuries of the Christian era. Skotnicki makes the interesting observation that the Christian concept of *purgatory*—a kind of prison of God for errant souls before they are released into heaven—emerged at roughly the same time as the concept of prisons for those considered dangerous to society. The religious, and the social, ideas appeared to develop at the same time, and were closely related (Skotnicki 2006).

The notion of *solitary confinement*, however, is often associated with the early American prison reform work of the Quakers. Believing that what the errant individual requires is quiet time to reflect on their mistakes, Quakers encouraged such reform projects as Eastern State Penitentiary in Philadelphia, which opened in the nineteenth century. The idea was not to severely punish, but to allow time for repentance and considering one's life. As an alternative to severe physical abuse, the Quakers suggested *solitary confinement* as a humane alternative. Psychologists, however, debate how "humane" such long-term isolation really is.

The eighteenth century had seen a major rise in interest among philosophers and religious leaders in Europe in the reforming of the often horrendous conditions of prisoners. Philosophers such as Jeremy Bentham saw prison reform as an important aspect of their social philosophy in the late eighteenth century in England. But solitary confinement as a concept was not unique to the Quakers. Schmid (2003) notes in her study of the history of prison reform, that Pope Clement XI in 1704 built the Hospice of San Michele as an early experiment, keeping persons in monastery-like enclosures, or *cells* in hopes that isolation and confinement would encourage repentance and reform. It was a similar belief that isolation, prayer, and long periods of time given to thought, would be more effective than inflicting pain and bodily harm, or other forms of physical punishments and public humiliations, that led to Quaker support of institutions such as Eastern State Penitentiary, built precisely to maximize isolation of individual prisoners. The very architecture of this prison was intended to look frightening to those outside by building it as a castle-like structure, as well as maximize separation and isolation for those within. But it was precisely this isolation that was considered by other visitors to this prison, such as Charles Dickens, to be inhumane punishment and a kind of "death." Eastern State itself was closed as a prison in 1971, and reopened as a museum in 1994. "Solitary Confinement" is today used only in short-term cases of severe isolation and punishment.

JAILHOUSE CONVERSIONS AND THE ROLE OF RELIGION IN MODERN PRISONS

There have always been stories of important *conversions* in prison. Perhaps most importantly in the twentieth century, Malcolm Little converted to a form of Islam, and became Malcolm X, one of the most important African American religious civil rights leaders in the twentieth century before his assassination by members of a rival Islamic movement. Such religious conversions have also raised difficult questions. In the late twentieth century, the celebrated conversion of a death-row inmate Karla Faye Tucker, raised difficult questions for conservative American Christians who normally support a strong prison system, and normally support capital punishment in large numbers. Tucker, who wished to serve out a life sentence, claimed to be completely transformed by her Christian conversion, and even married an assistant prison chaplain, and became a *model prisoner*. Tucker was finally executed on February 3, 1998, after a series of appeals, including many from prominent conservative Christian leaders who had previously supported capital punishment, particularly television evangelist Pat Robertson, who himself called for a suspension of capital punishment until it can be "more justly applied."

Such spectacular individual cases raise the issue of religious involvement in the prison system more generally, and also what the prison system is intended to accomplish. In many religious traditions, including Islam and Christianity, there is hope for the *repentance* and transformation of someone who is in the wrong. There is, in short, the possibility and the hope for some kind of *redemption*. Does this mean, however, that persons are to be reintegrated into wider society? The call for *punishment* as the goal of prison often overrides this belief in *redemption*, and thus any kind of reintegration is viewed with great suspicion.

It is often claimed that "jailhouse conversions" are too easily manipulated as merely a claim by prisoners seeking early release, parole, or special privileges. In their studies of the role of religion from the perspective of inmates themselves, however, social scientists have noted the issues associated with religious activity in prison are not simple.

On the one hand, religious involvement clearly offers benefits to prisoners. Time in chapel can often be a safe haven away from hostile prisoners, and can offer a form of friendship without the often associated *loyalties* that must be formed between prison *gangs* or *racial groupings*. Just having religious friends often serves to protect prisoners from the dangers of being seen as a loner without associates that *look out for them* in prison life. This is seen as equally important for prisoners who are Muslim as well as Christian. Finally, prisoners often sought the association with volunteers and religious leaders who represented some kind of regularized contact with *the free world*.

On the other hand, studies have also shown that prisoners themselves doubt that religious involvement earns them any *special favors*, and even prisoners who are not religiously active express doubts that the "religious ones" are getting any special treatment. Furthermore, studies also show that inmate involvement in religious activities actually contributes to building positive self-images by allowing inmates to deal with their mistakes, and build a "new life." In many cases, religious involvement helps them to face their mistakes by associating those mistakes with their "old life."

Do religious programs, however, actually contribute to transformation or "reform" of the individual prisoners, and perhaps even serve to reduce the rate of criminal behavior once they are released? This is normally a question of *recidivism rates*.

Recidivism refers to the frequency with which former prisoners are returning to prison because of further criminal behavior after serving time. The impact on religion on *recidivism* has been a subject of interest for social scientists who surveyed a wide range of studies on religious involvement and delinquency among youth, and concluded that "religion consistently had a negative effect on delinquency," and "religiosity was inversely related to delinquency" (Matthews and Blanchard 2005). That is to say, religious involvement among youth significantly reduced tendencies toward delinquent behavior.

PRISON MINISTRIES AND EXPERIMENTS

There are a number of prominent national Christian prison programs. Former White House aid Charles "Chuck" Colson, upon his own dramatic religious conversion before serving a short sentence for his involvement in the Watergate scandals in the Nixon White House, established Prison Fellowship, which is similar to other Christian Prison ministry projects such as *Kairos Ministries* who send volunteers into prisons to establish Bible studies and discussion groups. Encouraging letters are given to prisoners, written by volunteers with Kairos, and there are "graduations" from the program organized. A related organization, Kairos Outside, attempts to work with families of those who are imprisoned as a support group. Christine Money, warden of an all-male prison in Marion, Ohio, reported that in her fourth year as warden, the number of grievances filed monthly by prisoners had dropped from over 100 to single digit figures. Kairos Ministries claims that recidivism rates in the state of Florida were 15.7 percent among prisoners who had participated in only one session of their programs, and drops to 10 percent among those who are regular participants, as opposed to 23.4 percent for the general prison population. The recidivism rates are much higher nationally. Some estimates are as high as two-thirds of those released from prison will re-offend within 3 years.

Other studies have noted similar positive results with Native American prisoners by initiating Native traditional religious programs into prison life (Irwin, 2006), and there are many Islamic prison programs as well, especially since the founding of the first chaplaincy training program for Muslims in the United

States, located at Hartford Seminary in Connecticut, whose graduates work in hospitals, corporations, or prison chaplaincy programs. In Europe, the development toward regularized prison work among Muslims is further developed than the United States, and in London, a *Muslims Chaplaincy Association* was founded in 2007 to formalize the selection, training, and employment of Islamic chaplains working in the prison system.

THE NEW CONCERNS ABOUT RELIGION IN PRISON

In his article in the *World Policy Journal,* Ian Cuthbertson (2004) reports on the growing concern with radical *recruitment* in prisons—conversions to both Islamic and American "Christian" hate groups advocating religious or racial dominance. In testimony before the Senate Judiciary Committee, John Pistole of the FBI called American prisons, "a viable venue for radicalization and recruitment" for Islamic organizations. Cuthbertson, however, also points to the "utterly abysmal conditions" suffered by prisoners in penal institutions in Guantanamo Bay, Cuba, in Iraq, and Afghanistan, estimating that there were over 10,500 persons being held in these three places in 2004 (Cuthbertson 2004). The conditions themselves contribute to an openness to messages of radicalization. The concern is that prison conditions further encourage the spread of radical religious ideas, and that the British "shoe bomber" Richard Reid, and the American José Padilla—accused of trying to construct a radioactive bomb—were both converted to a radicalized version of Islam while in prison.

REFORM OR PUNISHMENT?

One of the most important sources of debate, therefore, is between those Americans who advocate the continued construction of prisons while denying *expensive programs* in those prisons (education and religious programs) which are seen as *coddling* the guilty (and thus these Americans have supported massive cuts in prison education programs). The common social attitude of *let them rot*, however, creates the very conditions of worsening radicalization and breeding of recidivism (gang violence in prisons that spills over outside the prisons) that leads to the increased need for prisons. It has been argued, however, that if prisons are only seen as places of punishment, and not treated in any way as potentially changing or *reforming* the prisoner—then the continued role of prisons as literal breeding grounds of crime and violence both inside and outside the prison will continue. The increased expenses of such *let them rot* policies will become increasingly crippling to state and national budgets (see Zehr 2005).

The arguments for prison reform, improved prison health and education programs, and continued religious involvement in prison ministry, can now include the growing alarm expressed by the fact that radical groups appear to be using the bad conditions of prison as a basis for recruiting prisoners to hate groups.

SUMMARY

The recent alarm at levels of prison *recruitment* into radical hate groups has re-opened the issue of the role of religion in prisons. Religious ideas were part of the very formation of the modern prison system, for better or worse, and religious involvement has always been some part of the prison system. Within the United States, two *sides* of the debate on religion and prisons have tended to harden their views.

As some more conservative political and religious attitudes in the United States toward crime have associated *getting tough* on crime with attitudes of *let them rot* in prison—and thus cutting education and other positive program benefits to those in prison—they are finding that they are actually increasing the problem of radicalization and recruitment in prisons, and increasing the levels of crime outside through gang activities. They find themselves having to argue for increased spending on prisons in order to *get tough*.

Among major religious traditions, Christianity has the strongest tradition of teaching about *visiting those in prison* and taking care of the imprisoned, undoubtedly because of the legacy of imprisonment and persecution during the first 300 years of Christianity. The advocates of increased health and education spending toward a potentially positive use of prisons as places of *penitence* and, hopefully, *redemption* and *transformation* have tended to focus on celebrity cases of "jailhouse conversion." Those who point to these cases would support increased programs that would eventually have the result of reducing social dependence on prisons that are becoming increasingly expensive. In short, more education and positive programs in prisons would result in the need for building fewer actual prisons.

See also Capital Punishment; Gambling and Religious Conscience; Separation of Church and State.

Further Reading: Clear, Todd, Patricia Hardyman, Bruce Stout, Karol Lucken, and Harry Dammer. "The Value of Religion in Prison." *Journal of Contemporary Criminal Justice* 16, no. 1 (February 2000): 53–74; Cooey, Paula. "Women's Religious Conversions on Death Row: Theorizing Religion and State." *Journal of the American Academy of Religion,* 70, no. 4 (December 2002): 699–717; Cuthbertson, Ian M. "Prisons and the Education of Terrorists." *World Policy Journal* (Fall 2004): 15–22; Davis, Angela. *Are Prisons Obsolete?* New York City: Seven Stories Press, 2003; Irwin, Lee. "Walking the Line: Pipe and Sweat Ceremonies in Prison." *Nova Religio, The Journal of Alternative and Emergent Religions* 9, no. 3 (2006): 39–60; Johnson, Byron, De Li Spencer, David Larson, and Michael McCullough. "A Systematic Review of the Religiosity and Delinquency Literature." *Journal of Contemporary Criminal Justice* 16, no. 1 (February 2000): 32–52; Kerley, Kent R., Todd Matthews, and Troy Blanchard. "Religiosity, Religious Participation, and Negative Prison Behaviours." *Journal for the Scientific Study of Religions* 44, no. 4 (2005): 443–457; Schmid, Muriel. "'The Eye of God': Religious Beliefs and Punishment in Early Nineteenth-Century Prison Reform." *Theology Today* 59, no. 4 (January 2003): 546–558; Skotnicki, Andrew. "God's Prisoners: Penal Confinement and the Creation of Purgatory." *Modern Theology* 22, no. 1 (January 2006): 85–110; Spann, Johnny. "Front Line Dilemmas." *Christianity Today* 50, no. 2 (February 2006): 38–41; Zehr, Howard. *Changing Lenses: A New Focus for Crime and Justice.* 3rd ed. Scottdale: Herald Press, 2005.

Daniel L. Smith-Christopher

JUST WAR

The tradition of just war theory asserts that, under certain conditions and restrictions, the use of force can be justified. Some contest the theoretical application of these normative rules to the ambiguities of war, whereas others—such as those in the pacifist tradition—reject any use of force as morally justified. The United States' pursuit of a war on terror provides a case-study for debate on the ethics of war.

THE ORIGINS OF JUST WAR THEORY AND ITS CONTENT

St. Augustine (354–430) is one the earliest theologians who discusses the notion of a just war (though just war was also discussed by Augustine's contemporary, St. Ambrose [c.339–97]). In *The City of God,* Augustine describes the misery of war even when just: "But the wise man, they say, will wage just wars. Surely, if he remembers that he is a human being, he will rather lament the fact that he is faced with the necessity of waging just wars; for if they were not just, he would not have to engage in them, and consequently there would be no wars for a wise man" (Augustine 1984, 861–862). Augustine believes that wars can be just if they comport with rationality, wisdom, and certain moral criteria such as self-defense, and the protection of the innocent against unjust aggression. St. Thomas Aquinas (1225–1274) appropriated the writings of Augustine and refined the criteria that constitute a just war. In his *Summa Theologiae,* Aquinas argues that just wars must be waged by competent authorities who possess a just cause and rightful intention (Aquinas 1920, q. 40. a. 1). Following Augustine, Aquinas defends ambushes (Aquinas 1920, q. 40. a. 3) as consistent with the just war criteria. These criteria were developed further by theologians such as Francisco de Vitoria (1486–1546).

From these thinkers and the historical development of the just war tradition, basic principles emerge. The fundamental normative principles that govern classical just theory and the moral use of force can be generally characterized into two criteria. The first pertain to the justification for going to war (*jus ad bellum*) and the ends of war, and the latter pertain to justified conduct in conflict (*jus in bello*) and the means of war. The criteria for *jus ad bellum* include the following conditions. Just cause includes the right to self-defense in the wake of an attack, but is also mandates that nations seek peace, not hateful revenge. Just cause is frequently interconnected with right intention; nations should protect innocent persons from unjust attacks, and restore a just order for the broader social common good. Last resort (ultima ratio) means the exhaustion of all diplomatic avenues before the use of force out of necessity. Legitimate authority addresses conscience, but also properly recognized governmental structures that must undergird carefully designed mobilizations of power and armed forces. The final *jus ad bellum* principle is some reasonable probability of success, which helps ensure that the loss of life remains minimal. This criterion received intense scrutiny during the Vietnam War; many determined that—after considerable loss of life—the conflict had reached an impasse, and it no longer was justified. In

JUST WAR THEORY AND TERROR

The September 11 terrorist attacks generated enormous debates about the ethics of war. How does one determine proportionality and discrimination when innocent civilians are killed? Do the rules of just war—which assume a Westphalian system of nation states—apply against disparate and clandestine terrorist cells whose suicide bombings violate laws of war? Can we make moral judgments about the American response to terrorism? Adopting an Augustinian realism, Jean Bethke Elshtain (2003) holds that just war theory does not promote a realpolitik *anything goes* strategy in responding to terror. Just war restrictions were followed by the United States in its subsequent attacks on Afghanistan: "We can see that the U.S. military response in Afghanistan clearly meets the just cause criterion of being a war fought with the right intention—to punish wrongdoers and to prevent them from murdering civilians in the future." Other thinkers such as Ronald Stone (2005), who also holds a realist position influenced by Reinhold Niebuhr and Paul Tillich, have articulated concerns regarding the legitimacy of the war on terror: "The war in Iraq was not justified by defense against terrorism directed against the United States" and "The 'war against terrorism' in its worldwide dimensions is misguided." Stone cautions that just war can easily morph into a triumphant militarism. He prefers a prophetic realism that mediates between just peacemaking and pacifism, on the one hand, and just war and militarism, on the other.

terms of the *jus in bello* principles, noncombatant immunity restricts violence against innocent civilians and bystanders; violent engagement can only occur against soldiers committed to battle. Additionally, proportionality stipulates that the goods to be achieved through the use of force must outweigh the destruction of the means. The use of force must be proportionate to the opposing force so as to avoid inflicting unnecessary suffering. There is considerable disagreement regarding the proportionality of the Hiroshima and Nagasaki bombings, which ended World War II, but at the cost of substantial death and suffering. Recently, some thinkers have begun to address postconflict aspects of war, or *jus post bellum,* which include peace treaties, reconstruction, and methods of reconciliation, and punitive aspects such as tribunals or trials for war crimes.

MORAL USE OF FORCE AND APPEALS TO SCRIPTURE: MARIN LUTHER AND MENNO SIMONS

In the Protestant tradition, there has been consistent appeal to Scripture as the normative use regarding the ethics of war and the moral use of force. Twentieth-century Theologians such as Reinhold Niebuhr (1892–1971) and Paul Ramsey (1913–1988) uphold the moral use of force, but these views derive from earlier theologians such as Martin Luther. Luther (1483–1546) was a Protestant reformer who firmly believed that God had entrusted humanity with the authority to use the sword, signifying the morally justified use of force. A scholar of Scriptural exegesis, Luther finds Scriptural grounds to support his claims: "Hence it is sufficiently clear and certain that it is God's will that the sword and secular law be used for the punishment of the wicked and the protection of the upright" (1 Peter 2:14). The use of violence is a necessary means, according to Luther, of confronting a world ravaged by the effects of sin. Luther develops a conceptual theological model to explain further the use of force. He submits that God creates two kingdoms, the kingdom of God and the kingdom of the world (that resemble, in some ways, Augustine's two cities). True believers in Christ, and those who are obedient to Christ, inhabit the heavenly kingdom. Consequently, "these people need no secular sword or law. And if all the world were composed of real Christians, that is, true believers, no prince, king, lord, sword, or law would be needed" ((Luther 1962, 368–369). By contrast, those in the kingdom of the world include the unrighteous; the sword therefore functions as a means to control the wicked and to protect the innocent.

If Luther were so committed to Scripture, how does he interpret Christ's use of the sword? Luther acknowledges that Christ does not use the sword (cf. Matthew 5:39). Nonetheless, Luther insists that Christ does not absolutely reject the sword: "Therefore, even though Christ did not bear the sword nor prescribe it, it is sufficient that He did not forbid or abolish it, but rather endorsed it; just as it is sufficient that He did not abolish the state of matrimony, but endorsed it, though He Himself took no wife and gave no commandment concerning it" (Luther 1962, 379). Luther extrapolates from Christ's teachings that one can never use the sword to promote one's own interests. This theological and ethical restriction resembles the basic premise of just war: force can only be used in the service of protecting the weak neighbor. The central difference between Luther and just war theory resides in Luther's negative anthropology, that is, his belief that humans are radically sinful, and this sinfulness threatens the earthly kingdom. Luther affirms, then, that individuals can and must undertake force to preserve order: "Therefore, should you see that there is a lack of hangmen, beadles, judges, lords, or princes, and find that you are qualified, you should offer your services and seek the place, that necessary government may by no means be despised and become inefficient or perish. For the world cannot and dare not dispense with it" (Luther 1962, 374–375). Luther's theologically grounded concern for order was famously illustrated in his repudiating the 1524–1525 Peasants' Revolt where an estimated 100,000 peasants were slaughtered.

If Luther finds Scripture as grounds for supporting the moral use of force, Radical Reformer and Anabaptist leader Menno Simons (1493–1561) uses Scripture as grounds for rejecting any moral use of force. Simons' followers became know as the Mennonites, one of the peace churches who practice pacifism. Simons appeals to text such as Isaiah 2:4: "He shall judge between the nations, and shall arbitrate for many peoples; they shall beat their swords into plowshares, and their spears into pruning hooks; nation shall not lift up sword against nation, neither shall they learn war any more." Simons contrasts the purity of the regenerated community and the depravity of the world; he emphasizes the retrieval of the discipline of the early Christian Church, and rejects the corruption of the present (Catholic) Church. Unlike Luther, who viewed the state's use of force as the divine wrath of God (cf. Romans 13:1–7), Simons abrogates any official relations between church and state.

JUST WAR THEORY AND IRAQ

The first invasion of Iraq in August 1990, and the second attack in March 2003, have received intense scrutiny: do these Gulf Wars satisfy the moral criteria established by just war theory? Defenders point to the role of diplomacy and the ends achieved (the liberation of Kuwait) as definitively just for the first Gulf War. However, others express reservation regarding the methods of *jus in bello*: "I have grave doubts about whether it was really necessary to bomb the Iraqi troops retreating from Kuwait as intensively as we did" (Miller 1992, 464). Jim Wallis has critiqued both Gulf Wars as having grave moral consequences for American soldiers and Iraqi soldiers, but he condemns the wars most emphatically, due to the enormous loss of civilian lives. Just war advocates argue that extremists have blended themselves with innocent civilians, thus requiring *on the ground* amendments to just war theory and the ethics of war. President Bush has argued that the establishment of democratic order and freedoms in Iraq justifies the tragic deaths of American soldiers. Critics argue that the conflict in Iraq has devolved into a civil war, that neither can be viewed in just war terms, nor can be justified on these terms (e.g., there is no probability of success).

In his 1550 text *On the Ban,* Simons advocates for radical *imitatio Christi* (imitation of Christ) as grounds for—in contrast to Luther—gainsaying the secular sword. For Simons, the use of force is never morally justified; rather, he recommends the ban as an alternative. Simons envisions two central moments, entering and departing from the Church. Baptism, which occurred as an adult, signifies entering the community as a member. The ban, whereby one is extruded by the community as a form of punishment, represents a response to sin and violence that does not itself enact violence. Simons derives the ban from Matthew 18:15–18: "If another member of the church sins against you, go and point out the fault when the two of you are alone. If the member listens to you, you have regained that one. But if you are not listened to, take one or two others along with you, so that every word may be confirmed by the evidence of two or three witnesses. If the member refuses to listen to them, tell it to the church; and if the offender refuses to listen even to the church, let such a one be to you as a Gentile and a tax collector. Truly I tell you, whatever you bind on earth will be bound in heaven, and whatever you loose on earth will be loosed in heaven." When one in the community has sinned, he or she is shunned by the community, and must leave the community for a period of time until the sinner has repented and the offense has been healed.

A CONSTRUCTIVE SYNTHESIS OF JUST WAR AND PACIFISM?

In 1983, the United States Conference of Catholic Bishops wrote a pastoral letter entitled *The Challenge of Peace: God's Promise and Our Response. The Challenge of Peace* is an important theological and ethical analysis of the use of force during a particularly volatile time of the Cold War. The Bishops hold that "[t]he Christian has no choice but to defend peace, properly understood, against aggression. This is an inalienable obligation. It is the *how* of defending peace which offers moral options" (United States Conference of Catholic Bishops 1983, paragraph 73; original emphasis). These moral options include just war defenses and military service, as well as the refusal to bear arms, conscientious objection, and active nonviolence. Are these two approaches—one which views violence as morally justified, and one which views violence as morally reprehensible—antithetical? Can one uphold both options as moral without being contradictory? The Church argues that the two approaches are distinct but complimentary: "They differ in their perception of how the common good is to be defended most effectively, but both responses testify to the Christian conviction that peace must be pursued and rights defended within moral restraints and in the context of defining other basic human values" (United States Conference of Catholic Bishops 1983, paragraph 74).

Building on the tradition of Catholic social teaching, The Bishops insist that the Christian has a responsibility to respond to unjust aggression. The solidarity of all humanity imputes a duty to confront aggression that corresponds with the tenets of just war theory: "This is why Christians, even as they strive to resist and prevent every form of warfare, have no hesitation in recalling that, in the name of an elementary requirement of justice, peoples have a right and even a duty to protect their existence and freedom by proportionate means against an unjust aggressor" (United States Conference of Catholic Bishops 1983, paragraph 78). However, the Bishops affirm that nonviolent means afford another way to confront this aggression. They identify nonviolent methods in Jesus' life and teaching, St. Francis of Assisi, Mahatma Gandhi, Dorothy Day, and Martin Luther King. The Bishops conclude that just-war teaching and nonviolence are "distinct but interdependent methods of evaluating warfare. They diverge on some specific conclusions, but they share a common presumption against the use of force as a means of settling disputes" (United States Conference of Catholic Bishops 1983, Paragraph 120).

Other thinkers hold that such a synthesis cannot be coherently achieved. Glen Stassen (1988) and other supporters of just peacemaking reject the coexistence of peace and war; they believe that peace-building, social justice, nonviolent direct action, and preventative diplomacy offer alternatives to the use of force. They focus on peace mobilization through the work of the United Nations, and religious and political organizations such as the Women's International League for Peace and Freedom, Mennonite Central Committee, Global Action to Prevent War, and Global Nonviolent Peace Force. Stassen asserts that conflict resolution, protection of human rights and religious liberty, communal cooperation, voluntary associations, and arms reduction foster the goals of just peacekeeping, including the abolition of war (Stassen 1998). Theologians such as Stanley Hauerwas (1984; 1985) and Michael Baxter have similarly called for the abolition of war as mandated by a Biblical witness of peace and justice. They insist that no mediation of just war theory and a pacifist perspective can be argued on coherent theological and moral grounds.

See also Apocalypticism and Nuclear War; Personal Pacifism versus Political Nonviolence.

Further Reading: Aquinas, Thomas. *The "Summa Theologica" of St. Thomas Aquinas.* Literally translated by Fathers of the English Dominican Province. 2nd and revised edition. London: Burnes, Oates, and Washbourne. 1920; Augustine. *Concerning The City of God against the Pagans.* A new translation by Henry Bettenson. Introduction by John O'Meara. New York: Penguin Books, 1984; Cahill, Lisa Sowle. *Love Your Enemies: Discipleship, Pacifism, and Just War Theory.* Minneapolis: Fortress Press, 1994; Christopher, Paul. *The Ethics of War and Peace: An Introduction to Legal and Moral Issues.* Englewood Cliffs, N.J.: Prentice Hall, 1994; Elshtain, Jean Bethke. *Just War against Terror: The Burden of American Power in A Violent World.* New York: Basic Books, 2003; Elshtain, Jean Bethke, ed. *Just War Theory.* New York: New York University Press, 1992; Hauerwas, Stanley. *Against the Nations: War and Survival in a Liberal Society.* Minneapolis: Winston Press, 1985; Hauerwas, Stanley. *Should War Be Eliminated?: Philosophical and Theological Investigations.* Marquette: Marquette University Press, 1984; Kleiderer, John, Paul Minaert, and Mark Mossa, eds. *Just War, Lasting Peace: What Christian Traditions Can Teach Us.* Maryknoll, N.Y.: Orbis Books, 2006; Luther, Martin. "Secular Authority: To What Extent It Should Be Obeyed?" In *Martin Luther: Selections from His Writings.* Edited and with an Introduction by John Dillenberger. New York: Anchor Books, 1962. First published 1523; Massaro, Thomas J., and Thomas A. Shannon. *Catholic Perspectives on Peace and War.* Lanham, MD: Rowman and Littlefield Publishers, 2003; Mattox, Mark. *Saint Augustine and the Theory of Just War.* London: Continuum, 2006; May, Larry, Eric Rovie, and Steve Viner, eds. *The Morality of War: Classical and Contemporary Readings.* Upper Saddle River, N.J.: Pearson Prentice Hall, 2006; Miller, Richard B. *Interpretations of Conflict: Ethics, Pacifism, and the Just-War Tradition.* Chicago: University of Chicago Press, 1991; Miller, Richard B., ed. *War in the Twentieth Century: Sources in Theological Ethics.* Library of Theological Ethics. Louisville, KY: Westminster/John Knox Press, 1992; O'Donovan, Oliver. *The Just War Revisited.* Cambridge: Cambridge University Press, 2003; Ramsey, Paul. *The Just War: Force and Political Responsibility.* Lanham, MD: Rowan and Littlefield, 2002; Stassen, Glen, ed. *Just Peacemaking: Ten Practices for Abolishing War.* Cleveland: Pilgrim Press, 2002; Stone, Ronald H. *Prophetic Realism: Beyond Militarism and Pacifism in An Age of Terror.* New York: T and T Clark International, 2005; United States Conference of Catholic Bishops. "The Challenge of Peace: God's Promise and Our Response." In *Catholic Social Thought: The Documentary Heritage,* eds. David J. O'Brien and Thomas Shannon. Maryknoll, NY: Orbis Books, 2002.

Jonathan Rothchild

L

LIBERATION THEOLOGY

Liberation Theology is a twentieth-century theological movement that intersects with grassroots struggles for social justice, especially throughout Latin America. Born out of the Roman Catholic Church, and especially the changes formed at the great church gathering known as "Vatican II" (in Rome in the 1960s), Liberation Theology includes an emphasis on the church's role as one that "relates believers to the modern world" (Gutiérrez 1988). Advocates of Liberation Theology interpreted this to mean that the church is to be an advocate for believers, especially poor believers. Liberation Theology took the *preferential option for the poor* as a rallying cry and, through Christian-based communities (regular gatherings for study and prayer), worked for social and economic justice for the poorest peoples. Connecting to other global movements such as feminism and environmentalism, Liberation Theology has continued to expand, despite resistance from inside and outside the Catholic and Protestant churches.

LEADING FIGURES

Leading figures in the Liberation Theology movement are Gustavo Gutiérrez of Peru, Juan Luis Segundo of Uruguay, Jon Sobrino of El Salvador, and Leonardo Boff of Brazil.

Peruvian Dominican priest and activist Gustavo Gutiérrez, defined the method of Liberation Theology as "critical reflection on Christian praxis in the light of the bible" in his 1968 address to the first South American Bishops' Conference (CELAM) at Medellín. *Praxis* became a central term in Liberation Theology generally, and the term—meaning *action*—sought to focus all Christian action toward transforming unjust social structures in favor of the poor and dispossessed. While educated in Europe himself (Catholic University of Louvain, University of Lyon, Georgian University, Rome), Gutiérrez worked most of his career in Peru, and he emphasizes that Liberation Theology must be "home grown." Theologies from Europe and America, however well intentioned, are not sufficient. The starting point of Liberation Theology, then, is specifically the experience of Latin Americans—and especially the unique context of suffering and economic depression.

One of the most prolific liberation theologians is the Jesuit priest Juan Luis Segundo of Uruguay. Segundo and Gutiérrez became good friends during their time together as students at Louvain. Called *the dean* of liberation theologians, Segundo has written extensively on the method of Liberation Theology. Segundo rejected a European-styled emphasis on individualized or *personal* readings of the gospel, and argued for a more *contextual* and social reading. The importance of the Bible for social situations—economic and political—was taught against an exclusively *personal* religion, only for the individual. In Liberation Theology, it was believed that these new interpretations of the Bible's message would give way to new, positive social structures.

Jon Sobrino, a Jesuit priest from El Salvador, writes extensively on the tradition of martyrdom within Liberation Theology. The way of being Christian in Latin America carries with it the mark of martyrdom, signified by the assassination of Monsignor Oscar Romero in 1980. While this particular death is well known, Romero is only one of the 70,000 victims killed by El Salvador's armed forces and paramilitary death squads during the 1980s and 1990s. In part, Sobrino's emphasis on martyrdom grows out of those deaths, as well as from being a member of the community of Jesuits who were assassinated by Salvadoran guards in 1989. Sobrino only escaped because he was in Thailand at the time. In the 1980s and 1990s Sobrino and his brother Jesuits carried on the work for social justice, pioneered by Monsignor Oscar Romero, with El Salvador's poor and disenfranchised. Sobrino questions the role of human cruelty and indifference in the world and challenges the "developed world" to recognize their complicity in the suffering of the world's poorest inhabitants.

Brazilian Franciscan priest Leonardo Boff is another leading figure in the movement. His book, *Introducing Liberation Theology,* written with his brother Clodovis Boff, has been the foundation for base communities in Brazil (Boff and Boff 1987). Boff specifically advocates the notion that authority and ministry can come *from below,* rather than from the church hierarchy. He was silenced twice by the Vatican, first in 1985, and again in 1991, for his "politicized" theology. After honoring a second year of silence, Boff left the priesthood and continues to act as an advocate for the poor and disenfranchised as an honorary professor of theology at the University of Rio de Janeiro.

VATICAN II

While Liberation Theologians trace their lineage back to Bartolomé Las Casas, who advocated for the rights of South American Indians already in the sixteenth century, the origin of Liberation Theology can be found more recently with a proclamation originating in the Second Vatican Council. The Vatican document, *Gaudium Et Spies* (Joy and Hope), calls for greater human equality, both social and economic. In the landmark Second Vatican Council held from 1962 to 1965, the council called for the Church to engage in a renewed involvement in the world, and to give attention to the dignity of all humans, specifically in political and economic aspects. As a result, one of the commitments to arise from the council was a sense of obligation for the church to relate to believers, especially the poorest of believers, through the liturgy and the relationship of the church to governments. The council furthermore articulated a concern for social justice over the accumulation of wealth. The council called for the Church to take a position of energetic conversation and exchange with the modern world in order to learn from, as well as teach, secular, non-Christian, and Protestant persons. Liberation Theologians enthusiastically took up this injunction to dialog with secularists, and freely incorporated social sciences into their theologies.

MEDELLÍN, 1968

In the wake of Vatican II and its new articulation of the Church's relationship to the world, liberationists like Boff and Gutiérrez focused on social sciences in dialog with theology in order to develop a *theology of liberation*. This method of constructive theology linked salvation and liberation as a way of understanding the relationship of God's free gift of salvation on the one hand, and human efforts at liberation on the other hand. While traditional theology has used Western philosophy as a basis for reflection, Liberation Theology uses the critical and liberating perspectives of the social sciences—including elements of Marxism—to identify the root causes of oppression, and to reflect critically on formulating Christian action to overcome this oppression in society. Liberation Theology is a new way of doing theology—a theology of praxis from the perspective of the poor, and through their struggle for justice and for liberation.

Because Liberation Theology calls for a new way of acting as Christians in the world, liberationists are activists first and foremost. This is reflected especially in the activities of *communidades eclesiales de base* or base Christian communities (called CEBs) in Latin America. CEBs were fully articulated at Medellín. The conference at Medellín, the first Latin American Bishops' Conference (CELAM), encouraged use of *communidades eclesiales de base* for organizing social, political, and religious justice among the poor and disenfranchised. A second goal of the CEBs was to render the Bible more accessible, utilizing the Bible as a tool for educating and empowering the poor.

CEBs are groups of between 5 and 30 individuals who meet to worship, read the Bible, and make plans for social justice in their communities. Reading the Bible through the lens of their struggle for justice, CEB members understand God as an advocate of justice. CEBs focus on education, teaching the members basic literacy skills through reading the Bible. For example, evidence of God's partisanship toward the poor and outcast is found in the Hebrew Bible. The role of God in Exodus is a particularly poignant passage for liberation theologians, and is emphasized in the CEBs (Exodus 3:7–8). Likewise, liberationists emphasize Jesus's solidarity with the poor and outcast, as seen in the Gospels. These biblical images then guide their Christian practice as disciples of Jesus, creating a relationship of solidarity between Jesus and the poor, shaping and guiding advocacy for social change.

Liberation is broad term within Liberation Theology, including not only the establishment of political and social justice and freedom from oppression for the poor, but also liberation from sin. When speaking of sin, liberationists tend to emphasize social sin, embodied in unjust societal and institutional structures such as racism and sexism. These unjust social systems lead further to individual sin. The bishops at Medellín condemned the "institutionalized violence" of poverty, and denounced capitalism and communism equally, placing blame for hunger and misery of the poor of the world on the rich and powerful. Following Vatican II, Liberation Theologians see continuity between justice and liberation in this world and the fullness of the Kingdom of God in the next world. Their primary focus, however, is on this world.

One of the first social theorists embraced by liberationists was Karl Marx, and this was clearly expressed at Medellín. While Liberation Theology specifically rejects the atheism of Marxism, and the apocalyptic notion of supernatural intervention in the political world, Marx provided important and necessary categories for understanding the experience of poverty and oppression in Latin America. Liberation Theology is founded upon a central notion of God's (and the Church's) preferential option for the poor that dictates its understanding of tradition, biblical texts, and philosophy. At Medellín, the conference of bishops took specific aim at the system of capitalism, arguing that it "militates against the dignity of the human person." Major components of Liberation Theology were formulated by Gustavo Gutiérrez, just prior to the conference at Medellín. Gutiérrez's book, *A Theology of Liberation,* marks the first full expression of Liberation Theology (Gutiérrez 1988).

The bishops at Medellín emphasized that Liberation Theology starts from an experiential perspective, more specifically, it begins from the experience of the Latin American poor. The focus is then on a *bottom up* approach to theology, as seen in the CEBs. Theology is not done in the ivory towers of distant first world academies, but rather by "'militant theologians' working with the pilgrim people of God engaged in their pastoral responsibilities" (Boff, 1987).

Leonardo and Clodovis Boff (1987) indicate that Liberation Theology has several themes:

- Solidarity with the poor
- Real faith requires liberating action
- God sides with the oppressed
- God is actively working to set up the Kingdom of God in history
- Jesus attacked oppression and his gospel is one of freedom from oppression
- God is found in the struggle of the oppressed
- Mary is a "prophetic and liberating woman"

- God supports the rights of the poor
- "Liberated human potential becomes liberative"

A quick examination of these themes shows several commonalities. First, there is a focus on the poor and the oppressed. Second, God has a clear preference for the oppressed and the poor. God, Jesus, and Mary are all invoked on the side of liberation. Finally, there is clearly a class emphasis at the root of Liberation Theology's analysis. While Gutiérrez and the Boffs rebel against oppression of any kind, including sexism and racism, at the bottom it is class oppression that is paramount for their articulation of Liberation Theology.

The tone for this type of class analysis was set at the *Medellín Document on Peace*, specifically the section titled, *Tensions between Classes and Internal Colonialism*. There, the bishops identify some of the problems as "Extreme inequality among social classes," "Forms of Oppression of dominant groups and Sectors," and "Power unjustly exercised by certain dominant sectors" (CELAM 1968). Likewise Gutiérrez, diagnosing the problem that leads to oppression and degradation of the poor, states quite clearly, "only a class analysis will enable us to see what is really involved in the opposition between oppressed countries and dominant peoples" (1988).

COMMUNIDADES ECLESIALES DE BASE (CEBs)

A detailed study of CEBs in El Salvador during the 1980s identified three ways CEBs contributed to politically mobilizing the poor. First, the local religious community was democratized in the CEBs, and through this mutual empowerment, those people were able to question institutional structures and existing systems of authority. Second, CEBs helped people develop leadership and organizing skills, especially in rural areas. Through the democratization of the CEBs, there was an emphasis on speaking in public, and working toward consensus rather than a hierarchical expression of power within the community. This gave individuals who would usually have said little about church or God or their community, an opportunity to participate in their church and community actively, leading to the second step of leadership and organization in order to change society at the grassroots level. For example, members of CEBs participated in community building projects and trade cooperatives. Lastly, CEBs strengthened collective identity among the poor, and helped them develop a sense of solidarity that comes from their struggle together. This solidarity then informs their relationship to each other, society, Jesus, and God. Cohesion at this local level leads to political solidarity and, in the case of El Salvador, participation in revolution. CEBs emphasized empowerment from the base, rather than from the top down, and functioned as the grassroots of Liberation Theology.

PUEBLA, 1979

The second South American Bishops Conference was held in Puebla, Mexico in 1979. The newly elected John Paul II attended this conference. There, he affirmed the conclusions of Medellín regarding the preferential option for the poor that the bishops had articulated at the first South American Bishops' Conference, but the Pope also cautioned against the misuse of secular political theories. He declared that Christ is not a political figure, nor a revolutionary, and said it was wrong to identify the Kingdom of God with an earthly political situation. He validated the liberationist's concern for social justice, while at the same time finding the use of secular social theories profoundly wrong.

VATICAN RESPONSE

Following Pope John Paul II's address at Puebla, the Vatican issued two instructions on Liberation Theology in the 1980s. The first, *Instruction on Certain Aspects of the Theology of Liberation*, was released in 1984. This *Instruction* has at its heart a rejection of the possibility that Marxist analysis can make any constructive contribution to Catholic theology. The *Instruction* rejects the idea that Marxism is science, and that Marxism provides a strategy for changing society. The *Instruction* denies that any of these elements can be removed from Marxism in order to give it any validity in constructive theology. While this *Instruction* does not use terms such as *heresy* or *errors*, the Vatican voiced concern that liberationists *deviated* from church teaching.

In 1986 the Vatican released a second instruction on Liberation Theology. *Instruction on Christian Freedom and Liberation* continues the themes developed in the first *Instruction* regarding Marxism, but this second *Instruction* is more hopeful about the possibility of achieving political liberation and freedom through social movements. The second *Instruction* acknowledges political uses of biblical narratives, such as Exodus, but subordinates political interpretations to "spiritual interpretations." *Instruction on Christian Freedom and Liberation* cautions religions against encouraging popular piety toward a "purely earthly plan" of liberation, calling that "nothing more than an illusion." The two instructions indicate that the aspect of Liberation Theology most alarming to the Vatican is the Marxist elements. Liberation Theology should be purged of its Marxist taint, and these *Instructions* offer guidance from the church of the issues of liberation, and the role of religion in political and social unrest.

SANTO DOMINGO, 1992

This fourth meeting of the South American Bishops' Conference was called to coincide with the 500th anniversary of Columbus' landing in the Americas. The theme of this conference was evangelization and human development. The conference emphasized the "preferential option for the poor" as articulated at Medellín. John Paul II spoke at the opening of this conference and called the bishops to practice a "genuine praxis of liberation" as set forth in the two instructions issued during the 1980s. Having effectively offered the final official word on Liberation Theology through the two instructions, the Vatican acted to change the role of the leaders of the movement. Throughout Latin America, liberationist priests and bishops were replaced with more conservative priests and bishops. And yet the Liberation Theology continues to be an important and effective voice in the Catholic Church, and to develop and grow in Latin America.

NEW DIRECTIONS

During the 1990s and into the twenty-first century, Liberation Theology has continued to use the CEBs to organize and expand. Because their emphasis is on *praxis* (*practice* or *action*), liberationists see Christianity as an active community of believers, and have continued to work with that goal in mind. Feminist and black theology, as well as ecologically informed theologies, have intersected with, and been woven into the fabric of Liberation Theology. One of the areas that both Boff (1995) and Gutiérrez (1988) focus on in their latest writings is the environment. Social solidarity has been expanded to include creation. Defending indigenous land rights and fighting for the respect for life at all levels is part of the humanistic endeavor of liberationists. Identifying the paradigms of development and consumption as the main causes of the worldwide ecological crisis, liberationists see the connection between the global environmental crisis, and the poor health and ever-increasing high rate of mortality of the earth's poorest inhabitants. Gutiérrez articulates this commitment as "poverty means death, unjust and premature death" (Gutiérrez 1988). The activism cultivated through CEBs, combined with the fact that the majority of the Catholic Church's constituency is poor, will continue to effect the way that theology is done, at least in those areas in the developing world most exploited by the developed world.

See also Bible and Poverty; Capitalism and Socialism.

Further Reading: Alves, Ruben A., and Elsa Tamez. *Against Machismo: Ruben Alves, Leonardo Boff, Gustavo Gutiérrez, Jose Miguez Bonino, Juan Luis Segundo . . . And Others Talk About the Struggle of Women: Interviews.* Yorktown Heights, NY: Meyer-Stone Books, 1987; Assmann, Hugo. *Theology for a Nomad Church: Practical Theology of Liberation.* Maryknoll, NY: Orbis Books, 1986; Boff, Leonardo. *Ecology & Liberation: A New Paradigm.* Maryknoll, NY: Orbis Books, 1995; Boff, Leonardo, and Clodovis Boff. *Introducing Liberation Theology.* Maryknoll, NY: Orbis Books, 1987; Gutiérrez, Gustavo. *A Theology of Liberation: History, Politics, and Salvation.* Maryknoll, NY: Orbis Books, 1988; Hennelly, Alfred T. *Theologies in Conflict: The Challenge of Juan Luis Segundo.* Maryknoll, NY: Orbis Books, 1979; Latin American Episcopal Council (CELAM). "Medellín Document on Peace." In *Third World Liberation Theologies: A Reader,* ed. Deane William Ferm. Maryknoll, NY: Orbis Books, 1968; Peterson, Anna L. *Martyrdom and the Politics of Religion: Progressive Catholicism in El Salvador's Civil War.* Albany: State University of New York Press, 1997; Second Vatican Council. "Gaudium Et Spies." 1965. Available at: http://www.rc.net; Segundo, Juan Luis. *Liberation of Theology.* Maryknoll, NY: Orbis Books, 1976.

Laura Ammon and Randall Reed

M

MARKETING RELIGION

Mel Gibson's film, *The Passion of the Christ* was the surprise box office hit of 2004. Generating in its first year more than $370 million in domestic revenue, the movie went on to garner more than $600 million from theater attendance revenues, and another $400 million in DVD sales.

Advertising, sales promotion, and ubiquitous publicity are what got people off their couches on a Friday night and into the local multiplex. But unlike other mediocre Hollywood films, *The Passion* had several elements that enhanced its box office potential: an A-list movie star as director and spokesperson, a story with a built-in audience, and a topic—religion—that readily lends itself to controversy. What are the issues raised in a market-driven economy like that of the United States when religious *products* become deeply involved in the economic system?

PROBLEMS IN RELIGIOUS MARKETING IN A MIXED RELIGIOUS AMERICAN CULTURE AND SOCIETY

At first, the controversy revolved around whether *The Passion* was anti-Semitic. That controversy was initiated and then exacerbated by the film's producers for months before the film's release. By framing the controversy as anti-Semitism, the producers opened up the film to a new market—Jews—an audience that would likely have otherwise avoided the film altogether. One of the issues raised by this aspect of the film's promotion, is whether *negative marketing* can itself be an effective tool in religious *products* as much as it is used in other product marketing (e.g., "bad reactions are better than no reaction," or more crudely, the old Hollywood adage: "There is no such thing as bad publicity").

As this controversy began to die down, a new one appeared. This latter controversy became a question as to whether Mel Gibson himself was anti-Semitic. It further became clear that Mr. Gibson's personal religious beliefs were based in strict pre-Vatican II Catholicism and therefore ultraconservative—controversial even in Catholic circles. The extent of his conservatism and possible anti-Semitism was fueled by stories about Gibson's father, who was widely reported as being anti-Semitic (he claimed that the Holocaust was mostly fiction), and was believed to have passed those beliefs down to his son.

Of course this was not the only publicity associated with the film. There were stories about Mel Gibson funding the movie himself. There were stories about how true to the Gospels the movie was. There were the typical stories about the making of the film. In sum, the publicity machine was humming in full force right up to the opening day. Even after the film opened, publicity ran for months, which is an unusual course of events for a Hollywood film. Stories subsequent to the film's release focused on audiences' response to the film. In particular, news stories centered around the idea that people viewed the film not so much as entertainment, but as a religious experience. There were several reports of audience members having heart attacks; one man confessed to a murder he had committed years ago; still others were moved to affirm or reaffirm their faith.

This free publicity, which was valued in the millions of dollars, was supplemented by other traditional film marketing elements. For example, there were e-mails from Amazon.com promoting the movie to anyone who had purchased religious or spiritual books, there were appearances by Mr. Gibson on a number of television talk shows and newsmagazines, and there were the typical commercials on television, and ads in local newspapers.

DIRECT MARKETING TO CHURCHES AND CHURCH ORGANIZATIONS

However, it was the marketing that most people did not see that drove the ultimate success of *The Passion*. Grassroots marketing, led by Gibson himself, was developed in conjunction with local churches throughout the country. Evangelicals, charismatics, and Roman Catholics were the target markets for this film. Thirty invitation-only screenings were held for high-level church leaders and the heads of prominent evangelical organizations. The first of these occurred in Colorado Springs, Colorado, home of many of these institutions, including the ultraconservative Focus on the Family run by James C. Dobson. The leaders of these organizations, and many others, were encouraged to purchase blocks of tickets for their institutions, and to suggest that the local churches do the same. More than $3 million in advanced tickets sales were generated through this campaign.

Church promotions began in December 2003—a full two months before the movie opened. The *Pastors' Action Kit* provided churches with information via the Internet (www.passionmaterials.com) on how to tie into *The Passion*. Promotional ideas included showing trailers of the film at church, putting up banners, inviting parishioners to attend a screening, and, of course, buying out an entire theater screening and taking the congregation. Sermon suggestions were promoted to correspond with the Christian calendar, and information about what aspects of the movie to discuss in relationship to these sermons was provided. There were also special materials targeted to the teen audience via church youth groups.

Just as in secular films, ancillary products were created in conjunction with the movie's release. These products included book tie-ins and coffee mugs like other Hollywood fare, but they also included crosses and—one of the most popular items—small and large pewter nail pendants on a leather string, which retailed for between $12.99 and $16.99. As with most major motion pictures, a soundtrack was created. *The Passion* soundtrack sold 50,000 units the day it was released, making it the third highest selling first-day soundtrack. Initially, this product, as with others associated with the film, was distributed primarily through traditional Christian bookstores. However, products were distributed more widely as the success of the film translated beyond the initial narrowly targeted groups.

WHY WAS *THE PASSION* IMPORTANT?

The Passion of the Christ showed in the most blatant of ways that religion is a product, no different from any other commodity sold in the consumer marketplace. *The Passion* started with a defined target audience, created secondary targets through promotion and publicity, and perpetuated the product's relevance through creating ancillary businesses. And while initially the objective was to sell a film, we can see from the sustaining campaigns and comments made by the director, that the ultimate objective was to promote religion itself.

Another reason why *The Passion* was important is that it furthered the notion that while religious practice is very much privatized, religious presentation and promotion has become widely acceptable within our culture. Many forms of religion are being advertised and promoted in a way never seen before. Churches advertise on billboards and in print media. Books sell us all types of religious and spiritual wisdom. Television has become overrun with religious content, with no fewer than eight channels presenting sermons and faith-based programming 24 hours a day, not to mention religious content in broadcast prime time and as regular content for nightly newsmagazines.

IS MARKETING REALLY NEW?

While the intensity of religious messages is new, marketing religion is not. It has been going on for centuries. When Gutenberg invented the printing press in the fifteenth century, for example, much of the early advertising was to sell Bibles. In America, the need for religious marketing stemmed from the First Amendment right to freedom of religion, something the Founding Fathers believed was fundamental to the establishment of the democracy. Choosing one's religion was as important a right as freedom of speech, or the right to petition the government against grievances. Establishing no state religion meant that people would be free to choose how to worship, or not to worship. With no state-mandated religion, religions had to compete for parishioners, and oftentimes that meant using marketing techniques, from simple print advertising to door-to-door salesmen, as evidenced by the Jehovah's Witnesses.

However, competing in the religious marketplace was simple in simpler times. For centuries, new Americans brought religion with them from their home countries, and passed that religion down from generation to generation. Houses of worship carried significance in the communities where they served because they were a place *for* community, as well as a place for worship. Going to church was not only about God, but also about making social connections. Churches were able to maintain their value and their numbers because social agents—family, work, and even the congregation itself—supported remaining in a single faith throughout one's lifetime.

This began to change as American society moved from agrarian to industrial. First, the opportunities to connect with other people presented themselves as part of daily life, particularly through one's place of business, thus usurping the church's monopoly on community building. Second, as the baby boom generation came of age in the 1960s, children rebelled against the older generation in myriad ways, including rejecting the faith of their parents. The flexibility to choose one's faith combined with reduced social stigma attached to not attending services meant that churches were no longer ensured a congregation. Finally, increasingly more sophisticated communications technologies—first the radio, and then television and the Internet—provided alternative forms of communication that could be used for connecting with others, as well as a means for distributing religious content. The church was no longer the only source of religious information—and in fact has become the least convenient one—and thus continued to erode in value.

This is not to say that religion or spirituality has diminished in acceptance. America is one of the most religious countries in the world, certainly the most religious industrialized country. Poll after poll touts the fact that 90 percent or more of Americans believe in some form of higher power, whether it is God, Jesus, Moses, Mohammed, Buddha, Krishna, or some other lesser known entity (though almost 75 percent claim to be Christian according to Simmons Marketing Research).

Not only are Americans religious, or spiritual, as some prefer to call it, but we readily buy products and services that relate to our faith. We do this because, as mentioned earlier, traditional religious institutions are not the primary source of spiritual sustenance for most people anymore. While nearly 8 out of 10 Americans claim belief in a higher power, only one out of three attends religious services on a regular basis. Specifically, only 26 percent of Americans go to church or synagogue regularly—that is, at least once a month—even though close to 90 percent believe in God. Doing the math, that means more than 60 percent of Americans get their faith from something other than a religious institution. People attend movies, read books, and participate in religious chat rooms, all of which are diminishing religious bodies' direct influence on religious consumers. Instead of going to church, we wear T-shirts with WWJD (What Would Jesus Do?) or Jewcy emblazoned on our chests. We buy Christian rock albums and New Age crystals. In fact, we spend more on religious/spiritual/self-help books than any other country, which makes total sense, given the size of the target market (79 percent of Americans), our faith beliefs, and our consumerist culture.

All of this is to say that religion as practiced in the United States is an autonomous, self-oriented religion. This individualized religious practice, famously noted by Bellah and his colleagues in the mid-1980s, was called *Sheilahism*, named after a nurse who created her own form of religious practice. Since that time, other scholars have seen this pastiche of religious practice as a continuing trend. More recently this *cafeteria religion* is believed to be increasingly fueled by a commodity culture.

In 2003, research estimates put the market for religious publishing and products at $6.8 billion, and growing at a rate of nearly five percent annually. This market is subdivided into three categories: books (the largest segment, with $3.5 billion in sales and a seven percent growth rate); stationary/giftware/merchandise (sales at $1.4 billion, and a 4.5 percent growth rate); and audio/video/software ($1.4 billion in sales and flat). Given the current interest in religious products, which continues to be fueled by *The Passion,* experts estimate that the market will grow at almost a five percent annual rate for at least the next three years, reaching $8.64 billion in sales (Seybert 2004, 50).

But even this tells only part of the story. Unlike other product categories, there is no standardized means for collecting data on religious products and services. Therefore, these numbers are misleading, and in fact significantly underreport the money consumers spend on these products and services. In the book segment, for example, there is little uniformity in what constitutes religious or spiritual content. Some religious-oriented titles can be categorized as fiction, or even science fiction in one store, as in the case of the *Left Behind* series, a fictional series based on the End Times, for example, and as religion in another. In terms of other media, these numbers do not include theatrical films like *The Passion of the Christ,* which in, and of itself, would add 14 percent to the total spending in the category. Nor does it include religious television, which is a viewer-supported, several billion dollar industry, and growing, as evidenced by the recent introductions of numerous digital channels dedicated to religious programming. These numbers do not reflect the money spent on religious seminars, lectures, or spiritual adventure travel. So from a consumer product and service perspective, what is being tracked is just the tip of the iceberg.

A good indication of where religious marketing is heading is evidenced by the fact that Wal-Mart, the behemoth of all retailers, has jumped on the religious retail bandwagon. In 2003, the company sold more than $1 billion in Christian book and music titles, and they are quoted as saying that they are "looking at this as a huge opportunity for the future" (Seybert 2004, 13).

WHY RELIGIOUS MARKETING HAS PROLIFERATED

There are two main reasons why religious marketing has permeated our culture. First, millions of Americans have been set free to choose their religion.

The ability to choose has created the *real* open market for religion. Yes, when the Founding Fathers chose not to force a particular religion on the country, they were promoting the proliferation of religious choices. However choice is no choice if the rest of society (and particularly your mother) makes you go to a specific religious institution. In addition to the elimination of familial pressure to attend religious services, there is no longer a social stigma attached to not attending church. Given the aforementioned statistics, you are more likely to see your neighbor in the local mall on Sunday than in your local church.

Second, in the last 20 years, the level of media saturation in general has reached a height never imagined. In addition to cable television, we now have digital cable, with the average home having the ability to receive more than 130 channels, not to mention direct broadcast satellite with its capacity to deliver several hundred channels to the home of anyone willing to pay for them. The Internet, with broadband access, has become a household item for many people, and where this is not the case, people readily access cyberspace in their workplace or at their neighborhood library. The media beast needs to be fed with content—all types of content. The simple fact that there is more media means that there is more *religious* media.

Tied into the proliferation of media is the ubiquitous advertising that goes with it. Our interactions with advertising have led us to expect certain things from marketers, specifically, convenience and entertainment. These expectations have migrated to the realm of spiritual practice. Religion is no longer tied to time and place; it can be practiced any time of the day or night via the media without going to a sacred space. So, traditional religious institutions have to compete not only with brick and mortar churches, but also with religion presented in other forms. The Internet, for example, presents information about all aspects of religious products and activities, from Beliefnet, a comprehensive site about all things religious, to opportunities to worship through online churches—everything from the Vatican to the Church of the Blind Chihuahua. A 2004 study called Faith Online, by the Pew Research Center, found that almost two-thirds of Internet users had used the computer for religious or spiritual purposes (Hoover, Clark, and Rainie 2004).

Television presents religious programming through 24-hour cable channels, including the Inspiration Network and the Prayer Channel, and Sunday morning religious infomercials too numerous to mention. Thus, seekers can receive the word of God in their homes 24 hours a day. This is not to say that the physical church or synagogue or mosque will disappear. Just as the VCR did not eliminate the local movie theater, the computer or plasma screen will not destroy the local place of worship. People like to experience events—religious or otherwise—in physical community. It does suggest, however, that traditional and nontraditional institutions have to compete with more entertaining forms of religious practice. In the same way that elementary schools have been forced to compete with *Sesame Street* over the past 30 years, religious institutions now have to compete against online churches, 24-hour religious networks, and even a recently announced 24-hour gospel music channel. If one does choose to go to church, consumers have a heightened expectation of being entertained, which is usually met with music and dramatic presentations. Moreover, believers expect an experiential practice, that is, a more personal connection to God wherein they experience His presence. Sermons from on high just won't cut it for the majority of today's religious consumers.

One of the most successful segments of religious media is the book publishing industry, which in the last few decades has become big business, and is getting bigger. Look at *The New York Times* bestseller list on any given week and you will see multiple religious or spiritual titles on it. For example, books by popular pastors, such as *The Purpose Driven Life* by Rick Warren and Joel Osteen's *Your Best Life Now,* have become perennials on this list.

See also Animation as a New Media; Graphic Arts; Religious Publishing; Western Cinema.

Further Reading: Beaudoin, T. *Consuming Faith: Integrating Who We Are With What We Buy.* Chicago: Sheed and Ward, 2003; Bellah, R., R. Madsen, W. M. Sullivan, A. Swidler, and S. Tipton. *Habits of the heart: Individualism and commitment in American life.* Berkeley, CA: University of California Press, 1985; Carrette, J., and R. King. *Selling spirituality: The silent takeover of religion.* London: Routledge, 2005; Cimino, R., and D. Lattin. *Shopping for faith: American religion in the new millennium.* San Francisco: Jossey-Bass, 1998; Clark, L. S., ed. *Religion, Media and the Marketplace.* New Brunswick, N.J., 2007; Einstein, M. *Brands of Faith: Marketing religion in a commercial age.* London: Routledge, 2008; Finke, R., and L. R. Iannaccone. "Supply-side explanations for religious change." *The Annals of the American Academy* (*AAPSS*) 527 (1993): 27–39; Hoover, S.M., L. S. Clark, and L. Rainie. "Faith online." Pew Internet and Public Life Project. 2004. http://www.pewinternet.org/pdfs/PIP_Faith_Online_2004.pdf (accessed February 17, 2005); Miller, V. J. *Consuming religion: Christian faith and practice in a consumer culture.* New York: Continuum, 2004; Moore, R. L. *Selling God: American religion in the marketplace of culture.* New York: Oxford University Press, 1994; Roof, W. C. *A generation of seekers: The spiritual journey of the baby boom generation.* New York: HarperCollins, 1993; Roof, W. C. *Spiritual marketplace: Baby boomers and the remaking of American religion.* Princeton, NJ: Princeton University Press, 1999; Seybert, J. *EPM's guide to the Christian marketplace: Selling books, music, gifts and videos to America's 218 million Christians.* New York: EPM Communications Inc., 2004; Twichell, J. B. *Shopping for God: How Christianity Went from In Your Heart to In Your Face.* New York: Simon and Schuster, 2007.

Mara Einstein

From Einstein, M. (2008). *Brands of Faith: Marketing religion in a commercial age.* London: Routledge.

MARRIAGE, SEXUALITY, AND CELIBACY

Contemporary debates on marriage, sexuality, and celibacy involve the function of sexuality (does it pertain more to procreation, pleasure, or some combination of both?), the indissolvable nature of marriage (is it more akin to a covenant or a contract?), and the fundamental right to marry (should same-sex couples be granted marriages?). The heart of these debates lies in a question about the resonance or dissonance between the Scriptural and traditional grounds of marriage, and contemporary practices.

THEOLOGICAL PERSPECTIVES ON SEXUALITY

One of the challenges for theological reflection concerns the function of sexuality. Procreation (Genesis 1:28: "Be fruitful and multiply") and union of one flesh (Genesis 2:24) grounds biblical claims about the importance of procreation as a gift from God. The Song of Songs celebrates sensual, bridal, and sexual imagery (e.g., Song of Songs 1:2: "Let him kiss me with the kisses of his mouth" and Song of Songs 4:5 "Your two breasts are like two fawns, twins of a gazelle, that feed among the lilies"). Mystical theologians such as Bernard of Clairvaux have implemented these images as part of the spiritual union with God. Pope John Paul II's theology of the body examines sex within the rubric of theological anthropology. Arguing that humans are the integration of mind and will, the Pope contends that the body expresses who we are as persons. Sexuality relates to the person because it represents the bodily expression of love, that is, mutual self-donation. The Pope views sexuality as a means by which we can love others as the union of body and person (Pope John Paul II 1981). These positive images must be juxtaposed with other descriptions of sexuality in Scripture, including the account of the fall in Genesis 3. Rather than a sense of intimacy, the text reveals "enmity between you and the woman" (Genesis 3:15), "pangs in childbearing" (Genesis 3:16), and hierarchy ("he shall rule over you," Genesis 3:16). The account of the fall represents a view of sexuality that is ambivalent and fraught with deconstructive tendencies. As Eve consented to the temptation of eating from the tree of the knowledge of good and evil (and thereby disobeyed God), later interpreters began to conflate sexuality, sin, evil, and estrangement from God.

Should any pleasure associated with sexual activity be valued in and of itself? Should sexuality be reserved exclusively for married persons for the purposes of procreation? Classical Christian theologians, drawing on Scripture and tradition, have promoted a vision of sexuality rooted in marital commitments, and designed by God for purposes of procreation. Contemporary theological ethicist Christine Gudorf critiques traditional Christian understandings of sexuality. She censures the view of thinkers such as Thomas Aquinas, who "maintained that sexual pleasure is something that humans have in common with animals" (Gudorf 1995, 83). Gudorf contends that such perspectives do not appreciate sexuality as a truly human good. She remains more concerned with the implications of Augustine's understanding of sexuality as irresistible. She writes that "the Augustinian understanding of sexual pleasure as an evil that robs humans of control of their actions and causes them to ignore the rights and needs of others has tended to prevail in American Christian culture" (Gudorf 1995, 83). More broadly (with respect to current notions of sexuality), this understanding has resulted in sexual avoidance, excuses for irresponsible behavior, and the misuse and abuse of women by men. By contrast, Gudorf insists that we can, and do control sexual pleasure, and we must strive for sexual pleasure that is consistently mutual. She argues that human beings are created for experiencing pleasure, and thus she does not believe that they should feel compelled to undertake celibacy.

She does not repudiate all forms of celibacy, but she cautions that pleasure remains central to the human condition: "Permanent celibacy, as any other form of pleasure deprivation, should be chosen only with the understanding that the individual accepts this deprivation as instrumental in procuring some greater pleasure, *and* has developed appropriate alternative avenues for satisfying the physical, emotional, and symbolic human desires normally satisfied by sex in this culture" (Gudorf 1995, 99).

In reconstructing Christian conceptions of sexuality, Gudorf submits that mutual sexual pleasure should be the ethical criterion for evaluating sexual activity. She argues that mutual sexual pleasure celebrates the goodness of sexuality without lapsing into hierarchy or abuse. Moreover, she believes that there is a Scripturally-grounded basis for mutual sexual pleasure: "Christianity has never really taken seriously the real wisdom of Jesus' injunction to love neighbor's *as oneself*: that love of neighbor must begin with love of self" (Gudorf 1995, 115; original emphasis). The mediation of love of self, and love of other, presents difficult challenges for theological interpretations of sexuality. Love of the self in ordinate ways is tantamount to sin, lust, and the inability to love the other without instrumentalizing them. The inundation of sexual images, their commodification, and their portrayal of women as submissive objective (e.g., pornography) render sexuality as impersonal (and thereby obviating the mediation of love of self and love of other). Sexuality, according to many contemporary theologians (e.g., Au 1989; Farley 2006; Cahill 1996), is naturally good, but it is also potentially destructive, in that individuals can experience alienation and suffer abuse. Freudian models of sexuality seem to undervalue the goodness of sexuality; they insist that persons must repress their sexual drives that inevitably lead to fixation and guilt.

THEOLOGICAL PERSPECTIVES ON MARRIAGE

Hebrew Scriptures

The Hebrew Scriptures depict marriage and procreation as fundamental to God's creation. Immediately following the creation of human beings in God's image, God declares that humans should "Be fruitful and multiply" (Genesis 1:28). Moreover, in the second creation account, God deems that human beings should not be alone (Genesis 2:18) and that marriage helps, in profound ways, to achieve relationality ("Therefore a man leaves his father and his mother and clings to his wife, and they become one flesh" Genesis 2:24). Genesis dedicates significant attention to family lineage, and God (YHWH) makes promises—secured in, and through covenant—that relate to the proliferation of these lineages. Despite the account of the Fall (Genesis 3) that introduces pain, enmity, and hierarchy into marriage, and the patriarchal assumptions and practices within marriage, fidelity, holiness, and righteousness are centrally located within marriage and family. God's covenant (see Exodus, the book of the covenant) establishes a model of loving trust between God and God's people that conveys the depths of the commitment of marriage (e.g., "Thou shall not commit adultery," Exodus 20:14).

NEW TESTAMENT

In the New Testament, Jesus upholds the sanctity of marriage as divinely instituted. He refutes adultery (consistent with the Mosaic code), but he also—intensifying and interiorizing the law—repudiates lust in the heart (Matthew 5:27–30); he also rejects divorce, and identifies marriage as grounded in God's intention for the world ("Therefore what God has joined together, let no one separate" Matthew 19:6). In terms of the question of not marrying (and, given that sexuality only was to occur within marriage, not engaging in sexual intercourse), Jesus affirms the varieties of celibacy: "For there are eunuchs who have been so from birth, and there are eunuchs who have been made eunuchs by others, and there are eunuchs who have made themselves eunuchs for the sake of the kingdom of heaven. Let any one accept this who can" (Matthew 19:12).

The New Testament, however, also presents challenges to the notion of marriage as the principal way of Christian living. In Luke 14:26, Jesus preaches: "Whoever comes to me and does not hate father and mother, wife and children, brothers and sisters, yes, and even life itself, cannot be my disciple." Furthermore, the apostle Paul affirms that the celibate life offers an appropriate model within the eschatological context: "I think that, in the view of the impending crisis, it is well for you to remain as you are. Are you bound to a wife? Do not seek to be free. Are you free from a wife? Do not seek a wife . . . Yet those who marry will experience distress in this life, and I would spare you that" (I Corinthians 7:26–27; 28). This affirmation of celibacy continued for centuries in the Christian tradition, particularly among religious communities. Consecrated virgins, monks, nuns, and priests took vows to uphold obedience, poverty, and chastity. Chastity reflected control of the body and the importance of the soul, where the only marriage that occurs is in the marriage with Christ.

THEOLOGICAL TRADITION

Early Christian martyrs frequently made choices that reflected a commitment to God over and above commitment to family (see Luke 14:26 reference above). The martyrdom account of Perpetua, for example, records her decision to give up her infant in order to give her own life for God. An important voice in defending marriage was St. Augustine (354–430), who developed an account of marriage, sexuality, and family in his treatise *On the Good of Marriage* (c. 401). Concerned about the lascivious and sinful dimensions of sexuality, but determined to defend the goodness of creation (and, by extension, the goodness of the Creator), Augustine insists that marriage is the only acceptable relationship for sexual intercourse. He articulates three goods of marriage: fidelity (a bond with one's spouse that functions as a remedy for lust); sacrament (a bond with God that is eternal and indissoluble); and offspring (children). Augustine characterizes the first two goods as the unitive goods or aspects of marriage, and the third good as the procreate good or aspect of marriage. He concludes that the unitive and procreative aspects are inseparable; hence, anything that severs them is not morally licit.

Between the fourth and thirteenth centuries, weddings were rarely performed by priests in churches (though priests would bless marriages after the civil ceremonies). Marriages were principally means by which economic and political ties could be strengthened, and offspring ensured the succession of property and possessions. A shift in the theological grammar used to describe marriage occurred in the Middle Ages. Theologians such as Thomas Aquinas, view marriage as a natural gift of God, but also a supernatural—in, and through the sacramental character of God's self-bestowal of God's sanctifying grace—and eternal gift. The Council of Trent (1545–1563) clarified further that Catholic weddings must occur in a church, and be performed by a priest, to ensure its sacramental character. In the early modern period up through the Second Vatican Council (1962–1965), the Church emphasized the communal dimensions of marriage, where the sacrament means that marriage consists of the relationship between spouses, but also the relationship with the church, children, and community. The sacramental character, the "unbreakable oneness" according to Pope John Paul II (1981), ensures that marriage is indissoluble.

MODERN CHALLENGES: THE RISE OF COHABITATION AND DIVORCE

Since the 1960s, the state of marriage in the United States has been under intense pressure. Many point to the cultural understandings and attitudes toward marriage as one of the catalysts for this pressure. On the one hand, cohabitation, or unmarried sexual partners living together, has risen dramatically. It is estimated that in 2000 there were more than 5.5 million couples cohabitating in the United States. Studies identify economic, cultural, religious (or lack thereof), and other factors as explanations for this rise in cohabitation. On the other hand, the rates of divorce also rose steadily from the 1960s, peaking in the 1980s, and reaching a plateau in the 2000s. Even as Jesus explicitly rejects divorce for any reasons (Mark 10:2–12 and Luke 16:18), divorce rates in the United States are highest in those states that constitute the *Bible belt*. Some thinkers point to the increasing cultural acceptance of divorce as the catalyst within religious and secular circles, whereas others suggest that legal mechanisms, such as no-fault divorce laws (whereby divorces can be granted simply for irreconcilable differences), exacerbated divorce rates. The notion that marriages are merely contracts, began to overtake understandings of marriage as covenant. Others insist that broader socioeconomic changes—for example, enhanced opportunities for women, the effectiveness of artificial birth control, the decline of religion, and the loss of morality—account for both of these phenomena. Some theologians, such as Rosemary Radford Ruether (2000) and Margaret Farley (2006), view some aspects of these phenomena as potentially positive, particularly for women. That is, women no longer need to sacrifice themselves solely for the good of the marriage. Others, such as Pope John Paul II, worry that they reflect selfishness, rather than selflessness, and cause grave harm to the institution of marriage and to children. The longitudinal studies of Judith Wallerstein have shed light on the potential long-term effects of divorce. For example, her studies indicate that children of divorced parents typically experience difficulties in establishing intimacy later on in life when they are adults.

COVENANT MARRIAGES

Louisiana, Arkansas, and Arizona have passed legislation for covenant marriages in their states. These marriages, which individuals would voluntarily select, require that individuals undertake various steps to ensure that marriage is a lifelong commitment. First, premarital counseling is mandatory before these states will grant a covenant marriage. Second, marital counseling is required if the marriage experiences challenges and there is contemplation of divorce. Third, there are restrictions on when and why divorces could be granted (e.g., period of separation and no irreconcilable differences). Other states have attempted such measures, but legislative debates have reached impasses. Some argue that states are attempting to implement a Judeo-Christian notion of covenant that might violate the separation of church and state. Others worry that the restrictions ascribed to such marriages limit personal freedoms and the pursuit of happiness. Only a small percentage of marriages in these states are covenant marriages, but some argue that their potential successes might inspire other states to develop such legislation in the hopes of strengthening marriages and improving the lives of children.

DEBATES REGARDING SAME-SEX MARRIAGE

Current Legal and Political Developments

In 1996, the United States Congress passed the *Defense of Marriage Act* (DOMA) in anticipation of the legalization of same-sex marriage. The act defines marriage as between a man and a woman, and stipulates that states do not have to recognize the marriage laws of other states that grant same-sex marriage. Furthermore, DOMA prevents same-sex couples from receiving any of the federal rights or benefits of marriage (which currently include over one thousand benefits). Forty-four states have adopted some version of the DOMA provisions. In 2000, Vermont created *civil unions* (which have been adopted as domestic partnerships in several states, including California, Washington, and Oregon), that allowed heterosexual and homosexual couples to have similar, but not equivalent, legal benefits. Defenders of civil unions claim that it protects and promotes the rights of all couples, whereas opponents of civil unions claim that such unions function as *separate but equal* and thus are viewed as (legally and socially) inferior to marriage. In 2003, the Massachusetts Supreme Court ruled that a ban on same-sex marriage violated the state's constitution by denying due process and equal protection under the law to same-sex couples. In May, 2004, Massachusetts became the first state to grant same-sex couples the right to marry. Several cities, notably San Francisco, seized upon the legalization and recognized same-sex marriages within their jurisdictions. This recognition prompted state legislatures to act to deny these marriages, and to implement mechanisms to prevent future same-sex marriages.

In November, 2004, 11 states voted to ban same-sex marriages. As of August 2007, 27 states have amended their constitutions to ban same-sex marriages. During the same time period, however, several countries, including Belgium,

Canada, The Netherlands, Spain, England, and South Africa, have legalized same-sex marriages. In November, 2006, Arizona became the first state to vote down a proposed amendment to ban same-sex marriages. It is difficult to predict political sentiment within the United States and outside of it, but it is clear that the political disagreements will remain quite polemical. A fundamental question within the political debate remains: Is there a fundamental right to marry? Political scientist Evan Gerstmann, for example, argues that such a right is a constitutionally protected right. Noting similarities between the United States Supreme Court's 1967 rejection of Virginia's antimiscegenation statute, and the desire of same-sex couples to receive legal recognition of their marriages, Gerstmann states: "There is a well-established, fundamental constitutional right to marry that is not limited to child-bearing couples" (Gerstmann 2004, 110). The fact that same-sex couples cannot have their own biological children should not, according to Gerstmann, preclude their legal right to marry one another. Gerstmann supports his claim by appealing to legal precedence and by asserting that though "the Constitution protects the right to bear children, it also protects the right to avoid having them by using contraceptives, to abort them, to bear them out of wedlock, and to raise them in nontraditional settings" (Gerstmann 2004, 92).

Theological Perspectives on Same-Sex Marriage

The Catholic Church condemns both homosexual acts, and proposals for legalizing same-sex marriage. In July 2003, the Congregation for the Doctrine of the Faith (CDF) (prefect, Joseph Cardinal Ratzinger) issued *Considerations Regarding Proposals to Give Legal Recognition to Unions Between Homosexual Persons*. The text begins by articulating the nature of marriage and its inalienable characteristics. Focusing on first two creation accounts' depiction of the biological complimentarity between men and women, and the function of sexuality therein, the text posits that "God has willed to give the union of man and woman a special participation in his work of creation" (CDF 2003, paragraph 3). Would same-sex marriage comport with such participation? The text gainsays any correlation with same-sex marriages: "There are absolutely no grounds for considering homosexual unions to be in any way similar or even remotely analogous to God's plan for marriage and family" (CDF 2003, paragraph 4). Engaging Scripture and Christian tradition, the CDF views homosexual acts to be a serious depravity and objectively disordered, though it does affirm that persons with homosexual tendencies should be accepted with respect, and not discriminated against in unjust ways. Persons with such tendencies are called to a life of chastity. The CDF insists that civil authorities cannot legitimate the "evil" of homosexual unions by legalizing them.

In constructing an argument again legal recognition of homosexual unions, the Church appeals to four different orders; the order of right reason, the biological and anthropological order, the social order, and the legal order. The order of right reason pertains to the natural moral law, where—following the model of Thomas Aquinas that civil law is the application of natural law to specific communities—"civil law cannot contradict right reason without losing its binding force on conscience" (CDF 2003, paragraph 6). The argument from the biological and anthropological order points out that homosexual unions cannot naturally procreate (and also should not utilize new reproductive technologies; see related entry on birth control and family planning). Moreover, the CDF contends that children raised by same-sex couples would not develop fully: "the absence of sexual complementarity in these unions creates obstacles in the normal development of children who would be placed in the care of such persons" (CDF 2003, paragraph 7). In terms of the argument based on the social order, the text claims that the institution would be redefined, thereby harming the common good. Individual pursuit of autonomy (and, in this case, the right to marry) cannot override, the text holds, the values of society. Finally, according to the argument from the legal order, marriage is legally sanctioned by the state because it ensures the succession of generations; as same-sex couples cannot achieve reproduction for the common good, it does not merit this legal recognition. The text concludes with a brief discussion about the role of Catholic politicians vis-à-vis legislation in favor of homosexual unions. The CDF notes that when legislative debates arise, "the Catholic law-maker has a moral duty to express his opposition clearly and publicly and to vote against it" (CDF 2003, paragraph 10). Among organized religious groups, some mainline Protestants and liberal Catholics support gay marriages, but white Evangelicals, Black Protestants, and conservative Catholics reject that legal right for homosexuals. These groups adopt similar positions to civil unions, though religious individuals defend it vis-à-vis gay marriage.

See also Abortion; AIDS; Female Subordination in Christian Thought; Homosexuality.

Further Reading: Au, Wilkie. *By Way of the Heart: Toward a Holistic Christian Spirituality.* New York: Paulist Press, 1989; Cahill, Lisa. *Sex, Gender, and Christian Ethics.* Cambridge: Cambridge University Press, 1996; De La Torre, Miguel A. *A Lily Among the Thorns: Imagining a New Christian Sexuality.* San Francisco: Jossey-Bass, 2007; Farley, Margaret. *Just Love: A Framework for Christian Sexual Ethics.* New York: Continuum International Publishing Group, 2006; Gerstmann, Evan. *Same-Sex Marriage and the Constitution.* Cambridge: Cambridge University Press, 2004; Gudorf, Christine. *Body, Sex, and Pleasure: Reconstructing Christian Sexual Ethics.* Cleveland: The Pilgrim Press, 1995; John Paul II, Pope. "Familiaris Consortio." 1981. http://www.vatican.va/holy_father/john_paul_ii/apost_exhortations/documents/hf_jp-ii_exh_19811122_familiaris-consortio_en.html; Kidder, Annemarie. *Women, Celibacy, and the Church: Toward a Theology of the Single Life.* New York: Crossroad Publishing, 2003; Loader, William. *Sexuality and the Jesus Tradition.* Grand Rapids, MI: W.B. Eerdmans, 2005; Ryether, Rosemary Radford. *Christianity and the Making of the Modern Family.* Boston: Beacon Press, 2000; Schneiders, Sandra M. *Seeing All: Commitment, Consecrated Celibacy, and Community in Catholic Religious Thought.* New York: Paulist Press, 2001; Scott, Kieran, and Harold Horell, eds. *Human Sexuality in the Catholic Tradition.* Lanham, MD: Rowman and Littlefield Publishers, 2007.

Jonathan Rothchild

MUSLIM MINORITIES IN THE WEST

Approximately 10 to 15 million Muslims live in Western Europe, and anywhere from 6 to 10 million reside in the United States. As a minority, Muslims have struggled to maintain their Islamic identity, safeguard their family values and lifestyle, and worship according to the tenets of Islam. Although the beginnings of Muslims in Western Europe and America were significantly different, the twentieth century has seen parallel experiences. Efforts by both Muslims and the West are being made to improve relations and coexist peacefully.

MUSLIM BEGINNINGS IN AMERICA

Today, Muslims with citizenship in America possess all of the rights of citizens, and are free to practice their religion in accordance with the constitution. However, the first Muslims to arrive in America were not free, but brought over from West Africa as slaves during the colonial era. Although some were religious scholars, they were not allowed to practice their religion, and were forced to accept Christianity. It was not until the 1800s that Muslims, mostly Arabs, came to the United States of their own free will. Poverty and political instability under the Ottoman regime were the deciding factors that caused them to immigrate. Arriving from Syria, Lebanon, Jordan, and Palestine they did not wish to create Muslim communities, but intended to return to their home countries. Nevertheless, many did not return to their homeland, sending for their families to join them. At the turn of the twentieth century, American Muslims practiced their faith within the home, seeking no recognition as a member of a religion different than that which was considered normal in America. Many assimilated into American culture, especially the youth, who attempted to become more like their white peers. Refusing to learn Arabic and turning to non-Muslim partners for marriage, the Muslim identity was beginning to disappear. In order to prevent the further erosion of their culture, American Muslims began to build communities in the hope of re-establishing their Islamic distinctiveness.

Muslim beginnings in America were humble, and documented evidence of the first Muslim groupings was found in the Midwest—North Dakota presumably the earliest. Syrians and Lebanese attended the first Islamic Center in Michigan City, Indiana, around 1914, which led to the formation of the Modern Age Arabian Society in 1924. Cedar Rapids, Iowa, saw the construction of a mosque in 1934, which is still attended and referred to as the *Mother Mosque of America*. New York City has been home to a Muslim population since the late 1800s. Polish, Russian, and Lithuanian Muslims created the American Mohammedan Society in Brooklyn in 1907. By the 1930s, the Moslem Mosque was established, and is still functioning. Today, Muslims from nearly every country in the world live in New York City, resulting in an increase in the number of Islamic centers, mosques, and schools. Chicago also saw an influx of Muslim immigrants, mostly Syrians and Palestinians, in the late nineteenth century, and by the early 1900s may have been the home of more Muslims than any other city in America. Today there is much cultural, racial, and ethnic diversity among the Chicago Muslim population. The Nation of Islam, an African-American heterodox group known as *Black Muslims*, established its base in Chicago.

By 1895, Muslims from the Punjab had arrived in California, Oregon, Washington, and Canada, and in 1947, the partition of India resulted in an increased immigration of Indian Muslims. Today, California is home to Muslims from all over the world, in particular to those from the Middle East, Iran and South Asia, as well as recent Muslim immigrants from Afghanistan, and refugees from some African countries. Los Angeles and San Francisco have seen the most growth, as evidenced by The Islamic Center of Southern California located in Los Angeles. Dearborn, Michigan, saw the first influx of Muslims when Sunni Ottoman Turks arrived in the early 1900s. After the launch of Dearborn's Ford Motor Company plant in the latter part of the 1920s, an Arab community began to grow. Today, large numbers of Lebanese, Yemeni, and Palestinian Muslims are settled in Dearborn where Sunni and Shi'i Arab Muslims enjoy a close relationship. Quincy, Massachusetts, due to its location as well as jobs created by the shipping business, became a home to Muslims, the majority being Lebanese, after 1875. Seven families consisting of Sunni and Shi'i, provided the inspiration for the establishment of the Islamic Center of New England.

NATION OF ISLAM

From the late nineteenth century and through more than half of the twentieth century, Muslims lived quietly without much notice from their fellow Americans. However, at the beginning of the twentieth century there were some converts to Islam. These new Muslims were mostly African Americans who were drawn to the racial and ethnic equality that was professed by Islam. In Detroit in the early 1930s, Wallace D. Fard claimed that he had just come from Mecca with a message of liberation for black Americans. According to Fard, they were the descendants of the lost ancient tribe of Shabazz. He encouraged separation from the white American oppressor, and established the *Lost-Found Nation of Islam in the Wilderness of North America*. Fard mysteriously disappeared in 1934, and Elijah Muhammad, formerly Elijah Poole, one of Fard's most ardent followers, became the leader of the *Nation of Islam*. Preaching a message of black militancy and separatism, he condemned white society for its oppressive policies toward blacks. He predicted the inevitable downfall of the white racist society, with the rise of the black community whom he referred to as a *Chosen People*. The teachings of Elijah Muhammad encouraged self-reliance, self-improvement, and empowerment, and forbade gambling, alcohol, drugs, and laziness. However, the Nation of Islam differed greatly from mainstream Islam. Its racist doctrine and the belief that Fard was Allah and Elijah Muhammad was the last prophet were antithetical to true Islam. The Five Pillars of Islam were not adhered to, and major Islamic traditions were not followed. Malcolm X, a renowned member of the Nation, initially followed the teachings of Elijah Muhammad's theology. However, in 1964, he went on a pilgrimage to Mecca and renounced his once firm belief that races could not coexist. On his return to the States, he declared himself a Muslim, rather than a Black Muslim. Malcolm X was assassinated on February 21, 1965, followed by the conviction of two members of the Nation. In the 1970s, with approximately 100,000 members, the Nation integrated with mainstream Islam, under the leadership of Elijah Muhammad's son, Warith Deen Muhammad. This, however, met resistance with Louis Farrakhan, who maintained that the original teachings of Elijah Muhammad were accurate. Claiming leadership of the Nation, Farrakhan continued to preach black militancy and separatism. In recent years he has led the Nation toward traditional Islamic practices, and claims that the Nation now meets the standards of mainstream Islam.

MUSLIM IMMIGRATION DURING THE 1960s

The 1960s saw an influx of Muslim student immigrants with the advent of the civil rights movement. Immigrant students established Muslim student organizations on many of the college campuses across America. Some returned home becoming influential in their own countries, while others remained. Many had been recruited by the United States, and eventually became professionals in areas of medicine, engineering, and other sciences. Muslims began to question what their role was to be in a non-Muslim society. Active participation in a non-Muslim government might not be considered permissible according to Islamic law. However, this issue would soon be addressed through American opinion, not Islamic decree.

CONFLICTS IN THE ISLAMIC WORLD

After the 1967 Arab-Israeli war, Arab Americans came under the scrutiny of the United States Government. The FBI spied on individuals and organizations within the Arab-American community and interviewed anyone associated with them—employers, neighbors, friends, and family. Already under suspicion, Muslims became increasingly singled-out as a threat to America with such events as the Iranian revolution, hijackings, and hostage situations. John L. Esposito writes, "Some saw these events as signs of an Islamic threat or a clash of civilizations, Islam versus the West. America's relationship with Muslims was seen within a context of conflict and confrontation. Islam was viewed as a foreign religion, distinct from the Judeo-Christian tradition. This reinforced a sense of 'us' and 'them'" (Esposito 2002). Instances were reported in which Muslim activists were arrested and their possessions confiscated, although there was no evidence of any wrong doing, and Palestinian activists, even though they were U.S. citizens, were threatened with deportation. Anticommunist laws were supplanted by antiterrorist legislation aimed mainly at Arabs. Arabs were not only excluded from political campaigns, but often campaign donations from Arab Americans were returned. Arab-Americans have regarded this unfair treatment as the intent of the U.S. government to marginalize them, and not afford them the same rights as non-Arab citizens, including freedom of speech. During the 1980s and 1990s, according to a study in Chicago, participation in civil activities was minimal, with the exception of a few Arabs who did not fit the typical physical description of Arabs, display their ethnicity, or openly express their opinion about U.S. foreign policy. Although there was improvement in the 1990s, Arabs still felt uncomfortable outside their own community.

One of the biggest problems in the American Islamic Community has been that Americans have had very little accurate information about Muslims. Within the last 40 years, negative stereotyping of Arabs and Muslims by the media has resulted in discrimination in the work force and society. While Americans have had little understanding of Muslim beliefs and customs, Muslims have struggled to define their identity within a pluralistic American culture. Issues, such as the role of women, education, worship traditions, the relationship between men and women, intermarriage, and the question of how devotion to one's faith integrates with loyalty to one's country, have created concerns within the Islamic community.

MODERN AMERICAN MUSLIMS

The modern American Muslim woman is outspoken in her demand for equality. The traditional separation of men and women during worship or in public meeting places in America is a choice that the woman is allowed to make. She also has the right to define her own manner of dress. Dressing conservatively has been the general rule, but that which defines conservative dress is up for discussion. Education is not only considered important for men, but is highly encouraged for women, as it is seen as a religious duty and a preventative measure against the repression of women that has plagued Muslim women in other countries. Marriage between men and women in America still favors the man. Although the man is free to marry Jews or Christians as long as his children are raised as Muslims, women, on the other hand, are restricted to marrying within the faith. This double standard, which leads to a lack of selection, results in the inevitable marriage of American Muslim women to men from their home countries. Another area in which Muslims have sought solutions concerns Muslim worship in America. In the past, imams were brought to America from Muslim countries. However, there existed a lack of understanding on the part of these foreign religious scholars concerning the unique set of problems that American Muslims face. Within the last couple of decades, American-born Muslims have been trained as imams in order to successfully handle these issues. Also, Muslims have reached out to Christians and Jews, participating in interfaith discussions. Probably the largest quandary facing American Muslims is the question of how to stay true to the faith and still be loyal to America. As America became involved in disputes with Muslim countries, the question of loyalty to faith or nation arose. The anti-Arab and anti-Muslim sentiment that accompanied these conflicts resulted in a shift in identification during the 1990s. Instead of identifying themselves as Arabs, Palestinians, or Jordanians, the Islamic community started to view themselves as Muslims first. Feeling rejected in the democratic society, the American Muslim began to turn to a transnational orientation focusing on the common ideals of Islam. This sentiment was to become a larger issue with the tragic events of September 11, 2001.

SEPTEMBER 11, 2001

The aftermath of 9/11 brought immediate attention to American Muslims. Terrorists espousing Islamic phrases and ideals, however distorted, placed the

Muslim community in a potentially volatile situation. President Bush, recognizing the potential for retaliation on Muslims, quickly beseeched all Americans to understand that Islam is a religion professing peace and not terrorism. As non-Muslim Americans have had to process the events of September 11, 2001, so too have Muslim Americans. Omid Safi (2006) describes three ways in which American Muslims have dealt with the situation. Initially, the perception among the Islamic community was that Muslims did not carry out the terrorism. Instead, a plot was concocted by the CIA or Israel's Mossad to vilify Muslims, in order to rationalize a violent retaliation on Muslim countries. Muslims all over the world held this view, and many American Muslims came to believe it as well. This type of thinking developed out of the disbelief that any Muslim could possibly perform such a monstrous act. After the realization that Muslims did engage in such activity, under an undeniable body of evidence, a rush to distance the true Muslim from the terrorist became paramount. Al-Qaeda was an aberration, and simply not representative in any way of the Islamic community. Finally, the third alternative is the realization that Islam can be interpreted in many ways, and can be used to justify violence. In fact, all the major religions can be construed so as to find a basis for good or evil acts. All three views are attempts by Muslims to understand and come to terms with a shocking event that has affected their entire lives.

In the post-9/11 era, a critical question remaining is: what will be the relationship between the American Muslim community and the rest of American society? A broad survey of mosque leaders taken in 2000 (Mosque in America: A National Study [MIA]), has been followed up by interviews in 2002 with the same mosque leaders, along with consideration of American Muslim literature pertaining to these concerns. The results have shown that almost all of the Muslim leaders wish to take part in American society without relinquishing their fundamental Islamic beliefs and traditions. There is a certain degree of trepidation concerning the secular and materialistic nature of American society, along with what Muslims view as the immoral behavior of Americans. Another issue that causes unease is America's foreign policy, which they believe to be biased and unfair. And although the Muslim community desires an active role as citizens, many are not comfortable with American demonstrations of patriotism. Many issues facing American Muslims also face European Muslims.

HISTORY OF MUSLIMS IN WESTERN EUROPE

Muslims have lived in Europe since the eighth century, and controlled Spain and areas of Italy and France, until Fernando of Aragon and Isabella of Seville began a campaign in the late fifteenth century to expel Muslims. Today, Muslims of virtually all ethnic groups reside in Western Europe. Most Western European countries such as Belgium, the Netherlands, Sweden, Spain, Denmark, Norway, and Austria are home to considerable numbers of Muslims, with France, Germany, and Great Britain being the most populated. Great Britain and France experienced some immigration before World War II, however, a greater influx occurred afterward. Educated Muslims, whose countries were no longer under colonial domination, sought work in the same European countries that had once been the colonizers. During the 1960s and 1970s, Europe's booming economy was creating jobs that required unskilled laborers. Over a million Muslims poured into Germany, France, and Great Britain. Soon, Muslim students sought higher education in Europe, and while many returned to their home countries, some stayed, either for political or economic reasons.

France, with five million Muslims, claims the largest Muslim population in Europe. Ten percent of its inhabitants are Muslim, and of those, many reside in major cities. Next to Roman Catholics, Muslims constitute the second largest religious group, and boast more than 1000 mosques. However, the Muslim experience in France has not been a positive one. At one time welcomed by the French to help with a labor shortage, working class Muslims are now accused of taking jobs that should belong to French citizens. Muslim girls wanting to wear the headscarf (*hijab*) have come under criticism due to the pressure by the French government to assimilate. Making matters worse are the influx of North Africans from Morocco, Tunisia, and Algeria—former French colonies. Violence in Paris, reportedly carried out by Algeria's Armed Islamic Group, and attacks against Jewish synagogues, have added to the already increased tensions. Many are expressing doubt that Islam can ever be harmonious with French secular culture. Most Muslims living in France do not have the privilege of voting, the same is true in Germany.

Between one and two million Muslims reside in Great Britain, most of which came from the Indian subcontinent. There are more than 600 mosques in Britain, many having been funded by Saudi Arabia. Since most Muslims have come from British Commonwealth countries, they enjoy full citizenship, participate in local politics, and occupy seats in the House of Lords and the House of Commons. But not all has gone smoothly for British Muslims. In the late 1980s, when Khomeini issued his fatwa on Salman Rushdie for the publication of the *Satanic Verses,* Muslims were targets of hostility. A speech was delivered in Oxford by the Prince of Wales in 1993, in which he admitted that "misunderstandings between Islam and the West continue."

CONCLUSION

While most of the Muslims in Western Europe are working class, Muslims in the United States are middle class, finding employment as doctors, intellectuals, and engineers. As a result, American Muslims have experienced more acceptance than European Muslims. Today, the American Muslim community (orthodox, heterodox, Sunni, Shi'i, or Sufi) is experiencing a trend of inclusion, and an acceptance of Islam as an American religion. In spite of the negative attitude toward Muslims following 9/11, a majority of American Muslims have reported that non-Muslim Americans have shown compassion and kindness, and have even offered protection. Although the history of Muslims in Western Europe is different than that of Muslims in the United States, many of the present-day concerns are the same. The struggle to retain their Islamic identity, uphold their family values and lifestyle, and the ability to carry out Islamic traditions, remain challenges for the Muslim minority in the West.

See also Islamic Nationalism; Nation of Islam.

Further Reading: Armstrong, Karen. *Islam: A Short History.* New York: The Modern Library, 2002; Bagby, Ihsan. "Isolate, Insulate, Assimilate: Attitudes of Mosque Leaders toward America." In *A Nation of Religions: The Politics of Pluralism in Multireligious America,* ed. Stephen Profero. Chapel Hill: University of North Carolina Press, 2006: 23–42; Cainkar, Louise. "No Longer Invisible: Arab and Muslim Exclusion after September 11." *Middle East Report* 224 (Autumn 2002): 22–29; Esposito, John L. *What Everyone Needs to Know about Islam: Answers to Frequently Asked Questions, from One of America's Leading Experts.* Oxford: Oxford University Press, 2002; H.R.H. The Prince of Wales. "Islam and the West." *Arab Law Quarterly* 9, no. 2 (1994): 135–143; McCloud, Aminah Beverly. "Islam in America: The Mosaic." In *Religion and Immigration,* eds. Yvonne Yazbeck Haddad, Jane I. Smith, and John L. Esposito. Walnut Creek, CA: Altamira Press, 2003: 159–174; Safi, Omid. "Progressive Islam in America." In *A Nation of Religions: The Politics of Pluralism in Multireligious America,* ed. Stephen Profero. Chapel Hill: University of North Carolina Press, 2006: 43–60; Smith, Jane I. *Islam in America.* New York: Columbia University Press, 1999; Suleiman, Michael W. "Arab-Americans: A Community Profile." In *Islam in North America: A Sourcebook,* eds. Michael A Koszegi and J. Gordon Melton. New York and London: Garland Publishing, 1992: 49–58.

Candace Lev

N

NATION OF ISLAM

The Nation of Islam (NOI) is a black, nationalist, religious, and political movement founded to empower African American people in light of ongoing racism and oppression that they were experiencing. The movement has come to be associated with controversial teachings, and its most famous member, Malcolm X. Since its inception in 1930, the organization has offered an alternative teaching and worldview that appeals to some African Americans who have otherwise given up on mainstream American values and Christianity as possible systems of liberation. The Nation of Islam is a unique, peculiarly American form of Islam that combines a black nationalist social, political, and economic program with a religious doctrine fused from Islam and Christianity. While mainstream Muslims (notably Sunni and Shi'ite Muslims), do not recognize the Nation of Islam as a legitimate form of Islam, the movement's leadership has always maintained that they are indeed Muslims, who have had to address very particular cultural and social ills within the United States, thus requiring a revised doctrine, that speaks to those ills. Most notably, mainstream Muslims specify that Islam is a universal religion, open to all people regardless of color. This differs significantly from the exclusivity of the Nation of Islam, which is a movement specifically targeted to African Americans, and is specifically not open to Caucasians, who are seen as the enemy, indeed, the devil incarnate.

The NOI developed out of a black nationalist, social context that preceded it in at least two other movements, including the first American Black Muslim group, the Moorish Science Temple Movement founded by Noble Drew Ali in 1913. While the NOI grew to be the most dominant form of African American Islam, Noble Drew Ali had previously presented a form of Islam to poor and disenfranchised black Americans in order to address many of the same issues that the NOI would later approach. Ali believed that a black nationalism would save black people from white hatred and bigotry that continued to plague them. The founder, and subsequent leaders of the NOI, would build upon this foundation laid by Ali. The Moorish Science Temple Movement would eventually decline following the death of its founder.

A second black nationalist movement was also instrumental in providing a context for the Nation of Islam. Marcus Garvey and his organization, the Universal Negro Improvement Association (UNIA), advocated a back to Africa program in 1916 as a means for African people throughout the world to have a foundation and homeland apart from European and American countries. Garvey's plan for the uplift and economic empowerment of black people throughout the Americas continued to play a dominant role for African Americans in the 1920s. He would gain the support of hundreds of thousands of black Americans who were willing to join him and build Liberia into a home base for Africans returning to the continent of Africa. Although Garvey would later be deported from the United States, following a conviction for mail fraud, and the movement crippled, Garvey's impact would continue to be felt in subsequent black leaders, including Elijah Poole, who would later become the leader of the Nation of Islam.

These prior movements illustrate a new consciousness among African Americans, a thought pattern characterized by confidence, independence, black theology, and a concept of self-help. These movements were appealing and compelling for a large number of African Americans over a period of years from 1900 to 1930, because they seemed to offer an alternative way of life, free from the restrictions and obstacles of racism. The Nation of Islam would simply tap into that consciousness and build on it in an enormously impactful way.

By 1930, the African American social context was ready to receive a teaching like the Nation of Islam. African Americans were dealing with vicious forms of racism in the forms of lynchings, Jim Crow segregation, and dehumanizing treatment in their daily lives. Black Americans felt that local and federal government agents were infested with the same racism as the people they encountered every day, and so could not be counted upon to change the system. Many African Americans began listening to the teachings of black nationalists who proclaimed that self-help was the only alternative. In particular, some African Americans began listening to the teachings of Fard Muhammad, (sometimes spelled Farad), who announced that Allah had come to rescue his people from their oppression. Fard Muhammad has remained a mysterious figure in terms of his heritage, birth place, and personal background. As a very fair-skinned black man, many have speculated about his origins, writing that he was perhaps Arabian or Polynesian, or any number of other nationalities. Whatever his ancestry, it is clear that he emerged in 1930, and began his ministry in Detroit, first appearing as a door to door salesman, who would offer more than just his wares to people. He spoke to poor and disenfranchised black people, offering them a message of identity, history, morality, communal responsibility, and empowerment. One of the people, who heard Fard Muhammad, was Elijah Poole.

The 1930s were a time of economic depression, following the stock market crash of 1929, and Elijah Poole, like most people of this time, found himself struggling to make a living for himself and his wife, when he met Fard Muhammad in 1931. Poole was so profoundly moved by these new teachings that he became Muhammad's most ardent pupil and disciple. He even came to believe that Muhammad was God in the flesh, a messiah figure. Consequently, the history and theology of the Nation of Islam would teach that Muhammad was the Great Mahdi, or messiah, who had come to liberate African Americans from their oppression. Poole joined with Muhammad, and learned history and religion according to this new perspective, ultimately becoming the leader himself. From this point on, Elijah Poole took the name Elijah Muhammad, following the teaching of Fard Muhammed that blacks should renounce their Christian slave names and take on Arabic or African names as befitting them as a people. As the Nation of Islam began to take shape, Poole would understand himself to be Fard Muhammad's messenger or prophet. Muhammad disappeared by 1934, leaving Elijah Muhammad to assume leadership for the organization.

One of the first things that Elijah Muhammad set out to do was to describe and articulate the teachings of his predecessor Master Fard Muhammad. (He began to do so as a person of very little formal education. He maintained that these teachings had to have been delivered by Allah, because he (Elijah) had not been well educated, and thus could not have made up these doctrines.) The basic teaching of the NOI under Fard and Elijah Muhammad was that God would appear to his people in the form of a messiah (Fard) in order to deliver them (black people) from their enemies (whites) and teach them how to destroy their white adversaries. Moreover, blacks should understand themselves to be descendants of the lost nation of the ancient tribe of Shabazz, from whom the founding prophet of Islam, Muhammad had descended. African Americans should further understand that though they were once "lost in the wilderness of North America," they are now "found," and being guided by God through Fard and Elijah Muhammad on the true teachings of who they are as a race of people. (This idea and these terms link to the biblical idea of the ancient Israelites who, according to the book of Exodus, wandered in the desert following their flight from Egyptian bondage. African Americans are thus like the Israelites for whom God has intervened against an oppressive political and social structure.)

For some African Americans who had been suffering under enslavement, racism, violence, and civil disenfranchisement, this type of program had wide appeal. NOI followers were empowered by teachings that affirmed their human dignity, even in this case, at the expense of demonizing all white people. African Americans felt that this teaching gave them confidence, and opportunities for self-improvement, despite the hatred and limitations imposed upon them by white society. Some African Americans found the NOI to be a refreshing alternative to more mainstream teachings by Christian ministers and accommodationist leaders, who cautioned blacks against radical doctrines and actions.

In addition to providing a theology and a genealogy, the NOI teachings inform a particular set of beliefs and core values for its members. The NOI teaches that Islam is the true religion for African Americans because it was a dominant religion in Africa prior to the slave trade. Some scholars, such as Sylviane Douf, have attempted to document the early practices of Islam on slave plantations. These numbers are largely lost to history because enslaved Africans were prohibited from practicing Islam, thus we have no exact count of African Muslims who were brought to the United States in bondage. Nevertheless, the NOI reclaims Islam for contemporary African Americans based upon this ancestral link. They believe that despite the large number of African Americans who are Christians, Islam is the true religion for all people of African descent.

Moreover, the Nation of Islam's program of uplift for African Americans is built upon certain values. These values include thrift, honesty, race solidarity, discipline, monogamy, and a concern for black history and Third World politics. Members of the NOI see themselves as united with other blacks around the world, and seek to be involved with justice issues in underdeveloped areas of Africa, and the Caribbean in particular. This form of race solidarity has, of course, been harshly criticized. As a black nationalist organization, the NOI can be characterized as a supremacist and separatist organization. One point of difference, however, from white supremacist groups, is that the members of the NOI perceive themselves to offer a haven to blacks *in response to* long-standing racism, discrimination, and violence. On the other hand, perhaps one major similarity between the two types of organizations is the perception each group has about the threat from the other. Each group claims to have an interest in self-preservation from the encroachment of the other racial group. In truth, they both hold similar ideological viewpoints, but maintain opposite extremes of the racial spectrum. The NOI strives to instill a strong sense of personal and communal responsibility in African Americans, challenging them not to depend on well meaning whites or anyone else for their social uplift. The NOI is firm in its teaching that black Americans have only themselves to look to for their progress; and this forms the basis for their exclusivity. Likewise, the group's sensationalist rhetoric against whites and Jews has caused a great deal of controversy throughout their history.

Many controversies have followed the Nation of Islam since its inception in 1930. Even the origins of the movement's founder, Fard Muhammad, are controversial. But even more detrimental than this relatively minor point, has been the construction and profession of a theology that identifies white people as devils. In a very elaborate cosmological and genealogical description of human origins, the NOI has described the creation of whites as a process of genealogical grafting from the original black people for the sole purpose of being an adversary to Blacks, and to undermine God's order.

More controversy ensued following the 1965 assassination of Malcolm X. While it is a matter of record that Malcolm was killed by Nation of Islam members, it has never been determined to what extent those members were following the orders of the NOI hierarchy. Given that Malcolm's assassination followed his public departure from the NOI over theological and personality issues, the dissension between the two of them was well known. Following a religious pilgrimage to Mecca, Malcolm began to rethink this version of Islam that he had grown so accustomed to, and to speak out about what he felt were its shortcomings. This was particularly difficult for Malcolm to do because he had considered himself to be reborn after his conversion to Islam and personal tutelage under Elijah Muhammad. Consequently, he was extremely close to Elijah Muhammad, and looked up to him as Allah's messenger and his own personal mentor.

Controversy began to erupt as Malcolm became aware of some of Elijah Muhammad's affairs and illegitimate children. Malcolm became severely disillusioned with his mentor, and began to rebel against his admonitions not to speak out against national politics. Malcolm also explored more traditional Sunni Islam, and built alliances with members of those communities. Elijah Muhammad began to see Malcolm as a loose cannon, whom he could no longer control. Tensions continued to escalate, resulting in Malcolm officially leaving the Nation in 1964. He would begin to formulate his own program for the uplift and empowerment of oppressed people, but he would do it as a Muslim free of racial exclusivity. Malcolm began to adopt the tenets of Sunni Islam as he continued the political work of liberating African Americans from civil rights' abuses. However, he would not live to see his vision unfold. In February of 1965, Malcom was shot to death while giving a speech at the Audubon Ballroom in Harlem, New York. His pregnant wife, Betty Shabazz, and their 4 young daughters were present. Some suggest that the NOI killed Malcolm because he was a traitor and publicly criticized Elijah Muhammad's teachings. Another theory claims that the assassins were planted by the FBI and CIA, who had been watching the movements of the black nationalist organization for many years. The theory asserts that plotting Malcolm's assassination would bring dissent, and the eventual downfall of the whole organization.

Elijah Muhammad would continue as leader of the Nation of Islam until his death in 1975. During his 44-year tenure, he continued his teaching for the uplift of African Americans over and against the inferiority of whites. Controversy would once again arise as two other leaders attempted to follow in his footsteps, his son, Warith Deen Muhammad, and Louis Farrakhan.

Schism in the movement occurred as Warith Muhammad and Louis Farrakhan set forth their agenda for continuing the movement. Each took their positions, and considered the other to be a false prophet. Muhammad aligned himself with Sunni Islam, and proceeded to take the movement along a nonracialized direction. Some of the older members, who had come in under Warith's father, did not accept this. Muhammad was severely criticized, and many members left to support Farrakhan. Minister Farrakhan ended up being the most persuasive, winning the larger following with the *old doctrine* as Elijah Muhammad had taught it. Thus, the 1980s saw the Nation of Islam beginning to stabilize with Farrakhan as its new leader.

Current leadership rests with Louis Farrakhan. Louis X, as he was known then, joined the Nation of Islam in 1957. Prior to joining, he had been a musician, living a fast, partying lifestyle. Although he had been aware of Elijah Muhammad and his teachings, Louis had been in no hurry to attend their meetings. He had been raised in the Episcopal Church, and did not feel compelled to give up the Christianity of his youth. Ultimately, however, he did listen to Elijah Muhammad, and became convinced of the truth of Islam for African Americans.

Louis converted to the NOI, changing his name to Louis X, and began his ascent in the movement as the head of the Fruit of Islam (FOI) in Boston. The FOI is the organization's security force. Farrakhan excelled in this role, advancing to captain, and then to minister of the Boston mosque that Malcolm X had started. Malcolm had thought well of Louis, and mentored him before leaving Boston. It was Malcolm's move that opened a place for Louis X to develop and gain recognition. Louis X would become Louis Farrakhan, and would become the national minister of the Nation of Islam. He has been credited with rebuilding the organization following the disarray of the movement in the aftermath of Elijah Muhammed's death.

Although Farrakhan has weathered a considerable amount of controversy since taking the leadership of the NOI, he maintains a reputation as the most influential black leader in the United States. He consistently draws tens of thousands of people to hear his public lectures. In addition, as a man now in his 70s, he seems to have mellowed in some areas of his teaching, and theology. For example, he has moved away from Elijah Muhammad's teaching that Fard Muhammad was actually God in the flesh. In 1999, he began to clarify this point, stating that Muslims believe in one God, and Fard Muhammad, revered though he may be among Nation of Islam members, is not to be understood as Allah.

The standout event for Minister Farrakhan is the Million Man March of 1995. This event called for African American men to gather in the spirit of atonement for self and community. As an extension of the Nation's traditional challenge for African American self-help and self-reliance, this landmark march was intended to inspire renewed moral discipline, and commitment of men to families and communities. The NOI was initially heavily criticized by women for being excluded from a gathering intended to uplift the whole community, but eventually the male-centered approach was accepted. The October 16, 1995, record-breaking gathering brought one million African American men to the nation's capital, reminiscent of the 1963 march lead by A. Phillip Randolph and Martin Luther King Jr. While that historical march addressed an audience of 250,000, the million man march was the largest all-black demonstration in American history, with an estimated one million attendees. (This number has been contested since the original event in 1995. However, the best estimate from the Boston University Center for Remote Sensing, using advanced photographic imaging is 837,214 with a 20% margin for error.) The NOI maintains that at least one million black men were in attendance (Boston University Press Release 1997).

Farrakhan and the Nation of Islam earned a good deal of notoriety on that date, and many believed it to be a turning point in the overall reputation of the movement. While it is true that Minister Farrakhan has many more mainstream followers than Elijah Muhammad had, many African Americans, and others, still consider the movement to be an extremist and separatist organization.

Perhaps what redeems the Nation of Islam is the movement's commitment to African American communities throughout the United States. The NOI, through the Fruit of Islam, has maintained a strong street presence in depressed and high crime neighborhoods in many major cities such as Chicago,

Detroit, Washington D.C., and New York. This unarmed, but highly trained, paramilitary security force, has played a significant role in maintaining civil order in many of these communities. Some of the most dangerous housing projects have been reclaimed by its residents with the ongoing help of the FOI guards.

In addition, Nation of Islam–owned businesses stand as models for African American entrepreneurship. Chicago, Illinois, is the headquarter city of the movement, home to the flagship temple Mosque Maryam, and the central location for the national newspaper, *The Final Call*. At its heyday, the Nation of Islam flourished with a flagship restaurant and entertainment venue, Salaam Restaurant, training academies, K-12 grade schools, the University of Islam, offices, bookstores, bakeries and other small businesses. Health and beauty products continue to be sold through the organization's Web site, and in *The Final Call* newspaper (www.noi.org).

As with many large institutions, the Nation of Islam has risen and fallen and risen again. It is a critical time in the life of the movement right now because of the health status of Louis Farrakhan. The minister is living with prostate cancer, and he has made statements that he will soon retire from his public role. However, no successor has been named. Although members continue to be hopeful for his recovery, and *The Final Call* continues to report that all is well, a new leader is destined to emerge in the very near future. The next stage in the history of the Nation of Islam imminently waits to be written.

See also Islamic Nationalism; Nationalism, Militarism, and Religion; Separation of Church and State.

Further Reading: Curtis, Edward E., IV. *Islam in Black America: Identity, Liberation, and Difference in African-American Islamic Thought.* Albany: State University Press, 2002; Gardell, Matthias. *In the Name of Elijah Muhammad: Louis Farrakhan and the Nation of Islam.* Durham: Duke University Press, 1996; Haley, Alex. *The Autobiography of Malcolm X.* New York: Ballantine Books, 1992 (1965); Lincoln, C. Eric. *The Black Muslims in America.* New York: Beacon Press, 1963; Muhammad, Elijah. *Message to the Black Man.* Chicago: Secretarius Memps Publications, 1997(1965); Murphy, Larry, ed. *Down By The Riverside: Readings in African American Religion.* New York: New York University Press, 2000; White, Vibert L. *Inside the Nation of Islam: A Historical and Personal Testimony by a Black Muslim.* Gainesville: University of Florida Press, 2001.

Darnise C. Martin

NATIONALISM, MILITARISM, AND RELIGION

Nationalism, militarism, and religion have always related to each other in ways that have been ambiguous and troublesome. All three draw on, and speak to some of our deepest human hopes and fears. They all, at least potentially, offer resources for creating secure and flourishing communities. Too often, however, they have interacted in ways that have created deep animosities and horrendous destruction, including the loss of millions of lives in the past century alone. How can that be possible when all three are so integrally linked to our basic identities as people?

An excellent way to begin deciphering these relationships is to reflect on Memorial Day. This typically American national holiday was instituted shortly after the Civil War as a way to honor the soldiers who died in American wars. The Memorial Day weekend in many American cities and towns involves special religious services in churches, synagogues, and other places of worship. Homes and businesses fly American flags. Many communities join with groups like the American Legion and the Veterans of Foreign Wars to organize parades and other activities honoring the service of military veterans. The tombs of veterans are decorated in local cemeteries. There are family gatherings and picnics.

Memorial Day brings together our American national, military, and religious traditions in a way that perhaps no other American holiday does. It draws on our deeply held American values of patriotism, religious faith, self-sacrifice, and family. It is both secular and sacred. Entire communities come together to dedicate themselves to the ideal of democracy, and the struggle against tyranny for which the military veterans are believed to have given their lives. Our other national holidays, such as Thanksgiving and the Fourth of July, do not combine all these values in the same way.

Another kind of national ceremony that offers further insight into the national, military, and religious character of our American nation is the funeral of a United States president, or other prominent national figure. The prominence of both religious and military traditions is on display in such funerals. Millions of Americans watch on their television sets as the funeral procession moves through the streets of our nation's capital.

There are religious services in the former leader's congregation or place of worship, and prayer or brief meditation by a prominent religious leader in the national memorial service in the Capitol Rotunda. Eulogies by political leaders draw on both national and religious symbols. There is a military band, a 21-gun salute, and elaborate military protocols as the casket is carried by pallbearers from all branches of the armed forces. There are few, if any, comparable civic rituals to draw on, even if the person being remembered was not overtly religious, or did not serve in the military. Such funerals are national ceremonies largely defined by military protocol and undergirded by religious symbolism.

ON NATIONALISM

It is assumed that each person in our contemporary world has a national identity. That identity defines who we are in a way that is similar to other social markers such as gender, culture, and language. For example, people living in southern Florida and North Dakota share a national identity even though they are geographically, and perhaps even culturally, much closer to Cuba and Canada, respectively. The defined borders of the United States, or of any other nation, stamp one's national identity. As the above example demonstrates, such national identity is extremely fluid. That is why rapid immigration is often seen as a threat by many people. They become alarmed that our nation is losing its basic national identity. And that is why national elites often insist on reinforcing national identities through such things as uniform public education, enforcing the use of a national language, and religious symbolism such as putting the phrase *In God We Trust* on our money.

Nationalism as an ideology has had tremendous political power in the modern world. Practically all successful political movements and revolutions have identified themselves as national struggles. It is understood as the foundation for our global world order. Yet it has produced no great thinkers, and is philosophically almost incoherent. That may be one reason why so many national political cultures around the world become rather banal and unimaginative after they have been in power for any length of time.

Unraveling the relationships between nationality and statehood can be especially perplexing. A nation has generally been understood as a people that identify themselves as having a common ethnic linage and shared history. In the modern world the notion of being a nation has evolved to include the right to political sovereignty within a given territory. The latter fits with Benedict Anderson's definition of a nation as "an imagined political community—and imagined as inherently limited and sovereign" (Anderson 1991, 6). Linking perceived national identities with the demands for an independent state has led to much conflict throughout the world. A dilemma of contemporary statecraft is finding ways to mediate such intractable claims.

For our purposes, Anderson's definition of a nation is better understood as referring to a nation-state. In many parts of the world, people from different national backgrounds come together to form a single state. Such states, like India and the United States, take on a hybrid national identity. As the continuing struggle for civil rights and religious pluralism in both of these countries indicates, building that kind of national society is never easy. It is always an ongoing project that is never completed.

That which makes a nation-state different from other kinds of communities, such as religious or cultural communities, is its defined geographical boundaries, and the claim to absolute sovereignty within its borders. To assert their sovereignty, nation-states claim the sole right to use violence and lethal force within their territory. They organize police and military forces to enforce that claim. Emerging and failed nation-states generally find it very difficult or impossible to control other armed groups within their territory.

Our contemporary world is divided into competing nation-states, each with its own military establishment to protect and advance the national interest. It is hard to even imagine a different kind of world, even though the nation-state as we know it emerged very late in human history. As recently as several hundred years ago all human societies were organized as clans, tribes, city-states, and larger realms. The borders between different realms, and even within realms, were not clearly defined. Furthermore, there was no exclusive right to the use of violence and lethal force within a realm. Local chiefs or lords generally maintained their personal constabularies or armies that were at the service of the realm during times of external threat. They also frequently fought against each other as they jockeyed for position within the realm.

The nation-state, as we know it, has evolved from European experience beginning in the sixteenth and seventeenth centuries. Popular political theories propose that state and military structures were formed as a *social contract* in which people gave up their autonomy in exchange for shared security. Political theorist Charles Tilly, however, claims that state making and war making went hand in hand in the emergence of the modern nation-state. State makers functioned as coercive entrepreneurs who extracted resources from the general population in order to fight wars to enhance their position against rival state making entrepreneurs. Though Tilly does not equate all statesmen and generals with murderers and thieves, he does claim that, "banditry, piracy, gangland rivalry, policing, and war making all belong on the same continuum" (Besteman 2002, 36).

Even though we may consider Tilly's analogy to be extreme, it helps us understand the relationship between nationalism and militarism. Whatever other functions national governments perform, they always insist on organizing and monopolizing violence. There are also significant differences in how national elites relate to the general population in their territory, as indicated by descriptive models such as a democracy, a monarchy, and a military junta. These models reflect the comparative strength and freedom of various civil society groups such as business associations, schools, labor unions, and churches within a nation-state. The more autonomy and clout such groups have the more open and democratic the society is likely to be.

As this analysis indicates, a central challenge in creating a more just and peaceful world is to recognize the connection between state making and war making, and to struggle against its systemic penchant toward violence and exploitation. Citizens always need to be vigilant in resisting concentrations of power and the tendency toward violence within their own nation-state. The sad saga of national leaders taking their country to war in order to enhance their own political power is all too common in human history.

ON MILITARISM

We need to distinguish the military from militarism. Militarism is a legitimate concern for human security that has gone awry. An increasingly urgent task is to differentiate between legitimate security structures and functions that promote security for all people, and the kind of militarism that glorifies brute force and violence. The latter is a perverse death instinct that actually mirrors authentic human love and community. It is inauthentic because it attempts to create community over against other communities that are characterized as evil. It quickly becomes perverse when all kinds of violence, including terror tactics and torture, are justified in the fight against the other. When we engage in that kind of struggle, we inevitably become the very thing we say we abhor.

Our media culture is full of the glorification of such violence. Heroes in movies and television shows portray a swashbuckling swagger that draws on ancient myths of redemptive violence. In actuality, it is far removed from the daily reality of the men and women who serve in the armed forces. There is a huge disconnect between such *mythic reality* and the *sensory reality* of police officers and soldiers carrying out their routine duties. Overcoming such myths is a central task in creating more effective and humane police and military forces. Too often, young recruits who join police and military forces already have their heads filled with dangerous mythic notions of glorified violence.

Contrary to such myths, the average person has a natural aversion to killing other human beings. Lieutenant Colonel Dave Grossman, an army psychologist, thinks that is a good thing. Military training designed to override our natural human instinct against killing our own kind has to be used with care, because it creates psychological damage. Killing causes deep wounds of pain and guilt that soldiers live with for the rest of their lives. In extreme cases, child soldiers in some parts of the world have been trained to be brutal killers with little moral compunction. Grossman is especially concerned that violent movies and video games targeted at our youth perpetuate the myth of redemptive violence, and actually condition young people to become killers (Grossman 1996).

ON RELIGION

All religions are rooted in the soil of a particular place and the shared life of a particular people. This means that our religious traditions are carried by our cultural and ethnic identities. That relationship makes it easy for religion to get caught up in social conflicts involving people from different cultural, ethnic, and national backgrounds. Religion is often used as a resource for group solidarity and courage in the midst of such conflicts. Even people who are not overtly religious can use religion in this way.

Furthermore, all religions draw on our human experience of the transcendent or divine, generally referred to as *God* in our English language. During times of conflict or war, the divine is thought to be on the side of our own people or nation. Americans, like people from other nations, always appeal to God during times of war. For example, in the lead up to the American invasion of Iraq, many Americans put flag decals and bumper stickers with the words *God Bless America* on their cars. National leaders will especially reach out for the support of prominent religious leaders during wartime.

At the same time, religion has the capacity to draw on the divine as a transcendent point of reference that brings all our activities into question. Consequently, the popular refrain of going to war with God on our side is turned on its head, and the very act of going to war is understood as a religious failure and lack of faith in God. Reliance on military strength for human security is brought into question. In the ancient Jewish scriptures, written millennia ago, a sage wrote, "A king is not saved by his great army . . . the war horse is a vain hope for victory" (Psalm 33:16–17). Likewise, the *Sutta Nipata,* one of the earliest collections of Buddhist scriptures, contrasts militarism with nonviolence. The Buddha proclaims, "I turn the wheel by peaceful means—this wheel is irresistible" (Saddhatissa 1995, III. 7.7).

All our major religious traditions predate the modern nation state by thousands of years, and have ample resources for resisting and subverting militarism and imperialism. For example, early Christian communities were solidly pacifist for several hundred years, and resisted being coopted by Roman imperialism. That changed in the fourth century c.e. when Emperor Constantine converted to Christianity. However, even after Christianity became the official religion of the Roman Empire, theologians such as Augustine developed just-war arguments to critique and curb military excesses. A big problem, of course, is that politicians and military leaders have always been quick to claim that the war they are waging is just, even though it does not meet just-war criteria. Too often, just-war arguments are coopted and used to support the kind of nationalist and militaristic agendas that they would resist if used honestly.

TOWARD A DIFFERENT FUTURE

The excesses of nationalism and militarism have become an increasingly toxic brew that divides our world into hostile enemy camps. That makes life ever more intolerable in our shrinking world where people of different cultures, ethnicities, and religions increasingly live in the same neighborhoods. Ever more advanced technology makes armed conflicts ever more brutal and destructive. Religions need to become more adept at not being swept up in national and military crusades. They also need to learn how to live side by side and work together for the common good in ever more pluralistic local communities.

A different future will require letting go of some ingrained ways of thinking about international relations, human security, and religious faith. It demands imagination and different tools for resolving conflicts. Our religious and national identities, in such a world, will serve the common goal of creating a just and peaceful world for all people. They will not be allowed to become the sources of division and bloodshed. We will recognize that peace and justice cannot be achieved through violent means.

The kind of world we want for our grandchildren will put more resources into strategic peacebuilding disciplines such as human development, diplomacy, and conflict transformation rather than pouring money and lives into ever more sophisticated armed forces and weapons' systems. It will recognize the dignity and interdependence of everyone, regardless of nationality or creed. And it will certainly draw on the contributions of transforming religious communities, national cultures, and security structures committed to the wellbeing of all people.

See also Amish; Hutterites; Just War; Personal Pacifism versus Political Nonviolence.

Further Reading: Anderson, Benedict. *Imagined Communities: Reflections on the Origin and Spread of Nationalism.* New York: Verso, 1991; Bainton, Roland H. *Christian Attitudes toward War and Peace: A Historical Survey and Critical Re-evaluation.* Nashville: Abingdon, 1960; Besteman, Catherine, ed. *Violence: A Reader.* New York: New York University Press, 2002; Grossman, David A. *On Killing: The Psychological Cost of Learning to Kill in War and Society.* New York: Back Bay Books, 1996; Hedges, Chris. *War is a Force That Gives Us Meaning.* New York: PublicAffairs, 2002; Johnson, Chalmers. *The Sorrows of Empire: Militarism, Secrecy, and the End of the Republic.* New York: Henry Holt and Company, LLC, 2004; Saddhatissa, H. *The Sutta Nipata.* London: Routledge/Curzon, 1995; Schirch, Lisa. *The Little Book of Strategic Peacebuilding.* Intercourse, PA: Good Books, 2004; Smith-Christopher, Daniel L., ed. *Subverting Hatred: The Challenge of Nonviolence in Religious Traditions.* Cambridge,

MA: Boston Research Center for the 21st Century, 1998; Yoder, John Howard. *When War is Unjust: Being Honest in Just-War Thinking.* 2nd ed. Maryknoll, N.Y.: Orbis Books, 1996; Zimmerman, Earl. *Practicing the Politics of Jesus: The Origin and Significance of John Howard Yoder's Social Ethics.* Telford, PA: Cascadia, 2007.

Earl Zimmerman

NATIVE AMERICAN RELIGIOUS FREEDOM

Generalizing about Native American religions is a daunting task. There are many different forms of Native American religion practiced by the various tribes found throughout the United States. For our purposes there are two central locations where Native American religious practice comes into conflict with various state and federal laws: (1) land use for sacred purposes, including burial rights; and (2) use of controlled substances in Native American religious practice. While monotheistic traditions such as Christianity orient their religious life around time, Native American religions relate to space and location rather than time. Because of the Native American understanding of the relationship of the tribe to the land, and religious identity as community-based rather than based on an individual to her or his own property and personal identity, Native Americans face a challenge demonstrating the sacred nature of areas such as the Black Hills, or creatures such as the endangered American eagle, to the United States government. Endangered species and national park land are understood to be *public* and protected, rather than part of the Native American religious landscape and heritage. Additionally, state and federal laws prohibit the use of controlled substances, yet the traditional use of peyote is part of some Native American tribal heritages, and therefore has offered constitutional challenges to the state and federal ban on peyote use through the Free Exercise of Religion Clause.

HISTORICAL CONTEXT

The history of the relationship between the United States government and Native Americans is painted in bloodshed and broken treaties on a canvas of forced relocation and constant pressure on Native Americans to break with their heritage and assimilate in mainstream American culture. From the early days of contact, the relations between the U.S. government and Native peoples has moved through various stages: government to government negotiations with sovereign nations, removal of native peoples from traditional lands onto reservations, forced assimilation, holding native lands in "trust" via the Bureau of Indian Affairs, and most recently, to self-determination and self-governance in the 1990s and early 2000s.

The Department of the Interior officially recognizes 561 indigenous groups in the United States. These groups consist of indigenous peoples who are eligible for programs and services from the U.S. government because of their status as natives. Because of this unique relationship to federal and state governments, Native Americans still may find that their property, civil, and political rights may be either diminished or extended by federal or state action.

United States' policy since the settling of the West has been to move the Native Americans onto limited reservations, by whatever means necessary, or force Natives Americans to adapt to mainstream U.S. lifestyles. Reservations are lands given to Native Americans usually in exchange for relinquishing tribal homelands. Throughout the course of U.S. government management of Native American reservations, there have been various Allotment Acts. These acts determine the location and size of a given reservation, and then determine how the reservation will be divided into individual land plots for the reservation inhabitants. Some of the Native American lands are held in trust by the U.S. government. These lands are not reservations per se, but are still considered Native lands. As part of the U.S. government trust for native lands, tribal lands are subject to the will of the U.S. government plans for redistribution, re-purposing, or reallocation. In many instances, allotment acts result in a reduction in size and purpose of trust lands, as well as individual land holdings. Often these changes in the allotment and purpose of trust and reservation lands rendered most agricultural practices infeasible and opened up "unused" reservation lands to white ownership, private development, or national park status.

While different presidential administrations and shifting domestic policies have kept this trajectory of containment on reservations and forced assimilation from being a consistent policy, the basic thrust of the federal government policy toward Native Americans has been to absorb Native peoples into the general population. This results in a kind of cultural extinction. This basic trajectory has been largely determined by the needs and demands of the U.S. government. Prior to 1968, those Native Americans living on reservations did not enjoy basic civil rights guaranteed to other U.S. citizens. Reservation residents were offered full United States citizenship in 1968 when the *Indian Civil Rights Act* was passed. Prior to this, Native Americans were considered extra-constitutional residents of the United States, living as sovereign peoples on reservations or parcels of land from various Land Allotment Acts. The rights and privileges of Native Americans prior to 1968 were subject to mercurial changes, due primarily to events and policies that had little or nothing to do with the Native Americans themselves. For example, some tribes were "terminated" because their reservation lands were discovered to be rich in natural resources. During the 1950s, the U.S. government dissolved some tribes, such as the Klamath tribe in southern Oregon, moved them from rural communities to urban relocation centers, and then ended any material support members of those former tribes had enjoyed through treaties and management of the land trust. Not only did this result in a loss of tribal lands, these policy changes deprived entire tribes of their homes, and means of sustenance. Significantly, this termination meant that tribal legal sovereignty was officially ended, and the application of traditional laws and values had to be adapted to state laws and regulations. Tribal termination, ultimately a policy of forced assimilation of Native Americans into mainstream American culture, meant the end of some federally managed land trusts, and the redistribution of Native lands to private ownership, almost always outside the tribe.

In the wake of other civil rights acts in the late 1960s, the *Indian Civil Rights Act* (ICRA) was passed. This law granted civil rights to Native Americans both on and off reservations. While this act did guarantee religious freedom to Native Americans living on reservations, the ICRA also emphasized individual property rights, rather than community or tribal property rights. Therefore, the ICRA weakened the authority asserted by the tribe to negotiate land use with the U.S. government, at the same time as it protected Native American individual rights. By putting a greater emphasis on individual rights and responsibilities, the Indian Civil Rights Act took some negotiating power away from the tribe as a whole. Reservations are considered nation within a nation, and native peoples are subject to federal and tribal laws (state criminal laws are prosecuted as federal offenses on reservations). The ICRA expanded individual rights, but it did not protect tribes or their members from federal actions designed to reduce tribal sovereignty, treaty rights, or aboriginal lands. Tribes can lose their lands to imminent domain, the quest for water rights, or other natural resources. In some instances, particularly in the southwest states of Arizona, New Mexico, and eastern California, reservation lands are some of the most desolate and uninhabitable lands in the nation. The recent development of Indian Casinos has enabled Native Americans to fight legal battles with private developers and the federal government when those organizations propose reclaiming the reservation, or areas around the reservation, for coal mining, oil refineries, or natural gas collection.

Ten years later, after passing the Indian Civil Rights Act, Congress passed the *American Indian Religious Freedom Act* (AIRFA). AIRFA is a nonbinding resolution that recognizes the Free Exercise of Religion Clause and applied that clause to Native American Religious Practice, but did not include any penalties for federal or private agencies who failed to comply with the law. Native American religious observation is often in conflict with federal policies. For example, sweat lodges and/or multi-day vigils in national parks, tobacco burning ceremonies, or killing federally protected creatures, such as the bald eagle, for religious and ritual purposes, all conflict with federal laws and mandates. Since much of the land Native Americans hold sacred is either part of a trust or in a public National Park, there are often conflicts over land use. When one of these practices comes into conflict with a federal law, a different federal agency enforces adherence to these laws. Until 1968, Native Americans could not appeal to federal or state courts for protection of their religious rights, because their status on the reservation was considered *extra-constitutional*, and as such, the reservation residents were not entitled to those protections guaranteed to U.S. citizens by the Constitution.

LAND USE

Because the relationship of the community to the land is such an important part of Native American religion, there are two areas where mainstream American culture, native culture, and constitutional protections collide: (1) traditional cultural use of public lands, such as the Devil's Tower in the Black Hills of Wyoming; and (2) desecration of graves through development or archaeological excavation. Rock climbers frequent the Devil's Tower (site of the film *Close Encounters of the Third Kind*) because it is a challenging and scenic climbing destination. Native Americans consider the volcanic tower a sacred place where they hold religious festivals and dances, especially during the month of June. In the 1990s, the National Park Service initiated a voluntary ban on climbing the tower in June. However, one climbing company challenged the ban, and the Wyoming courts found that the voluntary ban was an "unconstitutional support of religion" (see http://www.indianlaw.org/; and McLeod 2001). An executive order signed by President Clinton in 1996 mandated federal land managers to accommodate sacred sites wherever possible. While climbing at Devil's Tower during the month of June has declined steadily, there is no law or agency that protects Native American religious practices at the site.

A further complicated issue about land rights has developed with regard to burial sites and Native American remains. Here, the issue is not only about what kinds of uses and development are allowed on a specific site, but also the fate of artifacts and evidence of prehistorical humanity. In an effort to protect Native American burial sites, in 1990 congress passed the *Native American Graves Protection and Repatriation Act*. This law requires all federal agencies and public museums (for example, the Smithsonian) to identify Native American remains in their collections, and consult with tribes about those artifacts. If the tribe requests, the law requires the objects be repatriated and returned to the tribes. This also affects newly discovered remains, such as the site of discovery of Kennewick Man, the oldest known human skeletal remains in North America. He was discovered in the Columbia River gorge in Washington State, and the site was declared protected by the Graves Protection and Repatriation Act, and reburied. There are currently no archaeological excavations at the site of the discovery of Kennewick Man.

Unlike the issue of peyote, or even the voluntary 30-day ban on climbing the Devil's Tower, the Graves Protection and Repatriation Act has stirred up a great many debates about the ownership of intellectual authority over human prehistory. Critics claim that the law's original intent was to provide a form of cultural reparation, to give back to Native peoples artifacts of known sacred meaning. What has resulted, critics say, is that Native peoples are controlling the way objects and practices are interpreted, and have taken the law to an extreme where experts and scientists are unable to offer interpretations or displays of cultural artifacts without approval of Native Americans. Those Native Americans are not scientists or archaeologists or anthropologists, and are imposing limits on the intellectual use of Native American artifacts in understanding and interpreting human prehistory. The claim by some museum curators is summed up nicely by Edward Rothstein's words about the Smithsonian Institution's National Museum of the American Indian. "Tribes tell their own stories, not because they are most knowledgeable but because finally, they have control" (Rothstein 2006).

PEYOTE

The problem of Native American religious freedom is mostly clearly seen in the difficulties Native Americans have experienced with the legality of peyote use in religious rituals. Peyote is a button-like flower of a cactus plant that grows in the southwest and Texas. When ingested, peyote causes hallucinations and other altered states of consciousness. The Native American Church (NAC) uses peyote in its ceremonies. The NAC was founded in the early twentieth century as a way for Native Americans to preserve their traditions in a form that was recognized by whites and the U.S. Government. The NAC is not a public church, does not evangelize, and exists to protect and preserve Native American religious traditions. Within the religious practices of the NAC, peyote is used as a sacrament, a holy medicine given to humanity to guide, console, and heal. While the Native American church does not evangelize or accept converts, its controversial use of peyote has tested the relationship between federal and state laws, as well as the rights of Native Americans to the guarantee of freedom to practice their religion. In addition to challenging the complicated relationship between federal and state laws, the question of federal recognition of tribal identity is also a central part of the debate about peyote use in Native American religious practice.

In 1990, the United States' Supreme Court heard a case involving peyote use, *Employment Division v. Smith*. The court ruled that as long as a law did not target a specific group and could be generally applied to the whole population, it was acceptable. The details of this case involved the challenge of peyote use as a ceremonial substance. The court's decision supported the federal ban on peyote, denying use to Native American religious groups as an expression of religious life. Therefore, from the court's perspective, the use of peyote was outlawed for all persons, and while that law did affect Native American religious practitioners more than other groups, the law did not specifically target Native Americans, and therefore did not violate their freedom of religion.

When in 1994 congress passed the *American Indian Religious Freedom Act* (AIRFA), things changed. The AIRFA is one of many state and federal Religious Freedom Acts designed to counter current Supreme Court interpretations of the Free Exercise Clause. This act provided for the traditional use of peyote for Native American religious purposes. Since the AIRFA was designed to protect Native American use of peyote while still acknowledging its status as a controlled substance, the law served to protect those who can provide evidence of their status as Native Americans. Therefore, one has to be a member of a federally recognized tribe to be under the protection of the law. Those limits of this amendment have been challenged in several states, most recently in Utah. The State Supreme Court of Utah found that one did not necessarily need to be a member of a federally recognized tribe in order to use peyote for religious ceremonies. As it stands today, Native Americans can use peyote in religious ceremonies, though the requirement of belonging to a federally recognized tribe is currently subject to an individual state's interpretation of the AIRFA.

Federal recognition of tribes is also significant in determining who is a Native American, and what rights and privileges are granted to Native people through the federal government. This is a contested issue currently, not only because of the peyote laws, but also has a result of the relative affluence of some tribes due to reservation gambling.

Only recognized tribes can engage in gaming operations and casino businesses. Many tribes, such as the Ute in Colorado and the Quechan in western Arizona, have been using their gaming profits to buy back tribal land from private interests or the federal government. As casinos continue to be a growth industry for Native Americans, their ability to promote legislation and fight legal battles will develop. The American Indian Religious Freedom Act has given Native Americans solid legal ground to fight battles over religious freedom and their ability to preserve, protect, and continue their religious and cultural heritage.

See also Bible and Poverty.

Further Reading: Cousineau, Phil, ed. *A Seat at the Table: Huston Smith In Conversation with Native Americans on Religious Freedom.* Berkeley: University of California Press, 2006; Mazur, Eric. "'The Supreme Law of the Land': Sources of Conflict Between Native Americans and the Constitutional Order." In *American Indian Studies: An Interdisciplinary Approach to Contemporary Issues,* ed. Dane Morrison. Berlin, NY: Peter Lang, 1997; McLeod, Christopher. *In Light of Reverence.* Oley, PA, 2001, Bullfrog Films, CD-ROM; Rothstein, Edward. "Protection for Indian Patrimony That Leads to a Paradox." *New York Times*, March 29, 2006; Sink, Mindy. "Religion Journal: Peyote, Indian Religion And the Issue of Exclusivity." *New York Times*, August 14, 2004; Vescey, Christopher, ed. *Handbook of American Indian Religious Freedom,* new ed. New York: The Crossroad Publishing Company, Inc., 1991; Wilkins, David E. *American Indian Politics and the American Political System.* Lanham, MD: Rowman and Littlefield, 2002.

Laura Ammon

NEUROETHICS

Neuroethics has emerged as a subdiscipline of bioethics within the past decade. It has two major areas of concern: the ethics of neuroscience (e.g., the ethical questions associated with the practice of neuroscience) and the neuroscience of ethics (e.g., the basic issues neuroscientific study has raised about human beings as ethical creatures).

The contemporary challenges of neuroethics have as their source two broad streams of unprecedented development within the neurosciences. The first is the development of technology allowing researchers a fresh window into brain activity in human beings (for example, positron emission tomography [PET] scanning and functional magnetic resonance imaging [fMRI]). This capacity to capture psychologically meaningful variations in brain activity allows previously unimaginable access into a person's inclinations, attitudes, personality attributes, aptitudes, and decision making. How might we think about basing our decisions related to hiring, criminal cases, and national security, to name only three immediate applications, on these technologies? The second is the ability to alter brain function in human beings with chemicals (that is, through psychopharmacology) and brain-machine interfaces. Implants to counter hearing loss or to mitigate the effects of Parkinson's Disease, and the use of selective serotonin reuptake inhibitors (SSRIs—for example, Prozac or Zoloft) in cases of depression—these are therapeutic interventions with widespread public approval. But what of the use of implants or drugs among healthy persons—say, to increase mental alertness among college students or airplane pilots, or to provide superhuman eyesight for hunters or soldiers? In addition, advances in the neurosciences have eroded much of what we have imagined to be true about what it means to be human—for example, concerning the question of whether humans have immaterial minds (or souls) that control their behavior through the exercise of free will.

NEUROETHICS AND BIOETHICS

Many questions in neuroethics are at home within bioethics more generally. A representative list of these issues might include the protection of humans as research subjects, the relative safety of a new technology or pharmacological agent, privacy of research data, and obtaining informed consent (especially problematic with persons of diminished mental capacity). Issues of justice, or the fair distribution of resources, also apply: Who should have access to neurobiological tests and therapies? Who should pay? The issue of distributive justice becomes more pressing when the focus shifts from the treatment of persons with neurological disorders to the prevention of those disorders, and even more so when the focus shifts to the potential enhancement of those regarded as healthy. Additional questions arise: What course of action should follow the unexpected discovery of a neurological disorder during data collection? What is the role of predictive testing for future neurological illnesses, including testing of fetuses?

At many points, ethical questions facing neurobiology are familiar to ethical reflection in medical research and treatment. Even so, moving into the subfield of neuroethics raises the stakes on these concerns since many of the practices that concern us (for example, neuroimaging, psychosurgery, and psychopharmacology) are not peripheral to our subjective experience of self but intervene directly in the brain. That is, neuroscientific interventions have the capacity to reveal and shape, for good or ill, who we are as human persons at the most essential levels. Additionally, the potential of harm is exacerbated by the fact that, in spite of the remarkable strides forward made in our understanding of the central nervous system, there is much we do not know.

THE ETHICS OF NEUROSCIENCE

The ethical issues pertaining to the practice of neuroscience can be gathered under three headings: psychosurgery, neurological enhancement, and brain reading.

Psychosurgery

Skeletal remains from the distant past evidence early attempts at relieving psychic stress through surgery, but the term *psychosurgery* refers most prominently to its abuse in the early twentieth century in the indiscriminate practice of frontal lobotomy. This involved the insertion of a long, needle-shaped instrument through the skull just above the eyes, then swinging it back and forth, isolating the frontal lobes from the rest of the brain by destroying neuronal processes to and from the frontal lobes. This classic form of psychosurgery was successful in relieving psychiatric symptoms in some serious cases, but also introduced severe unintended consequences, including loss of social control, seizures, lethargy, and even death. Subsequent study has demonstrated the importance of the brain's prefrontal cortex in social behavior, ethical comportment, and decision-making, so, in retrospect, these grievous results are unsurprising. From the perspective of neuroethics, then, the first issue raised by psychosurgery in its contemporary versions is the problem of unintended consequences. In spite of the development of precision instruments and image-guided surgical procedures, the risk of permanent damage to areas of the brain not targeted for surgery and/or to adverse psychological affects is considerable. As a result, surgical interventions in cases of psychiatric disorder are closely monitored by review committees and reserved for severe cases involving, for example, otherwise uncontrollable obsessive compulsive disorder or epilepsy.

Is a candidate for psychosurgery capable of giving informed consent? (Note that the dysfunctional area of the brain targeted for psychosurgery may impair the patient's capacity to understand his or her own condition and the risks of surgery.) What if the person who emerges from psychosurgery lacks the memories of the person who agreed to surgery in the first place? What if she or he experiences significant personality change as a consequence of surgery? Because such central aspects of personal identity as consciousness, capacity for religiosity, or memory are not localized but distributed throughout the brain, psychosurgery has the real potential of altering the patient's sense of self. In such cases, a profession for whom the first principle is, "do no harm," is faced with the question whether the cure is worse than the disease. Psychosurgery is thus a therapy of last resort. Nevertheless, with increasing capacity for more precisely targeted surgical interventions we may anticipate that psychosurgery will become an option for more patients.

Better Brains? Neurological Enhancements

Neurological enhancements come in two broad categories: psychopharmacology and brain-machine interfaces. A number of drugs have therapeutic indications for which they were not approved by the Food and Drug Administration and not intended by their manufacturers. Methylphenidate (Ritalin) is a classic example. A pharmaceutical widely known for the help it provides for people with Attention Deficit Hyperactivity Disorder (ADHD), it also has the off-label effect of helping college students by enhancing their concentration and performance on exams. Methylphenidate illustrates another issue now endemic to psychopharmacological enhancement—namely, the increasingly fuzzy line between using a drug in the treatment of a disorder and using the same drug for purposes of enhancement of a healthy human being. The first problem is where to draw the line between "disorder" and health. Even those committed to a rigorous interpretation of the criteria might disagree on diagnosis. The second problem is that the baseline for prescribing this and other medications has a tendency to creep upward over time, with the result that increasingly less symptomatic persons find themselves on a Methylphenidate regimen. This example can be multiplied many times over with regard to pharmaceuticals that target not only anxiety, as in this case, but also mood and memory.

Memory is another interesting case, since here different uses of drugs are being explored. Memory-enhancing drugs are generally regarded as problematic for humans before middle age, since loss of memory among children and young adults is important to normal cognitive function. For older adults, however, memory enhancement might be welcomed, both as a treatment for dementia but also in cases of normal forgetfulness. What, though, of the use of drugs to achieve the opposite effect? What of the use of psychotropic substances to dampen memory in cases of trauma, whether with victims of rape or soldiers at war? Would the pharmaceutical dulling of pain also allow us as a society to forget the high costs of violence? If suffering is a means by which humans mature, would dampening the memories of suffering undermine the development of character? How do we adjudicate between the worthwhile aim of relieving suffering, on the one hand, and the erosion of our individual and societal character, on the other?

The general ethical concerns raised by the off-label use of drugs for neurological enhancement are threefold. The first is safety, since the drugs in questions have been studied and approved for therapeutic applications in cases of cognitive impairment rather than enhancement. The side effects of these pharmaceuticals may be judged as acceptable in instances of psychological dysfunction; can the same be said when enhancement of normal cognitive function is the goal? The second has to do with social equity and health. If Olympic sprinters are disqualified for enhancing their performance on the track, what should we make of persons whose performance on the SAT or ACT is pharmaceutically enhanced? Moreover, if some persons gain admission to colleges on the basis of their enhanced performance, what will the social pressure be on others to enhance their performance similarly? At some point, then, the definition of what constitutes "normal human attention" (or "normal mood" or "normal memory") may need to be adjusted, with the result that those without access to these enhancement drugs will fall further behind in terms of health and socioeconomic status. To push this issue further, psychopharmacological enhancements raise questions about our definitions of human health. When normal human performance is rejected as substandard, our definitions of health will be adjusted upward. What is healthy today, tomorrow is pathological. These lines of thought generally run against our tendency to applaud attempts at self improvement.

Much work on brain-machine interfaces remains largely experimental and is directed toward persons with impaired function. For example, attempts to enable paralyzed patients to communicate or to control the motion of prosthetic devices have enjoyed some clinical success, and researchers are working to create a bionic eye for those who suffer from loss of sight (much as cochlear implants have already restored hearing in some deaf individuals). Cyborgs or *technosapiens*—posthuman combinations of human flesh and machine—remain the stuff of science fiction, but this has not deterred anxiety among some regarding the future toward which we are heading. If neurotechnology advances along anticipated lines, it will do so amidst now-familiar questions: What does it mean to be human? Who will have access to these technologies? Who will pay? Will they be used for restoring the capacities of impaired individuals, or to enhance the capacities of normally functioning human beings? If for normally functioning human beings, to what end? The traction of this last question lies in the observation that much funding for electronic brain enhancement comes from the military.

Brain Reading, Mind Reading

When neuropsychologists refer to "mind reading," they are usually referring to the "theory of mind" that has its basis in "mirror neurons," those nerve cells that fire not only when a person is engaged in a certain activity but also when that person observes another engaged in the same activity. Such neural activity mirrors the movements of others, as well as their intentions, sensitivities, and emotions. Mirror neurons thus provide the neural correlates for important social capacities and behaviors, like empathy or imitation. Here, however, mind reading refers to our ability to use various forms of brain scans and images as a window into a person's decision-making processes, affective state, personality, truthfulness, consumer preferences, religiosity, and behavioral dispositions. This is not to say that neuroimaging is a regular tool in the arsenal of psychiatric diagnosis; this is true in relatively infrequent instances in which neuroimaging might indicate the neural correlates (or, in the case of lesions and atrophy, the lack of neural correlates) of observed behavior. Instead, neuroimaging has attracted attention for its ability to observe when persons are seeking deliberately to deceive (i.e., lie detection), to know in advance what a subject is thinking, to indicate those people or things to which a subject is attracted, or to disclose a subject's sexual preferences or predilections for social behaviors like violence or pessimism or extrovertedness. The potential applications are various: neuromarketing, lie detection and other modes of interrogation, background checks and security clearances, and screening for numerous professions, for example.

These applications of brain imaging raise a host of ethical concerns. The first is privacy—in this case, privacy at the most basic level of one's own unarticulated thoughts, feelings, and beliefs. Another concern is how quickly the sorts of experimental procedures that have thus far contributed to our understanding of the brain might be removed from their present location among scholars and other clinical experts, and placed in the hands of those lacking the requisite expertise. A related line of ethical concern is marked by the obvious distinction between a person's predisposition toward violence and one's actual violent behavior. Should we make life-altering decisions about persons on the basis of what they might do? That is, brain scans are neither as telling nor as easily interpreted as we might want them to be, particularly in cases that involve courtrooms and national security.

THE NEUROSCIENCE OF ETHICS

The most recent challenge to traditional views of the human person has come from the neurosciences, with its tightening of the mind-brain link. The resulting portrait of the human personhood impinges on traditional views in a number of ways, the most basic of which is our need no longer to postulate a second, metaphysical entity, such as a soul or spirit, to account for human capacities and distinctives. Though neuroscientists, philosophers, and theologians champion numerous ways to make sense of this emerging view of humanity, they tend to speak somehow of human life in terms of embodiment as physical persons. Faculties traditionally viewed as belonging to the "soul"—such as consciousness, religious commitments, the "real me"—are not dismissed but are understood as embodied human capacities.

The degree to which this physicalist or monist view is at home in the Jewish and Christian Bibles will come as a surprise to many, since it is widely assumed that these scriptures support a dualist portrait of the human person as body and soul. These scriptures are not concerned with defining human life with reference to its necessary "parts." Instead, they describe humanity in relational terms, with the human assessed as genuinely human and alive only within the family of humans brought into being by Yahweh. These scriptures do not locate the uniqueness of the human in terms of the human possession of a "soul," but rather affirm the human being as a biopsychospiritual unity. Indeed, within the Hebrew Bible and the Old Testament, the Hebrew term *nepheš*, sometimes translated as "soul," refers more basically to life and vitality—not life in general, but as instantiated in God's creatures. In short, the neuroscientific portrait of the human being as embodied, physical beings is on this point very much at home in the Jewish and Christian Scriptures. This biblical view stands in contrast, though, to the body-soul dualism of much of the world's population, including Jews and Christians. As a result, the challenge of the neuroscientific understanding of the human in physicalist terms is likely to be heard as a fundamental threat to traditional views of the human person.

The significance of neuroscientific work for ethics is, partly, this emphasis on the embodied nature of human existence, but it reaches further. A number of studies since the 1990s have demonstrated the tight link between neuronal processes and moral decision making—including, but not limited to, reviewing past decisions and their consequences, weighing options and potential rewards, and envisioning the future. Some background on two aspects of human formation will orient us here. First, neuroscientists have underscored the effects of environment on human development, drawing attention to how formative influences are encoded in the synapses of the central nervous system. Although our genes bias the way we think, feel, believe, and behave, the systems responsible for much of what we do and how we do it are shaped by learning, and especially through interpersonal experiences. Second, neuroscientists have demonstrated that the amygdala, that structure of the brain implicated in emotion, is networked with the brain's decision-making center such that, in normal brains, "thinking" is inescapably emotion-laden. Ethics, then, is not a matter of "cool reason" in decision making. Indeed, study of brain injuries has shown that damage to the emotion-processing center of the brain impedes real-life rationality and decision making. This means that moral reasoning and decision making are embodied capacities that involve predispositions and emotion.

These studies also have important implications for issues around ethical decision making in relation to traditional notions of free will. For example, injuries to the orbitofrontal cortex in childhood have been shown to lead to lifelong social and moral behavioral problems resistant to corrective interventions. Pathological lying has been tied to abnormality within the prefrontal cortex. Patients with damage to the ventromedial prefontal cortex, an area of the brain implicated in the generation of social emotions, display abnormally utilitarian patterns of moral judgment. Patients who evidenced a "sick will" (for example, inactivity, lack of ambition, autistic behavior, depressive motor skills, and behavioral inhibition) have been shown to have subnormal activity in the prefrontal cortex. Persons with schizophrenia lack the feeling of personal authorship of some of their own thoughts or actions, attributing them to an agency beyond themselves—hence, the sense of "hearing voices" and more general imagining of unreal persons and forces. Persons with certain brain lesions have a condition known as Alien Hand Syndrome—that is, one of their hands acts outside of the subject's voluntary control. One hand seems to function on its own accord, answering the phone, for example, choosing a blouse from the closet, or attempting to strangle the subject during sleep. Disorders of volition also appear among persons suffering from depression, a condition in which the inability of patients to initiate new goal-oriented activity is correlated with inhibition in the brain's frontal lobe and in the anterior cingulate cortex, parts of the brain implicated in executive functioning. Widely recognized impairment of the will arises in instances of addiction and substance abuse as regions of the brain related to signaling immediate pain or pleasure override those regions concerned with future prospects. Virtually everyone has had the experience of acting unselfconsciously—say, walking or driving or doodling—when the action is repetitive or habitual. Apparently, free will is not an all-or-nothing capacity.

These and other data have raised serious questions about long-held views of human freedom to act and the responsibility that is generally tied to that freedom. This, in turn, has raised difficult questions for institutions, including our court systems, that have typically tied responsibility to self-conscious agency. What if, when it comes to most of our behavior, we are on autopilot after all? Does this make us less responsible for our behavior? Since the prefrontal cortex, that part of the brain responsible for "executive function," begins to reach developmental maturity in late-adolescence and early adulthood, are teenagers responsible for actions that display a lack of impulse control? Because we diagnose schizophrenia as a brain disorder, should we punish a schizophrenic for criminal behavior arising from that disorder? What of the person who suffers a closed head injury in a car wreck, the result of which is the tearing of the neuronal processes that allow the prefrontal cortex to override her urges to lie or cheat; is she responsible for her behavior? If she refuses to participate in the combination of cognitive and psychopharmacological therapies that might restore her capacity to exercise self-control, is she then more responsible for her behavior? What of the real situation in which a man indicted as a pedophile is found to have a tumor displacing his right orbitofrontal lobe, an area of the brain commonly implicated in moral-knowledge acquisition and social integration? If, as was the case, upon removal of the tumor, his sexually lewd behavior discontinued, should he be regarded no longer as a threat and returned to his family and community? In short, can we tie moral and legal responsibility any longer to traditional concepts of free will, or must other definitions be explored?

Exploration of the neural correlates of consciousness, moral decision-making, memory, and other aspects of personal identity challenges both how we think about conscious self-determination and self-responsibility and, more broadly, almost all traditional images we have had of ourselves in the course of our cultural history.

See also Genetic Research; Health Reform Movements.

Further Reading: Bush, Shane S. "Neurocognitive Enhancement: Ethical Considerations for an Emerging Subspeciality." *Applied Neuropsychology* 13, no. 2 (2006): 125–36; Center for Bioethics at the College of Physicians and Surgeons of Columbia University. "Neuroethics: Implications of Advances in Neuroscience" (A Webcourse on Neuroethics). http://ccnmtl.columbia.edu/projects/neuroethics/index.html; Farah, Martha J. "Neuroethics." http://neuroethics.upenn.edu/index.html; Feinberg, Todd E. *Altered Egos: How the Brain Creates the Self.* Oxford: Oxford University Press, 2001; Gazzaniga, Michael S. *The Ethical Brain.* Washington, D.C.: Dana Press, 2005; Glannon, Walter, ed. *Defining Right and Wrong in Brain Science: Essential Readings in Neuroethics.* Washington, D.C.: Dana Press, 2007; Glannon, Walter. "Neuroethics." *Bioethics* 20, no. 1 (2006): 37–52; Glannon, Walter. "Psychopharmacological Enhancement." *Neuroethics* 1 (2008): 45–54; Illes, Judy, ed. *Neuroethics: Defining the Issues in Theory, Practice, and Policy.* Oxford: Oxford University Press, 2005; Levy, Neil. *Neuroethics: Challenges for the 21st Century.* Cambridge: Cambridge University Press, 2007; Moreno, Jonathan D. "Neuroethics: An Agenda for Neuroscience and Society." *Nature Reviews Neuroscience* 4 (2003): 149–53; Murphy, Nancey. *Bodies and Souls, or Spirited Bodies?* Cambridge: Cambridge University Press, 2006; Murphy, Nancey, and Warren S. Brown. *Did My Neurons Make Me Do It? Philosophical and Neurobiological Perspectives on Moral Responsibility and Free Will.* Oxford: Oxford University Press, 2007; Peterson, Gregory R. "Imaging God: Cyborgs, Brain-Machine Interfaces, and a More Human Future." *Dialog* 44, no. 4 (2005): 337–46; Sebanz, Natalie and Wolfgang Prinz, eds. *Disorders of Volition.* Cambridge, MA: The MIT Press, 2006; Tancredi, Laurence. *Hardwired Behavior: What Neuroscience Reveals about Morality.* Cambridge: Cambridge University Press, 2005.

Joel B. Green

NEW RELIGIONS AS GROWTH INDUSTRY

New religious movements have become big business, raising questions as to their methods of recruitment, financial practices, and legitimacy.

A new religious movement (NRM) is a spiritual or religious group that has emerged relatively recently, and is unaffiliated with an established religious organization. Contemporary times find many NRMs booming at a fast rate. This expansion is known as a *growth industry*, where an organization is in demand, expanding at a faster rate than the overall market. NRMs have become quite popular, no longer localized to a particular place, or limited to a specific group of people. As people seek answers to their ultimate questions today, they have instant and equal access to NRMs (as much as mainstream, established religions) through the Internet and mass media. As a result, the demand for information, materials, and contact with, by, and about NRMs has led to a flood of information, products, and services. From training seminars, to crystals, to red string Kabbalah bracelets, to Scientology stress tests, to Goddess cards, to books and articles written about new religious movements, new religious movements are big business.

WHAT IS A NEW RELIGIOUS MOVEMENT?

The term, *new religious movement*, arose as a designation for the many new religious organizations that formed in Japan post–World War II. At this time, new religious freedoms and social upheaval made fertile ground for such groups. The term was later used to describe other emergent religious groups around the globe.

The U.S. Immigration Act of 1965 lifted immigration restrictions from Asia, opening the doors to Asians, Asian religions, and their teachers. Groups, such as the Unification Church (Family Federation for World Peace and Unification—popularly known as the *Moonies*) and the International Society for Krishna Consciousness (ISKCON—popularly known as the *Hare Krishnas*), attracted largely young, white, middle-class disciples. Asian religious groups provided responses to their problems that were different from mainstream American traditions, and became popular and controversial for this very reason.

The innovative and turbulent 1960s and 1970s, also gave rise to other groups. While some employed more secular, psychological, and scientific methods and ideas, such as the Church of Scientology, others drew on ancient or hidden traditions, such as the Covenant of the Goddess, and the Order of the Solar Temple.

Other groups that had emerged in earlier times were also considered alongside these newer sects. They also posed an alternative to mainstream American religion. Some provided Christian alternatives, such as Christian Science, the Jehovah's Witnesses, and The Church of Jesus Christ of Latter-Day Saints (Mormonism). Others emerged from African (La Regla de Ocha—Santería), or Native American (The Native American Church) beliefs and practices.

Scholars debate how "new" a movement has to be to constitute a NRM. While some would date a contemporary NRM to as early as the nineteenth century (such as the Baháʾí Faith), others would argue that a new religious movement should have emerged no earlier than several decades prior to the contemporary moment. Regardless, NRMs aren't *new* in the sense that they pop up out of nowhere, in a vacuum. Some groups are centuries old or at least can trace their foundations to ancient origins. Indeed, NRMs often draw heavily on past revelations or traditions to authenticate their message. For example, Wicca claims an ancient past and lineage.

NRMs are often not religious in the traditional Western sense of belief in a deity/deities, faith coming from revelation, and/or ritual practice. The Church of Scientology, for example, has specifically denied the label of *religion* and instead emphasized its role in facilitating and maximizing personal development. The Self-Realization Fellowship, though it comes from a Hindu context, also does not require *religious conversion* or depend on any specific religious beliefs. Indeed, many groups have similarly avoided the label of *religion*, as it connoted the very thing that they found problematic, and the very thing new adherents were seeking to abandon.

NRMs are widely categorized as *movements* because the term covers a wide spread of organizational structure. Movements are generally fluid, but some new religious movements are highly organized and stratified.

TIMELINE

1830—The Church of Christ (later called The Church of Jesus Christ of Latter-Day Saints) is founded by Joseph Smith.

1844—The beginnings of the Bahá'í Faith, when the Báb (*gate*) starts teaching the local Persian Muslims about a coming prophet who would initiate a time of world peace.

1853—Mírzá Husayn'Alí receives a vision in prison that he is the Prophet foreseen by the Báb and is the fulfillment of all the world religions.

1930—Wallace Fard Muhammad teaches black power and Islam, marking the beginnings of The Nation of Islam.

1950—L. Ron Hubbard published *Dianetics: The Modern Science of Mental Health*.

1954—The Church of Scientology founded. The Unification Church founded by Sun Myung Moon.

1955—Jim Jones founds the Wings of Deliverance, later to be called The People's Temple. The group sees Jones as a prophetic healer and incarnation of Christ.

1965—A.C. Bhaktivedanta Swami Prabhupada arrives in the United States and forms The International Society for Krishna Consciousness (ISCKON).

1977—Maharishi Mahesh Yogi founds Transcendental Meditation as a modernization of classical yoga. The People's Temple is denied tax-exempt status and the group moves to Guyana, founding Jonestown.

1978—Mass murder-suicide in Jonestown; over 900 dead.

1986—Shoko Asahara (b. Matsumoto Chizuo) founds Aum Shinrikyo in Tokyo, Japan. The movement blends Hinduism, Buddhism, and Christianity.

1993—The Bureau of Alcohol, Tobacco and Firearms raids the Branch Davidian compound in Waco, TX. After a 51-day stand-off, ATF agents moved in and stormed the complex. Over 80 died in a resulting fire.

1995—Aum Shinrikyo members release sarin gas in Tokyo subway, killing 12.

1997—Combining Christianity with UFO beliefs, members of Heaven's Gate kill themselves outside of San Diego when the comet Hale-Bopp appeared to them as the sign of the ship arriving to take their souls to heaven; 39 people dead.

New religious movements are sometimes called *cults*. While the word *cult* most generally and specifically refers to a religious system of rituals, practices, and the people who adhere to it, the term today often carries a negative connotation of a controlling, distorted, even dangerous religious group. The term *new religious movement* is therefore a more neutral way to refer to a wider phenomenon of emergent religious/spiritual groups.

Every religion is at some point *new*, and NRMs are comprised by many different kinds of groups with widely divergent perspectives. While some new religious movements can indeed be dangerous to their adherents and to the general public, they are not all like this. Nevertheless, until NRMs gain the acceptance of mainstream society, establishing the legitimacy of a new religious movement is difficult.

WHO JOINS AND WHY?

New religious movements vary widely in their beliefs and practices; however, such groups often represent alternative worldviews and practices to the mainstream, and offer distinct responses to the problems of their day. These answers often seem more adequate than the *old* answers of established traditions. With widespread disillusionment in many *established* religious traditions, whether due to scandal or perceived backwardness, NRMs offer attractive alternatives to the mainstream.

New religious movements in America are comprised largely of white middle-class young people. Groups recruit largely from the middle to upper class. Adherents' families are generally well educated and financially stable. Many are in college or are college educated. They very much come from mainstream society. Nevertheless, people attracted to NRMs are largely dissatisfied with mainstream religion and society, are interested in religious/spiritual matters, and are actively seeking individually and independently for new answers to their life questions. Seeking to *find themselves*, people attracted to new religious movements want alternatives to the familiar, structured establishment of belief and practice.

People in search for answers to their personal and social problems of the day will often find complete answers in new religious movements. The strong community identity will provide security and stability; the communal cooperation will provide common goals for life-building; the discipline in practice will develop self-mastery and knowledge; and recruitment and financial activities may build self-esteem.

NRMs AND THE COURTS

While many countries grant their citizens religious freedom, conflicts between religion and the state are inevitable, and become more intense when considering the practices of new religious movements—practices many mainstream secular and religious people may find problematic.

New religious movements are often accused that they harm or endanger adherents. Court cases allege that they inflict psychological and/or physical trauma or death. These include practices such as kidnapping, brainwashing, mind-control, sexual abuse, alienation, harassment, harm or threat to families. This charge of endangerment and violence has also been leveled on a criminal, large-scale level. The mass murder–suicide in Jonestown is one example. Another well-known example occurred 1995, when Aum Shinrikyo released sarin gas on the Tokyo subway.

Another major legal issue for NRMs has to do with their status as a religious entity and their financial activities related to the organization. Tax exemption for religions and nonprofit organizations is accepted for many countries, the United States included. Here, the question involves whether particular new religious movements qualify as protected religions, and the legality of particular financial practices. An important issue raised in court cases is when an NRM becomes a legal religious entity. This is difficult, as these movements are not typically organized according to traditional Western understandings of a *religion*, nor do they always behave like one. Courts have to discern whether the group is a smoke-screen for illegal activities, or for convenient tax exemption. Some new religious movements are indeed quite wealthy and run business-like organizations, leading to questions as to whether or not they are legitimate *religions*.

The Church of Scientology has been under constant scrutiny for this very reason. The church has had trouble with the Internal Revenue Service and was involved in a 10-year legal battle with the Food and Drug Administration over controversial medical practices. It took 48 years for New Zealand to formally recognize in 2002 the Church of Scientology as a legal religious entity. Although Russia refused to re-register the church as a religion under their new laws on religion in 1997, the case was eventually taken to the European Court of Human Rights (*Church of Scientology Moscow v. Russia*), which sided with the church. In its decision on April 7, 2007, the Court found that the church was a religious entity entitled to the freedoms of association and of religion. The Italian Supreme Court ruled in 2000 that while Scientology is indeed a religion—and therefore tax exempt—its drug addiction program, Narconon, is not tax exempt. The Charity Commission of England and Wales rejected the church's application to register as a charity (giving it tax exemption like other religious entities registered as charities). Scientology was rejected as a religion, as British law requires a religion to include belief in a Supreme Being that is expressed in worship. Scientology is also involved in legal cases in other countries, such as Germany, where it is not accepted as a legitimate religion, and instead is seen as a dangerous cult.

The U.S. Supreme Court ruled in 1989 that Church of Scientology members could not deduct auditing and training courses from their federal income taxes. Such courses, though integral to church membership, and costing thousands of dollars, are payment for services, and not free church contributions. Auditing is the main practice in Scientology for the practitioner to gain control of the mind and achieve the state of *Clear*. Although the church argued that auditing is a religious practice for achieving enlightenment, and is comparable to the concept of tithing in other religious groups, the Court ruled that auditing is instead like church counseling, medical care, or other kinds of religiously sponsored services.

Other new religious movements have had similar troubles. Reverend Sun Myung Moon, founder of the Unification Church (*Moonies*), was convicted by the United States on tax evasion charges prior to the group's recognition as a tax-exempt organization. Pagan and witchcraft groups have not surprisingly been challenged on their status. While U.S. courts generally recognize them as religious organizations, the Supreme Court of Rhode Island revoked the Church of Pan's status. As the church's activities were entirely environmental in focus, they were ruled not a religion, and therefore not exempt. In such cases, mainstream religions can also get involved; for legal issues involving new religious movements have implications for all religious groups and their practices.

RECRUITMENT, FINANCIAL PRACTICES, AND THE BUSINESS OF NRMs

Recruitment and solicitation of funds have been particularly controversial for new religious movements, particularly their common method of public solicitation. Solicitation at airports and other public grounds has been banned in some places because it is argued that these practices are a public nuisance, or even deceptive. For example, ISKCON members were arrested in 1987 in West Virginia for allegedly soliciting money for their community under the false pretense of feeding the poor.

Critics of NRM solicitation practices argue that groups use deceptive practices like misleading donors/recruits on how the money is spent, who the specific group is, or what membership entails. Nevertheless, new religious movements do not have the forum that established religions have for gathering members and funds. Thus, public solicitation is often the most efficient way of *getting the message out*. Other groups organize side projects and products, establishing quasi-businesses, selling paraphernalia, vitamins or self-help books, offering cheap labor, designing websites, and so on. These practices are necessary for survival, but they also lead to questions of authenticity, legitimacy, and legality.

While some NRMs deny the material world and the accumulation of wealth (for themselves and their adherents), others either embrace it, or at least teach that both are possible. Thus, some new religious movements have been extremely successful in gaining financial capital. One way to do this is by targeting mainstream businesses. Whether it is through workshops, special seminars, or self-help books, some NRMs have found success targeting business professionals.

Organizations that offer seminars to train businesspeople have proliferated since the 1970s. These training seminars teach businesspeople techniques of management, developed out of their own beliefs, methods, and practices. For example, the World Institute of Scientology Enterprises offers programs for businesses, teaching them management practices developed from Scientology founder, L. Ron Hubbard; the Osho movement, founded by Bhagwan Shree Rajneesh, offers *Results Seminars*; and Maharishi Mahesh Yogi's Transcendental Meditation offers MBAs at its Maharishi University of Management.

Another way is for new religious movements to focus on the general public. The Church of Scientology offers personality, stress, and IQ tests. Marketed products, Internet sites, and self-help books are all ways that individuals can take advantage of the offerings of NRMs. Through all of these, the exploration and experimentation in the self allows new religious movements to spread their message and grow.

Seeking prosperity for oneself and one's organization seems counter to the traditional notion of religions as not-for-profit, and on individual disciples focusing on their own inner spiritual life. Yet, many groups who support these kinds of business practices focus on the holism of life. If the divine is in all things, the material world is not in distinction from the spiritual world. Thus, self-empowerment leads to life-empowerment, which leads to financial empowerment.

As movements grow and organize themselves, they naturally seek to attract followers, sustain themselves and grow. This requires that new religious movements finance the spread of their message. Thus, charges of financial impropriety and exploitation of vulnerable people who are seeking *alternatives* in their lives are inevitable. To combat these charges, NRMs must prove that they are "legitimate." To do so, they often point to experiential proof, revelation, and ancient wisdom in establishing their legitimacy. While new religious movements proliferate, they often rise and fall fairly quickly. Only time can tell if the new religions of today will become the mainstream religions of tomorrow.

See also Separation of Church and State; World Religion Aesthetics.

Further Reading: Ashcraft, W. Michael and Dereck Daschke, eds. *New religious movements: A documentary reader.* New York and London: New York University Press, 2005; Beckford, James A., ed. *New religious movements and rapid social change.* London: Sage Publications/Unesco, 1986; Bromley, David G. and Anson D. Shupe, Jr. "Financing the new religions: A resource mobilization approach." *Journal for the scientific study of religion* 19, no. 3 (1980): 227–239; Clarke, Peter. *New religions in global perspective.* New York: Routledge, 2006; Heelas, Paul. "Prosperity and the new age movement: The efficacy of spiritual economies." In *New religious movements: Challenge and response,* ed. Bryan Wilson and Jamie Cresswell. New York: Routledge, 1999: 51–77; Lewis, James R. *Legitimating new religions.* London: Rutgers University Press, 2003; Lucas, Phillip and Thomas Robbins, eds. *New religious movements in the 21st century: challenges in global perspective.* New York: Routledge, 2004; Melton, J. Gordon. "The fate of NRMs and their detractors in twenty-first century America." *Novo Religio* 4, no. 2 (2001): 241–248; Partridge, Christopher. *New religions: A guide: New religious movements, sects and alternative spiritualities.* New York: Oxford University Press, 2004; Richardson, James T., ed. *Money and power in the new religions.* Lewiston: Edwin Mellen Press, 1988; Saliba, John. *Understanding new religious movements.* 2nd ed. Lanham: AltaMira Press, 2003; Wilson, Bryan and Jamie Cresswell, eds. *New religious movements: Challenge and response.* New York: Routledge, 1999.

Tracy Sayuki Tiemeier

O

ORGAN TRANSPLANTS

HISTORY

Many people have forgotten that throughout most of human history, people died of diseases that are now completely treatable. Until recently, many bacterial and viral infections were lethal. Injuries to limbs led to death or required amputation because even a simple infection, say through a cut in the hand, was nearly impossible to stop once it became established. Not too many years ago, many women died soon after childbirth because of infections in the womb. Even women who survived childbirth often lost their babies to infections. If the umbilical cord was cut nonsterile instrument too close to the baby, bacteria would migrate down the cord stump and infect the child. Once infected, there was no way to save the baby. But current advances in medicine have changed our expectations. We all expect that any bacterial infection we might get will be cured because most bacterial infections can be cured with one of the dozens of antibiotics that have been discovered since the middle of the twentieth century.

Another frequent cause of death until the middle of the last century was organ failure. An organ might fail because it suffers a viral infection, is exposed to a toxic compound, or because it is weak from birth. Organ failure is when an organ, like the kidney, can no longer do the job for which it was designed. The kidney filters the blood continuously and removes wastes and other chemicals to keep its composition in perfect condition. We now know, for example, that the kidney forms the units that filter the blood (called nephrons) before a person is born. If a woman's body is undernourished before or during pregnancy, the kidney of her baby will make fewer filtering units than it needs during its life-time. Even in normal people, nephrons begin to disappear as a person reaches middle age. If a person starts life with too few nephrons, the kidney will be vul-nerable and potentially reach the point where it has too few left to filter the blood properly and the person might then suffer from kidney failure.

Heart failure has become a very common cause of hospitalization. The heart is said to be failing if it becomes too weak to pump enough blood each beat to keep the body healthy. People who have a failing heart often complain that their legs are swelling with fluid or that they cannot catch their breath when they are lying down. Many of these people's health deteriorates to the point where they cannot walk across a room. Up until the last few decades, people who had heart failure were prone to becoming weak and dying. Some have been helped by the drug Digitalis, derived from the "Fox Glove" plant, that helps the heart muscle beat stronger. This therapy often prolonged the lives of some people with heart failure but it too failed to stop the inevitable down-hill function of the heart. Despite good medical therapy, people with heart failure inevitably worsened and died from inadequate oxygenation.

For more than 200 years, medical scientists have had the idea that the best way to fix a failing organ is to replace it with a new one—organ transplanta-tion. This is not a new idea, the patron saints of surgery and pharmacy are the third-century physician twins Saints Cosmas and Damian (Nuland 1992). These physicians from Asia Minor refused money for their services and have been credited with a leg transplantation from a healthy Ethiopian or Moorish donor (probably involuntary) to a Caucasian bell-tower attendant. There is no record of the success of this surgery but it is certain there were issues with infection, surgical skill, and tissue compatibility.

During the twentieth century, this idea of transplantation became a reason-able possibility. Human surgery became very sophisticated. Anesthesia was per-fected with the invention of new anesthetics so that people would feel no pain during surgery. Operating room procedures became sterile and highly standard-ized. Surgery programs began rigorous training requirements that could last for 3–12 years after medical school to ensure that surgeons could perform very complex and difficult surgeries within their areas of specialty. By the middle of the twentieth century, surgeons had the skill to replace virtually any organ of the body.

However, the big hurdle that prevented successful organ transplantation in the early twentieth century was not surgical skill. It was organ rejection. The body's immune system is designed to reject any foreign tissue. Thus, if a person receives an organ from someone else, the body will naturally reject it. How does the body know that a new organ is not "self," that it does not belong to the per-son who needs it? The answer to this question has been known for only a short time. Cells have proteins on their outside surface that are unique to the person who made them. The proteins are called human leukocyte (white blood cells) antigens or HLA proteins. There are more than 200 genes that make up the HLA system. They make it possible for every person (except identical twins) to have his or her own unique protein complex on the surface of their cells. Each person gets genes from both of his or her parents. The closer the donor is related the more similar their HLA proteins to the recipient. Therefore, receiving an organ from a close relative causes less rejection than from someone who is not related. This immune reaction is a great system because it means that a person's immune system can recognize any foreign body that does not match its own protein complex and can then attack it to eliminate the threat. Sometimes a person's immune system makes a mistake and sees its own tissue as non-self. This condition is known as an autoimmune disease. Severe autoimmune diseases include lupus and rheumatoid arthritis.

Beginning in the 1950s organ transplants began to be successful. The first kidney transplant to a patient from a living relative was performed at the Brigham Hospital in Boston in 1954 (see sidebar). This was an amazing feat that was heralded around the world. The first lung transplant was performed in 1963. The year 1967 was an exciting time for transplantation. In that year, heart and liver transplants were first performed. Over the next decade medical scientists worked to perfect other kinds of transplantation. It became possible to think that any part of the body could be transplanted. In 1981 the first combination of

TIMELINE OF SUCCESSFUL TRANSPLANTS

1905—First successful cornea transplant by Eduard Zirm

1954—First successful kidney transplant by Joseph Murray (Boston)

1966—First successful pancreas transplant by Richard Lillehei and William Kelly (Minnesota)

1967—First successful liver transplant by Thomas Starzl (Denver)

1967—First successful heart transplant by Christiaan Barnard (Cape Town, South Africa)

1981—First successful heart/lung transplant by Bruce Reitz (Stanford, CA)

1983—First successful lung lobe transplant by Joel Cooper (Toronto, Canada)

1986—First successful double-lung transplant (Ann Harrison) by Joel Cooper (Toronto, Canada)

1987—First successful whole lung transplant by Joel Cooper (St. Louis)

1995—First successful laparoscopic live-donor nephrectomy by Lloyd Ratner and Louis Kavoussi (Baltimore)

1998—First successful live-donor partial pancreas transplant by David Sutherland (Minnesota)

1998—First successful hand transplant (France)

2005—First successful partial face transplant (France)

2005—First successful penis transplant (China)

2008—First successful complete full double arm transplant (Munich, Germany)

From: http://en.wikipedia.org/wiki/Organ_transplant.

heart and lung transplants was performed. Other organs that can now be successfully transplanted include small intestine, pancreas, heart and lung together, and the cornea.

There are three types of organ rejection that are named according to how quickly they can attack a newly transplanted organ. When an organ is rejected right at the time it is put in a new person's body, it is called *hyperacute* rejection. Hyperacute rejection happens when the person receiving the new organ already has antibodies against the proteins in the new organ. An example of this is when the two people have different incompatible blood types. All organ donors are tested for this problem before a new organ is transplanted into a person. Thus, this type of rejection rarely occurs. The second type is called *acute* rejection and begins during the first week and may continue for some months. Acute rejection is the result of HLA proteins that are recognized as foreign by the recipient. The third type is called *chronic* rejection. Chronic rejection is the result of a very slow attack on the transplanted organ by the immune system. It may cause organ failure many years after the new organ has been put into place.

The most important breakthrough in transplantation came with the discovery of immunosuppressant drugs. These drugs can prevent a person's immune system from attacking a transplanted organ. Unfortunately these drugs do not always work in people with chronic rejection. There are several types of antirejection drugs. Most work by inhibiting the ability of immune cells to attack the foreign cells. A new therapy involves the infusion of transplant acceptance-inducing cells (TAICs). These cells are modified to kill off the cells of the recipient that attack the donor organ. In time, TAICs may make it possible to have transplants without immunosuppressant drug therapy.

ETHICAL IMPLICATIONS

There are many ethical questions that surround the topic of transplantation. How can we be sure the donor is dead before the organ is taken? How should we define death? Does death occur when the heart stops or when the brain is deemed to be unable to function again? These problems are currently under hot debate (see Bernat 2008; Veatch 2008). A number of policies are in place to ensure that a person's brain is really dead before any organ can be taken.

Another problem is that some people believe that the heart holds the soul of a person and should not be placed in another person's body. The biblical imagery of the heart being the center for life and love has caused many religious groups to cautiously agree to this life-saving transplant. Heart transplant recipients do experience a profound sense of thankfulness to the donor's family for the chance at continued life but feel no transfer of the donor's spiritual attributes.

Perhaps the most important ethical issue is how to meet the demands for new organs. Organs are taken from people who have died from causes that do not harm potentially transplantable organs. Many of these people have gone on record as being organ donors when they die. In some states this can be noted on a person's driver's license. However, there are not enough people who die as donors each year to care for the number of people who are waiting for a life-saving organ transplant. Thousands of people are waiting for heart transplants every year. Sixty percent of them will never receive one. Who among them should get an organ when one becomes available? Who should be rejected from getting an organ when it becomes available? For example, if a person ruins his or her liver with excessive use of alcohol, should they be allowed to get a new liver? This question is asked several times a day in hospitals across the United States. Generally, the answer is no. Organ acquisition in the United States is governed by the Organ Procurement and Transplantation Network (OPTN) under contract with the U.S. Department of Health and Human Services by the United Network for Organ Sharing (UNOS). This system allows most medical institutions to allocate organs among themselves according to the most critical need of their patients.

Because of the intense pressure to obtain deceased-donor and living-donor organs, some countries have allowed so-called medical tourism whereby individuals with the financial means can purchase medical services and possibly organs. The intense desperation for survival associated with poverty could place families in a moral dilemma where organs (e.g., kidneys) could be sold. This ethical nightmare would cross the moral boundaries of most societies. In 1961 the United Kingdom passed the Human Tissue Act, which made organ sales illegal in Britain. The United States followed this lead in 1984 by enacting The National Organ Transplantation Act, which made organ sales illegal and set up the OPTN. This legislation has eliminated most organ sales within these two countries. There are advocates for selling organs to ease the pressure on the organ procurement process. Two books, *Stakes and Kidneys: Why Markets in Human Body Parts are Morally Imperative* and *Kidney for Sale by Owner,* make a case that thousands of people die each year who could be saved if a system was available for purchasing organs from voluntary donors who were fairly compensated for their life-giving tissues. A person's ethical view of this debate may be influenced by personal stories and the desperation people experience to save the life of a loved one.

On October 26, 1984, Dr. Leonard Bailey at Loma Linda University transplanted a young female baboon heart into a three-week premature human infant whose heart had stopped as a result of hypoplastic left heart syndrome. This baby was named "Baby Fae" and lived 21 days before dying of kidney failure. Even though the transplantation was done to prolong a human life until a human donor could be found, several organizations picketed the medical school claiming the procedure desecrated animal-human barriers or the baboon's rights (animal rights movement, People for the Ethical Treatment of Animals).

Xenotransplantation is the use of an organ from an animal for transplantation (i.e., cross-species transplantation). This has been attempted several times. For example, organs from pigs, chimps, and baboons have been transplanted into humans. However, organs from another species are even more likely to be rejected than human organs. Scientists have tried to find ways to use animal organs for transplantation without having them rejected. One way is to alter animal cells so that they make human proteins in place of their own proteins. This has been accomplished to different degrees in sheep and pigs. Pig heart valves are used in people every day. However, many people believe that animal tissues should not be used for transplantation either because it violates their view of the separation of species or because they are worried that animals will be raised and killed to support human life. Another view holds that it would be unethical to reject xenotransplantation if it could successfully save the lives of thousands of people.

Everyone wonders whether it will be possible to someday perform a brain transplant. It is a tempting wish that when your body wears out, you could take your brain and put in a new healthy body. The brain will, of course, be the most difficult to transplant. Perhaps it will never be done. The problem with a brain transplant is that the brain is connected to nerves that run to every part of the body and as of today it seems unlikely that all of the connections from one person's brain could be lined up perfectly with the cut nerves in another person's body. This problem is made worse by the fact that the number and position of the nerves in one person is quite different from those in another so it would be close to impossible to line up the nerves from the donor with the nerves of the recipient. There is also an ethical problem. The brain is the center of personhood. The mind, which is a product of the functioning brain, would move with the brain to the new person. Therefore, even if it were possible brain transplantation might never be seen as an appropriate surgery.

Organ transplantation has progressed quickly in the twentieth and early twenty-first centuries. As is often the cause in science, the ethical framework to make these tough decisions lags behind the technology. The political establishment does its best to keep up with the pace of scientific advancements and protect against abuses. Typically, religious institutions are the last to understand the pace and the moral ramifications. While it might seem to some people that the ethical issues surrounding transplantation are unimportant, the truth is that everyone in society must do their part in making ethical decisions. As many ethicists have rather dramatically argued, the future of the human race depends on it.

Further Reading: Bernat, James L. "Organ Donation after Cardiac Death." *The New England Journal of Medicine* 359, no. 7 (2008): 209–13; Cherry, Mark. *Kidney for Sale by Owner.* Washington, D.C.: Georgetown University Press, 2005; History of Transplantation. Available at: http://www.donatelifeny.org/transplant/organ_history.html; Manning, Jason. The Eighties Club, Baby Fae, 2000. Available at: http://eightiesclub.tripod.com/id302. htm; Nuland, Sherwin B. *Medicine: The Art of Healing.* Westport, CT: Hugh Lauter Levin Associates, 1992; Taylor, James Stacey. *Stakes and Kidneys: Why Markets in Human Body Parts are Morally Imperative.* Aldershot, UK: Ashgate Press, 2005; Truog, Robert D., and Franklin G. Miller. "The Dead Donor Rule and Organ Transplantation." *The New England Journal of Medicine* 359, no. 7 (2008): 674–75; Veatch, Robert M. "Donating Hearts after Cardiac Death—Reversing the Irreversible." *The New England Journal of Medicine* 359, no. 7 (2008): 672–73.

Dwight J. Kimberly

P

PERSONAL PACIFISM VERSUS POLITICAL NONVIOLENCE

Pacifists believe that they must not participate in any forms of violence, including military violence or even police violence. Among religious pacifists, their refusal to kill is based on ancient religious teachings, and a long history of practice. A recent variation of religious pacifism, however, believes that pacifists can and should participate in active movements for social and political change using tactics of persuasion, demonstration, economic pressures, and so on. This more assertive version of pacifism that arose in the twentieth century is known today as *nonviolence* or *nonviolent direct action*. These ideas are often defended on the basis of religious teachings, but have been heavily inspired by twentieth-century examples, like Gandhi's campaign for Indian independence from Britain.

THE ROOTS OF RELIGIOUS PACIFISM: CHRISTIANITY AND BUDDHISM

Many religious traditions, especially Christianity and Buddhism, seem to have clear teachings recorded in central documents (e.g., the New Testament and early Christian writings for Christians, and ancient Sutras for Buddhists) that strongly discourage violent actions. There is some debate among religious *pacifists* as to how much force can be justified in any situation based on these ancient teachings, but intentionally lethal violence is always considered to be prohibited by pacifists.

However, despite this ancient tradition that agrees that the written teachings have often been understood to encourage pacifism or nonviolence, later adherents of these religions often overrule or reinterpret the meaning of those ancient teachings to allow for modern participation in war and other forms of violence, especially when these religions (again, Christianity and Buddhism being particularly good examples) become the religions of nations or political systems.

THE RELIGIOUS ROOTS OF PACIFISM IN CHRISTIANITY

Most scholars of the Bible agree that the New Testament seems to present Jesus as a teacher of a very peaceful ethic. Perhaps most famous of all is his instruction to "love your enemies" (Matthew 5:44 and Luke 6:27) and the instruction to "turn the other cheek" when struck by others (Matthew 5:39 and Luke 6:29). Ultimately, Jesus' own death seems to be the ultimate expression of his nonviolent ethic. The other major New Testament writer, Paul of Tarsus, seems to interpret Jesus as teaching nonviolence also, because he writes in his moral instructions: "Bless those who persecute you; bless and do not curse them" (Romans 12:14); "Live in harmony with one another" (Romans 12:16), and "Do not repay anyone evil for evil, but take thought for what is noble in the sight of all. If it is possible, so far as it depends on you, live peaceably with all" (Romans 12:17–18). In sum, the overwhelming majority of early Christian writings suggest that for the first three centuries of the Christian movement, it was the teaching of the Christian leaders that Christians ought not to engage in any violence because of the teaching and example of Jesus.

In the fourth century, however, this peaceful tradition underwent significant changes. With the apparent conversion to Christianity of the Roman Emperor Constantine, Christianity was transformed from a minority religion among others within the Roman Empire, into the *official religion* of the Roman Empire by the end of the fourth century. By the early fifth century, all Roman soldiers had to be baptized Christians. As a direct result of this dramatic change of status, Christianity underwent significant changes, including accommodating itself to the violent needs of the Roman Empire, including the need to maintain a military and police force for the Empire itself.

The Just War

The earliest major expression of this change was the growth of the concept of the *Just War*. While there may be evidence for earlier forms of this idea, it finds its first major expression in the thought of the early Christian theologian, St. Augustine of Hippo (354–430 A.D.). This concept was a viewpoint that argued that, under certain very strictly defined moral and legal circumstances, war was actually permissible for Christians to participate in.

The ideal, however, of accepting martyrdom when facing life-threatening challenges was often still maintained in the folklore and stories of the saints in early and medieval Christianity, and remained an ideal ethic for Eastern (Arab and Asian) Christians, especially in the face of the rise of Islam beginning in the seventh century A.D.

In Western, especially European, Christianity, however, the idea of Christian *pacifism* or nonviolence as a normal Christian ethical ideal was revived by certain Christian protest movements before and after the rise of Protestantism. Followers of the Italian Christian preacher Pietro Valdes (d. 1218), whose movement exists today as the Italian *Waldensian* Church, were initially characterized by a commitment to nonviolence, and after the Protestant Reformation, groups such as the Quakers (*Society of Friends*) in England, and the Mennonites in Switzerland and Holland, revived Christian nonviolence/pacifism as central moral values of their interpretation of Christianity. Both Quakers and Mennonites maintain their commitment to nonviolence as a Christian ethic. Groups such as the Fellowship of Reconciliation were founded by Christians of all backgrounds, to be an organization where commitment to nonviolence is encouraged for any Christian from any church, Catholic, Protestant, and Orthodox.

THE RELIGIOUS ROOTS OF PACIFISM IN BUDDHISM

It is recorded in Buddhist sources that there was once a *prediction* that the young Buddha would grow to be a great *wheel-turner*—a phrase that was interpreted to mean *warrior* (e.g., rider of chariots). According to the earliest written teachings of Buddhism, the Buddha's first sermon was titled, *Turning of the Wheel of the Law*. This has been interpreted by Buddhist scholars to be his way of declaring that the famous prediction was *transformed* by the Buddha into a *Wheel of Peace*. This *wheel*, which became a central graphic theme of Buddhist art and iconography, is now often taken to refer to the classic teachings of Buddhism known as the *Four Noble Truths*. Of these four, there is included the *Eightfold Path*—a set of practical moral guidance for followers of Buddhism. For many Buddhists, included in their understanding of these practical steps of achieving spiritual wisdom, is a commitment to *ahimsa*—protecting all beings from harm or injury. This has included, for many Buddhists, a commitment to vegetarianism as well as a very personal *pacifism* in the classic sense.

The Path to Transformation of the Self

Christopher Queen writes that "The most significant contributions of early Buddhism to the practice of nonviolence . . . are its techniques to counter the three evil roots of action—hatred, greed, and delusion—the seeds of violence itself" (Queen 2007). This includes a meditative prayer technique that involves repeating prayers such as the following: "May I be free from enmity; May I be free from ill will." Buddhist approaches to pacifism and nonviolence, therefore, focus first and foremost on the individual's struggle to overcome violence within themselves, and in relation to one's immediate neighbors and contacts. This peacefulness is normally promoted by understanding one's own lack of permanence, and letting go of one's greed and desires. Combined with this view is also a profound sense of the interconnectedness of all existence, thus promoting a sense of interdependence that would question violent conflict and separations.

Toward Buddhist Activism

Although often associated by both Buddhists and non-Buddhists as a religion of spirituality and withdrawal from the *cares of this world*, Buddhist philosophy has developed a tradition of nonviolence that is more active, and has therefore been engaged in some similar debates about tactics and methods that other religions have also struggled with, namely Christianity. In the Mahayana tradition, for example, which teaches that everyone has the potential of reaching the *enlightened state* of the Buddha, there grew also the tradition of heroes of the faith who delayed their own ultimate enlightenment so as to assist their fellow humans—especially those in need or who are in danger. These heroes of the faith became known as *bodhisattvas* (literally, a being destined for enlightenment), and thus, there arose the beginnings of an ideal Buddhist who is active in the care of others.

Similar to Christianity's rise to power in the Roman Empire, forms of Buddhism became the state religion of a number of Asian kingdoms—Sri Lanka, Japan, Burma (Myanmar), and Thailand. In many cases, participation in warfare and violence were justified by Buddhist monks and philosophers, particularly where Buddhism itself was seen to be defended by military action by Buddhist societies. In response to general concerns about the increase in violence and warfare in the twentieth century, however, there have arisen new Buddhist movements advocating a much more active stance toward peacemaking and nonviolence.

Engaged *Buddhism*

The concept of *engaged Buddhism* is often associated with the teachings of Vietnamese Zen master, Thich Nhat Hanh, who began a movement of Buddhist monks opposed to the violence of both sides of the Vietnam War. In addition to speaking and teaching for peace, the public demonstrations of *engaged Buddhism* included marches, but also actions difficult for Western observers to quite understand, such as self-immolation of the Venerable Thich Quang Duc in the streets of Saigon in 1963. But the modern notion of *engaged Buddhism* has now expanded to include the largely nonviolent work of the Buddhist leader, the Dalai Llama, in his resistance to the Chinese occupation of Tibet, and the struggles of Aung San Suu Kyi, leader of the Democratic Burmese opposition political parties struggling against the military dictatorship of Burma. Included in this growing sense of *engaged Buddhism* has been the Soka Gakkai movement of Japan, especially under the leadership of Daisaku Ikeda. Each of these leaders and movements are typified by a much more involved approach to peacemaking and social justice issues—and similar to Christian developments—an approach to *pacifism* that seeks to be involved with the good, rather than merely avoiding the bad.

PACIFISM IN THE TWENTIETH CENTURY:
THE CASE OF CHRISTIANITY AND THE UNITED STATES

The United States Constitution gives the government the power to raise an army, so people can be drafted to fight. But, there is also an established right to conscientious objection (usually known as *CO status*); a right that dates from before the formal adoption of the American Constitution. As noted by the Section 6(j) of the Selective Service Act: "Nothing . . . shall be construed to require any person to be subject to combatant training and service in the armed forces of the United States who, by reason of religious training and belief, is conscientiously opposed to participation in war in any form." It seems certain that American law allows for this provision because of the early colonial presence of *Peace Church* groups such as the Quakers, the Mennonites, and the Brethren.

Traditionally, these *Peace Churches* practiced a form of *pacifism* in the United States and Canada that consisted largely of their *conscientious objection* to participation in military conflict. Such a religious opposition to participation in the military, however, usually does not result in a complete and total withdrawal from all modern active society. Members of all three groups participate actively in government service, business, and education, although avoiding those government agencies that would involve carrying weapons (police, border guards, and the military).

Extreme Pacifism

In some cases, however, the social practices of some Christian pacifist groups comes close to virtual withdrawal from the wider society—particularly in the case of the Amish, a radical religious expression of Anabaptist/Mennonite Christian theology. The Amish, radical pacifists since their founding in the sixteenth century in Switzerland, have a very minimal direct involvement with surrounding American or Canadian society (they are almost exclusively in North America, although there are small South American settlements). Many groups of Amish or Hutterites refuse to vote, participate in unions (even when they accept jobs in non-Amish factories), and have minimal involvement in economic systems of mortgages and banking. Many Amish groups dress in simple and plain forms of dress, and refuse modern forms of transportation, preferring the simple life of horse and buggy. They will interact with non-Amish, but will tend toward isolation, and have often become the subject of tourism in locations like Ohio and Pennsylvania. It is important to clarify, however, that the majority of *Peace Church* believers in North America believe that they should not only freely interact with modern society, but do their part toward working for positive social and political change in wider society. How can they do this without compromising their commitment to nonviolence? This is the difficult debate that is always ongoing among the members of these groups, and also debated among any Christians who agree that Christianity ought to be a nonviolent religious tradition.

DO PACIFISTS "DO THEIR PART"?

While there was large-scale resistance to World War I among American Christians, the famous American religious teacher, Reinhold Niebuhr, dramatically abandoned his own earlier pacifist convictions to support American participation in World War II, and accused those Christians who still remained *pacifist* of not being realistic about evil in the world, and "standing by" when they should be involved in fighting the threat of German and Japanese conquest. These kinds of pressures against Christian pacifist groups, while present during earlier American conflicts such as the Civil War and World War I, became much more intense during World War II. Niebuhr, and others who agreed with him, tended to accuse pacifist Christians of either *not doing their part*, or worse, *standing by* in the face of evil and tyranny. This pressure arising in the mid-twentieth century combined with the international impact of Gandhi's campaigns in India to give rise to the debates about *pacifism versus nonviolent action*.

CONSCIENTIOUS OBJECTION

Despite the fact that conscientious objectors willingly engaged in *alternative service* that typically involved building projects, wilderness projects, or medical work in nonmilitary facilities (and their terms of service usually exceeded military terms of service), there was a growing conviction among Christian advocates of pacifism that their resistance to evil ought to be more active and less *passive*. This was typically expressed by those who stated that they wanted to engage in political action supporting what they "were *for*, rather than what we are *against*."

In response, religious groups who try to maintain a modern commitment to the nonviolent implications of the ancient teachings of their tradition have developed more assertive forms of *pacifism* in order to show that a modern commitment to nonviolence need not mean a withdrawal from working for change in the serious social problems of the world.

Thus, for example, the oldest religious-based lobbying organization in Washington D.C. was founded by the Quakers (Friends Committee on National Legislation) with the expressed purpose of being more assertive about advocating political leaders for issues more in line with Quaker convictions about peacemaking and social justice. Beyond advocacy, however, others determined that there needed to be more engagement in *direct action*—assertive actions intended to exert political pressure for changes in political and legal life of wider society.

MODERN RELIGIOUS MOVEMENTS

Within both Christianity and Buddhism, but also among adherents of religious-based pacifism in Islam and Judaism, a significant change in debates surrounding religious pacifism and nonviolence occurred in the twentieth century with the political activity of Mahatma Gandhi (1869–1948) in India. Gandhi's development of nonviolent, but forceful and confrontational, tactics for seeking Indian independence from Great Britain, gave rise to new debates about what constitutes *nonviolence*. Gandhi's own religious roots in Hinduism, and his reading of the Christian Gospels, helped to inspire his formulation of political strategies and public tactics intended to pressure the British colonial government over India to grant total independence from British rule. These tactics included massive strikes of Indian workers, large scale demonstrations intended to embarrass the colonial governors or draw unwanted attention to abuses, and engage in large scale acts of noncooperation. Gandhi even experimented with attempts to economically undermine the colonial government by encouraging Indians to abandon or boycott imported products and, for example, wear only locally produced Indian clothing. The concept behind all these tactics was based on the idea that Indians can practice political and economic strategies that would make India *ungovernable* by an undesired foreign power, and thus the colonial powers will be forced to eventually accept Indian independence without large-scale lethal conflict. It was, in the minds of some, fighting a "war" without the lethal weapons and large scale casualties of warfare.

While it is arguable that others experimented with similar political tactics before Gandhi, such as Te Whiti (1815?–1907), the Maori leader whose movement based at Parihaka was nonviolently but forcefully engaged in tactics of resistance to British presence in New Zealand in the 1860s, Gandhi is often credited with transforming nonviolence into a political philosophy in a way that engaged the world media in unprecedented ways.

The Rev. Dr. Martin Luther King Jr. and Rev. James Lawson intentionally studied Gandhi's concepts and applied them to the American Civil Rights movement in the 1960s, including fasts, large-scale demonstrations and marches, and economic boycotts. Once again, the philosophical basis for the development of these forms of political pressure was explicitly religious, rooted in the teachings of Jesus according to both King and Lawson.

With the development of large-scale American public opposition to the continued war in Vietnam, however, debate among advocates of religious based nonviolence became more seriously involved in actions that for some, began to blur the difference between pacifism and violence. Two Roman Catholic Priests, Fr. Daniel Berrigan S.J., and his brother Philip (at that time also a priest) became associated with a more assertive form of Christian nonviolence that argued that destruction of property may be an acceptable tactic for nonviolent campaigns of social change. Beginning in 1967, the two Catholic brothers started a campaign of breaking into Selective Service offices, breaking open draft file cabinets, and throwing draft files into the street outside the offices. They would then gather outside and either pour blood upon them, or burn them with napalm, or both. These acts were intended to symbolize religious opposition to the war. The tactics further evolved to a stage where Fr. Daniel Berrigan actually led a group of religious protestors to break into an armament manufacturer's plant where the nosecones of actual missiles were produced. Quoting the famous Old Testament passage about "beating swords into plowshares" (Isaiah 2:2–4), Fr. Berrigan and others actually began to smash the missile parts with sledge hammers. The point, once again, was symbolic, although at the same time it was forceful and assertive. These tactics represented an escalation in the form of tactics considered morally acceptable within a commitment to nonviolence.

See also Amish; Hutterites; Just War.

Further Reading: Ackerman, Peter, and Jack Duvall. *A Force More Powerful: A Century of Nonviolent Conflict.* New York: Palgrave Press, 2001; Bainton, Roland. *Christian Attitudes Toward War and Peace: A Historical Survey and Critical Re-Evalution.* Nashville: Abingdon, 1979; Brown, Dale. *Biblical Pacifism.* 2nd ed. Nappanee, IN: Evangel Publishing House, 2003; Cahill, Lisa S. *Love Your Enemies: Discipleship, Pacifism, and Just War Theory.* Minneapolis: Augsburg, 1997; Charles, J. Daryl. *Between Pacifism and Jihad: Just War and Christian Tradition.* Downers Grove, IN: InterVarsity Press, 2005; Cole, Darrell. *When God Says War is Right: The Christian's Perspective on When and How to Fight.* Colorado Springes, CO: Waterbrook Press, 2002; Gan, Barry, and Robert Holmes, eds. *Nonviolence in Theory and Practice.* Waveland, MA: 2004; Holmes, Arthur. *War and the Christian Conscience.* 2nd ed. Nashville: Baker Academic, 2005; Johnson, James Turner. *Can Modern War by Just?* New Haven, CT: Yale University Press, 1986; Juergensmeyer, Mark. *Terror in the Mind of God: The Global Rise of Religious Violence.* Berkeley: University of California Press, 2003; Nelson-Pallmyer, Jack. *Is Religion Killing Us?: Violence in the Bible and the Quran.* New York: Continuum, 2005; Palmer-Fernande, ed. *Encyclopedia of Religion and War.* Routledge, 2003; Queen, Christopher. "The Peace Wheel." In *Subverting Hatred,* ed. Daniel L. Smith-Christopher, 2007; Sharp, Gene. *Waging Nonviolent Struggle: 20th Century Practice And 21st Century Potential.* Extending Horizons Books, 2005; Smith-Christopher, Daniel, ed. *Subverting Hatred: The Challenge of Nonviolence in World Religions.* 2nd ed. New York: Orbis Books, 2006; Wink, Walter, ed. *Peace is the Way: Writings on Nonviolence from the Fellowship of Reconciliation.* New York: Orbis Books, 2000; Yoder, John Howard. *When War is Unjust: Being Honest in Just War Thinking.* 2nd ed. Oregon: Wipf and Stock Publishers, 2001.

Daniel L. Smith-Christopher

PRAYER IN PUBLIC SCHOOLS

The First Amendment to the United States Constitution includes two guarantees about religion:

> Congress shall make no law respecting an establishment of religion, or prohibiting the free exercise thereof.

The phrase *shall make no law respecting an establishment of religion* prohibits Congress from enacting any laws that have the effect of creating an official religion in this country, or committing the government's resources to supporting or promoting any particular faith. But the Constitution also says "Congress shall make no law . . . prohibiting the free exercise of religion." This protects the individual's right to follow her conscience, both in determining what she believes, and what her beliefs require her to do.

Sometimes these two guarantees collide when people feel a need to practice their faiths in public settings. In the United States, the venue where the conflicts are greatest and most controversial is the public school.

HISTORY OF THE FIRST AMENDMENT AS APPLIED TO PUBLIC SCHOOLS

When the Constitution was first adopted, it had no explicit guarantee of religious freedom, other than a prohibition on using any "religious Test" as a prerequisite for public office. The framers assumed that civil liberties would be protected by the states, and that the Constitution did nothing to infringe them. But some Americans were concerned that, without clearer provisions in the new federal Constitution, the national government might act to undermine their rights. So, 12 amendments were proposed by the first Congress to address this worry. Of these, ten were ratified by the states, including the First Amendment.

The First Amendment is directed at the federal government: "Congress shall make no law . . ." Public schools in the United States are run by the states, or by the local governments created by the states, which are not mentioned in the First Amendment. (At the time the First Amendment was adopted, some states had established churches, a practice that persisted into the early nineteenth century.) After the Civil War, Congress proposed, and the states ratified, the Fourteenth Amendment, which includes a provision forbidding any state to "deprive any person of life, liberty, or property, without due process of law; nor deny to any person within its jurisdiction the equal protection of the laws." The United States' Supreme Court interpreted this provision to apply to religious freedom, declaring that the Fourteenth Amendment "incorporates" the First Amendment and religious freedom as part of the "liberty" that states must not infringe.

Since the middle of the twentieth century, the Supreme Court has decided a steady stream of cases dealing with the First Amendment in public schools. While there has been substantial confusion among the general public about what these cases mean, they can be summarized as follows:

- The Constitutional ban on laws *respecting an establishment of religion* (the Establishment Clause) prohibits national, state, and local governments from offering any kind of support to any religious faith, whether it be in the form of money, facilities, or endorsement.
- The Constitutional guarantee of religious liberty (the Free Exercise clause) allows citizens to practice their religious faith without interference from the government, unless there is a *compelling* issue of public safety or welfare. Even in the rare cases in which governments can restrict religious practice, the regulation has to be the least restrictive possible to achieve the compelling public purpose.
- In cases where a government agency has created a forum for public expression, it cannot restrict access to that forum based on the content of what is being expressed. In particular, it may not bar religious groups from using the forum because of the religious content of their speech or other activities.

TABLE OF SUPREME COURT CASES

Everson v. Board of Education of Ewing Township, 330 U.S. 1 (1947): Court applies First Amendment ban on establishing religion to the states.

Engel v. Vitale, 370 U.S. 421 (1962): Public schools may not sponsor or mandate a short nondenominational prayer.

Abington School District v. Schempp, 374 U.S. 203 (1963): Public schools may not sponsor or mandate the reading of the Lord's Prayer or other Bible verses.

Tinker v. Des Moines Independent Community School District, 393 U.S. 503 (1969): Public schools may not ban specific kinds of non-obscene speech, but may enforce content-neutral regulations for the purpose of maintaining order and a good learning environment.

Lemon v. Kurtzman, 403 U.S. 602 (1971): Public money may not be allocated directly to parochial schools because doing so violates at least one part of a three-part test: (1) whether the government action has a secular purpose; (2) whether the primary effect of the government action advances or inhibits religion; or (3) whether the action brings government into excessive *entanglement* with religion, such as resolving doctrinal issues or the like.

Widmar v. Vincent, 454 U.S. 263 (1981): Public university may not deny use of university facilities for worship, if they are available for other student or community groups.

Wallace v. Jaffree, 472 U.S. 38 (1985): Public schools cannot se aside a minute of silence expressly for meditation or voluntary prayer.

Board of Education of the Westside Community Schools v. Mergens, 496 U.S. 226 (1990): The federal Equal Access Act of 1984 is constitutional, requiring public schools to allow students to organize religious groups if the school allows students to form similar groups for nonreligious purposes.

Lee v. Weisman, 505 U.S. 577 (1992): Public schools cannot sponsor prayers of invocation or benediction at graduation ceremonies.

Rosenberger v. The Rector and Visitors of the University of Virginia, 515 U.S. 819 (1995): If other student-initiated groups are given student activities funds, a public university may not deny those funds to student-initiated religious groups.

Santa Fe Independent School District v. Doe, 530 U.S. 790 (2000): Public schools cannot sponsor prayers of invocation or benediction at athletic events.

Good News Club v. Milford Central School, 533 U.S. 98 (2001): Public schools may not deny access to religious groups to use their facilities after school if they have allowed access to other community groups.

Note: These cases can generally be accessed by doing an Internet search on the title of the case. Another good way to search for cases is through Cornell Law School at http://supct.law.cornell.edu, an outstanding website for legal materials.

CONTROVERSIAL IMPACT ON PUBLIC SCHOOLS

Some of the uproar about religion in the public schools is based on misperceptions. It is not true, for example, that prayer is banned in public schools. Students and staff may pray privately at any time. Students can also pray publicly in settings where they initiate the prayer themselves, and employees of the school do not exercise control over what is said. Students can also express their religious views at any time they choose, subject to the normal rules schools can impose to keep order and protect the educational environment.

Students may not force *captive audiences* to participate or observe. Nor may they interfere with class discipline, or disrupt the normal operations of the school. Otherwise, students are free to pray, study the scriptures, worship, and share their faith on school grounds to the same extent as any other kind of student activity and expression.

Employees, on the other hand, are restricted in some of the ways they might express their religious faith. Employees are free to practice their faith on their own time, or even with colleagues in settings that are entirely voluntary—after school hours in the faculty lounge, for example. But when students are involved, the Supreme Court has ruled that the employee's free exercise rights are limited by the students' right not to be subjected to a de-facto *established* religion. So, while employees can be present to preserve safety and proper order even when students have organized themselves for prayer or scripture study, the employees cannot participate in the religious aspects of the activity, or reward or punish students for their participation.

Setting aside the conflicts that arise from misunderstanding of the law—by parents, as well as school staff and administrators—there is still controversy among religious leaders and lay people about the current interpretation of the Constitution as applied to public schools. Some religious groups have essentially accepted the current rules about prayer and other religious activities in public schools. The conservative Christian group Focus on the Family offers resources describing current law, and suggestions for how to help students organize prayer meetings and share their faith on campus within the law. Moderate to conservative Christian attorneys pursue similar ends through organizations such as the American Center for Law and Justice, and the Christian Legal Society's Center for Law and Religious Freedom.

But others feel that the Constitution should be interpreted to permit more freewheeling religious expression on public school campuses, by students, community members, and employees alike. Most of the arguments fall into one of five categories:

- *The Christian nation argument:* the United States was founded as a Christian nation, and the Constitution should be interpreted in light of this. The ban on establishing a religion was not meant to exclude public expressions of Christianity by government officials, including teachers in schools.
- *The majoritarian argument:* In a democracy, when a community is in overwhelming agreement about what should happen in its schools, it should be able to implement that consensus.

- *The educational benefits argument:* There are positive educational benefits available to students from various religious activities.
- *The religious community argument:* All the major religions include a strong community emphasis, calling adherents to worship, study, or act jointly with others in public life, including school. True freedom of religion requires freedom to practice one's faith in this kind of community setting.
- *The religious accommodation argument:* Some of the private, individualized duties in many faiths have to be carried out in public, or at times of the day that bring them into the school setting. Schools need to find ways to accommodate these practices or they will be *prohibiting the free exercise* of religion.

The first two lines of argument are most often made by Protestant Christians in America, naturally, since most of the framers of the Constitution were Protestants, and Protestants are by far the group most likely to constitute a dominant majority in school districts in the United States. They are both essentially arguments from the basis of political theory, saying public religious activity is appropriate because of the kind of nation the United States is, either by definition in its founding documents, or by the political will of the current majority.

Other believers, however, including many Christians, object to the elevation of any specific faith to a privileged position in public institutions. For one thing, even in the most homogenous communities in America, there are strong differences among citizens about matters of religious doctrine. Sometimes the differences are major, involving fundamental issues about the existence of God (or gods). Other times the disputes are about issues that seem minor to outsiders, but are crucial to those who disagree, including issues ranging from the roles of men and women, to matters of ethics or lifestyle. Those who framed the Constitution had similar disagreements among themselves.

Whatever the differences, to assemble a *majority* involves one of three choices, all of which are unacceptable: forcing some people to accept or participate in expressions of faith that violate their consciences; compromising on important issues in ways that will put everyone in uncomfortable positions; or finding a way to gloss over the differences. The result, according to these critics, is a bland *civil religion* that masks living faith, and even distracts people from a true encounter with God.

Whatever the merits of the *Christian nation* or *majoritarian* arguments, they are clearly unpersuasive in the courts on *establishment of religion* grounds. There does not appear to be any realistic possibility that either approach will become the basis for American law in the foreseeable future.

The *educational benefits* argument shifts focus to the educational purposes of schools. If we hope for our schools to educate the entire person, then we should encourage students to reflect on their moral and spiritual duties by exposing them to stories of faith, and the basic teachings of religion. This line of reasoning is subtle and profound, and has several layers of appeal.

At the most surface level, the argument for religious expression in school addresses prosaic concerns like discouraging disruptive behavior, or encouraging scholarly virtues like discipline and hard work. If students are given a few moments at the beginning of the day to pray, to think about their duties to those around them, and to consider their deepest goals for their lives, there may be immediate and visible benefits in how well they do at their studies, and how smoothly the school operates. This has been a persuasive line of reasoning in the courts, which have accepted such measures of moments of silence to start the day, as long as school staff do not encourage (or discourage) students to use the time to pray or do other religious actions.

But the educational benefits of open religious practice or study in school might include more than just improving the educational atmosphere. If religion is an important factor in modern life, and if modern communications and transportation make it likely that students will encounter many faiths different than their own, then it might be valuable for students to learn about each other's faith in school. Study of religion and watching other faiths' practices would be good cross-cultural learning.

And there is an even deeper possible educational benefit. Since so much of students' time is spent in school, and since the public has a clear interest in developing virtuous citizens, then helping students to internalize solid values like honesty and caring for others is a public interest. Religion has traditionally promoted these kinds of values, a function that could be enhanced if religion and religious instruction were given freer rein in the public schools.

Focusing on educational benefits of exposure to religion in this way does not ask schools to favor one faith over another. In fact, schools would be encouraged to make space for encounters with as many religions as possible—at least all those represented among the student population in the school. Courts have been open to this kind of thing in schools, although they are still watchful, worried that activities that appear on the surface to be neutral toward various faiths might be mere covers for the advancement of one faith. For example, attempts by various states to provide for moments of silence before school have had mixed success in the courts. They have sometimes been rejected because people sponsoring the moments of silence went on record saying their goal was to encourage students to pray in school.

But the *educational benefits* argument is not always popular with parents, students, or even teachers. People worry that students may be converted to disfavored religions, either as a natural result of learning more about them, or because they have been recruited to a new religious faith by people abusing the freedom to practice their faith at school.

The final two arguments (the *religious community* and *religious accommodation* arguments) have had more success in changing school practices. These focus on the believer's attempt to live faithfully to his religion. Here, the religious freedom side of the First Amendment comes into full focus, and the concerns about establishing a religion are least prominent. The claim here is that schools need to be flexible in their operation to allow students and employees to participate fully in the schools without forcing them into a position of having to violate the commandments of their faith.

Courts have generally been willing to accept, and in some cases even to require, attempts by public schools to make changes in their operations or programs to accommodate those who find the standard school experience to be contrary to their understanding of God's will. For example, schools have had to reschedule athletic events to permit students to participate without violating religious Sabbath-day requirements. Schools have altered menus to accommodate religious diets; created space in the school, and time in the day to allow Muslims to conduct required prayers; allow students to opt out of dancing classes or other activities that violate their religious teachings; and many other forms of accommodation.

CONCLUSION

Courts in the United States developed their current interpretation of the First Amendment in a series of decisions since the mid-twentieth century. The boundary lines between what is, and what is not, permitted in the public schools are not yet settled firmly. But some areas of permissible activity have been clearly recognized, especially those involving voluntary nondisruptive activities organized by students. When students organize the events, and do not seek special privileges not offered to other student groups, they can pray, study the scriptures, support each other, and even share their faith gently with other students who consent to hear their message.

See also Separation of Church and State.

Further Reading: American Center for Law and Justice. http://www.aclj.org; American Civil Liberties Union. http://www.aclu.org/religion/index.html; Americans United for Separation of Church and State. http://www.au.org; Center for Law and Religious Freedom. http://www.clsnet.org; Dawson Institute for Church-State Studies (Baylor University). http://www.baylor.edu/church_state/splash.php; First Freedom Center. http://www.firstfreedom.org; Fisher, Louis and David G. Adler. *American Constitutional Law, Volume Two, Constitutional Rights: Civil Rights and Civil Liberties.* 7th ed. Durham, NC: Carolina Academic Press, 2007; O'Brien, David M. *Constitutional Law and Politics, Volume II: Civil Rights and Civil Liberties.* New York: W. W. Norton and Co., 2005, especially Chapter 6; People for the American Way. http://www.pfaw.org/pfaw; The Rutherford Institute. http://www.rutherford.org.

Ron Mock

PRIME TIME RELIGION

Father Ellwood Kieser, pioneer developer of Christian programming targeted for the secular audience and the founder of the Humanitas Award, complained in a 1994 essay that television producers had ignored the "most important part of the human psyche," and he cited the statistic that 94 percent of Americans said they believe in God, and that 41 percent attended a church or a synagogue. "[I]f religion is central to American culture," Father Kieser states, "it has been curiously absent from broadcast television in the United States" (Kieser 1997, 19).

The leader of a conservative Christian organization, the American Family Association, Donald Wildmon, used even stronger language during a conference on religion in television at the UCLA Center for Communication Policy in 1995. He claimed that religion had been "censored" from prime time television. "The message from TV is quite clear—religion hardly exists in American society and when it does it is not a good thing" (Wildmon 1997, 4).

Since 1995, however, TV landscape has included such popular religiously based programs as *Touched By An Angel* (1994–2003), *7th Heaven* (1996–2007), and *Joan of Arcadia* (2003–2005). Prior to that, Michael Landon's *Highway to Heaven* (1984–1989) told the story of Jonathan Smith, a probationary angel sent to Earth, helped people to find their way toward resolving their spiritual or moral crisis. While not specifically considered a show about religion, Christian faith and moral values played a central role in the characters and many of the stories in Landon's long running series, *Little House On The Prairie* (1974–1983), and the characters in *The Waltons* (1972–1981) also embraced Christian values as a central part of their daily lives.

Some critics believe, however, that television is the wrong place for religiously based dramatic programming. Thomas Plate argues that television is a medium for the entertainment of the masses. "It is not a spiritual medium ideally suited for inner reflection and communication with a Higher Being . . . The strength of American religion is in its diversity. But prime time television, as contradistinguished from an ever-increasing number of niche-nestling cable stations, cannot handle that level of diversity, nuance, or spiritual intimacy" (Plate 1997, 108–9).

Still other critics assert that programming in prime time is driven by commerce alone, and that networks derive their income from advertisers who are looking for a specific audience to sell their client's products to, and therefore are only interested in programs that will attract advertising dollars. Advertisers are often reluctant to have their product associated with any controversy, and so networks try to avoid alienating any group in favor of the other. "Television producers repeatedly note," Michael Suman reported in 1995, "that they are afraid that religion made public on television could lead to conflict. Many feel that religious portrayals are no-win situations that will only serve to offend on large group or another" (Suman 1997, 80).

The role television plays in influencing our lives cannot be denied. It is today's public forum where ideas are exchanged and attitudes are expressed, just as the Ancient Greek dramas were reflections of the current anxieties and concerns of the Greeks. We identify with the character's dilemmas in a television drama or comedy and find a certain catharsis in their attempt to resolve them. "Under the guise of entertainment, television teaches the hidden curriculum of society. Entertainment is our popular religion and television is its oracle" (Davis et al. 2001, xi–xii).

Beginning in the Twenty-First Century, there have been a number of television shows that have incorporated religious themes into the fabric of their stories, and because television often reflects the current feelings and sensibilities of the public, it is possible to find religious debate in even the most secular of shows.

LEADING THE RELIGIOUS LIFE IN TV LAND

Perhaps the most well known "show of faith" was the popular and long running *Touched By An Angel* (1994–2003), which chronicled the adventures of a group of angels sent down from Heaven tasked by God to intervene in the lives of people who are at some spiritual crossroad. What made this series compelling was not just how the guest characters were touched by the angels, but how the angels were touched by the experiences of the people they were sent to help. In one episode, for instance, the angel Monica (Roma Downey) is faced with experiencing racism first hand when she becomes African American. Often the angels would have doubts about their mission or their ability to actually help their assigned human, and the lessons learned in each episode were often those of the angels. There were no ultimatums handed to those who had strayed or were in crisis, but rather a helping hand, and an honest exchange, and divine intervention was rarely the norm. This gave a certain authenticity to the stories, and prevented it from drifting into pure dogma. The message of the show was clear; "God's got our backs," a message Americans were responsive to, and which explains its longevity. *Touched By An Angel*, however, was also criticized for its heavy-handed approach at morality and social issues; a tendency to oversimplify both the problems its characters are confronted as well as the solutions. While this can be chalked up to the time constraints of episodic television, it is easy to take away the message that the only requirement for divine intervention is to desire it, rather than take divinely inspired action. "Viewers must always remember that Touched by an Angel lives in the world of fantasy and fiction, not documentary or doctrine," Davis cautions us, "These stories are designed to make a point, but not to be taken literally" (Davis et al. 2001, 182).

7th Heaven (1996–2007) dealt with moral dilemmas and controversies within the household of protestant minister Eric Camden (Stephen Collins). Each week the faith of each family member was tested, especially as those controversies grew in scope and size. Being a family drama first, the episodes focused on character conflict, but the added element of religion often helped put a finer point on the message. The problems and lessons in the Camden household are simply presented: two of the boys deciding whether smoking is a bad thing; trusting someone's word, especially your own children; premarital sex. At the core of each episode, however, is the basic Christian message that love is the center of grace and forgiveness.

Forgiveness was a central theme in the short-lived and controversial *The Book of Daniel* (2006), a story about an Episcopal minister, Daniel, whose life is chock full of crisis. He is addicted to pain pills, his wife is battling alcoholism, his son is gay *and* Republican, his brother has run off with the parish's funds and on top of all that, he has been having conversations with Jesus himself!

Conservative Christian groups were outraged by the program, accusing its network (NBC) of being anti-Christian. Their list of complaints was large and long: openly gay characters, blasphemous portrayal of Jesus, and a negative view of clergy. Liberal Christian leaders, however, praised the show for its honesty in portraying an all-too-human clergyman who struggles with his faith. Through his conversations with Jesus—often heated—the burden on Daniel's shoulders is lightened ever so slightly, giving him the strength to forge out one more day in the hopes of doing better.

"What if God was one of us?" This is the question asked in the theme song of *Joan of Arcadia* (2003–2005), which tells the story of a teenage girl who talks to God. The unique conceit of the show is that God appears to Joan in many different human forms: a telephone repairman, a young child, and an elderly woman. God's requests to Joan often seem small and mundane, but in the end she realizes there was a greater purpose in performing the seemingly menial task. Joan is anything but happy about God's appearance in her life. Like most teenagers, she often bristles at authority—even the supreme authority—and is looking for fewer complications in her life, not more. But slowly Joan learns to accept the role God has given her, and tries her best to fulfill her assignments even though she doesn't fully understand them, often struggling with the "why me, God?" question common to prophets like Moses (Exodus 4:10–13), Jeremiah (Jeremiah 1:6), and even Jesus (Luke 22:42).

The struggle of faith was prominently explored in *Sleeper Cell* (2005–2006), which told the story of FBI agent Darwyn al-Sayeed, a devout Muslim who has been tasked to infiltrate a terrorist cell in the heart of Los Angeles. Darwyn is confronted daily with the cell members who call themselves soldiers of Islam, consider themselves devout Muslim's doing Allah's will, but as far as Darwyn is concerned, have perverted the faith. Yet even though Darwyn is quick to point out to his fellow FBI agents the difference between the Islam he follows and those in the cell, there are times when he can identify with their anger and their commitment. The biggest issue confronting Darwyn is how he, a man of faith, can survive in a secular world, especially as an FBI agent whose job is to take down fellow Muslims. He also finds himself falling in love with a non-Muslim woman, and breaking the Islamic law by having sex outside of marriage. In the end, however, Darwyn manages to retain his faith—albeit by a slender thread—and bring the terrorists to justice. Islamic scholar Amir Hussain praises *Sleeper Cell* for its positive portrayal of Muslims. "Such portrayals are crucial, for they offer a corrective to stereotypical representations. North American Muslims are better integrated into their societies than are their European counterparts, and these groups need to be presented on American television for what they are—part of the fabric of American life" (Hussain 2007).

SALVATION ON THE AIRWAVES

Often raw and ribald, *Rescue Me* (2004–present) presents the story of Tommy Gavin (Denis Leary), a firefighter profoundly affected by the events of 9/11, traumatized by his narrow escape in the twin towers and the loss of his cousin. His marriage is failing, his communication with his children is nonexistent, and his relationship with his fellow firefighters is strained to the breaking point. He acts out inappropriately, drinking himself into oblivion, finding himself trapped in an emotional nightmare that he can't seem to escape from. He is constantly haunted—literally—by the ghost of his cousin and other victims of the 9/11 tragedy. Yet Tommy is basically a good guy trying desperately to find his way back to a good life, although he is blinded by grief and guilt. In the third season, Tommy, now separated from his wife, enters his apartment and hears a strange noise coming from the spare bedroom. When he investigates (holding a baseball bat as a weapon against an intruder) he finds Jesus pulling out the nails from His cross with a hammer. For several episodes Jesus confronts Tommy with the truth of his life, and offers a simple message of salvation and love. The portrayal of Jesus was predictably criticized by conservative Christian groups as disrespectful, but others saw it as fresh way to express the teaching of Christ, who offers the same concept of salvation to Tommy—in a somewhat unusual way—as is found in the New Testament. In the end (although the series at the time of this printing is continuing into a fifth season), Tommy slowly finds his way to forgiveness and reconciliation.

Saving Grace (2007–present) also presents a character caught in the cross fire of a destructive lifestyle. Grace Hanadarko (Holly Hunter), a hard-living detective in Oklahoma City, runs down and kills a pedestrian after a long night of drinking. Horrified by what she's done, she asks God for help. That's when Earl, a tobacco-chewing, good old boy of an angel appears and tells her that he's been sent to warn her the path she's on will only lead to pain and suffering—not just her own but others in her life—and that if she doesn't change her ways pronto, she's headed straight for hell. He disappears and so does the pedestrian she hit. Grace chalks it up to an "alcoholic blackout thing," and a dream, so she soon finds herself back to her old ways. But Earl doesn't give up on her, and slowly we get a sense that Grace might find her way after all, if she becomes willing to have faith.

Salvation plays a pivotal role in the popular series *Lost* (2004–present). All the characters, who have survived a plane crash on a mysterious island, have a dark and unresolved past, and all are in need of some kind form of salvation. There is an epic battle of good versus evil on the island and the characters find themselves divided in loyalty to the island itself, and to the ultimate goal of rescue from the island. While God is never explicitly mentioned (although several characters reference their Catholic background), it is acknowledged (or at least argued) that some power higher than themselves is directly involved in their fate, and the fate of the island itself. "It's clear that *Lost* . . . [has] a certain degree of cosmic optimism," Ross Douthat argues. "With God (in some form) taking an active role in the narrative and nothing less than the fate of humanity hanging in the balance, it seems like a safe bet that the gates of hell won't prevail against the heroes. A price will be exacted along the way, but, however dark the story gets, the logic of eucastastrophe [a term coined by author J.R.R. Tolkien to describe a sudden turn of events at the end of the story, resulting in the protagonist's well-being] still holds, and with it the knowledge that the light will over come the darkness" (Douthat 2007, 24).

CREATED IN HIS IMAGE?

There has perhaps been no more unique portrayal of the theological debate on television than *Battlestar Galactica* (2003–present). Reimagined from the

1978 series of the same name, the current *Battlestar Galactica* portrays the last survivors of the human race, chased through space by Cylons, humanoid robots that had been created by man but have since declared war on their creators.

What drives the Cylons is a radical belief in "the one true God," and their mission is to destroy mankind. The humans, on the other hand, are polytheists, worshiping the familiar pantheon of Greco-Roman gods. While it is possible to see the Cylons as stand-ins for the Islamic fundamentalists in our own universe, nothing is that simple on *Battlestar Galactica*. Often the polytheistic humans are even more strict adherents to their "book" than their Cylon counterparts, and the Cylons seem to have broad-based tenets in their belief system, with no strict dogma or worship. But "both sides, despite their theological differences, seem bound to a common destiny in ways that neither understand; like Jews and Christians after Christ, they're joined in brotherhood and enmity, till the end of their quest or perhaps the end of time" (pp. 23–24). In fact, *Battlestar Galactica* goes out of its way to offer "a rich tapestry in which degrees of faith and differing doctrinal positions are treated sympathetically and sincerely" (Marshall and Wheeland 2008, 448). While *Battlestar Galactica* is about more than religious bigotry and misunderstanding (it certainly has its share of space battles), it is most certainly as dominant an element of the stories as it is in our daily existence here.

CONCLUSION

In the March 2004 edition of *TV Guide,* an article suggested that God had become a popular and sellable commodity on television. Religious leaders interviewed suggested that the media might be just picking up on the questions of faith Americans might have as a reaction to the traumatic events of 9/11 (Tatarnic 2005, 448). It might just be good business for broadcast networks to develop programs that allow spirituality and religion to be part of the storytelling in their television series, but more significant is the willingness of Americans to be open to watching these programs. Networks, as has been pointed out, are not driven by a social or ideological agenda; if people didn't watch, these programs wouldn't be on the air. Television's willingness to incorporate religious themes into its programming is also a reflection of America's openness to engage in the debate as well.

See also Aliens; Animation as a New Medium; Religious Film; Science Fiction; Western Cinema.

Further Reading: Abbott, Stacey, ed. *Reading Angel: The TV Spin-Off with a Soul.* New York: I. B. Tauris, 2005; Abelman, Robert, and Kimberly Neuendorf. "Themes and Topics in Religious Television Programming." *Review of Religious Research* 29, no. 2 (1987): 152–74; Davis, Walter T., Teresa Blythe, Gary Dreibelbis, Mark Scalese S. J., Elizabeth Winans Winslea, and Donald L. Ashburn. *Watching What We Watch: Prime-Time Television through the Lens of Faith.* Louisville, KY: Geneva Press, 2001; Douthat, Ross. "Lost and Saved on Television." *First Things: A Monthly Journal of Religion & Public Life* 173 (2007): 22–26; Hussain, Amir. "Muslims on Television." *Sightings* (2007). Available at: http://marty-center.uchicago.edu/sightings/archive_2007/0125.shtml; Kieser, Ellwood E. "God Taboo in Prime Time?" In *Religion and Prime Time Television,* ed. Michael

Suman, 19–20. Westport, CT: Praeger, 1997; Marshall, C. W., and Matthew Wheeland. "The Cylons, the Singularity, and God." In *Cylons in America: Critical Studies in Battlestar Galactica*, ed. Tiffany Potter and C. W. Marshall, 91–104. New York: Continuum, 2008; Plate, Thomas. "Religion and Prime Time Television." In *Religion and Prime Time Television*, ed. Michael Suman, 107–9. Westport, CT: Praeger, 1997; Potter, Tiffany, and C. W. Marshall, eds. *Cylons in America: Critical Studies in Battlestar Galactica*. New York: Continuum, 2008; Suman, Michael. "Do We Really Need More Religion on Fiction Television?" In *Religion and Prime Time Television*, ed. Michael Suman, 69–83. Westport, CT: Praeger, 1997; Suman, Michael, ed. *Religion and Prime Time Television*. Westport, CT: Praeger, 1997; Tatarnic, Martha Smith. "The Mass Media and Faith: The Potentialities and Problems for the Church in Our Television Culture." *Anglican Theological Review* 87, no. 3 (2005): 447–65; Warren, Hillary. *There's Never Been a Show Like Veggie Tales: Sacred Messages in a Secular Market*. Lanham, MD: AltaMira Press, 2005; Wildmon, Donald E. "It Is Time to End Religious Bigotry." In *Religion and Prime Time Television*, ed. Michael Suman, 3–8. Westport, CT: Praeger, 1997.

Remi Aubuchon

R

RELIGIOUS CONVERSION

In the United States, the First Amendment to the Constitution states that: "Congress shall make no law respecting an establishment of religion." The resulting *separation of Church and State* is usually taken to mean that the American government will give no legal or economic preference or privileges to any particular religious institution, nor will any religious institution be declared an *official religion* of the nation-state. Despite the numeric majority of professing Christians, therefore, America cannot be said to be a *Christian* nation, in the same way that many Western European nations still have actual *state churches* supported in part by tax dollars.

While the American tradition certainly affirms a rather generic sounding religious attitude (e.g., *In God We Trust*), and seeks to protect freedom of religion (to believe or even not to believe) it is clear that this religious "attitude" is not intended to be an affirmation of any particular religious tradition, but is considered generic enough to allow an affirmation equally from many different religious traditions, including Muslims, Jews, and many others. Part of this understanding of the First Amendment in the United States is the freedom to join any religious persuasion that one wishes, or equally, to leave any religious group that one chooses to leave.

However, toward the end of the twentieth century, and into the twenty-first century, conservative American Christian churches with extensive church-based investments in traditional missionary work (funding and staffing Christian missionaries around the world with the express intention to seek to encourage conversion to Christianity) have become increasingly vocal about conversion as a *human right,* and have pressured the United States government to make *religious freedom* a major aspect of foreign policy initiatives. Critics suggest that this amounts to American governmental support for the *right* of American churches to conduct foreign missionary work, in violation of the First Amendment. Is *conversion* a human right? Are conservative churches masking their missionary concerns behind generic language of *human rights*, and thus pressuring the U.S. government invest in making such missionary efforts possible?

FREEDOM OF RELIGION AND THE UNITED NATIONS

In fact, most countries are now signatories of the United Nations Declaration on Human Rights, and the two relevant articles are as follows:

Article 18.

Everyone has the right to freedom of thought, conscience and religion; this right includes freedom to change his religion or belief, and freedom, either alone or in community with others and in public or private, to manifest his religion or belief in teaching, practice, worship and observance.

Article 19.

Everyone has the right to freedom of opinion and expression; this right includes freedom to hold opinions without interference and to seek, receive and impart information and ideas through any media and regardless of frontiers.

While some Christians will tend to view Article 18 as permitting them to engage in whatever missionary activities they can manage to engage in, wherever they want—it is also true that many countries also interpret Article 19 to suggest that there must be some limitations on Western missionary work that can be seen as invasions of privacy, and even destructive of local culture and tradition. They would argue that missionary activity must not impose on the freedom to think differently than Christians!

However, such freedoms to change religious affiliation are not equally observed around the world—and the issue of *conversion* has emerged in the late twentieth century and early twenty-first century as a serious issue among many Americans in relation to their ideas about American foreign policy. Specifically, many American Christians, especially in more conservative Christian traditions, invest great amounts of time and energy into *missionary work*. This work has, as its explicit goals, the *conversion* of as many people as possible to Christian faith—and especially their own version of Christian faith.

It is clear, then, that missionary work in the twentieth and twenty-first century, especially the work sponsored by conservative Christian churches based in the United States, has emerged as a major controversy in American foreign relations—and not always in relation to traditionally Islamic societies. In the April 24, 2008 edition of the *New York Times,* writer Clifford Levy wrote about

President Putin's official encouragement of Russian Orthodoxy as the de-facto *state religion*. Concomitant to this preference, however, Levy wrote: "They have all but banned proselytizing by Protestants and discouraged Protestant worship through a variety of harassing measures, according to dozens of interviews with government officials and religious leaders across Russia" (Levy 2008). It is clear that a study of Eastern European churches more generally reveals a similarly cautious, or even hostile, attitude toward conservative American Christian missionary work.

CHRISTIANITY AS A MISSIONARY RELIGION

In the West, especially in British and American history, many Christian churches believe that it is an essential aspect of their faith to seek converts. While there have arguably been *missionary* efforts throughout the history of Christianity, it is also true that there was a significant change in missionary activity beginning in Britain in the nineteenth century. This is not coincidentally the same time as the height of British Imperial and colonial power, and many British Christian leaders saw the *hand of God* behind British strength around the world, and openly encouraged Christian missionary activity to be part of the British colonial presence throughout the Third World. As New Testament scholar R.S. Sugirtharajah points out, the alleged "missionary command" of Jesus in Matthew 28:19, and the reading of Paul's journeys in the Book of Acts (especially in Chapters 13–18) as "missionary" journeys, was radically reinterpreted in the eighteenth and nineteenth centuries in Great Britain (Sugirtharajah 2003).

These texts had been dormant and were largely disregarded by the reformers, yet were reinvoked in the eighteenth and nineteenth centuries during the evangelical revival that significantly coincided with the rise of Western imperialism. At this time, the Matthaean text came to be used as a template to institutionalize the missionary obligation, and Luke's alleged recording of Paul's missionary undertaking was fabricated as a way of perpetuating the myth that it was from the West that the superstitious and ignorant natives received the essential verities of God's message.

For many Christians, at issue is not that such words in the New Testament exist—at issue is their *interpretation* into actual policies and decisions of both Western governments and church organizations in the eighteenth and nineteenth centuries. The period of serious missionary activity in the west arose in the eighteenth century.

In 1780, the British Baptist William Carey began to read about the Pacific voyages of Captain James Cook (Hawaii, Australia, New Zealand, Fiji, Tahiti, etc.) and was inspired to begin writing about the Christian "obligation" to spread the Christian message to those who have not heard it. From this beginning, developing along with the rise of British power, the missionary movements gained strength and popularity both in Britain, the Continent, and especially in the late nineteenth century, in the United States as well.

This historical legacy of missionary work connected to government colonial policies (often referred to as: *The Bible and the Flag*) has created a highly negative stereotype about Western Christian missionary activity, since both British (in the nineteenth century) and American (in the twentieth and twenty-first century) missionaries were often viewed with suspicion by host countries. Since 1956, for example, India has begun to systematically attempt to limit foreign missionary presence and work in India, and particularly American missionary work in that massive developing nation has been the subject of controversy, and occasionally, open violence. More recently, however, the conflict over missionary activities is perhaps most serious in the twenty-first century in the context of Christian-Islamic relations and American foreign policy with these nations.

CHRISTIAN AND ISLAMIC RELATIONS—TWO MISSIONARY RELIGIONS

There is little doubt that the two most intensively *missionary* religions in world history have been Christianity and Islam. Despite partisan arguments on either side, it is true that both religions have spread by means of violence as well as preaching, and often both combined. It is furthermore the case that there are many Christians who are as critical of missionary abuses as non-Christians— including Native American Christians who have documented horrendously abusive Christian practices against Native peoples and cultures. Christianity most certainly followed the expansion of Western strength in Europe, beginning with the Christianization of the Roman Empire in the fourth century, into the rest of Europe through the Middle Ages, and continuing into the modern expressions of British and American conquests in recent centuries.

Islam, on the other hand, also spread by conquest outward from Arabia as well, beginning in the seventh century C.E., although it is not entirely accurate to suggest that Islam was any more violent in its expansion than was the Christian "West." The two traditions often debate with one another as to which has the *worst* historical record. Inevitably, however, Christianity and Islam have confronted each other in military and political borderlands that tend to mix politics and economics with religious differences in ways that are often violent.

CASES OF ISLAMIC AND CHRISTIAN CONVERSION: CONSERVATIVE AND LIBERAL CHRISTIAN RESPONSES TO TENSIONS WITH ISLAMIC SOCIETIES

Since the rise of openly violent tensions between the United States and many Islamic nations beginning in the twenty-first century, *conversion rights* debates have tended to focus on Islamic nations, although China and North Korea are often also included in the debates. Two recent cases illustrate the repercussions of *conversion* issues for American foreign policy.

The United States' military has maintained an extensive presence in Afghanistan throughout the twenty-first century. An Afghani case, therefore, attracted considerable debate. Abdul Rahman was an Afghani convert from Islam who became a Christian while working with Western medical workers in Afghanistan in 1990. When Mr. Rahman began legal proceedings to divorce his wife, and attempted to negotiate visitation rights with his daughter, however, he was arrested in 2006 by Afghan authorities on the basis of Afghani law that legally prohibits conversion away from Islam. Negotiations eventually led to his being allowed to seek asylum in Italy, but the case became a celebrated case in the West, used by Western press to raise the issue of conversion in Islamic nations, and especially in nations receiving significant Western and U.S. military and economic assistance.

A second case also stirred debate. Christian-Muslim relations in Egypt also present serious contemporary test cases. In March of 2008, a case went to the Supreme Constitutional Court involving the "reconversion" of several Egyptian Muslims back to the Christianity of their birth. In many of these cases, Christians legally became Muslims in order to marry a Muslim. This was considered the easiest way to get around some interpretations of Islamic law, which state that a Christian man cannot marry a Muslim woman, forcing some Christians to *legally* identify themselves as Christian, but then seek to *convert* back to Christianity after their marriages are complete. In Egypt, however, traditional Islamic law has been declared the main source of legislative precedent, and according to many interpretations of traditional Islamic (or *Shariah* Law) a Muslim cannot leave Islam on pain of death. Although 12 defendants were allowed to leave Islam, the case has stirred serious controversy both within Egypt (where relations between Egypt's historically Christian *Coptic* minority, and the Muslim majority, have always been delicate).

CONSERVATIVE AND LIBERAL CHRISTIAN RESPONSES

Hundreds of other cases of controversies stirred by attempted conversions can be cited, cases that must surely include harassment of Muslims in the West after the tragedies of 9/11 (the New York Trade Center destruction by religious extremists), and Christians in the Islamic countries, illustrated by the two cases above.

For Christians in more Liberal traditions, these issues were considered important enough to call a meeting of Christian and Muslim religious leaders in Chambesy, Switzerland in 1976, and a second major gathering, a joint Muslim-Christian Consultation on *Religious Freedom, Community Rights and Individual Rights*, was sponsored by the World Council of Churches at the MacDonald Center for the Study of Islam at Hartford Seminary (Connecticut) in 1999. Attempts by Christians from more liberal constituencies, such as the World Council of Churches, have moved in the direction of conciliatory statements and agreements with Muslim leaders on the issue of proselytizing and missionary work in traditional Islamic societies. However, it is often the case the more "liberal" Christian churches have different philosophies of missionary work, and often seek to be cooperative with host societies, or place much more emphasis on social and medical service without *ulterior motives* of converting local peoples.

More conservative Christian groups in the United States view such *dialogue* or even *cooperation* as compromising on the Christian responsibility to *spread the Gospel*. More conservative churches often consider social and medical missions to be largely a *strategy* to more effectively enable proselytizing the local population. Because of these organizations with clear goals of seeking increasing numbers of conversions (often featuring dramatic stories of conversions in their fund-raising literature), pressure to allow such missionary work has led many of these churches to pressure the American government to consider missionary work as a *human right*.

In fact, it is clear that pressures from (largely conservative) religious groups within the United States led the Clinton administration to include *conversion rights* in modern foreign policy debates, and led directly to the International Religious Freedom Act of 1998, which in turn created the U.S. Commission on International Religious Freedom. The act states that this commission

> shall have as its primary responsibility the annual and ongoing review of the facts and circumstances of violations of religious freedom and the making of policy recommendations to the President, the Secretary of State, and Congress with respect to matters involving international religious freedom.

Although the Commission's own literature suggests that this is a ". . . bipartisan federal body assess and propose U.S. foreign policy action to advance freedom of thought, conscience, and religion and other freedoms needed to protect people at risk of abuses, such as killing, detention, or torture," it is quite clear from the overwhelmingly conservative Christian appointees to the governing committee by the Bush administration, as well as the countries that are specified for particular concern, that governmental political interests are being mixed with religious concerns. Appointees tend to come from Christian organizations with deep commitments to very traditional missionary work. The Commission has recommended that the following 10 countries be designated as *Countries of Particular Concern*: Burma, China, Eritrea, Iran, North Korea, Pakistan, Saudi Arabia, Turkmenistan, Uzbekistanm, and Vietnam. These nations, with many foreign policy disagreements with the U.S. administration, seem selected for as much political impact as religious concerns.

CONCLUSIONS

Religious belief is most certainly an important and treasured human right. It seems clear, however, that freedom of religion in the American tradition has, until recently, been understood to allow freedom to all religious traditions equally, including their right to promote their faith traditions. There are clearly occasions, however, with *faith sharing* can become seen as unwelcome *proselytizing* in hostile societies. Some religious traditions see this as merely a challenge to persist, while others are willing to consider whether the criticism of methods may involve valid concerns about local cultures and faith traditions. Furthermore, some Christians see *service* (medical missions, building schools, and hunger programs) as ends in themselves, or as expressions of one's own Christian faith irrespective of the faith of those who receive these services, while other Christians see these projects as mainly a *means* to another end—seeking converts—and often measure the *effectiveness* of social projects by the number of resulting conversions. Should nation-states be involved in adjudicating between these two religious philosophies within Christianity?

Finally, when it comes to foreign missionary work sponsored by American private Christian organizations and churches, however, it is hard to escape the political legacy of *Bible and Flag*—that is—the incontrovertible fact that missionary work from Great Britain in the eighteenth and nineteenth centuries, and more recently from the United States, has almost always been a dubious mixture of religion and politics.

The attempt to use American governmental organizations as a tool to promote religious interests, therefore, is potentially disastrous both for the credibility of American policy interests as genuinely interested in all forms of religious and intellectual freedom, and the consistency and reputation of the religious traditions involved as well who, it would seem, would have serious interest in not being permanently associated with any particular national policies or nation-states that might be detrimental to their religious work.

See also Marketing Religion; Native American Religious Freedom.

Further Reading: Christian Post, The (pro-Missionary news service, often, features stories on Conversion rights and persecution of Christian converts). http://www.christianpost.com; Crusade Watch. (largely anti-Missionary Web Site) http://www.crusadewatch.org; Hefner, Robert W. *Conversion to Christianity: Historical and Anthropological Perspectives on a Great Transformation*. Berkeley and London: University of California Press, 1993; Human Rights Watch Report. "Politics by Other Means: Attacks Against Christians in India." 1999. http://wwwhrw.org/reports/1999/indiachr; Levy, Clifford. "At Expense of All Others, Putin Picks a Church," *New York Times*. Available at: www.nytimes.com/2008/04/24/world/errupt/24church.html; Ramet, Sabrina, P. *Nihil Obstat: Religion, Politics, and Social Change in East-Central Europe and Russia*. Duke University Press: Durham and London, 1998; Rashied, Omar, A. "The Right to Religious Conversion: Between Apostasy and Proselytization." Kroc Institute Occasional Paper #27, August, 2006. University of Notre Dame: The Joan B. Kroc Institute for International Peace Studies; Sugirtharajah, R.S. *Postcolonial Reconfigurations: An Alternative Way of Reading the Bible and Doing Theology*. St. Louis: Chalice Press, 2003; Tinker, George E. *Missionary Conquest: The Gospel and Native American Cultural Genocide*. Minneapolis: Fortress Press, 1993; U.S. Commission on International Religious Freedom. http://www.uscirf.gov/index.php?option=com_content&task=view&id=213&Itemid=40.

Daniel L. Smith-Christopher

RELIGIOUS DIPLOMACY

A variety of religious and spiritually motivated groups have supported official international diplomacy by mediating disputes and taking actions that promote world peace.

Merriam-Webster's Collegiate Dictionary defines diplomacy as "the art and practice of conducting negotiations between nations." Many political scientists

COMMUNITY OF SANT' EGIDIO

In 1968, a group of Roman Catholic high school students met in Rome to found an orga-nization, the Community of Sant' Egidio. They were committed to spreading the Christian gospel, to dialogue with followers of other religions, and to solidarity with the poor and weak. The leader of the community, since its beginning, has been Andrea Riccardi; in 1980 he also became professor of church history at Sapienza University in Rome. By 2007 the community had about 15,000 members, most of them in Italy, but others in more than 20 countries. They have worked in several countries in Europe, Asia, and Africa. In addition to their work in the Mozambique peace negotiations, they hosted meetings of parties in-volved in a military-political crisis in Algeria in 1994–1995.

today would modify this definition. They call the practice of officially conduct-ing negotiations and other ways of resolving conflicts, by nation-states, *track one diplomacy*. These activities can be helped by the work of nongovernmen-tal organizations: *track two diplomacy*. Nongovernmental organizations include many religious groups, and other groups that are motivated by religious or spiri-tual principles. Many such groups are actively involved in mediating disputes between nations or other conflicting groups. They also engage in actions that promote world peace: disease prevention, promoting human rights, economic development, building a climate of reconciliation, or spelling out principles of global ethics. All of these activities may be called religious diplomacy.

RELIGIOUS GROUPS INVOLVED IN RESOLVING CONFLICTS

A few examples show how religious organizations and religiously motivated groups have actively helped carry out negotiations between nations or conflict-ing groups within a nation.

One example is the Beagle Channel dispute between Argentina and Chile. A boundary treaty in 1881 had not clearly spelled out the ownership of three islands in the Beagle Channel, a narrow passage at the southern tip of South America. Over many decades the two countries had argued about this question. An attempt in 1971, to settle the question by arbitration, had failed. By 1978, Chile and Argentina were on the brink of going to war over this issue. Pope John Paul II sent an experienced Vatican diplomat, Cardinal Antonio Samoré, to South America. "The two countries agreed to submit the matter to mediation at the Vatican under the auspices of the Pope. The Pope, the official mediator, appointed a special mediation team headed by Cardinal Samoré to conduct the day-to-day mediation" (Princen 1987). Negotiations went forward slowly and deliberately, with several interruptions. The last interruption came when Cardi-nal Samoré died in 1983. A treaty settling the dispute was finally signed in 1984 and ratified in 1985.

A remarkable example of religious diplomacy led to the end of a civil war in Mozambique. Mozambique, in southeastern Africa, was a Portuguese colony until 1975. In 1964 an organization known as Frelimo had begun an armed revolt against Portugal to gain independence for Mozambique. A few months after the end of fascist rule in Portugal, that nation granted independence to Mozambique in 1975 and turned control of the country over to Frelimo, without any provision for elections. In 1977, an organization, which later changed its name to Renamo, began an armed insurgent movement against the government in rural areas of the country.

In the meantime, the Roman Catholic Archbishop of Beira (in Mozambique), Dom Jaime Goncalves, had become friends with a small Catholic lay movement that had started in Rome, the Community of Sant' Egidio. This community was devoted to tolerance, dialogue, and service to the poor. Beginning in 1984, members of the community were in Mozambique to seek the easing of restrictions on the Church, and to deliver food and medicine to people in desperate need. They developed contacts with leaders of both the government and Renamo.

By 1988, Frelimo and Renamo were both exploring the possibility for moving from civil war to dialogue. Beginning was difficult, because of intense mutual distrust. The Community of Sant' Egidio were perhaps the only people who were trusted by leaders of both Frelimo and Renamo. Representatives of both parties met in July 1990 at the Sant' Egidio headquarters in Rome with four men: Archbishop Goncalves; Mario Raffaelli, a member of Italy's parliament; and two leading members of Sant' Egidio, Andrea Riccardi and a priest, Don Matteo Zuppi. These four men were at first observers of the meetings; in August 1990 the two parties accepted them as mediators. Negotiations moved slowly, and with interruptions and constant difficulties. Meetings took place in various locations, but quite frequently at Sant' Egidio headquarters. Several nations became observers of the negotiations: the United States, Zimbabwe, Italy, and Portugal. By 1992, the United Nations were brought into the final stages of the talks. A peace agreement was signed in Rome on October 4, 1992. In 1994 the first national elections were held. The Frelimo candidate for president was elected with 53 percent of the vote. The 250-member National Assembly included 129 Frelimo deputies, and 112 Renamo deputies (Cameron 1994).

Another situation in which religious diplomacy played a role involved relations between the United States and North Korea. The United States became deeply concerned about North Korea's programs to develop nuclear energy and weapons in the early 1990s; by 1994, hostilities between the two countries had reached a crisis point; they did not have diplomatic relations with each other. U.S. President William Clinton asked former President Jimmy Carter to go to North Korea. North Korea's president, Kim Il Sung, invited president and Mrs. Carter to visit North Korea. The Carters also went as representatives of the Carter Center. After two days of talks in June 1994, "President Kim agreed to freeze North Korea's nuclear program in exchange for the resumption of dialogue with the United States": the first talks between the United States and North Korea in 40 years. These negotiations "resulted in two agreements, reached in October 1994 and June 1995, in which North Korea agreed to neither restart its nuclear reactor nor reprocess the plant's spent fuel" (Carter Center 2007).

JIMMY CARTER/THE CARTER CENTER

James Earl (Jimmy) Carter, Jr., was born in Plains, Georgia, in 1924. In 1946 he married Rosalynn Smith of Plains. He was governor of Georgia from 1971 to 1975 and president of the United States from 1977 to 1981. As president, he met with Egypt's President Anwar Al Sadat and Israel's Prime Minister Menachem Begin for 12 days at Camp David, Maryland. These meetings resulted in the Camp David Accords, and the 1979 Peace Treaty between Israel and Egypt. In 1982 Jimmy and Rosalynn Carter founded the Carter Center in Atlanta, Georgia, in partnership with Emory University. The Carter Center has undertaken a wide variety of programs around the world to promote human rights and democracy, and to resolve deadly conflicts. These programs have included negotiations, mediation, and monitoring elections in many countries, notably Palestine. Jimmy Carter received the Nobel Peace Prize in 2002.

Beginning in 1995, economic sanctions and a severe drought led to the deaths by starvation of hundreds of thousands of North Koreans. In 1999, the Carter Center joined several organizations, including CARE, Catholic Relief Services, Church World Service, and Mercy Corps International, in a project to increase food production in North Korea.

In contrast, some religious organizations are acting in ways that heighten international tensions. Christian Zionists believe that Jewish control of all Palestine is a necessary step leading up to the second coming of Christ. A major Christian Zionist organization in the United States is Christians United for Israel (CUFI). The founder of CUFI "claims his movement has raised more than $12 million to help settle new immigrants in Israel, including in settlements in the Occupied Territories" (Mearsheimer and Walt 2007). The spread of these settlements on properties owned by Palestinians is a major cause of increasing conflict.

INTERNATIONAL RELIGIOUS COOPERATION

Widely representative assemblies of Christians, and of many religions, have played varying roles in the quest for world peace.

In the context of the cold war, Josef Hromadka, noted Czech theologian, founded the Christian Peace Conference (CPC) in Prague in 1958. His aim was to provide churches in Eastern Europe with a Christian voice for peace, and to open dialogue between these Christians and Christians in the West and the third world. Useful dialogue did take place, but there were limiting factors. Most of the participants from North America and Western Europe were critical of United States' foreign policy; those from Eastern Europe were strong supporters of the Soviet Union's foreign policy. The conferences tended to produce resolutions that closely supported the views of the Soviet government.

The most fruitful CPC assembly took place in Prague in 1968. Czechoslovakia was celebrating its *Prague spring* under the leadership of Alexander Dubcek, moving toward democracy and *socialism with a human face*. Dialogue was more open than ever; conference resolutions were nearly free of Soviet political jargon. After

JOSEF HROMADKA

Born in 1889, Hromadka began teaching at the Jan Hus Faculty in Prague in 1922. He became a strong opponent of German Nazism; after the collapse of Czech democracy in 1938, he fled to the United States. He was a professor at Princeton Theological Seminary from 1939 to 1947. Six months after his return to Czechoslovakia in1947, communists took control of that country. At the first assembly of the World Council of Churches in Amsterdam in 1948, the two major speakers on international relations were John Foster Dulles from the United States, who was deeply critical of the Soviet Union, and Josef Hromadka, who expressed a positive attitude toward the communist government in Czechoslovakia. In 1958 he founded the Christian Peace Conference and became president of its Working Committee. He strongly supported Alexander Dubcek's reforms in 1968 and delivered a public letter of protest to the Soviet ambassador in Prague, when the Soviet Union invaded Czechoslovakia. He resigned the presidency of the Christian Peace Conference in 1969 and died three months later.

Soviet troops moved into Czechoslovakia in October, the atmosphere changed. Leaders from the Russian Orthodox Church took over the Working Committee of the CPC; in September 1969 they dismissed the Czech General Secretary, and Hromadka resigned the presidency of CPC in protest. The United States' Committee for the Christian Peace Conference protested, limited its attendance at CPC meetings, and changed its focus. Adopting a new name, Christians Associated for Relationships with Eastern Europe, it broadened its contacts to include Christians in Eastern Europe who dissented from Soviet policies. By the time the Soviet Union dissolved in 1991, the Christian Peace Conference had disappeared from the scene.

The first formal gathering of representatives from both Eastern and Western religious traditions was the World's Parliament of Religions, held in Chicago in September 1893. This gathering had two significant outcomes: (1) Hindu and Buddhist speakers at the Parliament were the first members of their traditions to make people in Europe and North America aware of the spiritual strengths and values of the religions of southern and eastern Asia; and (2) it inspired the beginnings of two series of inter-religious gatherings in the second half of the twentieth century.

The first of these series is the World Conference of Religions for Peace. The first world assembly of the World Conference of Religions for Peace (WCRP) met in Kyoto, Japan, in October 1970. This conference established an International Secretariat, with a permanent staff, in New York. Its first secretary-general was Homer A. Jack, an American Unitarian minister. He and his staff lobbied delegates to the United Nations for arms control and religious freedom; they chartered a boat to rescue refugees from Vietnam at the end of the Vietnam War. WCRP assemblies have met at four to seven year intervals, in Louvain, Belgium; Princeton, New Jersey; Nairobi, Kenya; Melbourne, Australia; Riva del Garde, Italy; Amman, Jordan; and most recently, in August 2006, again in Kyoto, Japan.

WCRP staff members have led peace negotiations in Ethiopia, Eritrea, Sierra Leone, Bosnia-Herzegovina, Liberia, Indonesia, and Sri Lanka. They have helped religious communities work together to assist orphans of HIV/AIDS. Religions for Peace has brought together leaders from different religious traditions for reconciliation and peace-promoting projects in Iraq and Israel/Palestine. It has brought women of faith together as peace-builders, especially in Africa and Latin America.

In Chicago in 1988, the Council for a Parliament of the World's Religions was formed, and began planning a new gathering on the 100th anniversary of the original parliament. Hans Küng, a Roman Catholic priest, was a professor of ecumenical theology at the University of Tübingen in Germany, and author of many books. In March 1989 he was in Chicago and called on the council to proclaim a *new ethical consensus* of the religions. The council invited him to prepare a draft outline for a declaration on a common ethic. During the next four years Küng consulted widely with representatives of many religions as he strove to draw up a minimum consensus of ethical principles that are shared by all of the world's religious traditions.

Some 8,000 people took part in sessions of the September 1993 Parliament of the World's Religions in Chicago. A 150-member Assembly of Religious and Spiritual Leaders was chosen to consider the statement that Hans Küng had prepared. Most of the members of that assembly signed the 24-page text as an initial *Declaration Toward a Global Ethic*. It covered a surprisingly wide range of topics, including human rights, nonviolence, economic justice, tolerance, truthfulness, and equal rights for men and women (Küng and Kushel 1993).

The council has organized further Parliaments of the World's Religions, which met in Cape Town, South Africa, in 1999, and in Barcelona, Spain, in 2004.

See also Just War; Nationalism, Militarism, and Religion; Religious Conversion.

Further Reading: The Carter Center. 2007. http://www.cartercenter.org; Christians Associated for Relationships with Eastern Europe. 2007. http://www.caree.info/caree/organization.shtml; El Fadl, Khaled Abou. "Conflict Resolution as a Normative Value in Islamic Law: Handling Disputes with Non-Muslims." In *Faith-Based Diplomacy: Trumping Realpolitik,* ed. Douglas Johnson. Oxford University Press, 2003: 178–209; Hume, Cameron. *Ending Mozambique's War: The Role of Mediation and Good Offices.* Washington, D.C.: United States Institute of Peace Press, 1994; Johnston, Douglas, and Brian Cox. "Faith-Based Diplomacy and Preventive Engagement." In *Faith-Based Diplomacy: Trumping Realpolitik,* ed. Douglas Johnson. Oxford University Press, 2003: 11–29; Küng, Hans, and Karl-Josef Kushel, eds. *A Global Ethic: The Declaration of the Parliament of the World's Religions.* London: Continuum Publishing Company, 1993; Mearsheimer, John J., and Stephen M. Walt. *The Israel Lobby and U.S. Foreign Policy.* New York: Farrar, Straus and Giroux, 2007; Princen, Thomas. "International Mediation—The View from the Vatican: Lessons from Mediating the Beagle Channel Dispute." *Negotiation Journal* 3, no. 4 (1987): 347–366; World Conference of Religions for Peace. 2007. http://www.wcrp.org.

T. Vail Palmer, Jr.

RELIGIOUS PUBLISHING

In what ways has the for-profit commercial and business success of religious organizations, products, and religious marketing influenced the practice, and the message, of religion in the United States? Do religious organizations, especially Christianity, have an unfair business advantage in a country that is largely sympathetic to the Christian tradition and often gives tax incentives to religious organizations? One way to examine these issues in the American context is to examine one of the most successful religious *industries* to emerge in American history—namely religious-based publishing.

THE SURGE IN RELIGIOUS PUBLISHING

Religious book publishing is the largest segment of the religious product category. Changes in the religious product category, primarily books and also movies, began in the mid-1990s. Most insiders trace these changes to the approaching millennium and its doomsday prophecies. At this time a book arose that took the religion category by storm—*Left Behind,* published in 1996. This phenomenally successful book, and then series of books, plus movies and even a video game, was based on the *end times* and what would happen to nonbelievers in the event of the apocalypse: they would be *left behind* on a darkened earth while true believers would be brought to Jesus. The series was embraced by Christian consumers, many of whom already believed that the end times were near. While their secular brethren were not as immersed in the doomsday belief, they, too, readily accepted these books. According to a *Time* magazine cover story, evangelicals made up only about half of the series' readership. In this same article, a Time/CNN poll found the 59 percent of Americans believe in the events in *Revelation,* a widely debated and interpreted book of the New Testament upon which the Left Behind series is based. Driving these apocalyptic beliefs were heightened concerns about the fate of the world, particularly in light of the events of September 11, and the subsequent anthrax scares. Sales of the series "jumped 60% after Sept. 11. Book 9, published in October, was the best-selling novel of 2001" (Gibbs 2002, 43).

MARKETING RELIGIOUS BOOKS IN AMERICA

The Left Behind series changed the publishing industry in a number of ways. First, the books crossed over from the traditional Christian market to the popular book market, opening up the series to a vastly wider audience. Second, *Left Behind* was the first Christian book to be sold in big box stores, and demonstrated for these retailers the revenue that was possible from the Christian market. Today Wal-Mart and Costco regularly stock the top Christian titles. Third, the series showed the level of success that could be achieved with Christian fiction, a segment not previously known for sizable sales.

Two other books solidified the crossover of Christian books into the mainstream: *The Prayer of Jabez: Breaking Through to the Blessed Life* (2000) and *The Purpose-Driven Life. Jabez* is a small book—only 93 pages long—that espouses prosperity through devotion. It inspired a whole new category—prayer books—which could be sold in multiple formats and targeted for specific audience segments such as women, parents, and children. *The Purpose-Driven Life: What on Earth Am I Here For?* provides 40 days of "points to ponder," "verses to remember," and "questions to consider." Published in 2002, this book has sold more than 25 million copies, and is the best-selling nonfiction hardcover book of all time (Warren 2002).

THE GROWTH IN RELIGIOUS PUBLISHING

While these three books sold phenomenally well, they were not the only publishing successes in the religion category. The 1990s saw an overall expansion of religious and spiritual books, making it the fastest-growing adult book category, and strong sales continued into the new millennium. While sales figures are heavily guarded by the industry, and there are mixed reports about the level of growth (one source says 50 percent, another 7 percent, another 4 percent), there is no disagreement that the category is growing. In 2004 there were more than 14,000 religious/spiritual books published, which makes it the fourth largest category only after fiction (28, 010), juvenile (21,161), and sociology/economics (17,518). In 2004 religious books sold $1.9 billion, up from $1.5 billion only four years earlier, and industry insiders expect the category to reach $2.5 billion by 2008. While still small in terms of the overall category (total book sales in 2004 was more than $28 billion), the important thing to bear in mind is that the industry overall remains stagnant due to competition from alternative media sources; the religion/spirituality category is one of the few areas of steady growth in book publishing.

Religious book executives—sellers as well as industry analysts—attribute this sustained interest in religion not to single book titles, but to a number of cultural factors, both personal and global. According to Lynn Garrett of *Publishers Weekly,* "Religion is just so much a part of the cultural conversation these days, because of global terrorism and radical Islam. People want to understand those things. They're looking to go more deeply into the religious traditions" (Charles, 2004, 11). Phyllis Tickle, former religion editor of *Publishers Weekly* and author of numerous books on religion, attributes the industry's success to something more personal—people's reluctance to change their public selves. "We are especially slow to express aloud religious beliefs or visibly pursue religious patterns that are too divergent from those of our community. Books are private. Books don't tell, especially in matters of the spirit" (Harrison, 1997, 22). Others have attributed the success to the aging of the baby boomers. Lyn Cryderman, vice president and associate publisher at Zondervan, home of *The Purpose-Driven Life,* has said, "They hit age 50 and they start asking, 'What significance do I have?' and 'What mark am I making?'" (Nelson and Garrett, 2004, S4).

SEGMENTING CATEGORIES AND AUDIENCES
FOR MAXIMUM GROWTH

Bibles remain the leading segment in the religious category, though most of them do not look anything like traditional, staid, black books of scripture. There are more than 50 different versions of the Bible, including the *King James Version* and *The New International Version* (NIV). There are numerous translations and specialized editions created for different audiences. One of the hottest demographics, for example, is the teen or young adult market. In terms of Bibles, products for this group have been some of the most successful—and the most controversial. *Refuel* and *Revolve* are Bibles that look like teen magazines, and are targeted at guys and girls, respectively. They feature tips on dating next to tips on how to live your faith. *Revolve* sold 150,000 copies in the first six months of its publication, making it the best-selling Bible in Christian bookstores.

Teens, of course, are not the only segment for Bibles. To appeal to more harried, older adults, publishers are creating religious texts that can be consumed in a minimal amount of time. *The 100-Minute Bible* gives readers the scripture in 64 pages, and *The HCSB Light Speed Bible* covers the key points of the Old and New Testaments in 24 hours. These books demonstrate a trend readily apparent in the secular market where producers cater to consumers' time constraints. For example, Stephen Hawking has recently published *A Briefer History of Time,* Shakespeare's plays are being produced in abridged versions that run less than two hours, and we're now seeing yoga classes that last for 30 minutes.

Christian Living is the second biggest segment in the religious book category, and an area that has shown significant growth in the last decade. Christian Living covers a broad spectrum of titles, but fundamentally it is about making Christianity widely accessible by relating religious and spiritual themes in a practical way to life and relationships. Included in this category are the *Left Behind* books, *The Purpose-Driven Life, The Prayer of Jabez, God Chasers,* and *The Passion of Jesus Christ,* among many others. These books are nondenominational, which gives them broad appeal and enables them to be sold through secular retail outlets. Also, because women are the primary purchasers of religious titles, Christian Living titles cater to their needs and interests, particularly in terms of family, relationships, and prayer. The importance of women to this market is evidenced by publishing house Thomas Nelson's Women of Faith division, which sponsors annual motivational conferences to further support this target audience. This group hosted close to 30 conferences attended by approximately 400,000 participants.

Kids have always been an important market for booksellers of all kinds. For the Christian market, books and other materials for Sunday school and for summer Bible classes are a big part of their marketing efforts. Campaigns targeting children have expanded into the secular arena due to the success of *Veggie Tales,* the first Christian children's video series to have significant crossover sales. These videos opened the door for other marketers, including book publishers, to release products targeting the *faith-based* youth market. Some of the larger publishers have special divisions, like Zondervan's ZonderKidz, which publishes the *Veggie Tales* books, and Tommy Nelson from Thomas Nelson, which publishes the New International Version of the Bible for kids.

Religious book publishing and retailing has seen extensive changes in the past decade. Broadly, the category has seen more nondenominational titles, a larger array of Christian Living titles that marry religion with popular culture, and increasing distribution through non-Christian retailers. There is considerable segmentation in the book business, with products targeting specific audiences like women, kids, and teens, and young adults. Like the secular marketplace, religious book publishers reflect the latest trends and tastes of consumers. In the wake of *Left Behind,* Christian fiction is exploding. Christian chick lit—fiction for women—is a particularly popular segment at this time. Religious diet books have also become a hot trend over the past five years.

NON-CHRISTIAN MARKETS

While Christian books have been garnering the vast amount of attention in the category (and sales), they are not the only successful titles. The New Age or spiritual titles have shown consistent growth for the publishing industry. The New Age made its first major splash in the book industry with the publication of Shirley MacLaine's *Out on a Limb.* This book was turned into a miniseries which aired in January 1987, which has been attributed as giving the segment a huge promotional boost. This is evident in that the same year New Age book sales were over a billion dollars, which was a 30 percent increase over the previous year.

Oprah has been instrumental in promoting so-called New Age authors, starting with Shakti Gawain's *Creative Visualization* concepts, and she introduced the world to Deepak Chopra and Marianne Williamson. New Age titles, too, are heavily promoted to women, but there are also titles for parents, kids, and other defined segments. Interestingly, just as there was increased interest in the *Left Behind* books after September 11, there was an increased fascination with psychic mediums following that event. Yet even before 2001, psychic mediums—people who profess to talk to the dead—were very popular, which many scholars also attribute to millennial fever.

However, until recently, the New Age had fallen into a bit of disfavor, and again Oprah may have been a factor here. In the 1980s the specialized Advice and How-to bestseller lists were created for the New Age category. Now these books are in little evidence. Until recently, they were replaced by Rachel Ray cookbooks and Dr. Oz diets (both of whom have been heavily promoted by Oprah). However, Oprah has returned as a force in promoting these books, most notably Eckhart Tolle's *A New Earth,* for which she created a 10-week online course.

BIGGER PLAYERS AND INCREASING CONSOLIDATION

The Christian book industry is an amalgam of a couple of large independently owned presses, a few multinational media conglomerates, a handful of mid-sized presses, and dozens of small independents. The two major independent religious publishers are Thomas Nelson and Tyndale House, publishers of the *New King James Bible* and *Revolve,* and the *New Living Translation (NLT)* and the *Left Behind* series, respectively. The major international conglomerates in this category are Newscorp (parent of Zondervan, publisher of *The Purpose-Driven Life* and the *New International Version* Bible, and HarperCollins San Francisco),

Bertelsmann (Random House), and Hachette (Warner Faith, which was part of Time Warner until it was sold to Hachette in 2006). Warner Faith is home to Joel Osteen, Joyce Meyer, and most recently Creflo Dollar. Mid-size presses include Multnomah Publishers (*Prayer of Jabez*), Harvest House (*The Power of Praying* series, a top-selling Christian series since 1995), and Shambhala Publications (producer of a wide range of alternative religion and New Age works, which are distributed through Random House's sales force).

An important contributing factor in the consolidation of the publishing side of the business is the change that has occurred in Christian retailing. Whereas once this retail segment was made up almost exclusively of independent Christian booksellers, now big box stores like Costco and Sam's Club, as well as mass-market retailers like Target and K-Mart, are key elements of any marketing plan. Wal-Mart—the retail behemoth that dominates sales in the vast majority of consumer products—has discovered the Christian market in recent years. According to *Forbes,* in 2003 Wal-Mart sold an estimated $1 billion in Christian-themed items. Wal-Mart has carried Christian-themed books and music for years, but it is only recently that the increase in consumer demand was enough to warrant additional attention and product lines. Wal-Mart's product lines vary by store, but in general, the retailer has approximately 550 *inspirational* music titles and 1,200 *inspirational* books, which are primarily Bibles and best sellers. And that is just media items. According to Wal-Mart's spokeswoman Danette Thompson, "In our jewelry department, we have seen an increase in sales of inspirational jewelry such as cross necklaces and Bible charms" (Howell, 2004, 4).

Whereas small independent retailers dominated this category even 10 years ago, now their numbers are significantly reduced. These independent booksellers are members of the Christian Booksellers Association (CBA), an organization whose membership shrunk from approximately 3,000 in the 1990s to 2,370 by 2004 (Italie, 2004, A16). Paralleling these figures is the decline in sales through Christian specialty stores. In the mid-1990s, retail sales in such stores were 70 percent of the market; by 2002 they had dropped precipitously to 40 percent (Seybert, 2004). In less than a decade, secular outlets had overtaken the majority of the category sales.

In addition, competition from online outlets has affected Christian publishing. *Glorious Appearing,* part of the *Left Behind* series, was the number-one fiction title on the Barnes and Noble Web site shortly after its release in 2004. The advances of secular online retailers into this space is particularly hard on Christian retailers, because online services are much more attractive to young consumers. Future book buyers are not establishing a habit of shopping at a Christian bookseller, which has long-term consequences for this industry.

CONCLUSION

Mergers and acquisitions have changed the face of the religious product marketplace. Multinational media conglomerates saw the money to be made in religion and turned their considerable marketing resources toward selling religious products. Suddenly, Wal-Mart and other big box stores saw that they, too, could generate major revenue from books like *The Purpose-Driven Life* and the *Left Behind* series. These distribution outlets also saw revenue in the movies, toys, and jewelry associated with these products. The introduction of Christian books, particularly, into mass merchandisers, increased competition exponentially in this category.

Moreover, secular producers have no compunction about using churches as marketers for their products. From movies to books, churches are increasingly becoming spokespeople and distributors for secular products. Just as our schools have become endorsers of soda and junk food, churches have become endorsers of religious media, providing an implied stamp of approval for little or no compensation.

The increase in mega-corporations and retailers into this arena has pushed the drive for profits, moving sacred content further and further into the realm of the secular. But at what cost? The best-selling books have all been criticized as being lightweight Christianity, if Christianity at all. Their authors are accused of pandering to reach a wider audience. The question is thus raised, 'How much of the religious message is itself being influenced by the attraction of sales?' Put more starkly, just as Christianity's transformation to the religion of the Roman Empire in the fifth century A.D. created major changes in the faith and practice of Christianity itself, how might Christianity's acceptance as a major player in the capitalist markets of the developed world also change its character and message?

Yet, this is the fundamental paradox of evangelicalism. Being an evangelical means you want to spread the good word, but—and this is the core issue—you have to spread the word to nonbelievers. In order to do this, you must reach beyond the protected walls of the church and into the secular marketplace. However, to compete against the ever-growing array of more fun, more entertaining, and less guilt-ridden discretionary leisure-time activities, religious institutions have to match their message to the marketplace. That message needs to become simple and easily digestible in a short period of time. It also has to be palatable to people who may not be at all interested in what the evangelical has to sell. So the product—the book, the music, whatever—becomes the marketing message, for example, the book is what gets people in the door of the church.

See also Marketing Religion; Prime Time Religion.

Further Reading: Aucoin, D. We Want to Know it All, but Please, Keep it Brief. *The Boston Globe*, November 19, 2005, D1, D5; Boorstin, J. For God's Sake. *Fortune*, November 24, 2003, 62; Chandler, R. *Understanding the New Age: Revised, Updated—The Most Powerful and Revealing Analysis of the New Age*. Grand Rapids, MI: Zondervan Publishing House, 1993; Charles, R. Religious Book Sales Show a Miraculous Rise. *The Christian Science Monitor*, April 9, 2004, 11; Dooley, T., B. Karkabi, and R. Vara. Returning the Favor/ Best Life Redux /Osteen's Megadeal Is One More Layer of Religious Crossover. *Houston Chronicle*, March 18, 2006, 1; Gibbs, N. Apocalypse Now: The Biggest Book of the Summer Is About the End of the World. It's Also a Sign of Our Troubled Times. *Time*, July 1, 2002, 40–53; Grabois, A. U.S. Book Production. Retrieved August 6, 2006 from http://www.bookwire.com/bookwire/decadebookproduction.html; Harrison, J. Advertising Joins the Journey of the Soul. *American Demographics*, June 1997, 22, 24–25, 28; Howell,

D. Christian retailing Ascending to New Heights. *DSN Retailing Today*, April 19m 2004, 4–5, 28; Italie, H. Specialty Books Hit Mainstream Success; But Christian Stores Struggle to Benefit. *Washington Post*, May 30, 2004, A16; Nelson, M. Z., and Garrett, L. Gimme that Old-time Spirituality. *Publishers Weekly*, March 22, 2004, S2; Packaged Facts *The U.S. Marketing for Religious Publishing and Products*. New York: Packaged Facts, 2004; Saroyan, S. Christianity, the Brand. *New York Times Magazine*, April 16, 2006, 46–51; Seybert, J. *EPM's Guide to the Christian Marketplace: Selling Books, Music, Gifts and Videos to America's 218 Million Christians*. New York: EPM Communications, Inc., 2004; Warren, R. *The Purpose-Driven Life*. Grand Rapids, MI: Zondervan, 2002.

Mara Einstein

From Einstein, M. (2008). *Brands of Faith: Marketing religion in a commercial age.* London: Routledge.

RELIGIOUS SYMBOLS ON GOVERNMENT PROPERTY

Abraham Lincoln famously described America's democratic dream as "government of the people, by the people, and for the people," a vision that is shared by billions of people around the world. The first commitment of democratic government, then, is to enact laws, carry out policies, and behave in ways that embody the aspirations and values of the people.

Many people draw their most important values and sense of identity from their religion. Since their faith is central to their lives, they long to live with others of similar convictions, so they can help each other build lives that draw upon and reflect their faiths. People have migrated, at risk to their lives, across oceans and continents, and settled in wildernesses, deserts, jungles, and other harsh environments to have a chance to build communities of faith. The United States was built in large part on the contributions of several different religious communities, from Puritans in Massachusetts, Quakers in Pennsylvania, Catholics in Maryland and the desert Southwest, Lutherans in the upper Midwest, Mennonites in several northern states stretching from Kansas to Pennsylvania, Baptists in the South, Mormons in Utah, and many others. A snapshot of the United States today would include the descendants of all these religious communities, and hundreds of others, stretching outside Christianity to include Jews, Moslems, Hindus, Buddhists, Bahai, and others.

But as soon as a political system is erected that incorporates more than one faith, a conflict arises: whose religious convictions get to be embodied in the policies and activities of the government? Should the workweek include a Sunday Sabbath day of rest, to accommodate Christian beliefs? Or Saturday, as most Jews and some Christians would prefer? Or Friday, in accord with Moslem beliefs? What should be taught in schools about the origins of the universe, or values of right and wrong, or the relative roles of women and men in life, and many other topics?

Conflict over religious dimensions of community life can get very intense because people believe the stakes are so high. If someone is teaching my children falsehoods about God and the universe and how they should live, they are threatening both the quality of life in this world and, possibly, dooming my children to eternal death rather than eternal life in Heaven. Unfortunately, human history is scarred with the battles over control of government policy between different religious groups, including some of the bloodiest wars in human history. As this is written, struggles over how to reflect people's religious faiths in their government are especially bloody in places like Iraq, Afghanistan, Pakistan, India, Lebanon, and Israel and Palestine.

America's founders were aware of this danger. So the First Amendment to the United States Constitution begins:

> Congress shall make no law respecting an establishment of religion, or prohibiting the free exercise thereof

With these words, the framers of the Constitution hoped to build a hedge of law around the deep passions evoked by our religious faiths. The principle of government *by the people* was given a limitation: even if most of the people wanted to, they would not be able to use the machinery of the federal government to establish their faith as the official faith of the entire nation. The *Free Exercise Clause* ("Congress shall make no law . . . prohibiting the free exercise [of religion]") guarantees that the government will not be used to suppress your faith. And the Establishment Clause ("Congress shall make no law respecting an establishment of religion . . .") prevents the government from favoring one faith, even when directed by a clear majority of the people.

This article will focus on how the Establishment Clause has been interpreted by the courts in the United States to determine whether it is constitutional for a government agency to display religious symbols, or engage in other religious activities or expression, such as prayers or slogans.

INTERPRETATION OF THE ESTABLISHMENT CLAUSE

At the time the First Amendment was ratified, some state governments had established churches, which included appropriations of tax money to the coffers of specific Christian denominations. These churches were disestablished over the next few decades, so that by the time the Fourteenth Amendment was ratified after the Civil War, there were no churches with official *established* status anywhere in the United States.

The Fourteenth Amendment says, in part:

> No state shall make or enforce any law which shall abridge the privileges or immunities of citizens of the United States; nor shall any state deprive any person of life, liberty, or property, without due process of law; nor deny to any person within its jurisdiction the equal protection of the laws.

The Fourteenth Amendment has been interpreted by the United States Supreme Court to *incorporate* various parts of the Bill of Rights, thereby extending civil rights protections to citizens against possible actions by the states. In the case of *Cantwell v. Connecticut* (1940), the Supreme Court ruled that the prohibition against establishing a religion was one of the rights incorporated in the Fourteenth Amendment, thus making official what had been observed in practice for a century: no state could *establish* a particular faith by specially favoring it over another faith.

But this leaves a wide range of issues, where democratic dynamics push government to reflect citizens' religious commitments, but the Constitution prohibits the government from anointing religion with its blessing. The Supreme Court has upheld some practices that bring religious faith into contact with the activities of governments, such as opening legislative sessions with prayer at the state level (*Marsh v. Chambers,* 1983); passing laws barring some commercial activity on Sunday (*McGowan v. Maryland,* 1961); displaying a Christian nativity scene on public property along with non-Christian symbols such as Santa Claus, reindeer, a Christmas tree, and Christmas presents (*Lynch v. Donnelly,* 1983); and granting property tax exemptions to religious worship organizations (*Walz v. Tax Commission of the City of New York,* 1970).

Other practices have been ruled unconstitutional, including laws requiring the posting of the Ten Commandments in public school classrooms (*Stone v. Graham,* 1980); school-organized prayers in classrooms (*School Dist. of Abington Township* v. *Schempp,* 1963), at football games (*Santa Fe Independent School Dist.* v. *Doe,* 2000) and at graduations (*Lee v. Weisman,* 1992).

These cases left laypeople (and lawyers) confused about what is, and what is not, permissible. Part of the problem is that the Supreme Court has not stuck to one single test for deciding matters. In some of the cases, the Court applied a three-part test first outlined in *Lemon v. Kurtzman* (1971):

1. Is the purpose of the government's action primarily secular?
2. Does it have the primary effect of encouraging or discouraging religious faith?
3. Does it threaten to entangle the government in the internal affairs of a religious group, especially in making judgments about questions of faith or doctrine?

School prayers, for example, do not meet the *Lemon* test, because courts have trouble believing the purpose of a prayer is not primarily religious. Multi-faith Christmas displays do better, because it is easier to defend them as having either no religious purpose, since so many contrasting faiths are on display, including completely secular symbols such as Santa Claus. But these simple generalizations do not seem to cover every case. If school prayers led by district employees, or involving captive audiences at games or graduations, are not constitutional, why is it constitutional to have Congress or a state legislature pay a chaplain to offer a prayer to open its daily sessions?

Sometimes the Court has taken pains to point out that religion has played a major role in American history, and still does in the lives of most Americans. This point is used in two ways. Some justices (especially William Rehnquist, Antonin Scalia, and Clarence Thomas) have employed it to argue that the framers of the First Amendment could not have meant to bar some inter-denominational expressions of religious conviction by the government. They point to many examples of official Congressional actions or Presidential addresses that invoke faith in God, including prayers, resolutions, proclamations, and other communications, which were made while the First Amendment was being ratified, and which continued unabated right after ratification. This is a classic *originalist* argument, insisting that the Constitution needs to be applied today consistently with how the original authors of the Constitution would have understood it when they adopted it. Thus, evidence that so many governmental leaders thought opening Congress with a prayer was not a form of establishing a religion, means the Establishment Clause was not seen at the time as covering interfaith prayers at government functions.

Most Supreme Court justices have not been originalists. They believe the Constitution should be applied in light of things we have learned since it was originally adopted. Thus, the original idea that *separate but equal* was an acceptable way to provide *equal protection of the laws* under the Fourteenth Amendment does not bind us today, according to the non-originalist view, since we learned long ago that *separate but equal* does not work as advertised. But even many non-originalists invoke the role of religion in American life to suggest that government acknowledgement of religion is acceptable if it is more descriptive than prescriptive—that is, if it objectively acknowledges or reports what people believe without endorsing or promoting (or criticizing) those beliefs. So a Christmas scene with secular symbols mixed in with religious symbols from a variety of faiths passes muster because it depicts (without endorsement) the range of views one could find in the community.

But other Justices see most forms of government recognition of religion as violating the Constitution, essentially on the grounds that anything that throws positive (or negative) light on a faith has the effect of helping (or hindering) it, and thus functions as an endorsement (or critique) even when it is not intended to be.

None of these three broad approaches has garnered enough support to command a stable majority of the Court.

SUPREME COURT CASES

Cantwell v. Connecticut, 310 U.S. 296 (1940): the First Amendment applies to the states, and prevents them from regulating public speech based on its religious content.

Everson v. Board of Education of Ewing Township, 330 U.S. 1 (1947): Court applies First Amendment ban on establishing religion to the states.

McGowan v. Maryland, 366 U.S. 420 (1961): States or localities may restrict commercial activity on Sunday.

Engel v. Vitale, 370 U.S. 421 (1962): Public schools may not sponsor or mandate a short nondenominational prayer.

Abington School District v. Schempp, 374 U.S. 203 (1963): Public schools may not sponsor or mandate the reading of the Lord's Prayer or other Bible verses.

Tinker v. Des Moines Independent Community School District, 393 U.S. 503 (1969): Public schools may not ban specific kinds of non-obscene speech, but may enforce content-neutral regulations for the purpose of maintaining order and a good learning environment.

Walz v. Tax Commission of the City of New York, 397 U.S. 664 (1970): states may grant tax-exemptions to houses of worship.

Lemon v. Kurtzman, 403 U.S. 602 (1971): Public money may not be allocated directly to parochial schools because doing so violates at least one part of a three-part test: 1) whether the government action has a secular purpose; 2) whether the primary effect of the government action advances or inhibits religion; or 3) whether the action brings government into excessive *entanglement* with religion, such as resolving doctrinal issues or the like.

Stone v. Graham, 449 U.S. 39 (1980): States may not require the Ten Commandments to be posted in public school classrooms.

Marsh v. Chambers, 463 U.S. 783 (1983): State legislatures may open their sessions with prayers from a chaplain employed by the state.

Lynch v. Donnelly, 465 U.S. 668 (1983): a local government may display a Christian nativity scene on public property along with non-Christian symbols such as Santa Claus, reindeer, a Christmas tree, and Christmas presents.

Lee v. Weisman, 505 U.S. 577 (1992): Public schools may not sponsor prayers at graduation ceremonies.

Santa Fe Independent School Dist. v. Doe, 530 U.S. 290 (2000): Public schools may not sponsor public prayers before school sporting events.

Van Orden v. Perry, 545 U.S. 677 (2005): A state may maintain a monument displaying the text of the Ten Commandments when there is no evidence the state had a religious motive for doing so and the display is in a context that does not communicate an essential intent to advance or endorse religious faith.

McCreary County v. American Civil Liberties Union, 545 U.S. 844 (2005): Counties may not post the Ten Commandments publicly when it is clear the intent for doing so was to endorse or advance religion.

Note: These cases can generally be accessed by doing an internet search on the title of the case. Another good way to search for cases is through Cornell Law School at http://supct.law.cornell.edu, an outstanding website for legal materials.

THE 2005 TEN COMMANDMENTS CASES

On June 27, 2005, the Court decided two cases involving displays of the Ten Commandments on government property. All of the dynamics that made this area of the law so murky were at work in these cases: competing visions of constitutional interpretation; contrasting views about the propriety of acknowledging religion on government property; even disagreement over how central religion has been in the development of the country. At first glance, the results were even more confusing than normal, since in one case the display of the Ten Commandments was upheld as constitutional, while in the other it was ruled to be impermissible. Each vote was five to four, with Justice Stephen Breyer voting in the majority each time.

In *Van Orden v. Perry* (2005), the state of Texas maintained a plaque on a six-foot tall monument on the grounds of the state capitol, on which was inscribed the Ten Commandments. The monument was donated in 1961 to Texas by the Fraternal Order of Eagles, a national service club, as part of a campaign against juvenile delinquency. The Eagles were hopeful that, if young people were more aware of the rules of behavior in the Ten Commandments, juvenile crime would diminish. The donation to Texas was part of a campaign in which similar monuments were donated to state governments around the nation. There were 16 other monuments of similar scale on the 21-acre grounds around the Capitol, none of the rest of which involved religious texts.

The inscription on the monument quotes from the Old Testament book of Exodus, although in somewhat condensed form. It starts in bold, centered text with Exodus 20:2, "I AM the LORD thy GOD" and then lists each of the Commandments. The text was framed by symbols—two stone tablets like the ones on which God wrote the original Ten Commandments, two stars of David (a Jewish symbol), and the Greek letters chi and rho (a Christian symbol).

In *McCreary County v. American Civil Liberties Union* (2005), two Kentucky counties tried three times to get the Ten Commandments posted on their courthouse walls. In the first attempt, the Ten Commandments were displayed by themselves prominently in the courthouse. The text of the display was similar to the one in Texas, except that the preamble "I AM the LORD thy GOD" was omitted. In Pulaski County, there was a ceremony when the display was hung in which a county official made comments about the existence of God. When the American Civil Liberties Union (ACLU) sued in court seeking an injunction ordering the displays to be removed, the counties each adopted a resolution explaining that the Ten Commandments were "the precedent legal code upon which the civil and criminal codes" of Kentucky were founded, and stating that county leaders shared with America's Founding Fathers an "explicit understanding of the duty of elected officials to publicly acknowledge God as the source of America's strength and direction." These resolutions directed that the displays be expanded to include eight excerpts from other historical documents in which there was some reference to God (such as Pilgrim's Mayflower Compact, and the passage from the Declaration of Independence in which the Continental Congress had said that all "men are endowed by their Creator with certain inalienable rights").

When the federal District Court ordered the displays removed because they lacked any secular purpose, and were distinctly religious, the counties created a third display. This one included nine documents of identical size, one of which was the Ten Commandments (in a more complete text). The others were the Magna Carta, Declaration of Independence, Bill of Rights, the Preamble to the Kentucky Constitution, Mayflower Compact, *Star Spangled Banner,* the National Motto (*In God We Trust*), and a picture of Lady Justice. Each document was accompanied by a statement of its historical and legal significance. The one for the Ten Commandments explained that they had "profoundly influenced the formation of Western legal thought and the formation of our country" and provided "the moral background of the Declaration of Independence and the foundation of our legal tradition."

These two cases reached the United States Supreme Court at about the same time, and were argued in the fall of 2004. The opinions in both cases were announced on the same day the following June.

In *Van Orden,* five justices voted to uphold the display of the Ten Commandments on the grounds of the Texas Capitol, while four voted to rule it was unconstitutional. In *McCreary,* five justices voted to rule the displays were unconstitutional, while four voted to uphold them.

The four justices who would have upheld both displays used two principal lines of argument. First, Justices Scalia, Rehnquist and Thomas argued that government was not barred from favoring religious practice, because the original Framers of the constitution would not have intended such a thing—an originalist argument. Justice Anthony Kennedy did not join in that view, but did agree with the other three justices that, in each of these two cases, the intent of the displays was secular: to reduce juvenile delinquency, in the Texas case, and to inform citizens of some of the main historical sources of the modern legal system, in the Kentucky case. Since there was a legitimate secular purpose, strong enough by itself to justify the creation of the displays, they would be acceptable under the *Lemon* test, or any other test, according to these justices.

The four justices who would have ruled all the displays unconstitutional (Sandra Day O'Connor, John Paul Stevens, Ruth Bader Ginsburg, and David Souter) used, either explicitly (in *McCreary*) or implicitly (in *Van Orden*), the *Lemon* test. They found that the displays had a primary religious intent, to go along with at least some religious effect on those who saw them. In *McCreary,* the religious intent was easy to discern in the second phase of the project, including the resolution that pointed to God as the source of America's strength, and in the focus on religious texts in the display. Whereas the four justices in the minority in *McCreary* generally ignored the first two attempts to get the display done, the majority opinion (by Souter) assumed that the motive behind the first two attempts was the genuine one, and the third version of the display with its assertion of broader educational goals, was an attempt to cover up the religious motive with "secular crumble."

The same kind of evidence was not available in *Van Orden,* so the four disapproving justices focused instead on the design of the monument and the lack of any attempt by Texas to integrate the 17 displays on the Capitol grounds into any kind of coherent treatment of Texas' legal, political, or social history. Since the context provided no clues about why the monument was there, other than the monument's own content, and since the monument featured the phrase "I AM the LORD your God" and religious symbols, according to these justices, people looking at the monument would be likely to see it as an endorsement of Judaism and/or Christianity.

Neither of these two views carried the day. Justice Breyer wrote a separate opinion in *Van Orden* in which he rejected the *Lemon* test for borderline cases where government connects itself to a message or symbol with religious content.

He saw *Van Orden* as just such a borderline case, requiring him (and his fellow justices) to exercise *legal judgment,* by looking at the entire situation to determine if there was anything about it that violated the purposes for the First Amendment, which were:

1. To assure the fullest possible scope of religious liberty and tolerance for all;
2. To avoid the public and political divisiveness that often grows out of religious differences; and
3. To maintain "separation of church and state" so that each authority (religious and political) can do the work for which it is best suited.

In *Van Orden,* Breyer thought there was no danger of observers being coerced or unduly influenced toward Judaism or Christianity by the old monument which had caused so little controversy for so long, and which was in a setting that did nothing to reinforce a religious message. But in *McCreary,* Breyer joined the majority opinion declaring the Kentucky displays unconstitutional, presumably persuaded that the history of the projects, with the clear evidence of religious purposes, moved that case out of the borderline region, so no special exercise of judicial judgment was required.

THE CURRENT STATE OF THE LAW ON PUBLIC DISPLAY OF RELIGIOUS TEXTS OR SYMBOLS

The results of the *Van Orden* and *McCreary* cases are instructive from a practical point of view, although not so much from a legal point of view. If a display of objects with religious content is to be attempted, it needs to be justified entirely by secular purposes fitting to the level of government, and needs to be carried out consistently with those purposes. A display about a secular topic—such as the history of the development of law, or about motives for settling a frontier—can include religious material pertinent to that purpose. So the Ten Commandments could go into a display on the history of the law. Or a diary from a settler expressing thanks for God's protection and commitment to a vision of serving God could be part of a display about frontier life. But these items would have to be justified based on their secular importance, tied to objective evidence that law draws important inspiration from the Old Testament (a difficult proposition for any individual state's laws, although perhaps not so difficult for the history of human law in general), or that large numbers of pioneers were motivated by religion (in some areas, a very easy case to make). These justifications cannot be added-on as afterthoughts, as ways to cover up what is really a religious motivation.

The unresolved differences on the Court trouble legal theorists, but they do tend to point remarkably clearly toward a fairly stable range of outcomes. If a government is considering a public display that is worth putting up without the religious symbol or text, and if the religious material is in the display only to make it more accurate (and thus does not over-represent the role of religious faith in the subject of the display), then it probably would pass Constitutional tests.

Nevertheless, it is important to note that the legal theory upon which future courts will judge these cases is still unsettled and even a little messy. Although the twin precedents of *Van Orden* and *McCreary* do go some way toward narrowing the scope of practical uncertainty, they did not clarify the legal definition of unacceptable government behavior in representing or displaying religious faith.

See also Prayer in Public Schools.

Further Reading: American Center for Law and Justice. http://www.aclj.org; American Civil Liberties Union. http://www.aclu.org/religion/index.html; Americans United for Separation of Church and State. http://www.au.org; Center for Law and Religious Freedom. http://www.clsnet.org; Dawson Institute for Church-State Studies (Baylor University). http://www.baylor.edu/church_state/splash.php; First Freedom Center. http://www.firstfreedom.org; Fisher, Louis and David G. Adler. *American Constitutional Law, Volume Two, Constitutional Rights: Civil Rights and Civil Liberties.* 7th ed. Durham, NC: Carolina Academic Press, 2007; O'Brien, David M. *Constitutional Law and Politics, Volume II: Civil Rights and Civil Liberties.* New York: W. W. Norton and Co., 2005: especially Chapter 6; People for the American Way. http://www.pfaw.org/pfaw; The Rutherford Institute. http://www.rutherford.org.

Ron Mock

RIGHT-WING EXTREMISM

In both the United States and Europe, the late twentieth century saw an upsurge in the formation of right-wing extremist groups and other groups often labeled as *Hate Groups* (advocating the expulsion or destruction of an entire people because of race or religion), and an accompanying upsurge in the number of anti-Semitic and racist incidents of harassment and violence. While most of these groups do not use explicitly religious arguments in defense of their ideologies and ideas, some of them most certainly do. In fact, in one recent study, it is stated that: "If there were one thread that runs through the various far-right movements in American history it would be fundamentalist Christianity" (Michael 2003, 65). It is important to know about these groups, particularly because they have found the Internet to be their most important modern tool of propaganda, and many of these groups have become quite sophisticated in their public presentation, often masking their true intentions behind quite normal sounding "research groups," "churches," or "cultural activities."

VARIETY OF GROUPS

Extremist movements, hate groups, and militias have been a part of the American landscape for many decades. The Ku Klux Klan, one of the most notorious of the American-grown terrorist organizations, was originally formed in 1865, based originally in Pulaski, Tennessee. It has been responsible for literally hundreds of lynchings and killings, mostly (but not exclusively) in the Southern United States, but dwindled into virtual nonexistence before World War I. The

Klan, however, was revived and refounded by a Christian pastor, William Simmons, in 1915, and advocated versions of the *Christian Identity* doctrine (see below), and recent Klan groups (there are now various splinter groups) have been implicated in violence and murders in the United States as recently as 1981.

Related extremist groups are the various *militias* that provide training in firearms and often advocate being *prepared* for an ideological battle or outright *war* between races or adherents of unacceptable beliefs.

Among less violent groups, but still advocating racism, are organizing groups such as the Council of Conservative Citizens (CCC), founded in 1985 in Atlanta, Georgia, and with a membership of 15,000 are now based in St. Louis, Missouri.

Finally, there are variations of the *Christian Identity* movements that take the form of a "church," often using names such as *Church of Aryan Nation* or *Christian Identity* in the title.

DEFINITIONS AND MEMBERSHIP

Scholars of right-wing groups define these movements in many different ways. How one defines these groups, obviously, has serious implications for how many movements fall within these definitions, and therefore impact on the statistics for how many such groups currently exist.

According to a 1996 study by the Center for Democratic Renewal (an important organization that is considered one of the main *watchdog* groups keeping tabs on right-wing extremism in the United States): ". . . there are roughly 25,000 'hard core' members and another 150,000 to 175,000 active sympathizers who buy literature, make contributions, and attend periodic meetings" (Michael 2003, 1).

In this study, the following break-down of right-wing groups in the United States is published:

Region	KKK	Neo-Nazi	Skin-head	Christian Identity	Other	Patriot/Militia	Total
East	16	23	6	1	30	16	92
South	69	28	6	20	54	51	228
Midwest	39	39	10	9	58	54	209
Southwest	9	9	12	2	23	36	91
West	5	31	6	14	51	60	167
Total	138	130	40	46	216	217	787

(Michael 2003, 2)

However, one of the main sources of information for right-wing extremist groups, the Southern Poverty Law Center, posts on their webpage a list of extremist groups active in the United States by state. For their list, and taking only the top ten states for active hate groups, there is a somewhat surprising comparison with the previous list, suggesting that these groups have a wider geographical distribution than one might presume.

1. California	80
2. Texas	67
3. Florida	49
4. South Carolina	45
5. Georgia	42
6. Tennessee	38
7. Virginia	34
8. New Jersey	34
9. Pennsylvania	33
10. Missouri	29

From: Southern Poverty Law Center: http://www.splcenter.org/intel/map/hate.jsp.

Studies of membership across the United States reported that the execution of Timothy McVeigh, the main conspirator of the Oklahoma City bombing of the Alfred Murrah Federal Building which killed 168 people, on June 11, 2001, seems to have slowed membership growth in various American hate groups. However, only a few months later, the attack on the Trade Center in New York City on September 11, 2001 stopped the downward trend in militia membership, and the movement began to pick up membership again.

CHARACTERISTICS OF EXTREMIST AND HATE GROUPS

Michael lists a number of characteristics that he suggests are generally common among extremist groups:

1. Small locus of identity—Groups tend to strongly identify themselves with very locally defined groups—at most a nation, but often a race within a nation, or a race within a region. Members are not interested in *recruiting* beyond a select few, because they view the rest of the world in highly negative terms;
2. Low regard for Democracy—Although most groups abide by federal rules, they often have a low regard for systems that give too much freedom to all people—including, of course, the excluded groups. This violates their sense of privileges that should be limited to a select group;
3. Anti-Government—Many groups view the federal government with great suspicion, and view the U.S. Government as hopelessly under the control of particular groups;
4. Conspiracy View of History—Groups view historical as well as recent events according to often very complex theories of conspiracy and control by some particular hated group;
5. Racism—Their views often exclude non-Caucasian races entirely, but in the case of those who also direct hatred toward Roman Catholicism, even Caucasian Catholics are not immune from being targeted by hateful propaganda. (Michael 2003, 5–6)

There can be differences, however, in certain categories of groups. Militia groups, for example, can be described somewhat differently, as suggested by Mulloy, who cites common denominators of members of Militia groups to include:

1. Conservative outlook, those who are worried about repressive government that imposes undesired limitations on them, usually including taxes and gun control;
2. *Week-end Adventurers*—Some of the less ideological members are simply those who enjoy dressing in camouflage and *playing soldier* in the woods;
3. Libertarian conservatives who argue against almost all forms of federal government, even if they accept some limited local government as valid;
4. Hardcore extremists who harbor an obsessive conviction that the United States, indeed the world, is in the grip of an all-powerful conspiracy (Mulloy 2004, 3–4). One can also add that:
5. Militia-type groups tend to be the most active in states where there is a high percentage of gun owners, current and retired military personnel, and law enforcement personnel.

For Americans who fall into any of these categories, two events in the 1990s stand out as national tragedies that fueled a great deal of anger and resentment among some Americans who already tended toward a conspiracy-theory of suspicion toward government. The first was the attempted arrest of Randy Weaver in Ruby Ridge, Idaho in August 1992. Weaver, a known white supremacist, was arrested for selling sawed-off shotguns to an undercover informant. When he did not appear for his trial, U.S. marshals went to his rural Idaho home to arrest him. The killing of the family dog led to a gun battle where Weaver's son Sam was killed, and a Federal Marshall was also killed. Weaver himself was wounded, and his wife was killed. The 11-day siege ended when another known member of a *Patriot Movement* cooperated with the Marshals and convinced Weaver to surrender.

The second event was the disastrous end of the police siege of the Branch Davidian religious movement near Waco, Texas, in February, 1993. The decision to force an end to a long stand-off resulted in the death of many members of this religious cult. After a 51 day stand-off, the FBI determined to invade the complex. In four hours, over 300 cannisters of tear-gas were injected into the complex, and a fire broke out that killed over 74 people, including children, who were members of the movement. Part of the ensuing controversy was stirred not only by the fact that the events were broadcast throughout the nation, but that many of the reasons cited by the government for their aggressive tactics did not turn out to be supported. For example, there was no evidence for the alleged child-abuse, and there was no evidence of drug dealing, much less drug producing laboratories, and no massive stock-piling of weaponry. There is even some suggestion that the government enforcement agency known as the ATF (Alcohol, Tobacco, and Firearms) wanted to *show off a success* in Waco in the light of upcoming Congressional discussions about the future of the agency and its federal funding.

While most Americans saw these events as isolated incidents involving religious extremists or troubled individuals, for those inclined to see conspiracies in the modern world, these events are cited frequently as "evidence" of deeper issues, and are often used in virulent literature used to stir up hatred, and support for extremist agendas.

WATCHING THE EXTREMISTS

Even through there are many organizations that compile information on various extremist and hate groups (including, of course, the FBI itself), there are four main organizations that are widely noted for reliable information on right-wing extremism, and are active in attempting to use legal means to limit their activities. These are:

1. The Anti-Defamation League (ADL), which was founded in 1913 in Chicago by attorney Sigmund Livingston as an organization intended to be a defense agency for Jews in the United States facing discrimination. However, the ADL had been active in organizing information and legal challenges against groups who advocate hatred and/or discrimination against many different minorities. Michael (2003, 15–16) even reports many cases of grudging respect for the ADL by many of the groups they have targeted for their effective use of legal challenges.

2. The Southern Poverty Law Center (SPLC) was founded in 1971 by two lawyers, Morris Dees Jr., and Joseph Levin in Montgomery Alabama. Sometimes considered controversial because of the major fund-raising success of Morris Dees, the charismatic central figure of the Southern Poverty Law Center, nonetheless the SPLC has emerged as one of the most effective agencies in combating hate groups in the USA (Michael 2003, 21–22). SPLC investigations have resulted in "civil suits against many white supremacist groups for their roles in hate crimes. More than 40 individuals and nine major white supremacist organizations were toppled by SPLC suits in the Project's first 17 years" (SPLC Web site).

3. The Center for Democratic Renewal, was founded in Atlanta, Georgia, in response to the November 3, 1979 shooting to death of five members of the Communist Workers' Party in Greensboro, North Carolina. This occurred when the Communist Workers' Party group attempted to engage in a counter-demonstration against Neo-Nazis and Klansmen who were marching in Greensboro that day. Surprisingly, no members of the Neo-Nazi or Klansmen demonstrators were ever convicted for the shooting. The organization engages in counter-demonstrations and is considered one of the more *activist* watchdog groups. Many of its members have strong Marxist sympathies.

4. The Political Research Associates was founded in Chicago in 1981, attempts to be "first and foremost a research organization" (Michael 2003, 27), and they work hard at establishing academic credentials to give their research a strong and trustworthy foundation.

THE "CHRISTIAN IDENTITY" MOVEMENT

Among the most explicitly religious groups in the far-right and extremist organizations is the movement known as *Christian Identity* (variant but related groups appear with names like Church of Aryan Nation, etc.). There are a number of specific groups that identify with variations on this train of thought, so it is important to briefly summarize some of the basic ideas that are encountered in many versions.

Among the most common ideas that feed the Christian Identity movement is a set of ideas known as *British Israelism* or *Anglo-Israelism*. This is the belief that the Caucasian races of Western Europe, and especially the Celtic and Germanic peoples, are direct descendents of the *Lost Tribes of Israel*. Thus, the "white" Americans and Commonwealth peoples (Australia, New Zealand, Canada, etc.) are descendents of Israelites, and thus have a special status before God.

In the United States, more virulent forms of the Christian Identity movement became deeply anti-Semitic, believing that they had "replaced" the Jews as the true "chosen people of God", and that today's Jews are "descendents of Satan" (Eatwell in press).

Among the most dangerous of the ideas circulated among Christian Identity followers is the notion of an impending great war between good and evil, largely to be fought between white people on the one side, and all non-whites aligned with the Jews on the other "side." Christian Identity adherents believe that there were many other people in the world before God made Adam and Eve, but that Adam and Eve were created white, and therefore the ones that God especially cared for. Eve, however, had sex with one of the pre-Adam peoples (therefore, non-white) and Cain was born from this union, and was the ancestor of all non-white peoples today. Abel, the true son of Adam, was the further ancestor of white people.

This is then mixed with (very loose) interpretations of, for example, selected portions of the New Testament Book of Revelation, which spoke (symbolically) of a war between good and evil that will finally bind and destroy evil in the world. Some extremist members within the Christian Identity movement advocate terrorist violence against minorities in the United States, even ahead of the "great war."

Members of Christian Identity movements have been implicated in violent acts in the United States, including;

Eric Rudolph's bombings of an Abortion Clinic in Birmingham, Alabama, and also a bombing at the Atlanta Olympics
Arsonists who burnt synagogues in California in 1999
A murder of a Gay couple in Redding, CA
The attempted murder of five individuals at a Jewish Community Center in Los Angeles, again in 1999

There appear to be international connections as well, such as the *Living Hope* Church founded in South Africa by Rev. Willie Smith in the late 1990s in reaction to the fall of the Apartheid racist regime there.

THE RESPONSE TO CHRISTIAN IDENTITY

Both Jewish and Christian movements have supported the *Watchdog* organizations such as the Anti-Defamation League and the Southern Poverty Law Center, but it is important to note some specific religious responses to some of the religious arguments of the Christian Identity movement. This response to the Christian Identity movement by progressive Christians takes a number of forms. Besides the general disapproval of racist violence in any form, even among Christians who would otherwise support legitimate use of firearms in police or military service, Christians would also cite Scripture.

Jesus was noted for his inclusive teachings, a *universalism* that often offended his own local societies. In the Gospel of Luke, for example, the Gospel writer speaks of the first public ministry of Jesus involving a teaching in his "home" synagogue. Jesus, according to this passage, risked his life in Luke 4: 16–30 to teach on God's universal love of all peoples. St. Paul also famously declared this same openness to all peoples: "There is no longer Jew or Greek, there is no longer slave or free, there is no longer male and female; for all of you are one in Christ Jesus" (Galatians 3:28). In fact, one of the most important aspects of early Christianity was precisely the openness of the young movement to accept people from any background and race (including, of course, Africans, Acts 8).

In fact, contemporary New Testament scholars would declare that there is not the slightest defense for the racist and violent teachings of Christian Identity in any normal reading and interpretation of the Christian New Testament, and Old Testament scholars typically read the Creation Stories of Genesis as religious story intended to teach important lessons, but not literal ancient history. But even in a literalist reading of the opening chapters of Genesis, there is not the slightest support for the racialized re-telling of the Adam and Eve story, nor the belief on *pre-Adamic* peoples.

In short, the biblical teachings advanced by the Christian Identity movement are classic cases of having one's political mind made up, and looking for biblical passages to twist into that political shape.

Finally, many analysts see the rise of hate groups and extremist groups to be indicative of social isolation and economic depression in many rural parts of the United States, and thus argue that such organizations are symptomatic of the frequently noted attempt to *scapegoat* or *blame* certain groups as somehow *responsible* for the difficulties that these Americans are facing. As religious beliefs are among the most deeply held convictions of modern Americans, it seems obvious that religious attitudes will often become mixed into the resentment and anger fueled by the ideologies of the extreme right.

See also Apocalypticism and Nuclear War; Hucksterism and Religious Scandals.

Further Reading: Barkun, Michael. *Religion and the Racist Right: The Origins of the Christian Identity Movement*. Chapel Hill: University of North Carolina Press, 1996; Eatwell, Roger. *Western Democracies and the New Extreme Right*. London and New York: Routledge, 2003; Eatwell, Roger. *Fascism and the Extreme Right*. London and New York: Routledge, In press; Hewitt, Christopher. *Political Violence and Terrorism in America: A Chronology*. Westport, CT: Praeger, 2005; Hewitt, Christop. *Understanding Terrorism* *in American: From the Klan to al Qaeda.* London and New York: Routledge, 2002; Juergensmeyer, Mark. *Terror in the Mind of God: The Global Rise of Religious Violence.* 3rd ed. Berkeley: University of California Press, 2003; Michael, George. *Confronting Right-Wing Extremism and Terrorism in the USA.* London and New York: Routledge, 2003; Mulloy, D. J. *American Extremism: History, Politics and the Militia Movement.* London and New York: Routledge, 2004; Robinson, B. A. "Christian Identity Movement." Ontario Consultants on Religious Tolerance. http://www.religioustolerance.org/cr_ident.htm; Smith, Brent. *Terrorism in America: Pipe Bombs and Pipe Dreams.* New York: State University of New York Press, 1994.

Daniel L. Smith-Christopher

ROCK MUSIC AND CHRISTIAN ETHICS

Rock and roll, as a specific music form, emerged onto the American scene in the 1950s. It brought with it a youthful sensibility that would forever change American culture. This new music form evolved from earlier musical genres, the blues, and rhythm and blues (R&B), bringing with it social, cultural, political, and religious challenges. Cultural and religious challenges were presented by the emergence of rock and roll from its R&B roots, and some of the sub-genres that would follow. In particular, this music can be related to traditional Christian values regarding the body and sexuality, how Christian musicians and singers have situated themselves within this complex social and religious context, and how some communities, marginalized from mainstream Christianity, have built underground music communities as alternative worship spaces.

Rock music was born into an American culture largely shaped by traditional 1950s Christian values, affirming among other things a conservative value system about the body and sexuality. Rock and roll music has always pressed up against this system from its beginnings out of the blues tradition to the present. The blues was itself considered a racy or emotionally raw type of music, created by black artists typically speaking about their experiences as poor and disenfranchised people. In addition to songs of social critique, they also created sexually suggestive lyrics and danceable tempos that encouraged listeners into seductive movements. Many "good Christians," both black and white, considered this music to be "the Devil's music," played in clubs called juke joints by, and for sinners. Moreover, it was the blues that gave us the term *rockin' and rollin'* as a euphemism for sexual intercourse in many songs, notably in a 1922 song called, *My Daddy Rocks Me (With one Steady Roll)*, by Trixie Smith.

Later in the early 1950s a white Cleveland, Ohio deejay named Alan Freed would be credited with using the phrase rock and roll to describe rhythm and blues, or black music. Freed's use of the term seemed to remove some of the racial stigma associated with the music, and it began to appeal to a wider mainstream audience. Black musicians would claim that rock and roll was a white imitation of the more authentic rhythm and blues, and thereby used to cut out many black artists who were banned from mainstream radio, television, and whites-only venues. White performers who began singing this music filled the void. Many attribute Elvis Presley's meteoric rise to fame and glory to this phenomenon. Songs from black musicians such as Chuck Berry, Little Richard, Louis Jordan, and a host of blues musicians would be copied by white singers such as Pat Boone and Elvis Presley, to great approval and fanfare from young white audiences.

However, race music or rhythm and blues, continued to cause great anxiety for white Americans of conservative social and religious values. Given that R&B as a distinct genre has been described as, *good time* music, or *body music*, appealing to the flesh more than the spirit, embodying the fervor of gospel music, the throbbing vigor of boogie woogie, the jump beat of swing, and the gutsiness and sexuality of life in the black ghetto, the challenge to mainstream values is evident. Likewise, the music introduced white teens to black urban lifestyles that were previously considered undesirable. In pre–civil rights' era America, integration was not yet the norm, and this music pressed the social and cultural status quo beyond most white Americans' comfort zone. The 2001 VH1 documentary, *Say It Loud: Black Music in America* presents vintage news footage of an outraged white man exclaiming that, (rock and roll) promotes interracial dating, dancing, and that "the White man's children will be driven to the level with the n***!"

Nevertheless, white teens had become captivated by this music and the lifestyle it projected. "Whites had long reified Black culture as perpetually fascinating but feral, alluring but alarming, sensual but sordid antithesis to the dominant white one" (Ward 1998). So exuberant to hear and experience this music, white teens went to great lengths to acquire it. As rock and roll and R&B were scorned by the older mainstream population, race music was not readily available except in black neighborhoods. White teens pressed the boundaries even more by venturing into these areas and listening to the growing number of radio stations who played this music late at night. Much to the dismay of the white mainstream, rock and roll was already changing American culture. By the time of the so-called British Invasion, blues-inflected rock music could not be stopped, as famous rock and roll artists like the Rolling Stones, the Who, Eric Clapton and Steve Winwood would openly declare their admiration and indebtedness to the often unrecognized blues men of the Mississippi Delta region from which the genre arose. In the June 12, 2008 issue of *Rolling Stone* magazine, the cover article focused on these musical relationships.

Not only were the cultural bounds being transcended, but traditional religious values were being challenged by the lifestyle that rock and roll projected. The music was considered to promote rebellion against social and parental authority, experimentation with drugs, and promiscuity. This was in direct opposition to conservative Christian moral codes about the body and sexuality. In contrast, all Christians were encouraged to control bodily passions, and remain celibate until marriage as a mark of being saved, and biblical obedience. However, teenagers during these early years of rock's emergence were being presented with an alternative that seemed to pull them away from the Christian moral code deemed to be a hallmark of American values.

Older white mainstream audiences were not the only ones struggling with the changes that rhythm and blues now transformed into rock and roll presented, many traditional African American Christians also struggled with the dichotomy between sacred and secular music. For many older African Americans acquainted with Negro spirituals and tame forms of gospel music, this new style of music was seen as pulling many of the traditional artists away from the church, and into a sinful lifestyle playing the Devil's music. This notion was so strong that an urban legend developed around the idea that many artists who had crossed over into rock and roll had sold their souls to the Devil in exchange for fame and wealth. When some of these musicians met with untimely deaths or misfortune, the urban legend was reiterated as the Devil coming to collect his due. Thus, the divide between the things of God and the things of the world was deep and pervasive. Prior to rock and roll, many Christian blues musicians would create secular music under other names. The backlash from the church community was so great that artists feared family and church rejection, and that ultimate disparagement, being called a backslider in faith. The well known gospel standard, *Precious Lord, Take My Hand* was written by one of the most well known blues/gospel artists of the twentieth century, Thomas Dorsey. As a "blues man," Dorsey was known as Georgia Tom, and his reputation for suggestive lyrics followed him among church people, some of whom accepted his *gospel blues* and some who did not. Dorsey's career is a quintessential example of artists who have traversed back and forth between the worlds of sacred and secular due to a deeply instilled sense of Christian morality. Dorsey was known to venture into the blues world for a time, and then become reconciled to the church again, for a time. This vacillation between genres was a hallmark of his career.

An additional layer of this issue has to do with an attempt by black Americans to fit with a white mainstream religious sensibility. Since *gospel blues* was considered raucous and inspired people to spontaneous dancing and disorderly worship styles, many traditional black ministers saw this music as perpetuating notions of blacks as unsophisticated wild Africans. Instead, some of these ministers wanted to appropriate the more structured, European-styled forms of worship in order to present black people as respectable and cultured. The mainstream American Christian aesthetic dictated what legitimate religion and worship style should look and sound like. Thus, many black musicians who wished to remain within the fold of good Christian morality found themselves restricted to secular music, and those who wanted to explore the realms of worldly music found themselves marginalized or outcast.

With the emergence of rock and roll in the 1950s, and ever since, some of the most famous artists in music have had to navigate through this complex territory. Little Richard, James Brown, Sam Cooke, Aretha Franklin, Marvin Gaye, B.B. King, Gladys Knight, Tina Turner, and Al Green represent just a fraction of artists who have had to address such a struggle. In particular, Sam Cooke grew up in the Baptist church and joined the gospel group the Soul Stirrers, later becoming the lead singer. The group was extremely popular as they traveled from church to church throughout black communities. However, Cooke stood out from the group, and was recognized for both his handsome looks and his smooth, soulful voice. He began to be recognized by the mainstream audiences as well, and despite the internal conflict he felt, between secular and sacred, he began to have bigger dreams of performing crossover music to white and integrated audiences. Cooke was the most famous gospel artist in the 1950s to transition into the mainstream market. His 1957 hit, *You Send Me*, was the impetus behind that success. Tragically however, Cooke's rise to stardom would be stopped short by the 1964 shooting in a Los Angeles motel that ended his life. The shock of his unexpected death affected not only the public and his loved ones, but record company executives who had high hopes for Cooke's crossover success from gospel to R&B to pop.

This dynamic also played out among white southern artists who stepped out into secular music. Some of these artists came from conservative, evangelical backgrounds that prohibited joining in with rhythm and blues and rock and roll on both social and religious grounds. Where racist attitudes prevailed among these whites, they did not believe in the racial integration this music promoted. Likewise, religiously they objected on grounds of a perceived rejection of God for the Devil and his worldly things. Some of the artists who nonetheless transcended these categories include Elvis Presley, Jerry Lee Lewis, and Johnny Cash among many others. As an example, Jerry Lee Lewis was routinely publicly vilified by his ultra-conservative cousin, Jimmy Swaggart, noted televangelist and church musician. Swaggart would often include the notorious escapades of his famous rock and roll cousin in his sermons as a cautionary tale, warning his congregation and Christian television audiences away from pursuit of worldly things.

Many contemporary artists continue to be caught in the push pull dynamic between the church and the secular world, such as Marvin Gaye, Prince, and Tupac Shakur. We have a rich library of music that symbolizes the internal conflict many musicians felt. Notably, songs from Marvin Gaye and Prince serve as examples of sacred/secular duality. Both musicians wrote and performed songs reflecting a strong belief in God, as well as songs celebrating free sexuality. Gaye's songs from his classic album, *What's Goin' On*, are in stark contrast with *Let's Get It On* and *Sexual Healing*. However, these sexually themed songs include references to masturbation being "not good," and being "sanctified," a term used often by those in the Pentecostal/Holiness church of Gaye's childhood to describe the holy lifestyle. Likewise, Prince's suggestive lyrics and performance style is well known and documented. He is a convert to the Jehovah's Witnesses religion from the Seventh Day Adventist faith of his youth. In interviews of recent years he has denounced the bad language and lewd stage behavior of his past on the basis of his devout religious practice.

This dichotomy has also been written about extensively regarding the rap artist Tupac Shakur, whose music was often perceived as promoting a *thug life* or being part of the angry, violent gangsta rap genre of hip hop music. However, he has also been described as a sensitive, insightful poet speaking to a generation of young people who could relate to his experiences and conclusions. Although he was not reared in the church, his lyrics routinely addressed such theological issues as God, death, redemption, and the afterlife, within the context of young black urban life, much as earlier Blues and rock and roll lyrics did in their contexts. By many accounts of those who knew him, his public *thug life* stood in contrast to his more reflective, spiritual tendencies. For some he embodied the inner turmoil evident in Marvin Gaye's *Trouble Man*, a song reflecting right and wrong dualism within a person. Tupac's inner conflicts were writ large through his celebrity and his ultimate early death.

Another contemporary music form that emerges from this historical trajectory in which we see tension between conservative Christian values and popular music, is the underground dance sub-genre. The dance music scene is a complex one, and will not be thoroughly discussed here, but briefly summarized, as it represents another layer of tension between Christian values and popular music, as well as a response from a community marginalized by that value system. The issue remains sexual morality, but in this instance regards homosexuality, and the traditional Christian teaching against it.

Contemporary dance music has evolved from the R&B trajectory via rock and roll, soul, funk, and disco. Dance music today is often referred to as electronic music. However, this broad category does not do justice to the extensive sub-genres of techno, trance, house, and the multiple sub-sub genres within those. For our purposes here, I will refer to house music, specifically the sub-sub genre, gospel house. House music is a particular form of dance music with origins in the nightclubs of Chicago and New York following the demise of disco. Typically, the clientele were black and Latino gay men who had been part of disco, but found a new form of expression with house music. The term *house,* is a reference to one of the most famous dance clubs in 1980s Chicago, The Wherehouse, where this music was created and played by djs on turntables into the late night and early morning hours. A similar following was happening in New York City at the legendary, but now defunct club called the Paradise Garage.

House music clubs represented safe spaces where gay men and those sympathetic to them could find a place to be themselves in an affirming community and dance to the music they loved. Out of this context arose the sub- sub-genre of gospel house music. In this form, djs and producers create remixes of established gospel songs, or create new songs with a gospel musicality, but with lyrics that actually replace some of the sin-oriented language with words of God's unconditional love and acceptance of everyone. Like the blues, some of these songs are written to critique the so-called good Christian, who is found to be hypocritical, overly judgmental, and exclusive in their own personal behavior. One of these songs, *You Don't Even Know Me*, describes the singer's feelings of being judged for his sexuality, but not known for the type of person he is. Other songs are straight forward praise songs directed to God the father and/or Jesus as redeemer of all humanity, but without going through the Christian church as mediator. Some of these titles include, *We Lift Our Hands in the Sanctuary*, where the sanctuary is actually the club where the "worship" is happening on the dance floor; and, *He Is*, in which God is recognized and praised as a loving creator of all. For many gay men who have lost their family connections and church affiliations because of their sexuality, the dance clubs have become spaces for reclaiming fragments of their traditional faith in alternative ways, which do not diminish their humanity. Gospel house music has become a refuge for those gay men who still value their Christian faith, and the clubs allow them to create their own family connections and worship spaces. The music allows them to maintain their connection to God, but bypass the tension with traditional values that generally ostracize and marginalize them.

The Christian moral codes regarding the sanctity of the body, control of physical passions through monogamous, married sexuality have been part of the fabric of American values throughout the nation's existence, and yet as we have seen, it has been thoroughly challenged by popular music of the blues, R&B, rock and roll genres, and sub-genres for at least a century. Conservative Christians have tried to preserve what they perceive as a certain sanctity to life, and where they have felt challenged they have pushed back. One of the ways that has been effective is the establishment of the music rating system in 1985, which requires that explicit music of any genre be labeled as such. This was a move by the Parents' Music Resource Center (PMRC), a group led by Tipper Gore, wife of senator and later Vice President, Al Gore, with a mission to educate and inform parents about the music their children were listening to. They connected growing trends in teen violence, pregnancy, and suicide, to song lyrics with explicit references to sex, drug use, and violence, particularly in songs performed by hard rock bands and rap artists. Like the mainstream parents of earlier decades, the PMRC claimed that "the change in rock music was attributable to the decay of the nuclear family in America." Gore asserted that "families are havens of moral stability which protect children from outside influence, and that without the family structure rock music would infect the youth of the world with messages they cannot handle" (Gore 1987). The group was also concerned about Satanic or occult, anti-Christian teachings being integrated into music to subconsciously influence teen listeners. Artists such as Pink Floyd, Ozzy Osbourne, and Led Zeppelin were accused of *backmasking*, or adding contents to music that could only be heard if the record was played backwards. The PMRC met with a backlash from many musicians who affirmed their right to freedom of expression, and protests against censorship. Today, the PMRC is not as vocal or public as they once were; however, perhaps they do have the last word, because explicit lyric labeling is now a standard in the music industry.

Rock music and Christian ethics have often been at odds in American culture. We have seen that there has been a push-pull relationship since the music form and its sub-genres emerged in the 1950s. Then and now, the hottest points of contention have been centered on social, cultural, and religious values, specifically sexual morality. The music itself continues to reflect the internal struggle of America and this homegrown art form. At once we may be enticed by the infectious rhythms and sense of freedom the music promotes, and simultaneously repelled by the lyrics we hear and the behaviors we see. Both the music and Christian values continually propel us in American culture to examine and re-examine who we are, and what we actually value.

See also World Religion Aesthetics.

Further Reading: "All Things Considered." *National Public Radio*, January 11, 2005; Altschuler, Glenn C. *All Shook Up: How Rock and Roll Changed America*. Oxford: Oxford University Press, 2003: 23; *Associated Press Newswire*, May 27, 2001; *The Observer* (UK publication), April, 2004; Fikentscher, Kai. *You Better Work: Underground Dance Music* *in NYC.* Hanover, NH: Wesleyan University Press, 2000; Gore, Mary Elizabeth (Tipper). *Raising PG Kids in an X-Rated Society.* New York: Bantam Books, 1987; Reed, Teresa. *The Holy Profane: Religion in Black Popular Music.* Lexington: University Press of Kentucky, 2003: 152; "Senate committee hearing on the recording industry." Sept 20, 1985; Shaw, Arnold. *Honkers and Shouters: The Golden years of Rhythm and Blues.* New York: Macmillan, 1978: xvi–xx, 34; Ward, Brian. *Just My Soul Responding: Rhythm and Blues, Race Consciousness and Race Relations.* Berkeley: University of California Press, 1998: 39, 241.

Darnise C. Martin

S

SAME-SEX MARRIAGE

Same-sex marriage is a major civil rights issue that has been heavily debated on legal, political, moral, and religious grounds. Clashing views of personal rights, competing definitions of marriage and its purpose, and differing moral and religious beliefs on sexuality and gender are the driving forces behind this issue.

BACKGROUND

Same-sex marriage is one of the most hotly contested political issues in the twenty-first century. Quite possibly, no other social issue today has been more passionately debated in churches, courtrooms, state houses, and living rooms across the nation. The federal government continues to weigh in on the topic, although most legal experts agree that it is a states' rights concern. Schools, popular culture, health and religious institutions, families, and communities have all played important roles in shaping cultural perceptions about same-sex marriage, and about homosexuality and sexual identity more generally. Gay celebrities such as Rosie O'Donnell, Melissa Etheridge, and Elton John have announced their weddings to the press, setting an important public precedent for other same-sex couples. While there is a great deal of disagreement among gay rights' activists about the merits of marriage privileges for lesbians, gays, and bisexuals (LGB), many claim same-sex marriage as one of their primary goals. Opponents claim that marriage has been, and should continue to be a sacred commitment exclusively between a man and a woman. The administrations of William J. Clinton (1992–2000) and George W. Bush (2000–present) have publicly supported legislation opposing same-sex marriage, and conservative religious sectors continue to oppose it, and homosexuality more generally. Why the controversy? Why so much dissent within, and among groups about the importance of securing or prohibiting same-sex marriage rights? Differing moral and religious beliefs on sexuality and gender, as well as divergent perspectives on the role of the state in regulating people's private lives, contribute to the controversy. While some claim that allowing same-sex marriage would contribute to the erosion of *family values* in the Unites States, proponents argue that same-sex marriage would help to establish equality under the law for gays and lesbians. Broadly speaking, public opinions about same-sex marriage, and about the institution of marriage in general, underscore broader debates on citizenship, religion, and what it means to be a "proper" American.

WHAT IS MARRIAGE?

Marriage rights include a range of laws and policies, and concern legal as well as moral and religious dimensions. A civil marriage is typically a ritual-ized ceremony of commitment between two people to share a life together that is legally sanctioned by the state. The marriage license, issued by local govern-ment authorities, becomes a binding contract that provides access to numerous government protections and benefits that ensure financial and social security for couples and their children if they choose to create a larger family unit. Mar-riage is considered a core institution in the United States, and is often consid-ered important for social well-being and stability. Over 1,000 federal laws and benefits alone are tied to marriage. Marriage is also considered a core institution in religious communities, and religious institutions are very often the places that civil marriages are performed in conjunction with religious ceremonies based on church traditions. This intersection of church and state creates a contested terrain where conflicts arise on how marriage is defined, who has the right to define it, and ultimately who has the right to marry.

SUPPORTERS OF SAME-SEX MARRIAGE

Many liberal ideologies view the right to marry as a basic civil right that is denied same-sex couples based on discrimination against lesbian, gay, bisexual, and transgender individuals as a class of citizens. This view holds that marriage is a secular institution that should not be denied any citizen who wishes to claim this right. The argument continues that the denial of the right to marry inter-feres with an individual's right to life, liberty, and the pursuit of happiness, and violates a person's right to equal protection under the law. The 1967 Supreme Court decision *Loving et Ux. v. Virginia* (1967), which found laws banning inter-racial marriage as unconstitutional, is often used as a comparison to the ban-ning of same-sex marriage today. Justine Warren wrote in the majority decision, "marriage is one of the basic civil rights of men [*sic*]" and the freedom to marry is "one of the vital personal rights essential to the orderly pursuit of happiness by free men [*sic*]" (*Loving et Ux. v. Virginia* 1967).

While many gay rights activists support same-sex marriage, some believe that legalizing same-sex marriage would not in itself bring equality to gays

FAMOUS CASE 1

On February 12, 2004, Del Martin, age 84, and Phyllis Lyon, age 81, became the first legally married same-sex couple in U.S. history when, on the twelfth day in office, Mayor Gavin Newsom of San Francisco, California instructed the County Clerk to allow same-sex marriages. Mayor Newsom interpreted the marriage ban to be discriminatory and in violation of the equal protection clause in the California State Constitution. Intimate partners for over 50 years, Martin and Lyon's legally sanctioned marriage was short lived when on August 12, 2004, the California State Supreme Court declared that Mayor Newsom did not have the legal authority to change state marriage laws. Del Martin and Phyllis Lyon founded the first national lesbian rights organization, Daughters of Bilitis, in 1955.

On May 15, 2008, the Supreme Court of California overturned the state's ban on same-sex marriage. Beginning June 16, 2008, same-sex couples could legally marry in the state of California.

and lesbians, because it does not challenge the exclusionary nature of the institution of marriage, nor the state's role in regulating sexuality. For example, some scholars argue that marriage creates *selective legitimacy* as it necessarily privileges some couples over others and so, by definition, is discriminatory. Yet others argue that there are other more important issues to address than same-sex marriage: hate crimes and antigay violence, job discrimination, social and economic policies that privilege heterosexual over gay families, and lack of access to health care are just some of the issues that create additional daily inequalities and hardships for lesbian, gay and bisexual people according to this view.

DEFENDERS OF TRADITIONAL MARRIAGE

More conservative ideologies view marriage as a fundamental institution protected by the state to support a union between a man and a woman. In this view, marriage is seen as an institution that furthers procreation, protects the rearing of children, ensures the caretaking of families based on traditional gender roles, and creates financial security for the stability of society. For some religious traditions, marriage is viewed as an institution based in religious principles and ceremonies that do not support the right of same-sex couples to marry. Not all religious communities ban same-sex marriage, and heated debates have taken place within, and among religious communities about their views and institutional policies on same-sex marriage. There is a lack of consensus on this issue. Currently, some large churches that support same-sex marriage include the United Church of Christ, the Unitarian Universalist Association, the Episcopal Church, and the Evangelical Lutheran Church. The United Church of Christ has over one million members and is considered to be the first major U.S. Christian denomination to support same-sex marriage. The case for denying same-sex marriage is often based in religious beliefs that view homosexuality as morally wrong and against biblical teachings. The Christian Coalition, one of the most powerful conservative lobbying organizations in the nation, has developed an explicit political agenda to counter the same-sex marriage movement. According to conservative Christians, allowing same-sex marriage is considered an attack on traditional Christian notions of *family values* and on the institution of marriage; an institution they perceive as already unstable due to high divorce rates, single-parent families, and pregnancy without marriage.

STATE AND FEDERAL RESPONSES

Federal and state governments have played important roles in shaping the debate over same-sex marriage. It became a topic of significant national debate in 1993 when the Supreme Court of Hawaii in *Baehr v. Miike* (formerly known as *Baehr v. Lewin*) ruled that the denial of marriage licenses to same-sex couples was sex discrimination. This ruling fueled national fears that same-sex couples would marry in Hawaii and then return to their home states and expect their marriages to be recognized. In reality, states had the legal right to deny these marriages. The underlying debate was primarily a moral one about who should have the civil right to marry. Religious institutions wanted to maintain the power to decide this question for themselves and for society at large, and politicians began to see this as a possible wedge issue between conservatives and liberals to be exploited for political gain. As it turned out, same-sex marriages were never granted in Hawaii, because a state constitutional amendment passed after the ruling that defined marriage as a union between a man and a woman. This ruling, however, set the stage for the national dialogue that continues until today.

Because of the Hawaii ruling, and other cases that were making their way through state court systems, a few states began to pass legislation that defined marriage as a union between a man and a woman. This type of legislation, known as *defense of marriage* legislation, continues to be pushed as a way to disallow same-sex marriage legislation from being passed. While the federal government had historically taken the position that marriage law was a states' rights issue, it decided to enter the dialogue. In 1996, the U.S. Congress passed the *Defense of Marriage Act* (DOMA), which President William J. Clinton (1992–2000) signed into law. DOMA defined marriage, for federal purposes, as a union between one man and one woman. It also allowed states to not recognize the marriage laws of other states that grant same-sex marriage. As same-sex marriage proponents pointed out, this second clause was not necessary, as states already had this right. At the time the federal Defense of Marriage Act passed, no states allowed same-sex marriages. Nonetheless, following its enactment, a flood of states began passing their own state-level Defense of Marriage bills. Currently, 41 states have such laws. This appears to be a strong reaction to a hypothetical situation, but the passage of the Defense of Marriage Act represented the social sentiment that homosexuality is an illness, deviant and/or sinful, and that gay people do not deserve this right. In addition, to further reinforce this, numerous states went on to amend their constitutions to define marriage as a union between one man and one woman. To date, 19 states have amended their constitutions (National Conference on State Legislatures 2006). Many states also have strong citizen movements organized to oppose these legislative initiatives.

SAME-SEX MARRIAGE AND CIVIL UNIONS

Thus far, two types of legal partnership frameworks have been proposed for same-sex couples: marriage and civil unions. Same-sex couples currently are denied the right to legally marry in almost every state, although in some states they are allowed to form civil unions. The Massachusetts law came into effect in 2003, following the legal case of seven couples that were refused marriage licenses by city or town clerks and challenged the state law. In November 2003, *Goodridge v. Mass. Department of Public Health* was ruled on by the Massachusetts Supreme Court. The court ruled that the ban on same-sex marriage violated the state's constitution by denying due process and equal protection under the law to same-sex couples. The court argued that civil marriage is a government-created secular institution that all citizens have a right to benefit from, and that central to the state's legal definition of personal freedom and security is the assumption that the laws of the state will apply equally to all citizens. Based upon this ruling, the state legislature initially passed a "separate but equal" civil union law that conferred state rights and benefits to same-sex couples. Later, the Massachusetts Supreme Court ruled that a "separate but equal" civil union created second-class citizenship, and that it was not constitutionally acceptable. Rather, the court argued, only civil marriage would meet the standard set by the court (*Goodridge v. Mass. Department of Public Health* 2003). On May 17, 2004, Massachusetts became the first and only state to grant same-sex couples the right to marry. Obtaining the right to marry in Massachusetts was a historic moment for LGB people and their supporters. For the first time ever, same-sex couples had equal legal status with heterosexual couples, and in this regard it was seen as a civil rights' victory by supporters of same-sex marriage rights.

However, the backlash from the Massachusetts decision is significant, and continues today. Many same-sex marriage opponents fear that a case may someday be heard by the U.S. Supreme Court that will universally overturn the ban on same-sex marriage. As a result of this decision, President George W. Bush and other conservative politicians are calling for an amendment to the U.S. Constitution to further define marriage as a union between one man and one woman. In January 2005, the U.S. Senate Judiciary Committee passed a resolution to amend the federal constitution. In the spring of 2006, First Lady Laura Bush indicated in public statements that she does not believe a constitutional amendment defining marriage between a man and a woman should be used as a campaign strategy in the mid-year election cycle, illuminating how significant of a wedge issue same-sex marriage is between conservative and liberal politicians and their supporters. At the same time, the Majority Leader of the Senate, Republican Bill Frist, called for a debate of the full Senate on the constitutional amendment resolution. He claims an amendment to the U.S. Constitution is important in order to stop the attack on marriage by "activist judges" who are overturning defense

FAMOUS CASE 2

May 17, 2004 marked a historic day in the expansion of civil rights for same-sex couples when the first legally sanctioned marriages were performed in the state of Massachusetts. The Massachusetts State Supreme Court ruled in November of 2003 that the laws prohibiting same-sex couples from marrying violated the state constitution. Seven couples had sued for the right to marry. Massachusetts and Connecticut are the only states that currently allow same-sex couples to marry. A State Supreme Court decision in Vermont requires same-sex couples to have access to the same benefits that married couples are given; creating a *separate but equal* status called a civil union.

Do such unions promote equality? Should they be viewed as equivalent to marriage?

---

of marriage laws in states. Although such a resolution has not yet progressed through Congress at the time of this writing, President Bush and other conservative politicians and religious sectors continue to support it.

Opposition to same-sex marriage also continues at the state level, where there has been a significant push to amend state constitutions to define marriage as a union between a man and a woman. In some cases, those amendments also void domestic partnership laws. Currently, 19 states have successfully amended their constitutions; a victory for opponents who fear that the institution of marriage will deteriorate if marriage rights are extended to gay and lesbian couples. Proponents point out that these *defense of marriage* laws have had unintended consequences for same-sex as well as heterosexual couples. For example, in the state of Ohio, the constitutional amendment effectively banned same-sex marriage, and all domestic partnership arrangements in the state. This more encompassing attack made void, among other things, domestic violence laws that protected intimate partners in nonmarital relationships, and domestic partner laws and policies for heterosexual couples. Seven additional states currently have amendments to ban same-sex marriage on their ballots.

CONCLUSION

The debate over same-sex marriage will likely continue into the foreseeable future. It is difficult to determine what the outcome will be in the legal and public policy arenas. To date, most state and federal legislation continues to ban same-sex couples from marriage laws. Only two states have granted this right, and perhaps one or two more will grant this right in the near future. While numerous municipalities (over 60) have set up domestic partnership registries that offer recognition to same-sex and opposite-sex partners, states play the leading role in making major public policy decisions in this arena. At the same time, federal politicians opposing same-sex marriage continue to push for more significant federal action by amending the U.S. Constitution. While Americans have increasingly shown more support for same-sex marriage in general population surveys, the votes still show a largely divided public on the issue. However, the majority of Americans do not feel the U.S. Constitution should be amended to ban same-sex marriage. And so, the debate continues.

See also Homosexuality; Marriage, Sexuality, and Celibacy.

Further Reading: Boswell, John. *Christianity, Social Tolerance, and Homosexuality.* Chicago: University of Chicago Press, 1980; Brandzel, Amy. "Queering Citizenship? Same-Sex Marriage and the State." *GLQ: A Journal of Lesbian and Gay Studies* 11, no. 2 (2005): 171–204; Cahill, Sean. *Same-Sex Marriage in the United States: Focus on the Facts.* Lanham, MD: Rowman and Littlefield, 2004; Chambers, D. 2001. "What If? The Legal Consequences of Marriage and the Legal Needs of Lesbian and Gay Male Couples." In *Queer Families, Queer Politics: Challenging Culture and the State,* eds. Bernstein and Reimann. New York: Columbia University Press, 2001: 306–337; Chauncey, G. *Why Marriage? The History Shaping Today's Debate Over Gay Equality.* Basic Books, 2004; de Sève, Jim. *Tying the Knot.* Outcast Films, 2005; Epstein, Steven. "Gay and Lesbian Movements in the United States: Dilemmas of Identity, Diversity, and Political Strategy." In *The Global Emergence of Gay and Lesbian Politics: National Imprints of a Worldwide Movement,* eds. Barry D. Adam, Jan Willem Duyvendak, and André Krouwel. Temple University Press, 1999: 30–90; Eskridge, William. *The Case for Same-Sex Marriage: from Sexual Liberty to Civilized Commitment.* Free Press, 1996; Gerstmann, Evan. *Same-Sex Marriage and the Constitution.* Cambridge University Press, 2004; Glassman, Anthony. "United Church of Christ Endorses Marriage Equality." *Gay People's Chronicle,* Cleveland, Ohio, July 8, 2005; Goldberg-Hiller, Johnathan. *The Limits to Union: Same-Sex Marriage and the Politics of Civil Rights.* University of Michigan Press, 2002; National Conference on State Legislatures. "Same Sex Marriage Policy Information." 2006. http://www.ncsl.org/programs/cyf/samesex.htm; Sullivan, Andrew. *Same-Sex Marriage: Pro and Con.* Knopf Publishing Group, 2004; United Church of Christ Coalition for Lesbian, Gay, Bisexual and Transgender Concerns. 2006. http://www.ucccoalition.org; Warner, Michael. *The Trouble with Normal: Sex, Politics, and the Ethics of Queer Life.* Harvard University Press, 1999; Wolfson, Evan. *Why Marriage Matters: America, Equality, and Gay People's Right To Marry.* Simon and Schuster, 2004.

Jack Balswick and Judith K. Balswick

SANCTUARY MOVEMENT

In the 1970s and 1980s undocumented Central Americans fled civil war and brutal conflicts in their home countries of El Salvador, Guatemala, and Nicaragua for the United States. These people were not officially recognized as refugees by the United States' government. The Sanctuary Movement is a grassroots, religious-based, ecumenical coalition that provides support and advocacy for these undocumented people. After the fall of the Berlin wall and the U.S. economic and foreign policies that changed in its wake, the Sanctuary Movement continued to be a group advocating for the just and equitable treatment of immigrants. The movement continues today to work for change in U.S. foreign and domestic policy toward illegal immigrants and migrant workers.

The Sanctuary Movement began in the early 1980s as a response to several different events. The first, the assassination of Oscar Romero on March 24, 1980, brought the unstable political situation in El Salvador home to many American Catholics, Jews, and Protestant peace tradition churches. Romero's assassination was followed in December 1980 by the brutal rape and murder of three U.S. nuns and a lay worker in El Salvador. While the Reagan administration was largely silent on these issues, these events mobilized American churches and synagogues. In addition, an influx of immigrants across the borders of California, Arizona, New Mexico, and Texas caused a humanitarian crisis on the border, and the tremendous human suffering and anguish spurred action by churches in order to aid in the plight of those undocumented immigrants.

On March 24, 1982, the second anniversary of Romero's assassination, Rev. John Fife of Southside Presbyterian church in Tucson, Arizona, along with five churches in Northern California, issued a declaration of public safety, and stated that their churches and synagogues were safe havens for Salvadoran and Guatemalan refugees. Through this network of churches, the Sanctuary Movement worked to raise public awareness of the situation in Central America, and to find legal means to help the undocumented migrants. The Sanctuary Movement sought to rectify a failure in U.S. immigration policy toward people who the U.S. government had classified as undocumented workers. Instead, the Sanctuary Movement understood these people as refugees seeking political asylum, and sought to change U.S. immigration law accordingly. The Sanctuary Movement believed that answering the humanitarian need of these refugees was a higher law than the U.S. policy that did not recognize Central Americans seeking political asylum. Moreover, the Sanctuary Movement put itself at risk as the U.S. government referred to the refugees as illegal immigrants, and helping those immigrants enter the country, or providing them with support was illegal.

Many of these religious people were moved by the plights of the refugees, who told stories of torture, disappearances, and brutality. Within the movement, however, there was tension over the issue of what kind of relationship the churches should have toward the official U.S. policy, and to what extent the movement should challenge the law. While many churches understood their work on the behalf of Central Americans as civil disobedience, others understood churches to have a responsibility to protest and actively disregard laws that were unjust or violated human rights. Many sanctuary workers held the U.S. position on Central America to be a violation of its own laws, and therefore conceived of their actions as a necessary response to the unjust and hypocritical position of the Reagan administration. Sanctuary workers argued they were upholding humanitarian laws the United States had put into place years before, to deal with Vietnamese and Laotian refugees. Others understood their work with the refugees to be a kind of religious practice, born from their faith, and in response to Leviticus 19:33–34, which was a central part of the declaration of the Sanctuary Movement. "Remember that you were a stranger, and do justice by the stranger, for remember you were strangers in the Land of Egypt. When a stranger resides with you in your land do him no wrong. Treat him as you would treat yourself, for remember you were strangers in the Land of Egypt." This division led to a separation of foci within the movement itself.

There are two different orientations within the Sanctuary Movement. The first is humanitarian. This perspective understands the goal of the churches to be one that is upholding basically good but inadequate immigration and amnesty laws. Rather than understanding their support of Central Americans as critical of the United States' policies, this perspective believes their actions are enforcing a policy that has been misinterpreted, and will eventually return to the interpretation that recognizes undocumented Central Americans as refugees. The second orientation is political, and understands the Sanctuary Movement's actions as acts of civil disobedience, which they identify as "civil initiative," against the unjust and indefensible policies of the U.S. government. The political perspective seeks an alliance that will build a coalition among refugees from all parts of the world (for example, Haiti), and among social justice movements, regardless of faith perspective.

The *founders* of this movement are Quaker Jim Corbett (1933–2001), Rev. John Fife of Southside Presbyterian Church in Tucson, and Fr. Ricardo Elford, a Roman Catholic priest. From a Quaker heritage, Corbett had been working on social justice issues for most of his life. He dedicated the latter years of his life to help Central American refugees seek legal support from the United States' government and, when that support was not forthcoming, helped refugees stay in the United States illegally. The goals of the Sanctuary Movement were to provide assistance to detainees who were applying for political asylum, to provide social services for refugee communities, to actively protest human rights abuses in Central America by writing and sending telegrams to Congress, to organize press conferences, and, through selling Central American arts and crafts, raise public awareness about the plight of those Central Americans. From these origins three centers emerged—the Arizona borderlands, Northern California, and Chicago. By declaring churches subject to a higher law, movement workers hid refugees, and eventually helped them relocate through the underground railroad that developed though the efforts of churches and synagogues committed to the movement. The Chicago Religious Task Force on Central America (CRTFCA) eventually became coordinator for the underground railroad that helped Central American refugees resettle in the United States or Canada. The Tucson Ecumenical Council (TEC) focused on getting immigrants into the United States and acted as a legal advocate for them. While TEC and CRTFCA initially worked together, eventually the two groups became irreconcilably divided over issues of how to treat the political usefulness of refugees to achieve policy change in the United States. The Chicago group decided to strategically focus on high-profile immigrant cases that would be more likely to sway public opinion, allowing other immigrants who, for one reason or another, could not stand the public scrutiny, to be deported. The Tucson group, on the other hand, was committed to settling all immigrants who came to them for help, regardless of the publicity. The two groups evolved into a national grassroots resettlement effort (TEC and San Francisco and Bay area churches and synagogues), on the one hand, and a national network of antiwar activists (CRTFCA) on the other. This distinction was based primarily on proximity to the U.S.-Mexico border, and the immediacy of the humanitarian crisis brought on by the challenges of border crossing.

At its height in the mid-1980s, the Sanctuary Movement included 200 religious orders and congregations across the United States, and more than 600 religious organizations, including the National Federation of Priests' Councils (representing more than 33,000 Catholic priests). Notably, the National Association of Evangelicals did not sign the Sanctuary Declaration, and distanced itself from the movement. In 1984, Jim Corbett was awarded the Letelier-Moffitt Human Rights Award on behalf of the movement.

The first effort in the Sanctuary Movement was to bail out people who had been held in detention centers in the Southwest. Corbett, along with other pastors in the Southwest, raised $100,000 to bail out a hundred refugees who had been abandoned in the desert and left to die in the harsh conditions. However, even after that bail out, many were sent back to El Salvador, even though they had reason to believe that their lives were in danger if they went back. There were two methods that members of the Sanctuary Movement used to help people find a safe haven in the United States. The first method involved helping Central Americans cross the Mexico-U.S. border and bringing them to member churches who would offer them help with legal fees in order to apply for asylum, acquire housing, and other kinds of support. This was the most legally risky for members of the movement, because it openly violated the U.S. law forbidding aid to illegal immigrants. The second method involved U.S. sanctuary workers traveling to Central America in order to accompany Central Americans to the Mexico-U.S. border. This avoided the legal risks of transporting illegal aliens in the United States, because they did not actually cross but just helped them too the border, but was very dangerous for the Americans in El Salvador, Guatemala, or Nicaragua, who could be targeted by governmental or paramilitary groups who caused the refugees to flee in the first place. The members who traveled to Central America and helped refugees come to the United States were subject to suspicion in Central America, and possible detention or imprisonment in El Salvador, Guatemala, Nicaragua, and Mexico as they made the journey north with the refugees.

In 1985 the Department of Justice (DOJ) brought charges against 14 members of the Sanctuary Movement, though ultimately only 11 faced trial. The majority of the defendants in the DOJ case against the Sanctuary Movement came from the TEC. The DOJ had infiltrated the Southside Presbyterian Church through an informant, and put together a case against the movement. The DOJ charged the Sanctuary Movement members with alien smuggling, conspiracy, recruiting, transporting, and harboring illegal aliens. Over 100 persons were listed as un-indicted coconspirators. The government argued that the undocumented Central Americans were criminals, illegally entering the United States for economic prosperity and not because of political persecution. During the trial, the government sought to differentiate religious action and political action, accusing the Sanctuary workers of conflating the two, and taking immigration law into their own hands. While the defendants were optimistic that the movement would be vindicated, the focus of the trial was not on the reason for the illegal immigration, or even the definition of refugees versus illegal immigrants, but rather, the prosecution focused on the efforts of movement members to evade or circumvent U.S. law. The judge banned testimony about persecution in the refugees' home countries and the defendants' motives for providing sanctuary. In the end, eight of the sanctuary workers were convicted. They were sentenced to probation, and forbidden to participate in any further Sanctuary Movement activities.

The Reagan administration's official position was that Central American immigrants were not refugees but were "seeking a better life for themselves by finding better employment" in the United States, according to Elliott Abrams in 1983 during his tenure as Assistant Secretary of State for Human Rights and Humanitarian Affairs. From the point of view of the Reagan government, to grant Central Americans asylum would be tantamount to admitting those people were in fact persecuted, and would expose the involvement of the U.S. government in that persecution. The Reagan administration saw the Salvadoran and Guatemalan immigrants as illegal aliens who should be deported. The Reagan administration minimized the human rights' violations in El Salvador and Guatemala, emphasizing instead the leftist leanings of the guerrillas in those countries. The crux of the debate about the Sanctuary Movement hinges on this issue. If the immigrants are illegally entering the United States as economic immigrants aided by U.S. citizens, as the Reagan administration argued in the trial, then those citizens are breaking the law.

The Sanctuary Movement's defense hinged on the interpretation of United States law regarding political asylum and refugees. They argued that the U.S. government had laws that protected people seeking political asylum, and in the case of El Salvador and Guatemala, the government was ignoring that law. The Sanctuary Movement argued that they were not committing acts of civil disobedience, but civil initiative, upholding laws their government disregarded. The Sanctuary Movement attorneys argued that the workers were not "smuggling," because their immigrants were refugees who had legitimate asylum claims.

Despite the trial and the criminalization of their activities, the Sanctuary Movement continued to help Central American refugees throughout the 1980s. During the 1990s and early 2000s, the Sanctuary Movement often worked with refugees from Africa. They also continued their work with illegal immigrants from Mexico and Central and South America. Currently, the New Sanctuary Movement has expanded, and includes legal and humanitarian agencies as well as churches and synagogues across the country. The movement is self-consciously faith-oriented and maintains a strong connection to Christian social justice initiatives. The New Sanctuary Movement website pledge includes this statement: "The New Sanctuary Movement is a coalition of interfaith religious leaders and participating congregations, called by our faith to respond actively and publicly to the suffering of our immigrant brothers and sisters residing in the United States" (www.newsanctuarymovement. org). Recognizing the complex economic and historical context of immigration in the United States, the New Sanctuary Movement seeks to change legislation that discriminates against immigrants, and to protect immigrants from hate, discrimination in the workplace, and forced deportation.

In conjunction with several border-area churches, including the American Friends Service Committee, Southside Presbyterian Church supports humanitarian aid programs such as No More Deaths (No Mas Muertes). No More Deaths is an organization whose "mission is to end death and suffering on the U.S./Mexico border through civil initiative: the conviction that people of conscience must work openly and in community to uphold fundamental human rights" (www.nomoredeaths.org). The organization was given the Oscar Romero Award for Human Rights in Houston, Texas on April 2007. This award recognizes the organization's contribution to humanitarian aid along the U.S.-Mexico border. The award was presented to Daniel Strauss and Shanti Sellz, who were arrested for offering medical aid to migrants in the Sonora Desert. Because the United States has no official policy regarding humanitarian aid on the border, activists such as Strauss and Sellz are in danger of being charged for violating federal laws regarding transporting and harboring illegal aliens. Strauss and Sellz were charged with transporting undocumented migrants in 2005, when they transported three severely ill migrants to a hospital. In September 2006 the charges were dismissed. The case against Strauss and Sellz drew international attention to the region and the problems of the U.S.-Mexico border area.

What remains to be seen is the future of such sanctuary movements. With the rise of border vigilantism like the Minutemen, and the current rhetorical invective against illegal immigration coming from conservatives and even some Democrats, the future looks uncertain for these movements. It is difficult to see how movements concerned with humanitarian issues can stand against the new rise of nationalist xenophobia that has dominated the nation's discourse. The 2005 failure of immigration reform, showed the power of these anti-immigrant forces. What will remain are small groups and churches who will focus on the needs of these people regardless of the vagaries of politics or law. They will continue to follow their "higher law."

See also Bible and Poverty; Immigration.

Further Reading: Coutin, Susan Bibler. "The Culture of Protest: Religious Activism and the U.S. Sanctuary Movement." In *Conflict and Social Change Series*, eds. Scott Whiteford and William Derman. Boulder, CO: Westview Press, 1993; Coutin, Susan Bibler. "Smugglers or Samaritans in Tucson, Arizona: Producing and Contesting Legal Truth." *American Ethnologist*, vol. 22, no. 3 (August 1995): 549–571; Davidson, Miriam. *Convictions of the Heart: Jim Corbett and the Sanctuary Movement*. Tucson, AZ: University of Arizona Press, 1988; Golden, Renny and Michael McConnell. *Sanctuary: The New Underground Railroad*. New York: Orbis Books, 1986; Lorentzen, Robin. "Women in the Sanctuary Movement." In *Women in the Political Economy Series*, ed. Ronnie J. Steinberg. Philadelphia: Temple University Press, 1991; No More Deaths/No Mas Muertes. http://nomoredeaths.org; Sanctuary Movement Homepage. http://www.newsanctuarymovement.org/pledge.htm; Southside Presbyterian Homepage. http://www.southsidepresbyterian.org; Tomsho, Robert. *The American Sanctuary Movement*. Austin, TX: Texas Monthly Press, 1987.

Laura Ammon

school with an interpreter. The majority held that the presence of the interpreter would not "add to the religious environment" and therefore did not constitute either excessive entanglement or promotion of religion (www.findlaw.com).

Additionally, in *Witters v. Washington Department of Services for the Blind*, the Court held that a tuition grant could be given to an individual who wanted to go to a Christian college without violating the establishment clause. Using the Lemon test, the Court found that because the aid was going to the individual, the state was supporting the individual, not the institution. Therefore, even if a religious school ultimately benefited, the purpose of the program was secular in intent, did not create an entanglement between church and state, and did not support religion. Thus, the program did not violate the establishment clause. The combination of *Zorbrest* and *Witters'* decisions gave the Court license to allow public school teachers to teach in private schools in *Agnostini*.

More recently, the Court has continued in the permissive tradition of *Cochran* and *Lemon* in *Mitchell v. Helms* (2000) (www.findlaw.com). The Court here once again asserted the ability of the states to provide material for religious schools. However in *Helms*, the latitude of the states was significantly expanded to include computers, and other instructional materials. The majority was divided on how broadly its decision was applicable, with Rehnquist, Scalia, Thomas, and Kennedy arguing for a very open policy of government support, while O'Connor and Breyer were more restrained in their concurring opinion (www.findlaw.com).

VOUCHERS

In 2002, the Supreme Court addressed the issue of vouchers with a suit that tested the constitutionality of a voucher program established in Cleveland, Ohio (www.findlaw.com). The Cleveland Scholarship and Tutoring Program (CSTP), ratified by the Ohio Legislature in 1995, is a voucher program that provides parents a voucher that can be used to pay for tuition at private or religious schools. The program is need-based, giving those families whose income is below 200 percent of the poverty level 90 percent of tuition costs or $2,250 (whichever is less). Families above 200 percent of the poverty level received 75 percent or $1,875 (whichever is less). These figures have since been raised, and are now linked to the Consumer Price Index. Originally the program included only K-8th grade students in the Cleveland Municipal School District (though only students who did not require separate special education), but was expanded in 2003 to 2004 to include 9th grade and above. Since the Court ruled, the program has been made statewide. This established the first large-scale voucher program.

The program allowed parents to use the vouchers to enroll their children in private charter schools. The majority of schools affected by the voucher program were in fact religious schools. The law was challenged on the grounds that it provided monetary support of religious institutions, thus violating the establishment clause of the First Amendment.

The first opinion was from a three-judge panel from the Sixth Circuit Court of Appeals, which had ruled against the Cleveland voucher program. In *Simmon-Harris v. Zelman* the majority ruled "there is no neutral aid when that aid principally flows to religious institutions." However when the Supreme Court reviewed the ruling it took a quite different approach (www.findlaw.com).

It would seem that the controlling decision for such a case such as *Zelman* would be *Lemon*. However the recent events had made it clear that *Lemon* might ultimately be sidelined. The request of the Bush (Sr.) administration to review the Lemon decision, indicated that conservatives felt the Lemon test was too restrictive. Justice Rehnquist had also noted that Lemon was not as solid as it once had been, and had been questioned at various points by a variety of justices and ignored in some key establishment cases.

Likewise, when it came to the issue of public funding of parochial schools, the history of the Court was much more unpredictable. In *Agnostini v. Felton* the majority consisted of Justices O'Connor, Rehnquist, Scalia, Thomas, and Kennedy. This five to four decision showed that the Court had changed its thinking on the establishment clause. Justice O'Connor's comments in her opinion are very telling, "What has changed since we decided *Ball* and *Aguilar* is our understanding of the criteria used to assess whether aid to religion has an impermissible effect." In *Agnostini* the answer to that question was clearly it did not create an "impermissible effect" (www.findlaw.com).

The issue of vouchers is much akin to both *Agnostini* and *Witter*. If vouchers are given to the parents and not directly to religious schools, the logic of *Witter* would prevail. By the Court's current understanding of the Lemon test, such aid would not be seen to infringe on the establishment clause. The combination of the conservative block on the Court, coupled with the moderates of O'Connor and Kennedy, could very well have been expected to find vouchers constitutional.

Clearly the major issue, as court history might indicate, is whether this was another attempt at public funding for religious institutions. As the appeals' court quote above indicates, that court concluded it was, and therefore found it unconstitutional. The Supreme Court, however, took a different view. It ruled that the program was secular in its intention; it provided parents of the Cleveland schools an opportunity to choose to send their children to a number of schools; public, private, and religious. That Cleveland has a large number of religious schools, and therefore a large number of parents who availed themselves of the program (82%) sent their children to private religious schools, was ultimately immaterial. As Justice Rehnquist said in his opinion,

> To attribute constitutional significance to the 82% figure would lead to the absurd result that a neutral school-choice program might be permissible in parts of Ohio where the percentage is lower, but not in Cleveland, where Ohio has deemed such programs most sorely needed. (www.findlaw.com)

In her concurring opinion Sandra Day O'Connor addressed the math of this decision explicitly. Reiterating that there are in fact a number of options aside from private religious schools, Justice O'Connor notes,

When one considers the option to attend community schools, the percentage of students enrolled in religious schools falls to 62.1 percent. If magnet schools are included in the mix, this percentage falls to 16.5 percent. (www.findlaw.com)

Additionally, the fact that only partial scholarships are provided for religious institutions, while magnet and charter schools are provided full funding, is more evidence that the establishment clause has not been violated because money as an incentive was clearly focused on nonreligious options.

Justice Rehnquist wrote the opinion of the court. The basis of the decision for him was not *Lemon,* but was ultimately based on those precedents where the court had focused on individual choice (*Muller v. Allen, Witters v. The Washington Dept. Services for the Blind,* and *Zobrest v. Catalina Foothills School District*). In each of these cases, Rehnquist argues, the right of individual choice trumps the challenge to the establishment clause. As long as individuals make the choice where the money is spent, and there are nonreligious alternatives, there is no violation of the establishment clause to be found.

While Justice Rehnquist did not find *Lemon* relevant in his decision, Justice O'Connor did. In her concurring opinion she argues that the court was, in fact, still upholding *Lemon* as modified by subsequent cases. Instead, Justice O'Connor talks about a "refinement" of *Lemon* by reiterating Justice Rehnquist's theme of "choice."

> What the Court clarifies in these cases is that the Establishment Clause also requires that state aid flowing to religious organizations through the hands of beneficiaries must do so only at the direction of those beneficiaries. (www.findlaw.com)

It is the beneficiaries who choose where the state money may go, and thus it does not create a constitutional violation.

Since the Courts' decision in *Zelman* a number of states have started their own local voucher programs, though most are small pilot programs. Ohio leads the nation once again by establishing the first state-wide voucher program. Nonetheless, the benefits of voucher programs in terms of student achievement are still highly debated. The studies that have been done have found mixed results, and have been hampered by the small sample size of most voucher programs. At this point, the battle over vouchers has shifted to the state courts, where they have been ruled unconstitutional in two states (Florida and Colorado). Other states, however, may soon join the fray, and congress looks to take up a national program sometime soon. There is no doubt that the issue of vouchers will continue to be important in the United States debate on education.

FAITH-BASED INITIATIVES

The other issue that pertains to the issue of public funding of religious institutions is President George W. Bush's program of government support for faith-based charities engaged in social services work. Starting in 2001,

President George W. Bush signed a series of Executive Orders that brought into being the Faith-Based and Community Initiatives Office. These orders also established Faith-Based and Community Initiative centers throughout the various departments of the executive branch (Justice, Education, HUD, Labor, etc.). The goal of these orders was to break down barriers restricting the application of government monies to faith-based organizations for community service. Importantly, from the perspective of public education, the requirement of the *No Child Left Behind* legislation that mandated supplemental educational services (such as after-school tutoring, summer intensive programs, etc.) for failing schools, has now become an available venue for faith-based organizations.

The legal history of this program has been mixed, with lower courts deciding for the Bush administration in late 2005, but the Faith-Based Initiative Office was forced to suspend another grant program because of the threat of a lawsuit (Cooperman 2005, A25). No cases have made it as high as the Supreme Court yet.

However, the question of the program's constitutionality remains. It is possible the court will find the program constitutional in the end. The argument for deciding this was laid out by Justice Rehnquist in his dissent in *Edwards v. Aguillard* (www.findlaw.com). There, Rehnquist argued that motivation was not a determinant in deciding establishment. Rehnquist, in fact, makes this argument in regards to social services when he says, "We surely would not strike down a law providing money to feed the hungry or shelter the homeless if it could be demonstrated that, but for the religious beliefs of the legislators, the funds would not have been approved. Also, political activism by the religiously motivated is part of our heritage." Provided that bureaucratic structures are in place that insulate the proselytizing functions from the social functions, it is possible that this program would pass the Lemon Test.

However, two additional considerations should be noted. First, the Supreme Court has had a history of divining intentions behind a law. In the Louisiana *Balanced Treatment Act* (which allowed teaching creationist alternatives to evolution in the public schools), the legislature had discussed at length in hearings the constitutional issues, and specifically formulated the law in an attempt to avoid those issues. The Court, nevertheless, determined that the true intent was the promotion of a religious belief, not the offering of "all the evidence." While the facts in the case of President Bush's program would certainly be different, if the Court thought that the intent of the program was the advancement of religious institutions, it may well rule that the program violated the establishment clause.

Second, exclusive aid of religious institutions was specifically banned in *Everson*. This decision included both the privileging of one group over another, or the help of religion in general. Much of the controversy regarding Bush's program is vis-à-vis different religious groups. For instance, will the Nation of Islam be included despite its leader's comments on Jews? Will neo-pagan groups, like the Wiccans who many Christians see as a satanic threat, be eligible? Any attempt to distinguish between prima facie religious groups may quickly run afoul of the establishment clause.

With the change in the makeup of the court from the Rehnquist court to the Roberts court, any prediction regarding the constitutionality of Faith-Based Initiatives becomes difficult. However, it is worth noting that the GAO's report on Faith-Based Initiatives in 2006 shows that governmental departments are not making the necessary distinctions that the Court has in the past required (GAO 2006). Appropriate *safeguards* were mandated in the Executive Order 13279 in 2002. However, the GAO's report indicated that such *safeguards* have not been explicitly given to Faith-Based Organizations participating in the program and that much confusion remains. It may be that ultimately it is this that becomes the grounds upon which the program is challenged.

CONCLUSION

The battle over the establishment clause continues on in American public discourse and jurisprudence. The handful of words provided by the framers of the Bill of Rights has actually produced a host of court cases, as the practical meaning of those words is defined and redefined by the Supreme Court. The makeup of the Court continues to be important in what sort of decisions it ultimately reaches. With new members joining the Court it remains to be seen whether the path the Rehnquist Court took will continue.

With the continued criticisms of public schools that have followed the passage of the *No Child Left Behind* law, the turn to private alternatives may increase. The decision on vouchers still shows that while the Court has previously been reluctant to give carte blanche to public funding of religious schools, it has opened the door to see them as an alternative, particularly in districts that are considered *failures*. What future decisions will hold, remain to be seen.

See also Homeschooling; Separation of Church and State.

Further Reading: The text of all Appellate and Supreme Court decisions may be found at http://www.findlaw.com; Belfield, Clive R. "The Evidence on Education Vouchers: An Application to the Cleveland Scholarship and Tutoring Program." National Center For The Study of Privatization in Education. January 2006; Black, Amy E., Douglas L. Koopman, and David K. Ryden. *Of little faith: the politics of George W. Bush's faith-based initiatives.* Washington, D.C.: Georgetown University Press, 2004; Bush, George W. "Rallying the armies of compassion." Washington, D.C.: Executive Office of the President, 2001. http://www.purl.access.gpo.gov/GPO/LPS18666; Cooperman, Alan. "Bush's Faith Plan Faces Judgment." *Washington Post,* October 20, p. A25; Eastland, Terry ed., *Religious liberty in the Supreme Court: the cases that define the debate over church and state.* Washington, DC : Ethics and Public Policy Center, 1993; Government Accountability Office. "Faith-Based and Community Initiative: Improvements in Monitoring Grantees and Measuring Performance Could Enhance Accountability." GAO-06-616. June 19, 2006; Moe, Terry M. *Schools, vouchers, and the American public.* Washington, D.C.: Brookings Institution Press, 2001; Noll, James Wm. ed., *Taking sides. Clashing views on controversial educational issues.* Introduction by James Wm. Noll. Guilford, CT: McGraw Hill/Dushkin, 2004; Peterson, Paul E., Bryan C. Hassel, eds. *Learning from school choice.* Washington, D.C.: Brookings Institution Press, 1998; Pulliam, John D., and James J. Van Patten. *History of Education in America.* 7th ed. Columbus, OH: Prentice Hall, 1995, 1999; The White House. "Unlevel Playing Field: Barriers to Participation by Faith-Based and Community Organizations in Federal Social Service Programs." Washington, D.C.: The White House, 2001. http://www.purl.access.gpo.gov/GPO/LPS16590.

Randall Reed

SCIENCE FICTION

Mary Shelley's 1818 classic, *Frankenstein,* tells the story of a man who aspired to play God and a creature in search of his own existence, expresses the themes of man's relationship with God, and demonstrates the conflict of the spiritual (or supernatural) versus the material and the sense there is a greater order and purpose in the universe have captivated authors and readers alike for generations.

Publisher's Weekly reports that interest in religiously oriented science fiction (SF) has been steadily increasing, prompting many publishers to reprint past titles that have long been considered classic SF–religion hybrids such as *A Canticle For Leibowitz* (see the following section "Apocalyptic SF Visions"). *Publisher's Weekly* also observed that perennial titles such as Frank Herbert's Dune trilogy and Philip Pullman's The Golden Compass series continue to be popular with each new generation of readers (McKee 2007, xi). Both of these popular series explore the battle of good versus evil, our search for the meaning of our human existence, and the search for salvation. Novels such as Mary Doria Russell's *The Sparrow* and *Children of God,* which chronicle the adventures of Jesuit priest Emilo Sandoz on the planet Rakhat, or the Left Behind series by evangelist minister Tim LaHaye and writer Jerry B. Jenkins, have religion or religious characters as the focus of their story.

Many literary pundits have declared that religious themes have no place in science fiction and that when religion becomes a dominant element in a story, it leaves the realm of speculative "science" (the argument being that science and religion are incompatible) and moves into fantasy—it can be argued that in many ways the two are inextricably intertwined. In fact, many science fiction novels and short stories center around the battle between science and religion. "Science fiction creates a mystic point of view that doesn't deny the other side of the world, the devil's madness," says Greg Bear, a top-selling science fiction author (Winston 2001, 35). What is our quest to reach for the stars, or our need to explore the unknown, if not a search for a better understanding of our place in the universe, the meaning of our existence, and our relationship with God? "SF peers into the mystery of the unknown," Gabriel McKee argues, "bringing our most ancient cosmic questions into the future and anticipating the answers we may uncover. Whether the gods we find are powerful aliens, immortal versions of ourselves, or vast cosmic minds, the future is certain to hold countless secrets to surprise and inspire us" (McKee 2007, 20).

THE BATTLE OF SCIENCE AND RELIGION

In the West, science and religion (a.k.a. the secular and divine) have been at each other's throats for over a millennium, and for much of this antagonistic history, the Church used an iron fist to quash anything that might reek of heresy or contradiction to its teachings, especially when it came to the nature of the universe or the creation of the Earth. In the Age of Enlightenment, science and secularism fought back with ardent fervor, the most obvious result being a separation of church and state. This era also created an attitude within the scientific community that there was no place for religion in science; that, in fact, religion was the enemy of science. Reason and not faith should dictate truth.

Not surprisingly, many authors of science fiction have made this conflict the centerpiece of their stories. Some have taken the not so subtle position that science is indeed evil, possibly in league with Satan himself. Much of this stems from an identification of science as representing not only humankind's focus on the material world but also our hubris at believing we are the center of the universe. Others have explored the premise that because the existence of God cannot be scientifically proven, God cannot possibly exist; not necessarily a direct challenge to faith, but a claim that the two are forever separate. Another group of SF stories explore the idea that faith and religion are not only compatible with science but also indeed intertwined. Some stories offer speculation that science might one day be able to prove the existence of an intelligent force that could be called God, others warn that God can never be proven by science. Only faith can prove God's existence, confirming the famous Buddhist expression, "if you meet Buddha on the road, kill him," which somewhat dramatically expresses the notion that the divine can only be seen through the eyes of faith, and will never be manifest in the material world. As Gabriel McKee states, "[s]cience can determine the value of an empirical theory, but not a spiritual experience, just as theology is of little practical use in the questions of chemistry or physics" (McKee 2007, 154). Arthur C. Clarke's famous 1953 short-story *The Nine Billion Names of God* gives the somewhat chilling warning that if we were able to scientifically prove the existence of God, it would probably mean the end of our own existence.

The unapologetic Christian author C. S. Lewis is best known for his fantasy series, The Chronicles of Narnia, an allegorical expression of faith and salvation. Lewis also penned the classic science fiction trilogy, *Out of the Silent Planet* (1938), *Perelandra* (1943), and *That Hideous Strength* (1945), which while directly portraying science as aggressively evil and contrary to Christian ideals, simultaneously puts forth the notion that scientific exploration may end up confirming the existence of Christ. In the first book, *Out of the Silent Planet*, we are introduced to Edwin Ransom, a philologist (a language historian) who is kidnapped by an evil scientist and finds himself on another planet. The scientist and his industrialist partner have brought Ransom to offer him up as a human sacrifice to the local indigenous people in the hopes of securing the rights to mine their valuable natural resources. Ransom escapes and finds himself among a primitive but kindly race that takes him in and gives him shelter. Because of his skills as a linguist, he is quickly able to communicate with them. Soon, he is introduced to the spiritual leader of the indigenous people who is, at least to Ransom, a manifestation of Jesus Christ. Ransom is able, with the help of this manifestation, to defeat the evil scientist and save the planet from exploitation. In the second novel, *Perelandra*, Ransom again must do battle against his nemesis, now on a planet, Perelandra, that is just beginning to awaken to the presence of God. This time, however, the scientist is outright possessed by Satan, and an epic battle for the souls of the inhabitants of Perelandra ensues and Ransom barely survives. In the final installment, *That Hideous Strength*, the battlefront is taken to Earth itself (a.k.a The Silent Planet). Satan's minions are now in control of scientific and technological development, preparing to ensnare humankind's souls through their dependence on their inventions. In the end, the faithful (led by Ransom) are able to defeat evil and save the world.

A similar if more secular view is explored in Kurt Vonnegut's *Cat's Cradle* (1963). Through hubris, greed, and the quest for power, "ice-nine" is inadvertently unleashed upon the world, freezing solid all liquid and any organic organism that it comes in contact with. The result is a bleak world with a dwindling population of humans whose only refuge is Bokononism, a wry and cynical religion/philosophy, that exposes for its followers the folly of man's efforts but unfortunately does nothing to forestall the inevitable destruction of Earth. Much of Vonnegut's intent is to make us painfully aware of a journey driven by aggressive technology at the expense of improving our own enlightenment.

In Ben Bova's The Grand Tour series, religious fundamentalists control the world while governments and scientists struggle under severe restrictions to conduct explorations of other planets. This time the religious faithful are the villains. While the New Morality movement allows the exploration of other planets, it condemns any science that may contradict their literal interpretation of the Bible, which includes any research into alien life because the discovery of other life forms would be in direct opposition to the creation story in Genesis. The hero-scientists of Bova's series are constantly battling the close-minded government authorities, putting themselves at risk in the cause of advancing science.

A common theme in SF, however, is the harmonious melding of both science and faith. This is the case in Philip Jose Farmer's *Jesus on Mars* (1979), where astronauts in the near future discover an entire civilization living in underground caverns on Mars. The inhabitants are a mixture of an extraterrestrial race called Krsh and humans whom the Krsh had taken from Earth in the year 50 C.E. Included in that group of humans was Matthias, the so-called 13th Apostle, who replaced Judas Iscariot (Acts 1:24–26). Matthias converted not only his fellow passengers on the Krsh's spacecraft but also the Krsh on Mars to the belief that Jesus was the Messiah foretold in the Hebrew Scriptures. What the modern astronauts discover is a society founded on strict first-century Jewish law (like Judaism on Earth, it has evolved and adapted over the centuries, but in a very different way than its terrestrial counterpart) including purity and food restrictions, as well as a form of early Jewish Christian beliefs. Like first- and second-century believers, however, the Kirsh consider themselves Jewish yet believe Jesus was the true Messiah chosen by God but not a divine being himself. At the same time, these Martians are literally light years ahead of the earthlings technologically, and they see no conflict in their belief system and their scientific research. In fact, they firmly believe that science is a true gift from The Merciful One, and is almost a form of worship. Of course, the greatest surprise of all for the astronauts is the fact that Jesus—or a form of Jesus—is still present on Mars!

THE EPIPHANY OF PHILIP K. DICK

In 1974 prolific science fiction author Phillip K. Dick, best known for his novel *Do Androids Dream of Electric Sheep?* (1968) from which the classic science fiction film *Blade Runner* (1982) was based, had an experience that changed his life and the focus of his work—a close encounter with God.

After being administered sodium pentothal during a routine wisdom tooth extraction he sat at home in a daze and in pain. When a young girl delivered pain medication to his home, she was wearing a goldfish charm around her neck, which, she explained, was a symbol worn by early Christians. Dick had a sudden epiphany and a period of intense revelation was put into motion. Dick referred to this as *2-3-74* (February–March of 1974), which prompted him to spend the rest of his life writing an 8,000-page journal he called *Exegesis*. It also spawned a trilogy of novels *VALIS* (1981), *The Divine Invasion* (1981), and *The Transmigration of Timothy Archer* (1982).

Dick also believed he was given certain revelations, including knowledge the cause of his infant son's illness. His work is considered by some scholars to be much like Augustine's in the sense that he was not afraid to document his internal dialogue, fearlessly exploring his struggle to understand his soul, warts and all, in order to grasp the divine.

Dick, however, had always been interested in the spiritual and Christianity. Much of his earlier work explored or integrated religious themes or icons.

Eventually the voices faded and the quest for the meaning of his religious experience began to lose some momentum. While he continued to write the *Exegesis* journal, he was never able to find any definitive answers, nor did he really expect or perhaps even want any.

MESSIAH OF THE FUTURE

Messiah figures (or literary stand-ins for Jesus) are surprisingly prominent in many SF novels. As the story progresses in Farmer's *Jesus on Mars*, we discover a Jesus that is based on the Gnostic model of Christ; a being of energy that has manifested itself in the body of the earthly Jesus. Richard Orme, captain of the astronauts and a devout Baptist, struggles to reconcile his understanding of the Christ his faith professes versus the Jesus he now meets on Mars. As Jesus prepares for his second coming to Earth, Orme finds himself struggling with his doubts while desperately wanting to believe this Christ is the savior foretold in scripture.

In Lewis's *Out of the Silent Planet*, we are also introduced to an extraterrestrial Christ, called Oyarsa, although his identity is more obscured than Farmer's Jesus. Oyarsa has been charged with protecting Malacandria (a stand-in for Mars), and explains to Ransom that each planet has its own Oyarsa assigned to it. The Oyarsa of Earth, however, has turned evil and Ransom is appointed by the Malacandrian Oyarsa to rescue it. Ransom, of course, does not find himself worthy but is persuaded that he is Earth's only hope for salivation. He reluctantly returns to his home planet, ready to shoulder the task appointed to him.

Not all SF messiah's, however, are heroic. Walter Tevis's classic 1963 novel, *The Man Who Fell to Earth*, tells the tale of an alien sent to Earth to save his dying planet. In the course of his stay, he becomes corrupted by all the human weaknesses available to him, which are substantial, causing him to eventually go mad and ultimately fail to rescue his planet from destruction.

Another flawed messiah is portrayed in Robert Heinlein's Hugo Award–winning *Stranger in a Strange Land*, which chronicles the adventures of one Michael Valentine Smith, a human raised on Mars by the native Martians, who returns to Earth bringing the Martian religion. On Earth he establishes The Church of All Worlds, which promotes free love, man's own divinity, and other controversial tenets that eventually cause the authorities to condemn him as a false prophet.

Arguably, the most famous messiah of the future is Superman, created by Jerry Siegel and Joe Shuster in a time when Earth (certainly the United States) was in desperate need of hope and salvation. In the first 1938 issue of Action Comics, Superman takes on corrupt government officials. Throughout his long popular life in comic books, Superman battled criminals and helped guide the mythical city of Metropolis toward a moral code ("truth, justice, and the American way").

The parallels to Superman (or his Krypton name, Kal-el—a pseudo-Hebraic phrase that can be roughly translated as "all that is God") and the Jesus portrayed in the Gospels is striking. He is sent to Earth by his father not only to save him from the destruction of his planet, Krypton, due to the hubris and stubbornness of its leaders but also in the hopes that he can save another planet that is bent on destroying itself. "They can be a great people, Kal-el," his father tells him. "They wish to be. They only lack the light to show the way. For this reason above all, their capacity for good, I have sent them to you, my only son." Over the years, Superman has continued in popularity, spawning several feature films, long-running television shows, and Saturday morning cartoons. During the last 70 years Superman has adapted to each current age and accompanying crisis but always maintains his code of ethics, never wavering in both physical and moral strength. "There are inherent messianic qualities in the SF concept of the superhero," McKee says. "An individual with exceptional abilities who sacrifices part of his or her life for the greater good" (McKee 2007, 143). In other words, we long for a hero of superior abilities or intellect who will save us from our own apocalypse, a subject that is also prominent in science fiction

APOCALYPTIC SF VISIONS

Perhaps no other literary genre is more preoccupied with eschatology (i.e., the end of the world) than science fiction. In many ways the apocalyptic sensibility may well be the defining trait of SF and "is also the key to understanding not only how religious themes are explored in SF, but how *all* SF is religious. The contemplation of the world as it should be (or how it *must not* be) is at the core of all SF, and this utopian impulse parallels the goals of human religion" (McKee 2007, 240).

Walter Miller's inventive *A Canticle for Leibowitz* (1959) chronicles a monastery during three distinct eras. The first part takes place in the postapocalypse of our own time, where the monks studiously copy the documents of St. Leibowitz, still puzzling over many of arcane and obscure fragments, including a shopping list. They are constantly wondering how and why the "ancients" disappeared, oblivious to the obvious (unlike the reader) that the world was brought to the brink of destruction by a nuclear holocaust. The second part follows the rise to a new civilization through the eyes of the church authorities as they scramble for power and control much like the medieval church did. The third and final section of the book finds the monks on the verge of another nuclear holocaust, and the church powerless to stop it. Clearly a product of the fear and concern of the 1950s and 1960s that the world was at the brink of nuclear war, Miller sought to remind the reader that unless we learn the mistakes of the past, we are inevitably doomed to repeat them.

CONCLUSION

While some may argue that religion is not compatible with science fiction, the brief survey above does much to dispel that theory. Science fiction has always provided an insight into our own time, and gives us insight into the consequences of our present actions. "Whether the futures it presents," McKee argues, "are bleak or bright, SF is always concerned with salvation. By warning us of our current folly or presenting paradises of the future, SF hopes to improve the human condition" (McKee 2007, 128).

See also Aliens; Cosmology.

Further Reading: Bertonneau, Thomas, and Kim Paffenroth. *The Truth Is out There: Christian Faith and the Classics of Science Fiction.* New York: Brazos, 2006; Clarke, Arthur C. *The Collected Stories of Arthur C. Clarke.* New York: Orb Books, 2002; Farmer, Philip Jose. *Jesus on Mars.* Los Angeles: Pinnacle Books, 1979; Heinlein, Robert A. *Stranger in a Strange Land.* New York: Putnam, 1961; Lewis, C. S. *Out of the Silent Planet.* New York: Scribner, 2003; McKee, Gabriel. *The Gospel According to Science Fiction: From the Twilight Zone to the Final Frontier.* Louisville: Westminster John Knox Press, 2007; Miller, Walter M. *A Canticle for Leibowitz.* New York: Bantom Spectra, 1959; Oropeza, B. J. *The Gospel According to Superheroes: Religion and Popular Culture,* ed. B. J. Oropeza. New York: Peter Lang Publishing, 2005; Schenck, Ken. "Superman: A Popular Culture Messiah." In *The Gospel According to Superheroes: Religion and Popular Culture,* ed. B. J. Oropeza, 33–48. New York: Peter Lang Publishing, 2005; Shippey, Tom, ed. *The Oxford Book of Science Fiction Stories.* Oxford: Oxford University Press, 2003; Winston, Kimberly. "Other Worlds, Suffused with Religion." *Publisher's Weekly,* April 16, 2001, 35–39.

Remi Aubuchon

SEPARATION OF CHURCH AND STATE

HISTORICAL BACKGROUND

It is sometimes said that the United States is a secular nation with the soul of a church. That cliché has grown out of the colonial experience of European settlers coming to North America seeking religious freedom. Many had a fervent desire to escape the corruptions of European Christendom, and to establish faithful religious communities in a new world. These early settlers brought their different forms of Christian faith with them. Anglicans predominated in the first colony in Virginia. The Puritans, with their distinctive Covenant Theology, settled in New England. The Quakers, pursuing their *holy experiment* of love and religious tolerance, founded Pennsylvania and invited other peace-church groups such as the Mennonites and Dunkers to join them. Catholics, as a persecuted English minority, founded Maryland. A few Jews were also among the earliest European settlers.

We dare not forget that Native Americans had followed their own indigenous religious beliefs and practices for thousands of years before the first European immigrants arrived. Though they were tragically misunderstood and almost annihilated by the Europeans, their religious traditions, involving a deep reverence for nature, persisted and contributed to our American religious landscape. Soon, African slaves were being transported to the colonies, bringing their distinctive forms of African religiosity with them. American religious communities would be much poorer without their contributions to our music, communication, and human relationships.

The United States was religiously pluralistic from its earliest colonial history, even though various expressions of Protestant Christianity dominated in the first centuries. Consequently, it has always had a complicated national religious identity. A dominant early strand of American religious identity is rooted in the Covenant Theology of the early Puritan settlers in New England, who saw themselves as God's chosen people in a new world. Yet another is the more secular Anglo-Saxon social tradition involving the political philosophy of John Locke, which greatly influenced American founders with ideas of natural rights, liberty, and the private ownership of property.

Such enlightenment philosophy was adamantly opposed to the political establishment of any religion in the United States, partly because of the sad history of protracted religious wars in Europe. Free-church minorities such as the Quakers and Baptists also fought for religious freedom. In any case, the reality on the ground was that we were a diverse nation of immigrants who have brought their own religious and cultural traditions to their adopted land. Consequently, the formal separation of church and state was a foregone conclusion when the Constitution of the United States was written in the summer of 1787. The First Amendment guaranteed freedom of religion and separation of church and state with the statement, "Congress shall make no law respecting an establishment of religion, or prohibiting the free exercise thereof."

SECULAR AND SACRED

Religious and secular strands of national identity coalesced into a unique American understanding of its *manifest destiny* to conquer the wilderness and create a distinctly new society (often referred to as *American exceptionalism*) in its restless westward expansion as a young nation. This self-identity informed the drive to create American institutions of political democracy, economic capitalism, and religious freedom. Using a biblical metaphor, Americans have always seen their nation as a *city on a hill* serving as an example to other nations. Even though there was religious freedom and no formal establishment of religion, few questioned that the United States was a Christian nation with a distinct Protestant identity.

Throughout American history, religious and secular traditions have interacted with each other, often supportively, and sometimes antagonistically. The energetic young country gained ever more territory and global influence, even as it disavowed imperialist interests. This injected an intense religious quality into our American national identity. It operates even more effectively because it is defined as secular in American liberal ideology, rather than being identified with a particular religion.

RELIGION AND POLITICS

Even though there is a formal separation of church and state in the United States, religion has always had significant influence, both for good and for ill, in the public life of our nation. It has often been recognized that religious ethics, such as honesty and self-sacrifice, undergird the republican virtues that make a functional democracy possible. Without such virtues, the slide toward some form of totalitarianism is inevitable. Conversely, religion has been used by those preaching social intolerance and military adventures against supposed national enemies. Politicians have always been tempted to use religion for such less than honorable ends, and religious leaders have always been tempted by the perks that come from the cozy association with such political power.

The separation of church and state in America has been designed to counter the negative effects of a too cozy relationship between politics and religion in our public life. Alexis de Tocqueville, an astute nineteenth-century French commentator on democracy in America, has observed how religious American society is in comparison to European societies. He concluded that this was actually a result of the separation of church and state, because a too close association with political power is detrimental to religion. The close association of church and state in Europe has tied European Christianity to the hated excesses of authoritarian states (Tocqueville 1969).

Some have taken this to mean that there should be an impermeable *wall of separation* between church and state, or religion and the public square. They seek to relegate religion to the private sphere. Others insist that such a position misinterprets the intent of the First Amendment and weakens American democracy by stifling religious voices in public debate. They point to the contributions of religious movements to past advances in social justice. For examples, the early labor movement, and the civil rights' movement grew out of, and depended on religious communities and religious leaders in America. There has always been a healthy tension between those who seek to limit religious expression in the public square, and those who welcome its participation in a vibrant democracy. How do we promote religious freedom and yet respect the intent behind the separation of church and state in the U.S. Constitution?

CIVIL RELIGION

As noted above, messianic religious sensibilities inform some of the worst traits associated with American imperialism and notions of *manifest destiny*. Nevertheless, a judicious public theology is needed to undergird republican virtues, and to facilitate working together for the common good. It is sobering to recognize that much of what is good and what is bad in American history is rooted in our public theology.

Astute sociologists acknowledge the function of religion in the creation and maintenance of human society and a habitable world. A temperate and constructive public theology recognizes the transcendent, and does not see the nation-state or any other human construct as an end in itself. That which is most alarming and worrisome about American public theology or civil religion is the tendency to see the nation itself as the ultimate point of reference.

Robert Bellah (1980) has characterized the fault line in American public life as the antithetical tensions between republicanism undergirded by self-sacrificial virtues and liberal constitutionalism that thinks the good society can be achieved by citizens motivated by self-interest alone. These tensions were already present in the founding of the United States as an independent nation. The presence of active American religious communities that promote moral virtues and practice the common good has helped to counteract the self-interest of liberal constitutionalism. The end of such self-interest can only be the corruption of republican virtue, and will end in some form of totalitarianism.

Bellah was concerned that American society had already traveled far down that path in the last half of the twentieth century, and worried about the future of America as a republic (Bellah 1980). The recent *war against terrorism* and the related focus on *homeland security* bring up the same issues in a more dramatic way. The gradual curtailment of civil liberties for the cause of national security poses a real and alarming threat to our democratic way of life.

In the middle of the past century, Will Herberg, another perceptive student of religion and society in America, reflected on the transition of the United States from a predominately Protestant society, to one that he characterized as Protestant-Catholic-Jew (Herberg 1983). The 1950s was a highpoint in American religious life; more people were church members than ever before in our history. Yet, at the same time, America was becoming increasingly secular in its social outlook. Herberg was fascinated by that contradiction, and probed more deeply into the social transition that was taking place (Herberg 1983).

President Eisenhower was a quintessential American when he declared, "Our government makes no sense unless it is founded in a deeply felt religious faith—and I don't care what it is" (Herberg 1983, 85). That statement would have been nonsensical in the not too distant past, but it now made complete sense to the average American. Herberg argued that it made sense because the prevailing religion was what he called the American Way of Life—an individualistic, optimistic, and pragmatic faith in all things American. The various denominations and religious groups were understood as distinct expressions of that American civil religion.

Especially troubling was the tragic divorce between religions faith and public morals in American society. The majority of Americans said that their private religious beliefs were personally meaningful, but had no real effect on their politics or their business practices. And they were united in their opposition to *godless Communism,* which was the much vilified American national enemy. Herberg saw this as a great reversal of historic Christian and Jewish faiths (Herberg 1983). Insofar as they spoke of God, it was with reference to the God who sanctioned the American Way of Life. The secularization of religion in America was complete. Nevertheless, American religion was close to the people, and had a vigor that offered some hope that it could perhaps still serve a more critical and constructive function in American society.

CHRISTIAN WITNESS TO THE STATE

Christians have traditionally recognized that the state serves a necessary God-given function of encouraging the good and restraining evil (Romans 13:1–7). Nevertheless, Christians have also recognized that the state is prone to become its own final authority. Such idolatry usurps the place of God, and leads to the abuse of its power in ways that are self-serving and destructive. Its authority can influence people to thoughtlessly carry out horrendous atrocities and violations against human dignity (Revelation 13:1–4). Not only crude forms of fascism or totalitarianism embody that kind of idolatry. It is true every time that a nation sees itself as the unique bearer of manifest destiny, or claims the right to act unilaterally.

Participants in this controversy need to remember that the state is not an abstraction; it is individual elected government officials, teachers, bureaucrats, police officers, judges, and soldiers serving in assigned roles. Together, these people become a corporate entity that enables humans to live together in community. The Bible speaks of such corporate entities as the "powers" that structure our lives (Colossians 1:15–17). The Bible also teaches that the "powers" have a shadow side (Ephesians 6: 12). Every known state includes a greater or lesser degree of oppression and injustice that concerned citizens need to struggle against. And every state ultimately claims the sole prerogative to use lethal force within its territory.

Christians argue that the church is also not an abstraction; it is individual members, pastors, teachers, service workers, and bishops or conference pastors. Together, all these people become a different type of corporate entity that is also political in its own way.

GROWING RELIGIOUS PLURALISM IN AMERICA

The United States has always been a nation of diverse people bridging the ethnic, cultural, and religious differences from their countries of origin. At first that was commonly thought of as people from different European backgrounds. The Native Americans, Blacks and Asians among us were routinely marginalized and ignored. Even so, the challenge was always recognized as seen on the motto of the Great Seal of the United States printed on the loose change in our pockets: *E Pluribus Unum—From Many One*. Two questions immediately arise: "Who are the many? How do we define the one?" Those related questions have shaped much of the social, cultural, and religious discourse in our country.

Each wave of new immigration raised fears the pluribus was too great and would destroy our unum. When floods of Irish and Eastern European immigrants began arriving on our shores in the late nineteenth and early twentieth centuries, some Protestant church leaders were sure that Catholics were antidemocratic and could not make good Americans. Prejudiced Americans known as *nativists* were especially hostile toward Catholics, Jews, African Americans, and Asians. Hate groups such as the Ku Klux Klan sprang up, strict limits were placed on the immigration of Jews, and a movement was even started to return blacks to Africa. The Chinese Exclusion Act was passed by the U.S. Congress in 1882. Finally, the Johnson Reed Act in 1924 effectively closed immigration from outside of Western Europe. The unum in this exclusive interpretation meant WASPs—White Anglo-Saxon Protestants.

A more tolerant response to the pluribus is seen in the vivid image of America as a *melting pot* assimilating the *many* into the *one*. Newcomers would shed their native customs and cultures to fit into the new American nation that was being created. The image begs the questions of how much difference could be assimilated, and the nature of the one being created. Would each language, culture, and religion contribute to the "one" or was it predetermined by the dominant Anglo-Saxon culture of the first settlers? Some argued that a more perfect unity would be achieved by drawing on the gifts and energies of those from all parts of the world.

When the immigration quotas based on national-origins was lifted in 1965, it opened the door to immigration from Asia and other places. Since then, according to religious scholar Diana Eck, Muslims, Hindus, Buddhists, Sikhs, and others have arrived from every part of the globe, forever changing the religious landscape of America (Eck 2001). We have now become the world's most religiously diverse nation. It is still too early to tell if these new religious traditions will be fully assimilated into the American Way of Life as Protestants, Catholics, and Jews have been. Might it be possible that they will contribute new life and that, together, we can forge a more critical and constructive relationship with American society? Perhaps Will Herberg's hope for such a revitalized American religious community may still become a reality.

See also Nationalism, Militarism, and Religion.

Further Reading: Bellah, Robert N. and Phillip E. Hammond. *Varieties of Civil Religion.* San Francisco: Harper and Row, 1980; Berger, Peter L. *The Sacred Canopy: Elements of a Sociological Theory of Religion.* New York: Doubleday, Anchor Books, 1967; Cherry, Conrad, ed. *God's New Israel: Religious Interpretations of American Destiny.* Revised ed. Chapel Hill, N.C.: The University of North Carolina Press, 1998; Eck, Diana L. *A New Religious America: How a "Christian Country" Has Now Become the World's Most Religiously Diverse Nation.* New York: HarperSanFrancisco, 2001; Herberg, Will. *Protestant-Catholic-Jew: An Essay in American Religious Sociology.* Chicago: The University of Chicago Press, 1983; Marty, Martin. *Pilgrims in the Own Land: Five Hundred Years of Religion in America.* New

York: Penguin Books, 1984; Stephanson, Anders. *Manifest Destiny: American Expansion and the Empire of Right.* New York: Hill and Wang, 1995; Stout, Jeffrey. *Democracy and Tradition.* Princeton N.J.: Princeton University Press, 2004; Tocqueville, Alexis de. *Democracy in America.* Translated by George Lawrence. Edited by J.P. Mayer. New York: Doubleday, Anchor Books, 1969; Williams, William Appleman. *Empire as a Way of Life.* Oxford: Oxford University Press, 1980; Wink, Walter. *Engaging the Powers: Discernment and Resistance in a World of Domination.* Minneapolis: Fortress Press, 1992; Wuthnow, Robert. *Christianity and Civil Society: The Contemporary Debate.* Valley Forge, PA: Trinity Press International, 1996; Yoder, John Howard. *The Christian Witness to the State.* Scottdale, PA: Herald Press, 2002.

Earl Zimmerman

T

TERRORISM

Terrorism and religion have become linked in many people's minds, probably because so many recent examples of terrorism have been conducted by people claiming religious motives. Prominent religious skeptics have seized upon these recent episodes to charge that religious faith causes terrorism. Recognized religious leaders vehemently deny the charge, pointing to the many official statements they have issued condemning terrorism as a heinous sin. But many terrorists themselves have justified their actions based on their faith.

Given the intense emotions surrounding the practice of terrorism, by terrorists and potential targets alike, it is not easy to get a clear picture of religion's role in terrorism. One of the first problems is defining terrorism clearly enough so we can identify it when it happens. Without a clear definition of terrorism, it becomes a label anyone can use to criticize their enemies' violence and portray them as demons. If one cannot move beyond *one person's terrorist is another person's freedom fighter* terrorism is nothing more than violence someone disapproves of.

Political scientists insist terrorism is a specific form of violence, with its own roots and dynamics. While scholars have offered over 100 different definitions of terrorism, among all the variations in the details there is a reasonably clear consensus on its central features. *Terrorism is lawless violence directed at noncombatants in order to generate fear as a means to a political goal.* This definition leaves some questions unsettled (such as whether the violence needs to be directly lethal, or the cause unjust, or even whether governments can be terrorists), but it captures the main features of terrorism.

Although terrorist violence is a crime, terrorism as defined here, is clearly distinguished from general criminal violence, since criminals are motivated by personal gain or revenge, not political goals. Terrorism is also distinguished from warfare because the violence is lawless and directed at noncombatants, whereas war is primarily conducted by governments under the legal authority granted them by their constitutions, and is generally focused on opponents' armed forces.

A careful definition of terrorism also helps clarify some of the complex dynamics of various forms of political violence. For example, it is important to be clear about who is the ultimate target of a terrorist act. The destruction of the World Trade Center on September 11, 2001 was not primarily aimed at the people working there. The attackers apparently did not care about any of the specific individuals in the buildings. The main goals were to change how Western governments relate to the Muslim world: reducing support for Israel, reversing the spread of Western secular and Christian ideas into Muslim lands, disrupting the economy, and so on. The attackers wanted people to die, horribly and on-camera, so the rest of us would be shocked and scared into changing our attitudes and actions. That is the hallmark of terrorism—the people who do the dying are not the real targets of the action. They are useful to the terrorists only as vessels of conspicuous suffering, dramatic tools with which to capture the world's attention.

Under this definition, assassination of political leaders is not always terrorism. If the intent is focused on eliminating the leader, as when Lee Harvey Oswald shot U.S. President John F. Kennedy, there is very little terroristic about the act. But if the assassination is intended to spread fear and thereby influence the actions of other government officials, then the act can be treated as terrorism, even if the specific leader killed was also a target. For example, the assassinations of a series of leaders in Lebanon in the first decade of the twenty-first century are appropriately labeled as *terrorism*, since their purpose was clearly to intimidate other potential leaders.

Nor are acts of war generally terrorism. The main objective of attacking soldiers is to kill them and thereby weaken the enemy's forces. Any spillover fear affecting policymakers on the other side is usually a secondary consideration, although sometimes operations against soldiers are designed with these secondary effects in mind. But the dynamics are different when the targets of violence are themselves in the business of inflicting lethal force. The impact on civilians and their policy-making leaders is buffered by the specialized status soldiers have as people prepared to risk their lives in lethal conflict. Terrorists recognize this, too, which is why civilians are chosen for their attacks. If civilians going about their normal routines can be reached by a terrorist, then other citizens cannot console themselves that only soldiers are at risk.

RELIGIOUS VIEWS CONCERNING THE ETHICS OF TERRORISM

Leaders in every major religion have denounced terrorism. There are no major proterrorism faiths.

However, there are many faiths, and many authorities within faiths, which honor or endorse revolutionary violence at least under some conditions. Endorsement might be explicit and direct, in the form of statements from church leaders, major conferences, or sermons. Or it might be implicit, such as the display of photos or other "hero" treatment for the revolutionaries. And if the revolution succeeds, those who fought are eligible to become national heroes, part of the pantheon of greats who helped found the nation or defend the faith.

The line between revolutionary violence and terrorism can be hard to draw, particularly if the definition of terrorism includes any reference to the justness of the cause. Generally, the justice of the cause does not matter to scholars in labeling activity as terrorism, which is why it is excluded from the consensus definition cited above. But this is not always reflected in how religious communities respond to the violence around them. All human groups have trouble seeing their own actions objectively, and tend to endorse some violence committed by their own communities that they would condemn if committed by others. But religious groups may have an extra layer of incentive to defend violence done in their behalf: they see themselves as defending God as well as themselves.

If God is the sovereign creator—a belief shared by a wide variety of faiths—God has the authority to order actions that would be outside the authority of any human agency, including governments. If God gives us all life, God can define the terms of the gift, and revoke it, in ways humans have no right to do to each other. If God's purposes require the slaughter of civilians, humans are not in a position to second-guess.

This introduces a justification for terrorism that is unavailable to someone not acting on God's behalf: that God commands it. Conceivably, someone who is convinced that God is commanding the placement of a bomb might do so even if, up to the moment of receiving the command, the bomber thought such acts were heinous crimes. After all, radical obedience to God is a central teaching of a wide variety of faiths.

If a possible terrorist comes to believe that God endorses an act of violence against civilians—that a terrorist attack is part of a *holy war*—he may be more likely to take an action that would normally be unthinkable. Nonbelievers have noted this, and used it to buttress claims that religious belief encourages terrorist violence.

However, there are factors in religious faith that also discourage terrorism. For example, some believers are *pacifists,* especially among Christians and Buddhists, but also in other faiths. Pacifists generally believe all lethal violence is wrongful, which would include terrorist violence.

Other restraints on violence apply even to nonpacifist believers. Most Christian groups teach a *just war* ethic, which permits war only if several conditions are met, including:

1. The war has a just cause—including defending against an attack by an enemy, or coming to the aid of an ally who has been attacked.

2. The motive for going to war is just—generally including self-defense or correction of clear injustice, but not including vengeance, territorial expansion, or other enrichment.
3. The war is initiated by a proper authority, meaning as authorized by the constitution of a legitimate sovereign government.
4. The war is the last resort. All nonlethal means of accomplishing the goals of the war must have been tried and found unavailing.
5. The means employed in the war are proportionate to the issue at stake. A nation cannot take a small offense as pretext for a large war.
6. The war is conducted justly. Noncombatants cannot be the primary targets of any attack, and are to be protected from the killing insofar as possible.
7. The war has a reasonable chance of success. Because people will die, war may not be undertaken unless the deaths are likely to accomplish some greater good. There is no room in just war theory for heroic stands against all odds, because honor is never a good reason to kill an enemy.

Islam also has restraints on violence, including the principle of the rule of law, which forbids killing an innocent person, or anyone not properly convicted by a competent court. Suicide bombing also violates the Islamic prohibition on suicide. The Koran also contains passages that encourage Muslims to live peacefully with those of different faiths. Furthermore, Muslims consider their faith overall to be a religion of peace, noting that Islam (meaning *submission*) and salaam (meaning *peace*) are connected at the heart of the faith.

But both Christianity and Islam illustrate some of the complexity of discerning whether a faith is, on the whole, encouraging or discouraging to terrorism. The classic formulation of just war requirements is not universally accepted among nonpacifist Christians. Some Christians are drawn to what amounts to a modern version of holy war, and would emphasize radical obedience to God over human-made standards such as just war criteria.

Furthermore, Christianity is not monolithic, with hundreds of denominations and sects. The Bible includes texts on violence that different groups interpret in different ways. Many Christian denominations are created when groups split over these different interpretations. The most radical Christian groups tend to be isolated organizationally and socially from the mainstream of Christianity, so that the firm statements against terrorism issuing from the main centers of the faith have little or no bearing on these fringe groups.

Islam is perhaps even more decentralized, lacking the hierarchy of most Christian denominations. The Koran's teachings are read differently by various schools of Islamic thought. Imams at various mosques may follow one or another of these schools of thought, which may attract or repel worshippers considering attending that mosque, but there is not the kind of strict enforcement of denominational doctrines found in most of Christianity. The result in Islam is a sort of marketplace of ideas, with leaders gaining or losing influence based on how appealing Muslims find their teaching to be.

Judaism, with its three broad divisions of Orthodox, Conservative, and Reformed, and smaller groups and debates within these divisions, also includes radical groups who accept some terrorism as acceptable. Hinduism, with its inherent diversity arising from its relative nonexclusivism, also has generated among its vast diversity some groups willing to kill civilians for political and religious ends.

In fact, all the largest religions share this feature of diverse interpretation of the teachings of their faith, including about violence. This means the interplay is complex in each faith between influences encouraging terrorist violence and those discouraging it. Perhaps faiths with fewer members and more organizational unity ought to find it easier to corral those who might be tempted to endorse terrorist violence, steering them back toward more orthodox views, and preventing extremist groups from forming in their ranks. Yet there are several examples of smaller religious groups turning to terrorist tactics, such as the Sikhs in India, who staged spectacular assassinations of government officials, or the tiny Aum Shinriko sect in Japan, responsible for an attack on Tokyo subways.

RELIGIOUS INSIGHTS INTO COMBATING TERRORISM

Although religion's official doctrinal stance against terrorism has not been entirely successful in steering believers away from the practice, religion does suggest some avenues for understanding and addressing the causes of terrorism. Terrorism can be analyzed as a spiritual problem.

One approach sees terrorism as an example of *spiritual deformation*. Religious leaders speak of *spiritual formation* as the process by which a person's spiritual life grows toward a healthy ideal. Terrorism, by contrast, involves the deformation of the terrorist's soul into something twisted and monstrous.

Terrorism has its roots in a *corrosive grievance*. The potential terrorist suffers from an ongoing sense of having been wronged. Over time, as the sense of victimization persists without resolution in forgiveness or justice, the grievance intensifies, and cuts its way toward the center of the personality. The potential terrorist allows his life to be dominated by his obsession about the grievance, and whoever he sees as responsible for it. He begins to see his entire life story as orbiting around the wrongs done to him. A *myth* grows up around his grievance, that is, a powerful story (much of which may be true) that explains where the grievance came from and what caused it.

Thus begins the spiritual deformation of the terrorist. His bitterness becomes his idol. Even his relationship with God is filtered through his grievance, which explains how the divine call to peace is missed, and everything in his faith that steers toward violence is magnified.

Corrosive grievance leads to another form of spiritual deformation, *dehumanizing hatred* of the perceived enemy. The myth surrounding the grievance requires at least one villain, some malevolent person or being who is seen as having unjustly caused the suffering. Once a villain has been identified, accounts are developed explaining the villain's incentive and power to create such misery. The more pervasive the corrosive grievance in the life of the potential terrorist, the more menacing the villain becomes. Typically, the potential terrorist begins to dehumanize his villainous enemy in two ways. First, he sees the enemy's motives as far simpler, and more purely evil, than any real human being. Actions that spring from complex motives in most humans are seen as springing entirely from the villain's extraordinary depravity and malice toward the victim and his community. Thus the villain is seen as subhuman, with fewer and more guttural motivations than real humans.

Second, the potential terrorist sees the villain's influence in events that begin to stretch well beyond the actual reach of the villain's power. Aggrieved Palestinians, for example, often say that the United States could just order the Israelis to end their occupation of the West Bank and Gaza, remove the Israeli settlements in those areas, and sign a peace agreement favorable to Palestine. When these things do not happen, the blame is laid squarely at the feet of the United States for not snapping its fingers to bring them about. So the United States becomes superhuman, and thus no longer requiring empathy for weaknesses, indecision, mixed motives, or good intentions gone awry. A superhuman villain gets what it wants, so everything bad that happens to the potential terrorist must have been chosen by the superhuman.

A villain that is superhuman or subhuman (or both) has ceased to be human at all. Thus, the spiritual scarring of corrosive grievance can interfere with the potential terrorist's ability to see humanity in others. Seeing himself in an overwhelming unjust world surrounded by subhuman and superhuman enemies, the potential terrorist has seriously degraded his potential for empathy and reconciliation so central in so many religious faiths.

Once under the influence of corrosive grievance and dehumanizing hatred, the potential terrorist turns into an active terrorist when he succumbs to *political despair* (the belief that there is no remedy for his situation through conventional political channels), and embraces the *myth of effective violence* (the belief that important things can get done—maybe *only* can be done—through violence). Finding in violence an avenue for accomplishing change denied him through conventional politics, the terrorist begins planning his attack.

Working under religious models of terrorism in this vein, believers have designed strategies for preventing and combating terrorism. To forestall the growth of corrosive grievance, believers have worked toward early intervention in areas of poverty, hunger, and lack of education. Dehumanization has been eased with personal contacts among potential adversaries, including everything from evangelistic teams, to relief projects and sports' competitions. Believers trying to live up even in part to their faiths' commands to love others, have accelerated these service and rehumanization projects, delving deeper into the needs and perceptions of those living in what we might call *preterrorist* conditions.

There have been repeated calls among various faiths for efforts like these to be expanded as quickly and widely as possible. In Western countries, where governments are kept legally, organizationally, and mostly financially separate from religious groups, the believer's work of preventing and combating terrorism falls to nongovernmental organizations (NGOs) founded by members of the faith.

CONCLUSION

While no leading religious group has ever officially endorsed terrorism, the picture is muddied by the dissenting voices of extremists, and the inability of some religious groups to recognize terrorism in the violence of those fighting on their behalf. The charge that religion feeds terrorism is plausible if one focuses on the unique dynamics involved in acting for, or defending God, but there is counterevidence that religion dissuades some from using violence. Furthermore, faith offers a powerful vehicle for understanding terrorism that has led to significant efforts to prevent it.

See also Nationalism, Militarism, and Religion.

Further Reading: Carr, Caleb. *The Lessons of Terror.* New York: Random House, 2002; Juergensmeyer, Mark. *Terror In the Mind of God.* Berkeley: University of California, 2000; McKeogh, Colm. *Innocent Civilians: The Morality of Killing in War.* New York: Palgrave, 2002; Mock, Ron. *Loving Without Giving In: Christian Responses to Terrorism and Tyranny.* Portland, OR: Cascadia Press, 2004; Pillar, Paul. *Terrorism and U.S. Foreign Policy.* Washington, D.C.: Brookings Institution, 2001; Reich, Walter, ed. *Origins of Terrorism: Psychologies, Ideologies, Theologies, States of Mind.* Washington, D.C.: Woodrow Wilson Center Press, 1998.

Ron Mock

UNIVERSAL HEALTH CARE AS RELIGIOUS ETHICAL ISSUE

Universal health care is a broad concept that denotes health care coverage that is extended to all citizens, typically of a country or region. Universal health care coverage programs vary widely, and are typically discussed in terms of their economic costs and benefits. For instance, in terms of health care access, the absence of adequate health insurance due to lack of affordability remains the primary obstacle to acquiring health care services. At any given time, at least 44 million Americans lack health insurance. This issue has a particularly urgent appeal among religions, since service to, and advocacy for those people whose social condition puts them at the margins of society and makes them particularly vulnerable to discrimination, are directives many traditions share.

THE BASIS OF THE PROBLEM

Traditionally, universal health care is a concept often rejected by society. Most often, this objection has to do with the economic factors that a move to such a system would entail. Individuals worry about the cost of such a move, and the impact that it may have on taxes and services they receive. However, many of these objections may stem from an individualistic approach to universal health care. An appeal to universal health care as a religious ethical issue provides a different way of recognizing the social nature of humans, and a commitment to a health care that moves beyond the economic impact.

Universal health care often involves confusion, particularly in regards to one's political, moral, and cultural goals. Clearly, there has not been a single, clear blueprint for such a move, either sponsored by the government or a member of a community. As such, the confusion that people feel around this topic is understandable.

To understand health care access in terms of its social dimensions, one must understand the reality of health care in the United States. For instance, it is often the case that people in the United States believe that universal access to health care would be too costly. In fact, however, recent data reveals otherwise. The United States spends at least 40 percent more per capita on health care than other industrialized nations with universal health care. Further, federal studies by the Congressional Budget Office and the General Accounting Office show that single payer universal health care would save $100 to $200 billion per year, despite covering all the uninsured and increasing health care benefits.

Another *myth* that many Americans believe is that universal health care would deprive them of needed services. However, studies have revealed that citizens in universal health care systems have more doctor visits and hospital stays than in the United States. In fact, around 30 percent of Americans have problems accessing health care due to payment problems or access to care, far more than any other industrialized country. About 17 percent of the U.S. population is without health insurance. About 75 percent of ill, uninsured people have trouble accessing/paying for health care.

PRINCIPLE OF HUMAN DIGNITY

Many religious traditions incorporate some notion of human dignity, which stresses the intrinsic worth that inheres in every human being. From the Catholic perspective (among other Christian perspectives), the source of human dignity is rooted in the concept of *Imago Dei,* in Christ's redemption, and in our ultimate destiny of union with God. Human dignity therefore transcends any social order as the basis for rights, and is neither granted by society, nor can it be legitimately violated by society. In this way, human dignity is the conceptual basis for human rights. While providing the foundation for many normative claims, one direct normative implication of human dignity is that every human being should be acknowledged as an inherently valuable member of the human community and as a unique expression of life, with an integrated bodily and spiritual nature. In Catholic moral thought, because there is a social or communal dimension to human dignity itself, persons must be conceived of, not in overly-individualistic terms, but as being inherently connected to the rest of society. Because the tradition emphasizes the integral nature of our body and spirit, the human body takes on a great deal of significance and value. Therefore, issues of health, and access to health care take on greater importance.

The implications of this conception of human dignity impacts religious traditions as it pertains to a range of human life issues, including universal health care. For example, the principle is foundational for an understanding of the common good, justice, and ultimately the right to health care. Other perspectives, both religious and secular, may conceive of human dignity in similar terms, with a similar sense of its inherent worth or value.

Evangelical bioethicist Nigel M. de S. Cameron (2005) sees religion as an important part of a universal access to health care. He draws upon the notion of biblical anthropology—the Christian idea of what it means to be human—and its roots in Scripture to note this involvement. The foundational elements of human dignity are found in the Book of Genesis, and offer a radical starting point for every discussion of human dignity and rights. This application within the context of universal health care offers a radical assertion of the unity and common dignity of the human race in the "Maker's" image.

Drawing on these notions, it is apparent how different religious traditions may impact the argument for universal access to health care. This task may draw on those concepts developed though Tradition (i.e., justice) or those found in Scripture (i.e., creation). In either case, many religious traditions may find a common voice with regard to health care access that draws upon the values outlined by physician and theological bioethicist Daniel Sulmasy: human dignity, compassion, solidarity, and invoking the common good.

HUMAN RIGHTS

Many religious traditions appeal to human rights. These can be understood as the basic claims that persons have on society simply due to their being human. Grounded in the concept of human dignity, no individual or institution can legitimately fail to recognize and respect these claims or rights, which makes them absolute rights. According to Catholic social teaching, human rights are claims to the minimum conditions necessary for life in community, and which allow one to fulfill one's moral responsibility in life, for instance, universal access to health care.

Although some rights imply duties on the part of the right-holder, all rights imply duties on the part of others. In terms of universal health care, there exists, then, a duty *for* governments to provide this *right* (to health care) to all persons. Human rights are closely linked to the concept of justice. Without some notion of justice, there is neither a basis for deciding which claims or rights must be respected, nor to determine which are of the utmost importance. Further, since human rights are claims that persons have on society, the concept of human rights is also closely linked to the concept of the common good.

THE RIGHT TO HEALTH CARE

From the perspective of Catholic moral teaching, the *right to health care* for all is not an optional stance. Rather, the right to health care is a human right founded on human dignity and the common good. Considered as such, health care is more than a commodity, in so far as it is an essential safeguard of human life and dignity that ought to be provided for, and to everyone. This absolute right to health care, however, should not be understood as an unlimited entitlement, but as a right that carries with it corresponding duties regarding justice, stewardship, and the common good.

PRINCIPLE OF RESPECT FOR PERSONS

All individual human beings are presumed to be free and responsible persons, and should be treated as such in proportion to their ability in the circumstances. Individuals who are particularly vulnerable, are entitled to appropriate protection, which includes access to health care.

This principle may be given different content, depending on one's conception of personhood. From the Catholic perspective, there are a number of anthropological considerations that have significant implications for this principle. For example, human persons are integrated body-spirit beings created in the image and likeness of God, with four integrated dimensions of human life: biological, psychological, social, and spiritual. The human person, then, can be understood in four interrelated ways: as a bodily subject, that is, we are not merely spirits that possess bodies, but we are body as much as we are spirit; as a knowing subject for which knowledge is a good, both as an end in itself, and as a means to fulfillment; as a social subject whose primary context is that of person situated in community; and as a self-transcendent subject, insofar as we are related to God in our created nature, through God's loving creation, and in our ability to participate in that creation. As a subject, and not merely an object, a human person must be treated with respect in such a way that recognizes his or her human dignity, which includes access to health care.

PRINCIPLE OF THE COMMON GOOD

In general, the common good consists of all the conditions of society and the goods secured by those conditions, which allow individuals to achieve human and spiritual flourishing. The social teaching of the Catholic Church insists that the human community, including its government, must be actively concerned in promoting the health and welfare of every one of its members, so that each member can contribute to the common good of all. This teaching is encapsulated in the principle of the common good, and its corollary principle of subsidiarity. According to this understanding, the principle of the common good has three essential elements: (1) respect for persons; (2) social welfare; and (3) peace and security. All three of these elements entail the provision of health care in some way as an essential element of the common good.

Insofar as the common good presupposes respect for persons, it obligates public authorities to respect the fundamental human rights of each person, in this instance, health care. Society should allow each of its members to fulfill his or her vocation. Insofar as it presupposes social welfare, the common good requires that the infrastructure of society is conducive to the social well being and development of its individual members. In this respect, it is the proper function of public authorities to both arbitrate between competing interests, and to ensure that individual members of society have access to the basic goods that are necessary for living a truly human life; for example, food, clothing, meaningful work, and education, and health care.

JUSTICE

Justice is a crucial notion to reflect upon in the context of access to health care. Justice helps move beyond the individualistic orientation, which can permeate this discussion. The object or purpose of justice is that we give each person his or her due, and give each person those goods and services he or she rightly expects from us. Justice is about duties and responsibilities, about building the good community. Justice is not simply a question of what we might like to do for people, not a question of how we might be generous to others. Rather, it is a question of what we simply must do for others on the basis of our common humanity.

When considering the concept of justice, it is important to distinguish between five different types of justice: (1) commutative justice, which refers to that which is owed between individuals, for example, in conducting business transactions; (2) contributive justice, which refers to what individuals owe to society for the common good; (3) legal justice, which refers to rights and responsibilities of citizens to obey and respect the rights of all, and the laws devised to protect peace and social order; (4) distributive justice, which refers to what society owes to its individual members, such as, the just allocation of resources; and (5) social justice, which appeals to the values of human dignity and human flourishing.

Theological bioethicist Gene Outka offers a classic example of how justice may be used in distributing health care resources (Outka 1988). Outka rejects merit, social worth, and ability to pay as grounds for health care decision-making. His rejection of these three factors as the basis for decisions regarding health care, are widely accepted by scholars of justice. Using one's ability to pay as the basis for health care seems to dispute the basic premise of distributive justice. Likewise, the merit of a person and their contributions to society are inadequate basis, within this distributive framework, on which to make health care decisions. Both *sinners and saints* can get seriously ill, and health care needs may arise before or after someone is *socioeconomically* useful (such as the very young or very old).

Additionally, the question of universal access to health care may be linked to aspects of social justice. This organic approach to societal needs emphasizes the wholeness of the human person within her community, and resonates with issues of solidarity. In the context of access to health care, this emphasis on social justice tends to be defined in terms of an obligation to furnish basic health care to those in need. Such a notion draws out the *dynamic vision* for an integrated society in which we are all responsible, even co-responsible for one another. Certainly, then, it makes sense to work out this notion in terms of providing health care access to all on the basis of social justice.

Closely aligned with this social justice theme is a preferential option for the poor. The Catholic social tradition, clearly affirms a responsibility to this concept. This is especially true in health care and *structural justice* that ensures access for all. For instance, the U.S. Catholic bishops in their *Resolution on Health Care Reform* (1993) assert, "every person has a right to health care. This right flows from the sanctity of human life and the dignity that belongs to all human persons, who are made in the image of God." They draw upon the notion of social responsibility and stress "the biblical call to heal the sick and to serve 'the least of these,' the priorities of social justice and the common good," the "virtue of solidarity" and "the option for the poor and vulnerable." Such a notion of social justice opens the way to critique, and challenges institutions that are part of today's economic systems and their concern about *the bottom line*.

See also AIDS; Health Reform Movements.

Further Reading: Battista John R. and Justine McCabe. "The Case for Single Payer, Universal Health Care for the United States." Connecticut Coalition for Universal Health Care. 4 June, 1999. http://www.cthealth.server101.com/the_case_for_universal_health_care_in_the_united_states.htm; Cahill, Lisa Sowle. "Bioethics, Relationships, and Participation in the Common Good." In *Health and Human Flourishing: Religion Medicine, and Moral Anthropology,* eds. Carol Taylor and Roberto Dell'Oro. Washington. D.C.: Georgetown University Press, 2006; Cahill, Lisa Sowle. *Theological Bioethics: Participation, Justice, Change.* Washington, D.C.: Georgetown University Press, 2005; Curran, Charles E. *Directions in Catholic Social Ethics.* Notre Dame, IN: Notre Dame University Press, 1985; Daniels, Norman. *Just Health Care.* New York: Cambridge University Press, 1995; de S. Cameron, Nigel M. "The Sanctity of Life in the Twenty-first Century." In *Toward an Evangelical Public Policy,* eds. Ronald Sider and Diane Knippers. Grand Rapids, MI: Eerdmans, 2005; Keane, Philip. *Health Care Reform: A Catholic View.* Mahwah, N.J.: Paulist Press, 1993; Keane, Philip. *Catholicism and Health-Care Justice: Problems, Potential and Solutions.* Mahwah, N.J.: Paulist Press, 2002; Kelly, David F. *Contemporary Catholic Health Care Ethics.* Washington, D.C.: Georgetown University Press, 2004; Mouw, Richard. *He Shines in All That's Fair: Culture and Common Grace.* Grand Rapids, MI: Eerdmans, 2001; Outka, Gene. "Social Justice and Equal Access to Health Care." In *On Moral Medicine: Theological Perspectives on Medical Ethics,* eds. Stephen Lammers and Allan Verhey. 2nd ed. Grand Rapids, MI: Eerdmans, 1998; U.S. Bishops. "Resolution on Health Care Reform." In *Origins* 23, no. 7 (1993); Walzer, Michael. *Spheres of Justice.* New York: Basic Books, 1983.

Robert V. Doyle

V

VEGETARIANISM AS RELIGIOUS WITNESS

Many Christian, Hindu, Buddhist, and Jaina religious groups advocate vegetarianism as an important aspect of religious practice. Additionally, many nonreligious organizations advocate vegetarianism as an expression of compassion for animals and the environment.

Christians regard vegetarianism as an expression of humility. In many parts of the world, meat is generally associated with wealth and high living. Medieval religious orders of the Catholic Church regarded vegetarianism as an important expression of asceticism, including the Cappadocians and Cistercians. Today, the Trappists maintain a largely vegetarian diet, in accordance with the Rule of St. Benedict (ca. 530), chapters 36:9 and 39:11. During the nineteenth century, many American Protestant movements advocated a vegetarian diet to encourage cleanliness and health. For several years, Brigham Young (1801–1877) observed vegetarianism. The Mormon text, *Word of Wisdom,* transmitted by Joseph Smith in 1833, advocates consumption of meat only in winter, or at times of famine. The Seventh Day Adventists, founded by Ellen White (1827–1915), promote vegetarianism, and are known for their longevity and good health. In 1864, she wrote: "God gave our first parents the food He designed that the race should eat. It was contrary to His plan to have the life of any creature taken. There was to be no death in Eden. The fruit of the trees in the garden was the food man's wants required." John Harvey Kellogg (1852–1943), the inventor of corn flakes and promoter of vegetarianism worldwide, was a Seventh Day Adventist. A 2001 study at Loma Linda University showed that "the life expectancy of a 30-year-old vegetarian Adventist woman was 85.7 years, and 83.3 years for a vegetarian Adventist man. This exceeds the life expectancies of other Californians by 6.1 years for women and 9.5 years for men." Leo Tolstoy (1828–1910) championed Christian vegetarianism, writing that "how deeply seated in the human heart is the injunction not to take life!" (Tolstoy) In addition to health benefits, many Christians consider vegetarianism an important way to reduce dependence on fossil fuel and to conserve water (see below). Among Christian youth, some are adapting a *straight edge* lifestyle that rejects tobacco, alcohol, drugs, and the consumption of meat.

Hindu vegetarianism developed within India more than 2,500 years ago, primarily among followers of Krishna. Although the earliest texts of Hinduism, the Vedas, do not specify a particular diet, the cow eventually became sacred within Hinduism, and the consumption of beef was forbidden. The *Mahabharata*, a religious epic, includes several chapters on the benefits of vegetarianism, stating that "Nonviolence is the highest religion (*dharma*)" and that "those who renounce the eating of meat gain great merit." Mahatma Gandhi (1869–1948) followed a vegetarian diet scrupulously as part of his campaign to unseat the British through staunch adherence to the principles of nonviolence, truthfulness, and his belief that "there is enough in the world for everyone's need, but not enough for everyone's greed." Though Indian cuisine might include chicken and mutton, a significant portion of Hindus follow a lacto-vegetarian diet, drawing protein from milk products including yogurt and cheese, and a complement of rice and legumes.

Perhaps the most famous activist Hindu vegetarians are the Bishnoi community. Founded by Jabheswara (1451–1536) in 1485, this movement advocates protection of both trees and animals throughout Rajasthan in western India. He composed 29 rules to be followed by all members of this community, which include the following:

18. to be compassionate towards all living beings;
22. to provide common shelter for goats and sheep to avoid them being slaughtered in abattoirs;
23. to not castrate bulls;
28. to not eat meat or nonvegetarian dishes.

In another of his works, the *Jambha Sāra,* he lays out six rules to avoid violence, including prohibitions against animal sacrifice, releasing water creatures back into the water, making certain that the firewood and the cow dung used for fuel do not have any creatures or insects that might be accidentally burnt, avoiding harm to bullocks by not sending them to the butcher, and protecting the deer in the forest. As vegetarians, they eat only a lacto-vegetarian diet, and have supported and inspired environmental activism throughout India. In modern times, Bishnoi have established the All India Jeev Raksha Bishnoi Sabha, a wildlife protection organization, and the Community for Wildlife and Rural Development Society. They maintain an active Web site, which includes the posting of an award winning film about their movement, *Willing to Sacrifice* (www.bishnoi.org).

Buddhists, particularly in China, practice vegetarianism because of a firm belief in reincarnation. The Buddha (566–486 or 490–410 B.C.E.) included stories of his past lives in many of his sermons. He told of his adventures in animal and plant births, including when he lived as a tigress, a crow, and several times as a monkey. The *Lankavatara Sutra,* a Mahayana Buddhist text popular in China, proclaims that "we have been born and reborn so many times that there is not one animal among us who in some past birth has not been our relative, whether mother or father, sister or brother." Buddhists in Southeast Asia generally subsist on alms for food, and will accept whatever is given. The Japanese diet relies heavily on fish, and in Tibet's rugged climate, people, even Buddhist monks, eat Yak meat to survive. However, in Chinese Buddhist temples where the monks grew their own food, a tradition of vegetarian food with heavy reliance on tofu developed. Many American Buddhists follow a vegetarian diet. Zen teacher Philip Kapleau (1912–2004) claimed that to cherish all life is the hallmark of a true Buddhist.

Jainism, of all the world's faith traditions, holds most assiduously to vegetarianism as a core tenet of its religious teachings. The earliest known Jaina teacher, Tirthankara Parshvanath, lived around 800 B.C.E. in northeast India. According to Jainism, the soul, which is particular to each individual, and eternal, has become encrusted with karma through the course of countless rebirths. The practice of Jainism entails sloughing off all karma, which in this tradition has the physical character of being colorful and sticky. Acts of violence cause one's karma to thicken and adhere more tightly to the soul, hence constricting and concealing its true nature as energy, consciousness, and bliss. By purposeful acts of nonviolence, including the observance of a vegetarian diet, one is able to gradually release karmas and advance toward the goal of liberation (*kevala*). The Jaina diet generally includes milk products, but many contemporary practitioners have adopted a no-dairy vegan diet.

From the secular side, organizations such as the Humane Society and the Royal Society for the Prevention of Cruelty to Animals have included vegetarian advocacy as part of their mission. With the rise in awareness about the deleterious effects of climate change and the limited resources of fossil fuel, a renewed secular advocacy of vegetarianism has emerged. According to the United Nations, 18 percent of all greenhouse gases come from livestock, more than from cars and airplanes. The rearing of livestock requires vast tracts of land both for grazing and for growing fodder. Fodder crops (corn, alfalfa, and soybeans) require huge amounts of water and petroleum-based fertilizer. According to a study at the University of Chicago, the average meat eater in America generates 1.5 tons of carbon dioxide each year that could be avoided by following a vegetarian diet. For reasons of one's personal health, and for the health of the environment, many people are reducing or eliminating their consumption of flesh foods.

See also Health Reform Movements.

Further Reading: Adams, Carol. *The Sexual Politics of Meat: A Feminist-Vegetarian Critique.* New York: Continuum, 1989; Bishnoi Movements. http://www.bishnoi.org; International

Vegetarian Union. http://www.ivu.org; Lappe, Frances Moore. *Diet for a Small Planet.* New York: Ballantyne Books, 1991; Seventh Day Adventists. http://www.adventist.org; Singer, Peter. *Animal Liberation.* New York: Avon Books, 1975; The Meatrix. http://www. themeatrix.com; Waldau, Paul and Kimberley Patton, eds. *A Communion of Subjects: Animals in Religion, Science, and Ethics.* New York: Columbia University Press, 2006.

Christopher Key Chapple

W

WESTERN CINEMA

Religious themes have found expression in art throughout the history of mankind in paintings, sculpture, literature, and theater, so it should come as no surprise that the medium of the motion picture, invented in the late nineteenth century, would also be influenced and inspired by religion. In observing religious art throughout the ages, it becomes evident that the artist's own social location influences the way in which an artist portrays a particular religious theme, and the same is true for the medium of film, especially in Western cinema, where the portrayal of Jesus reflects the cultural *zeitgeist* of each decade.

Often the most successful Christ-themed films have been those that have not overtly portrayed the person of Jesus, but rather have come from a *sideways* viewpoint, such as *Babette's Feast* or *Jesus of Montreal,* or tell the Gospel story using an historical character other than Jesus as the protagonist, such as *Barabass* or *The Robe.* Sometimes, it has been safer for the film-maker to use stories from the Old Testament such as *David and Bathsheba* or famously, *The Ten Commandments.* In other seemingly secular films, especially those who have a *lone hero* as the protagonist, the story of Jesus may unconsciously be its inspiration, such as *Platoon* or even *Resident Evil.* It has even been argued that George Romero's *Night of the Living Dead,* is heavily laced with religious symbolism!

JESUS IN FILM

Before it even premiered, Mel Gibson's *The Passion of the Christ* (2004) was caught in a maelstrom of controversy. The strident public dialogue around Mel Gibson's film highlighted the already deep divisions in America between secular and religious, becoming a galvanizing element for the culture war that had been raging in politics for a decade. While Conservative Christians hailed it as the most authentic portrayal of Jesus on film, Jewish advocacy groups condemned it as an anti-Semitic screed. Other public groups protested that it was overly bloody and violent; gore hiding behind the sacred portrayal of Christ's death. A large and ever-growing base of conservative Catholic and Evangelical Christian savvy in the ways of the Internet also contributed to the success of the film, by making it their *cause celeb,* urging churches around the country to encourage members to attend the film, almost as a way of defending the faith against the faithless. Jewish *bloggers* also jumped onto the electronic bandwagon, condemning it for the film's less than flattering portrayal of the Jews, implying that they were directly responsible for Jesus' death, and playing down the role of the Roman authorities. Adding fuel to the flame was Mel Gibson's father declaring to the media that the Holocaust never happened.

The rhetoric rose in volume as the date of the premiere came closer and closer, propelling the subject of the film onto the front pages of every major newspaper in the United States, assuring that the film would become a blockbuster at the box office, grossing more than $350 million between Ash Wednesday and Easter Sunday.

While it is possible to view *The Passion,* in spite of its graphic portrayal of the torture and execution of Jesus, as just another in a long line of *Passion Plays* that had appeared since the invention of the moving picture itself, it also stands as the most current example of how religious cinema affects and reflects the culture and era that it was produced in. Filmic *Realism* has become an important box office draw in the last decade, and much of the promotion for *The Passion* billed it as the "real" version of Jesus' suffering and death. By using the term *real* the filmmakers did not necessarily mean that it was based on some heretofore unknown source other than the gospels, but rather that the depiction of how he was treated, how his wounds were inflicted, and how he died was realistic. The box office success of movies claiming to be "based on a true story," the ever-increasing demand for realistic depiction of violence (ironically aided by technical advances in special effects), and the film-going public's apparent taste for stark drama, all served as the platform by which Gibson was able to present his version of the events. At the same time, there were many political and religious upheavals that also served to make *The Passion* both controversial and profitable.

This was not the only time, however, that the portrayal of Jesus on film created both adulation and ire. The first popular religious film to be shown in the United States was the *Passion Play of Oberammergau* in 1898, which had been performed every ten years in Bavaria since 1634. The film ran for 20 minutes and consisted of 23 scenes, but even this Jesus film was surrounded in controversy. Having declared itself an authentic recreation of the centuries old traditional passion play, the *New York Herald* reported the film was not shot in a Bavarian village as promoted, but on a rooftop in New York City with professional actors! This revelation, however, had absolutely no negative effect on the public, which flocked to see it all over the Northeastern United States, and then it was eventually purchased by an itinerant preacher who showed it all over the country at revival meetings. Many versions of the Christ story were made in the early years of cinema, and all were assured box office success, but perhaps the most successful and critically acclaimed filmic portrayal of Jesus in the silent era was D.W. Griffith's three and a half hour epic, *Intolerance* (1916). The Jesus story is one of four parallel stories, but stands as not only spectacular, but equally controversial to Mel Gibson's *Passion* in its portrayal of the Jews, but unlike Gibson, gave into Jewish groups and refilmed the crucifixion scenes with Roman soldiers instead.

Each generation and culture has brought its own version of Jesus to the screen, each claiming to be an authentic portrayal, but it usually ends up reflecting the time and place that the film was produced. All of them have had their share of controversy. Martin Scorsese's filmic adaptation of Kazantzakis' *The Last Temptation of Christ* (1988) was widely condemned by Christian organizations for its depiction of Jesus as *neurotic* and indecisive, yet one could easily argue that the decade of the self-focused 1980s created an introspective Jesus. Scorsese explained that his desire to make the film was born out of his own personal belief in Jesus as fully human and fully divine, hoping to show what that struggle must have been like. He assumed most believers would see the film as an extension of the same temptation Jesus was subjected to in the dessert. He never expected the negative reaction the film received. As Scorsese explains:

> Over the years I've drifted away from the Church, I'm no longer a practicing Catholic, and I've questioned these things. Kazantzakis took the two natures of Jesus, and Paul Moore, the Episcopal Bishop of New York, explained to me that this was Christologically correct: the debate goes back to the Council of Chalcedon in 451 C.E., when they discussed how much of Jesus was divine, and how much human. I found this an interesting idea, that the human nature of Jesus was fighting Him all the way down the line, because it can't conceive of Him being God. I thought this would be great drama and force people to cake Jesus seriously—at least to re-evaluate His teachings. Most non-Christians also misunderstand the importance many believers give to images of Jesus . . . through the Kazantzakis novel I wanted to make the life of Jesus immediate and accessible to people who haven't really thought about God in a long time. (Thompson and Christie 2004, 124)

Though both were originally stage musicals born in the late 1960s, *Jesus Christ Superstar* (1973) and *Godspell* (1973) had very little in common with each other. *Godspell* featured Victor Garber as a hippie-mime Jesus. The music was upbeat and hopeful, and in many ways the text was truer to the Gospels than other Jesus films. In contrast, Norman Jewison's brooding *Superstar* was filmed in and around Israel, and captured the tension of the conflicts in the Middle East using modern images (not always successfully) juxtaposed with traditional representations of first century life. It also featured a racially diverse cast, and Carl Anderson's powerful presence as Judas brought a great amount of heartfelt gravitas to a role usually played with much mustache-twirling. The Weber-Rice rock opera score (by then well known) was oddly disquieting when played against the backdrop of the Judean desert. While commercially successful, it stirred up an enormous amount of controversy from many sides. Jewish groups condemned it as anti-Semitic. Equality groups considered the casting of a black actor as Judas to be racist. Conservative Christian groups considered the portrayal of Jesus as a *superstar* to be just too much.

The 1960s featured handsome and hip Jeffrey Hunter as Jesus in Nicholas Ray's *King of Kings* (1961), which has sometimes been derisively subtitled by critics, *I Was A Teenage Messiah* partly because of Ray's previous cult hit *A Rebel Without a Cause* (1955) and Hunter's good looks. With a running time of three hours, the story was a pastiche of the gospels' accounts combined with *imagined* scenes and characters, which most reviewers considered flabby and boring. It was, in fact, a box office disaster.

Another Jesus of the 1960s was portrayed by the Swedish actor Max Von Sydow, in George Stevens's *The Greatest Story Ever Told* (1965). Stevens claimed that he was going to make an "authentic" version of the Jesus story, but as many critics pointed out, Stevens ultimately succumbed to a more traditional, almost tableau (i.e., pageant) presentation.

Possibly the most powerful Jesus film in the 1960s (or, arguably, for all time) was *The Gospel According to Matthew* (1964) by avowed atheist and member of the Italian Communist Party, Pier Paolo Pasolini. While viewers today may not appreciate its raw, sometimes jarring cinematic style, it is imbued with an urgent energy that is certainly not present in its languid contemporaries. Passolini was attracted to what he perceived as a revolutionary spirit present in Matthew, proclaiming that he was the most "worldly" of all the evangelists. Further, he says he had in mind "to represent Christ as an intellectual in a world of poor people ready for revolution" (Stern, Jefford, and Deboua 1999). Pasolini made a controversial choice casting non-actors in many of the key roles, most notably Jesus portrayed by Enrique Irazoqui, a 23-year-old student from Spain, who in contrast with the usual placid portrayals of Christ, is at times, restless, impatient, and often just plain angry. Since Pasolini had the reputation of being Italy's *enfant terrible,* critics were expecting the worst prior to its release. Police were stationed in front of the theatre the night of its premiere, expecting angry protesters to disrupt the showing, but reaction was fairly contained and mild. While it was no darling of conservative Catholics, many were impressed with the respectful portrayal of the Matthian narrative. Pasolini even dedicated the film to Pope John XXIII.

Denny Arcand's *Jesus of Montreal* (1989) deserves special notice. It is not a strict portrayal of the life of Jesus, yet comes closest to possibly the most honest representation of the Christ story. Ostensibly about a troupe of French Canadian actors staging a somewhat controversial version of the Passion Play, it follows Daniel, the actor who portrays Jesus, as he becomes profoundly affected by the experience, eventually leading to his death (ultimately resurrected as many of his donated organs save the lives of others in an incredibly affecting montage at the end of the movie) thus changing the lives of his action troupe. Arcand's secondary theme of the degradation of art, often influences his choices in the use of biblical text and history. Perhaps one of the most brilliant moments of the film is when Daniel interrupts a commercial audition at a theatre by destroying the video equipment, much like Jesus overturning the money-changer tables in the Temple. This thematic intertwining and the off-center portrayal of Jesus (e.g., an actor playing Jesus) gives enough distance so that the charge of irreverence can never be charged.

As can be seen from the above-abbreviated survey, portraying Jesus in film has been a risky business for filmmakers. When attempting a pious, traditional representation, a movie often falls into a wooden *iconic* portrayal, usually boring the audiences. As Adele Reinhartz argues, "[t]he irony is that whereas the Gospels have inspired profound ideas and beliefs that have shaped Christian spirituality through the two millennia since Jesus' lifetime, their transformation on the silver screen almost always results in a superficial, shallow, simplistic representation of Jesus, his life and his significance for humankind" (Reinhartz 2006, 3). If, on the other hand, the filmmaker attempts a nontraditional rendering of Jesus, such at Scorsese's *Last Temptation of Christ,* the film is immediately branded as disrespectful, or worse, heretical. But not all films with religious themes are about the life of Christ. Most, in fact, are allegorical canvases reflecting current events and social sentimentalities, as was the case in postwar America in the 50s.

SAND, SANDALS, AND APPLE PIE

The decade of the 1950s was fraught with worldwide tension and uncertainty. The Korean War, the Soviet expansion into neighboring countries and their acquisition of the atom bomb that created a fear of an all-out nuclear holocaust, and the paranoia created by the activities of the House Committee on Unamerican Activities, certainly contributed to the tension during the decade. At the same time, the United States experienced a boost in its economy, and with that, along with a triumphant end to WWII, came a certain sense of national identity that had heretofore not been present.

At the same time, the 1950s gave us an unprecedented amount of religious spectaculars such as *The Robe* (1953), *The Ten Commandments* (1956), *Quo Vadis* (1951), *David and Bathsheba* (1951), *The Silver Chalice* (1954) and *Ben Hur* (1959), that became huge box office favorites. Given the uncertainty and anxiety of the times, this was no mere coincidence.

Gerald Forshey argues in his book, *American Religious and Biblical Spectaculars,* these films were not-so-subtle reflections of current issues. The unyielding Ramses in *The Ten Commandments,* and the erratic but dangerous Nero in *Quo Vadis* and *Silver Chalice* could easily have their counterparts in Hitler, Stalin, and Khrushchev of the contemporary world. "The use of history in religious and biblical spectaculars serves to keep us aware of our traditions and responsibilities," Forshey says, "imparting a sense of identity as both Americans and Judeo-Christians" (Forshey 1992, 10). This, according to Forshey, blurs the line between patriotism and religion, often using "faith" as a stand-in for "freedom."

When these so-called *Sandal and Sand* epics are viewed though the lens of political commentary, certain themes make themselves clearer. The story of Moses fighting the tyranny of a totalitarian dictator leading his people to a land of freedom. The 1959 version of *Ben Hur* differs significantly in its allegorical content from its earlier predecessor made in 1923 in its concern for the then current issue of the tensions in the newly established state of Israel and its Arab neighbors.

Forshey observes that the protagonists of these films were skeptical, burnt out, perpetually in a crisis of faith, much like the returning WWII veterans now disenchanted with the power of their nations and the global political landscape (Forshey 1992). In other words, what was our sacrifice all about? Most of the biblical epics' themes center around a very American-centric view of international affairs: often a righteous hero or force (America) transforming an unrighteous nation (the Soviet Union). Often even the publicity would blatantly state this agenda outright. In speaking of *Quo Vadis,* the studio press release stated that it wanted to make a film that "would carry a message of beauty and inspiration to the people of the earth" (Forshey 1992, 34). While there was much in these films to satisfy secular tastes (love and romance, epic battles and action sequences, and lush, exotic locations) most of these stories focused on the religious conversion of the unbeliever, and his rejection of the values of a powerful but corrupt government, leading ultimately to the hero's dedication in joining the forces of good to fight against the evil empire. This combination translated into great box office success for almost a decade and a half.

THE CHRIST STORY IN WESTERN CINEMA

Up until now, we have been discussing the actual depiction of the life of Jesus, and epic stories from the Bible, or those centered in biblical times. Consciously or unconsciously, however, Western Cinema popularizes the notion of a lone hero who sacrifices himself/herself for the greater good, or for an individual who represents humankind and has therefore been influenced by the story of Christ. Joseph Campbell identifies this as the *mono-myth* in *The Hero with a Thousand Faces* wherein he includes the Christ story as part of the collective myth of birth and rebirth (George Lucas famously used Campbell's study when writing *Star Wars*) (Campbell 1949). There are so many examples of Christ figures in films that it is beyond the scope of this article to present a comprehensive list. Instead, it might be easier to set criteria for deciding just what constitutes a "Christ" figure. I suggest five:

1. A mysterious figure that arrives in a crisis.
2. Some kind of gift is offered; either teaching, affection, or example.
3. Sacrifice; usually themselves.
4. Resurrection. This is a key element just as it is a key theological element in Christianity. *It is not a Christ story without a resurrection.*
5. Encounter with the figure is salvific or life-changing.

While there are many "save the day" hero-films, the list gets a little narrower and, frankly, interesting, when adhering to the above list. Here are a few recent examples:

Sermon on the Battlefield: *Platoon* (1986)

Oliver Stone's Academy Award–winning film about a young innocent, Private Chris Taylor, caught between the forces of good and evil (Sgt. Barnes) in the jungles of Vietnam in the form of two Platoon sergeants, Elias (who represents the Christ figure) and Barnes (evil incarnate). Taylor, baptized by his first wound, finds himself attracted to the animal fierceness of Barnes, yet greatly affected by the natural humanity of Elias. Eventually Elias sacrifices himself to prevent Taylor from following the same path as Barnes. Initially, Barnes appears to have killed Elias, but as the platoon is helicoptered out of the combat zone, Taylor witnesses Elias still alive—after Barnes had reported Elias had been killed by the enemy—running away from the advancing enemy, and eventually is gunned down, splayed on the ground, in a crucified position. Taylor looks over at Barnes, realizing the truth, breaking free of Evil's grip and illusion. The resurrection is subtle, but present: earlier in the movie, Elias tells Taylor he plans to come back as "wind, or fire—or a deer . . . yeah, a deer," and at the end Taylor wakes up to find a gentle deer watching from the edge of the forest. Taylor, through Elias's sacrifice, has learned the true nature of war and evil.

The Food of Salvation: *Babette's Feast* (1988)

A mysterious French woman arrives on the desolate shores of an isolated Danish Island employed as a cook by two elderly sisters who have been isolated against the sensual joys of life such as food, love, and happiness by a restrictive religious code taught to them by their father, a fire and brimstone preacher. Slowly, Babette introduces the unworldly sisters to the pleasure of good food, which breaks down the rigid beliefs inherited by their strict father. To commemorate the 100th anniversary of his death, the sisters decide to hold a dinner, and Babette begs the sisters to allow her to prepare the feast. Babette, who has won the lottery and can finally leave the tiny Danish village for her beloved France, sacrifices all her money on the ingredients for the meal, which puts the sisters, and their church followers, in a state of harmonious ecstasy. Babette's resurrection comes in the form of the meal itself; she is reborn as the great restaurateur that she was in France, once again able to fulfill her role as one who can enlighten the senses and thereby cleanse the soul. Her salvific power is evident in the bonding of the church members, and at the end of the film, dancing as if they were children again.

Saving the Future of Mankind: *Terminator 2: Judgment Day* (1991)

The old Terminator model, having been reprogrammed, returns from the future as the protector of the young and reluctant John Connor (who will eventually lead the rebels against the machines) against the seemingly unstoppable new threat of a new Terminator model sent to destroy him. During the course of the film, he gives future leader Connor, lessons in how to survive and, more importantly, how to believe in something worth fighting for. The Terminator eventually sacrifices himself in order to save Connor, and thus saves the future of the human race. The resurrection is subtle and convoluted, since the Terminator dies in the past but is created in the future; he will come again to rescue Connor.

The Sacrifice of Love: *Pirates of the Caribbean: At World's End* (2007)

In the first installment of this trilogy, Will Turner is found at sea by Elizabeth Swann. Upon first sight, he is instantly in love with her, and throughout the three films is constantly risking his life for her, eventually sacrificing his mortality in the third installment to save Elizabeth and his father. Through his sacrifice, evil is vanquished and everyone gets their moral compasses reset. He is resurrected as the new Davy Jones, charged with ferrying souls to the other world.

CONCLUSION

Religion and religious themes have played an important role in the imaginations of artists since recorded history, but those themes have arguably become much more visceral, and therefore more powerful since the invention of the motion picture. Very often these films become reflections of our own time and social location, mirroring the current political climate, moral attitudes, or our collective fears, as we have seen from Griffith's *Intolerance* to Gibson's *The Passion of the Christ*. Interestingly, the most powerful religious themes are often hidden in films that seem anything but religious, due in large part to our culture's unconscious assimilation of the Christ story into our every-day imagination. This phenomenon is not limited to Western cinema, but plays a role in Indian Films (even the Bollywood Spectaculars) and other world cultures. Indeed, there is a good chance we can find the sacred in any expression of art if we look hard enough.

See also Prime Time Religion; World Religion Aethetics.

Further Reading: Baugh, Lloyd. *Imagining the Divine: Jesus and Christ-Figures in Film.* Franklin, WI: Sheed and Ward, 1997; Beck, Avent Childress. "The Christian Allegorical Structure of Platoon." In *Screening the Sacred,* eds. Joel W. Martin and Conrad E. Ostwalt. San Francisco: Westview Press, 1995: 44–54; Bergesen, Albert J., and Andrew M. Greeley. *God in the Movies.* New Brunswick: Transaction Publishers, 2000; Butler, Ivan. *Religion in the Cinema.* Edited by Peter Cowie. The International Film Guide Series. New York: A. S. Barnes and Co., 1969; Campbell, Joseph. *The Hero with a Thousand Faces.* 1st ed. Bollingen Series. New York: Pantheon, 1949; Cawkwell, Tim. *The Filmgoer's Guide to God.* London: Darton, Longman, Todd, 2004; Dwyer, Rachel. *Filming the Gods: Religion and Indian Cinema.* New York: Routledge, 2006; Exum, J. Cheryl, ed. *The Bible in Film—the Bible and Film.* Boston: Brill, 2006; Forshey, Gerald. *American Religious and Biblical Spectaculars.* Westport, CT: Praeger Publishers, 1992; Landres, J. Shawn, and Michael Berenbaum, eds. *After the Passion Is Gone: American Religious Consequences.* Walnut Creek, CA: AltaMira, 2004; Locke, Maryel, and Charles Warren, eds. *Jean-Luc Godard's Hail Mary: Women and the Sacred in Film.* Carbondale: Southern Illinois University Press, 1993; Martin, Joel W., and Conrad E. Ostwalt, eds. *Screening the Sacred.* San Francisco: Westview Press, 1995; May, John R, ed. *New Image of Religious Film.* Kansas City: Sheed and Ward, 1997; May, John R, and Michael Bird, eds. *Religion in Film.* Knoxville: University of Tennessee Press, 1982; Paffenroth, Kim. *Gospel of the Living Dead: George Romero's Visions of Hell on Earth.* Waco, TX: Baylor University Press, 2006; Paietta, Ann C. *Saints, Clergy, and Other Religious Figures on Film and Television, 1895–2003.* Jefferson, N.C.: McFarland and Co., 2005; Plate, S. Brent, ed. *Representing*

Religion in World Cinema: Filmmaking, Mythmaking, Culture Making. Vol. 2, Religon/ Culture/Critique. New York: Palgrave Macmillan, 2003; Reinhartz, Adele. "History and Pseudo-History in the Jesus Film Genre." In *The Bible in Film—the Bible and Film,* ed. J. Cheryl Exum. Boston: Brill, 2006: 1–17; Silk, Mark. "Almost a Culture War: The Making of *the Passion* Controversy." In *After the Passion Is Gone: American Religious Consequences,* eds. J. Shawn Landres and Michael Berenbaum. Walnut Creek, CA: AltaMira, 2004: 348; Stern, Richard C., Clayton N. Jefford, and Guerric Debona, O.S.B. *Savior of the Silver Screen.* Mahwah, N.J.: Paulist Press, 1999; Stichele, Caroline Vander, and Todd Penner. "Passion for (the) Real? The Passion of the Christ and Its Critics." In *The Bible in Film—the Bible and Film,* ed. J. Cheryl Exum. Leiden: Brill, 2006: 18–36; Tatum, W. Barnes. *Jesus at the Movies: A Guide to the First Hundred Years: Revised & Expanded.* 2nd ed. Santa Rosa, CA: Polbridge Press, 2004; Thompson, David, and Ian Christie. *Scorsese on Scorsese: Revised Edition.* London: Faber and Faber, 2004; Wright, Melanie J. *Religion and Film: An Introduction.* New York: I. B. Tauris, 2007.

Remi Aubuchon

WORLD RELIGION AESTHETICS

the image *per se* is neither God nor any angel, but merely an aspect or hypostasis (*avasthā*) of God, who is in the last analysis without likeness (*amūrta*), not determined by form (*arūpa*), trans-form (*para- rūpa*).

(Coomaraswamy 1995, 129).

Divine representation in Hinduism is a highly complex subject and requires a great deal of discussion and nuance. It is possible to describe, in broad terms, some of the key ideas that relate to the material religious image, however. At first sight, one may be impressed by the sheer number and variety of images associated with Hindu worship. Yet, the multiplicity of divine images in Hinduism may be derived from a synthesis of images and names that stammer toward apprehension of the divine. It is *māyā*, or delusion, to adhere to a particular image as if it were in fact, the Ineffable. Brahman is thought to give devotees sight of divinity (*darsan*) in order to please and bless worthy worshipers. Before *darsan* is granted, the worshiper entreats the divine to enter in the sacral image (*murti*). At the end of the ritual, the worshipper bids the deity farewell, and thus renders the object profane. Interestingly, despite the preponderance of divine images in Hinduism and Bollywood productions, religious animation in India is a rather recent phenomenon.

In the Japanese religious aesthetic tradition, the Void is a formless Reality that flows through time and space—and it is apprehended in between, in a state of *mindlessness* (*mushin*). Richard B. Pilgrim, reflecting on the concepts of *between* (*ma*) and *emptiness* (*kū*), observes that they relate to Shinto, Buddhism, and the Tao Te Ching, and that they are variously understood. According to Pilgrim's analysis of the Japanese tradition, artistic ability is dependent on the artist's aesthetic intuition and receptivity to experience (Pilgrim 2006). Nature is spiritualized and approached by those who empty themselves of self. A religious ideal and aesthetic is to experience immediately the flow between time, space, and the spiritual. However, it is necessary to use visual or spoken language to refer to the Formless. Consequently, Zen Buddhists use religious imagery to ritualize Reality. For other Buddhists, shrine statues more closely mediate the reality they represent. Pilgrim quotes the Japanese poet Basho: "To learn [in this art] means to submerge oneself within the object, to perceive its delicate life and feel its feeling, out of which a poem forms itself" (Pilgrim 2006, 153). It may be that multimedia anime engenders something of the immediacy and holistic experience idealized in traditional Japanese religious aesthetics. If long exposure to cartoons (and other forms of multimedia) does in a sense *entertain us to death*, might a new form of mindlessness be fostered through what may at times be a religious art form? If so, how does this square with the traditional self-emptying, or kenotic, ideal?

Islam does not take such an ambiguous stance towards the arts and theology. In fact, the Qur' ān and hadith writings condemn attempts to depict God and foster artistic stylization of all living things. Lois Isben al Faruqi relates Islamic theological aesthetics to the doctrine of tawhid (Isben al Faruqi 1995). This monotheistic teaching regards God as absolutely holy and above all of creation. Nothing is to be compared with God, and all figural art is forbidden. As such, Islamic art is intentionally symbolic and ordered to illustrate ideas. In particular, through beautiful patterns, Islamic art attempts to broker mere insights or intuitions into God, and intimate who the human person is in relation to God. Sufis, alone, mystically view all things and persons as symbolic of the Numinous. Recently, an Islamic artist introduced figural cartoons (not animated) to represent each attribute of Allah (see also Isben al Faruqi 1995). His aim is to provide material suited for the religious education of modern children. Understandably, this has been a controversial move, and it remains to be seen whether or not these characters will be seen in an animated feature.

A study of Jewish theological aesthetics is sensitive to the seemingly divergent views in the Torah. Against the biblical prohibition to make or worship an image (Exodus 20:3–5) are injunctions to decorate cultic space and objects (Exodus 25:18–22). God even gifts, inspires, and commissions Bezalel "for workmanship of every kind" for one of these religious art projects (Exodus 31:3–5). There are scriptural indications that Solomon's ornate temple was adorned with figural images (1 Kings 7:27–37, 8:6–7) as well. Archeological findings in Dura Europos (modern day Iraq) and at Bet Alpha, a sixth-century synagogue, also reveal figural art—in addition to Greek influence—in Jewish liturgical space. In fact, Jewish artisans who signed their work at Bet Alpha, depict God's hand stretched toward Abraham. Figural art and Hellenistic symbols are evident at the burial sites of prominent rabbis too.

Interpreting this and other ancient data to reflect ambivalence in Jewish theological aesthetics, the Altshulers suggest that "norms regarding idolatrous imagery" varied from one community to another (Altshuler and Altshuler 1995). While there may be plurality in artistic form and content, however, Jewish usage seems more consistent. Torah, in fact, only proscribes images for profane use, not for sacred space. Torah further indicates what spirit is required for crafting cultic art. Might these distinctions actually serve catechetical and liturgical, doxological ends? Does Disney's animated *Prince of Egypt* cohere within the norms for imagery established by the Torah? Are its religious symbols within this medium fixed within profane or sacred "space"? Where is that space, in fact, located? By whom, how, and to what purpose is animated religious imagery usage determined? Are these things determined by the viewer, television/theater, virtual space (if posted online), the production company, agents, commercial sponsors, culture(s), the originating scriptural tradition, and/or others, collectively?

Theological aesthetics has been, at least at some point in history, a topic of interest to all major Christian denominations. The Bible attests to the perennial human desire to see God. Paul explicitly refers to the beauty of Christ, God Incarnate, if only fleetingly. Drawing on scriptural (particularly John 1:18; 2 Corinthians 4:18; 1 John 1–3), philosophical, and other historical sources, Patristic reflection on aesthetics is seminal, tangential, rather than sustained. The earliest systematic Christian treatise on this topic is Pseudo-Dionysius's *The Divine Names,* written around 650 C.E. Later, Justin Martyr refutes iconoclastic claims of idolatry with his *First Apology.* Other significant apologetic works are *The Divine Institutes* by Lactantius and some letters of Gregory the Great. In the Medieval East, there is lengthy, positive treatment of the icon by John of Damascus and Theodore of Studios. Western theologians of the period, notably John Scotus, Bonaventure, Thomas Aquinas, Julian of Norwich, Nicholas of Cusa, Bernard of Clairvaux, William of St. Thierry, and Meister Ekhart developed Patristic themes such as beauty and goodness, and the vision and praise of God through the arts. Dallas G. Denery II's study correlates late Western Medieval enthrallment with, and suspicion of, perspectivist optics with its conception of the human person, the *imago dei* (Denery 2005).

Iconoclast polemic and conciliar documents of the Reformation period reveal a divergent spectrum of Christian theological aesthetics; Jean Calvin's writings place him and his followers at the apophatic extreme, whereas the Catholic Church maintains its more kataphatic, sacramental approach to the arts. Martin Luther and Huldrych Zwingli maintain more moderate positions.

Later in the United States, Puritan theologian Jonathan Edwards writes enthusiastically and extensively on the beauty of God, nature. Edwards presents virtue as both beautiful and beatifying. Another American theologian, Friedrich D. E. Schleiermacher, highlights the partial quality of individual manifestations of the Beautiful. John Henry Newman sees apprehension of beauty and its motivational power as something distinct from the *visio dei* grasped by human conscience. Newman also describes human conduct in terms of beauty. Aesthetics developed by philosophers Immanuel Kant, Georg Hegel, and Søren Kirkegaard significantly contribute to the theological discussion. It is not until the twentieth century, however, that interest in theological aesthetics explodes.

Gesa Elsbeth Thiessen notes that theology has had to contend with World Wars I and II, nihilism, secularism, and is now contextualized by a period remarkable for its lack of common, definitive values. In this postmodern or even post-postmodern time, theological reflection delves further into such topics as imagination, creativity, art, faith, and seeing God, who reveals Godself as the Beautiful One. Artistic style, technique, and even movements, too, range over an unprecedentedly broad spectrum. Even everyday life is "aestheticized," according to Thiessen, and she asserts that art displays have somewhat displaced traditional sacred spaces in brokering kinds of contemplative experiences (Thiessen 2004, 203–204). Whereas the Impressionists tried to discover and memorialize the ephemeral flash of a moment, disclosing their contemplative insights into reality, animated film exploits these moments, not singly but by *rolling* directed, constructed scenes together. How are cartoons, then, a "disclosure of truth"—to use David Tracy's phrase? Where is the *locus* of truth in religious animation: the originating message and its Origin, the animator, the animation, the inspired viewer, or some complex interplay among them? What is the faith dimension of religious animation itself?

Pope John Paul II, aware of new psychology and language evident in, and engendered by the modern cultural milieu, calls for a New Evangelization, one that will integrate these phenomena in rendering the Gospel message intelligible to modern people (Pope John Paul II at the beginning of the Third Millennium, http://www.ewtn.com/library/papaldoc/jpmil3.htm). At the same time, the Vatican is critical of the secularism, "suggestive power," and value content of the media that is incompatible with that of the "culture of the Beatitudes" and Christ himself (Pontifical Council for Culture 1999, 10). Church documents speak explicitly of the evangelizing and catechetical value of beautiful art. Nowhere are cartoons explicitly mentioned, though the documents do not outright deny their religious potential. Thinkers such as Harvey Cox advise against taking a theological, highbrow approach to art over and above popular culture. As such, it will be important to specifically consider the theological aesthetics of cartoons, and religious animation in particular. This evaluation should grapple not only with their storytelling potential and value content, but also attempt to confront the kind(s) of psychology associated with these products. How does this psychology compare to that of conversion, faith, and contemplation in children and adults? How will Christian communities be intentionally responsive to this new psychology in order to foster personal encounter and decision necessary for discipleship? How will these communities contend with anti-religious sentiment and syncretism evident at times in products such as *South Park* and some anime?

See also Graphic Arts; Western Cinema.

Further Reading: Altshuler, David and Linda Altshuler. "Judaism and Art." In *Art, Creativity, and the Sacred*, 1995: 155–63; Baugh, Lloyd. *Imagining the Divine: Jesus and Christ-Figures in Film*. Franklin, WI: Sheed and Ward, 1997: 8–9; Beck, Avent Childress. "The Christian Allegorical Structure of Platoon." In *Screening the Sacred*, eds. Joel W. Martin and Conrad E. Ostwalt. San Francisco: Westview Press, 1995: 51; Campbell, Joseph. *The Hero with a Thousand Faces*. 1st ed. Bollingen Series. New York: Pantheon, 1949: 349; Coomaraswamy, Ananda K. "The Origin and Use of Images in India." In *Art, Creativity and the Sacred*, ed. Diane Apostolos-Cappadora. New York: Continuum International, 1995: 127–37; Denery, Dallas G., II. *Seeing and Being Seen in the Later Medieval World: Optics, Theology, and Religious Life*. Cambridge: Cambridge University Press, 2005; Forshey, Gerald. *American Religious and Biblical Spectaculars*. Westport, CT: Praeger Publishers, 1992; Isben al Faruqi, Lois. "An Islamic Perspective on Symbolism in the Arts."

In *Art, Creativity, and the Sacred,* 1995: 164–78; Landres, J. Shawn and Michael Berenbaum, eds. *After the Passion Is Gone: American Religious Consequences.* Walnut Creek, CA: AltaMira, 2004; Paffenroth, Kim. *Gospel of the Living Dead: George Romero's Visions of Hell on Earth.* Waco, TX: Baylor University Press, 2006; Pilgrim, Richard B. "Religio-Aesthetic Tradition in Japan." In *Art, Creativity and the Sacred*, 1995: 138–54; Pontifical Council for Culture. *Toward a Pastoral Approach to Culture,* May 23, 1999 (10); Pope John Paul II. Theological Aesthetics, 203–4; *Redemptoris* Missio (37); Reinhartz, Adele. "History and Pseudo-History in the Jesus Film Genre." In *The Bible in Film—the Bible and Film,* ed. J. Cheryl Exum. Boston: Brill, 2006; Stern, Richard C., Clayton N. Jefford, and Guerric Debona, O.S.B. *Savior of the Silver Screen.* Mahwah, NJ: Paulist Press, 1999: 191–92; Stichele, Caroline Vander and Todd Penner. "Passion for (the) Real? The Passion of the Christ and Its Critics." In *The Bible in Film—the Bible and Film,* ed. J. Cheryl Exum. Leiden: Brill, 2006: 23; Tatum, W. Barnes. *Jesus at the Movies: A Guide to the First Hundred Years: Revised & Expanded.* 2nd ed. Santa Rosa, CA: Polbridge Press, 2004: 3–4; Thiessen, Gesa E. *Theological Aesthetics: A Reader.* Grand Rapids, MI: Eerdmans, 2004; Thompson, David, and Ian Christie. *Scorsese on Scorsese.* Revised ed. London: Faber and Faber, 2004: 124.

Deborah Pavelek

BIBLIOGRAPHY

Breger, Marshall J. *Public Policy and Social Issues: Jewish Sources and Perspectives*. Westport, CT: Praeger, 2003.

Brockopp, Jonathan. "Islamic Ethics of Life: Abortion, War, and Euthanasia." In *Studies in Comparative Religion*. Columbia: University of South Carolina Press, 2003.

Campolo, Tony. *Red Letter Christians: A Citizen's Guide to Faith and Politics*. Ventura, CA: Regal, 2008.

Cohen, Cynthia. *A Christian Response to the New Genetics: Religious, Ethical, and Social Issues*. New York: Rowen and Littefield, 2003.

Curran, Charles. *Catholic Moral Theology in the United States: A History*. Moral Traditions. Washington DC: Georgetown, 2008.

De la Torre, Miguel. *Doing Christian Ethics From The Margins*. New York: Orbis, 2004.

Dorff, Elliot. *Contemporary Jewish Ethics and Morality: A Reader*. Oxford: Oxford University Press, 1995.

Dorff, Elliot. *Love Your Neighbor and Yourself: A Jewish Approach to Modern Personal Ethics*. New York: Jewish Publication Society of America, 2003.

Fasching, Darrell J., and Dell Dechant. *Comparative Religious Ethics: A Narrative Approach*. New York: Wiley-Blackwell, 2001.

Greenspahn, Frederick. *Contemporary Ethical Issues in the Jewish and Christian Traditions*. New York: KTAV, 1986.

Hashmy, Sohail H., ed. *Islamic Political Ethics: Civil Society, Pluralism, and Conflict*. Ethikon Series in Comparative Ethics. Princeton: Princeton University Press, 2002.

Heyer, Kristin. *Prophetic and Public: The Social Witness of U.S. Catholicism*. Moral Traditions. Washington DC: Georgetown, 2006.

Jung, Patricia Beattie, and Shannon Jung. *Moral Issues and Christian Responses*. 7th ed. Belmont CA: Wadsworth, 2002.

Paris, Peter J. *The Social Teaching of the Black Churches.* Minneapolis: Augsburg/Fortress Press, 1985.

Pearson, James M., and Kelly Hahn. *Minefields in the Marketplace: Ethical Issues Christians Face in the World of Business.* Schuler, NE: BMH Books, 2005.

Rasmussen, Larry L., and Bruce Birch. *Bible and Ethics in the Christian Life.* Minneapolis: Augsburg, 1989.

Rispler-Chaim, Vardit. *Islamic Medical Ethics in the Twentieth Century* . Social, Economic and Political Studies of the Middle East and Asia. Leiden: E.J. Brill, 1993.

Sajoo, Amyn. *Muslim Ethics: Emerging Vistas.* London: I.B. Taurus, 2008.

Sanders, Cheryl J. *Empowerment Ethics for a Liberated People.* Minneapolis: Augsburg, 1995.

Snyder, T. Richard. *The Protestant Ethic and the Spirit of Punishment.* Grand Rapids: Eerdmans, 2000.

Stassen, Glen H. *Just Peacemaking: The New Paradigm for the Ethics of Peace and War.* Cleveland: Pilgrim Press, 2008.

Stivers, Robert L., Christine E. Gudorf, Alice Frazer Evans, and Robert Evans. *Christian Ethics: A Case Method Approach.* 3rd ed. New York: Orbis, 2005.

Stott, John R.W., John Wyatt and Roy McCloughry, eds. *Issues Facing Christians Today.* Grand Rapids: Zondervan, 2006.

Zoloth-Dorfman, Laurie. *Health Care and the Ethics of Encounter: A Jewish Discussion of Social Justice.* Studies in Social Medicine. Chapel Hill: University of North Carolina Press, 1999.

ABOUT THE EDITORS AND CONTRIBUTORS

Daniel L. Smith-Christopher is Professor of Theological Studies at Loyola Marymount University. Dr. Smith-Christopher specializes in Biblical Theology, especially Biblical and Theological issues in relation to contemporary issues of social justice and peace. He also serves as Director of Peace Studies at LMU. Among his most recent books is *Subverting Hatred: The Challenge of Nonviolence in World Religions* (1997, 2007), and a book on reading the Bible for Peace and Justice titled: *Jonah, Jesus, and Other Good Coyotes: Speaking Peace to Power in the Bible* (2007).

Laura Ammon (PhD Claremont) is Assistant Professor of Religious Studies at the University of North Florida. Dr. Ammon teaches and conducts research in Patristic and Medieval Christianities, Christianities in the Early Modern World, Theories of Religion, and Women in Christianity.

Remi Aubuchon, in addition to his current work in Theological Studies, is an accomplished American screenwriter. He is a respected theater director who trained under an American Film Institute Directors Fellowship, but found himself in demand as a screenwriter. He wrote segments for HBO's miniseries *From the Earth to the Moon*. He created, wrote, and produced the television series *The Lyon's Den*. He served as the executive producer of *Summerland*, a co-executive producer and writer for the second season of *24*, and is co-creator and wrote the pilot for the *Battlestar Galactica* prequel series *Caprica*.

Jack Balswick (PhD Iowa) has taught at Fuller Theological Seminary since 1982. His research in marriage and family issues, and religious mental health, has led to more than 50 articles, monographs, and books, the more recent of which are *Family Pain* (1997) and *The Family: A Christian Perspective of the Contemporary Home*

(1999). Jack's newest book is *Parenting for Life: Building Family Relationships that Last,* coauthored with his wife, Judy, and with Boni and Don Piper (2003).

Judith K. Balswick is Senior Professor of Marital and Family Therapy in the Department of Marriage and Family, School of Psychology at Fuller Theological Seminary in Pasadena, CA.

Gerald Beisecker-Mast is Professor of Communications at Bluffton University in Bluffton, Ohio. Among his most recent books are *Separation and the Sword in Anabaptist Persuasion: Radical Confessional Rhetoric from Schleitheim to Dordrecht* (2006), and *Teaching Peace: Nonviolence and the Liberal Arts,* co-edited with J. Denny Weaver (2003).

Paul Boudreau is a priest of the Catholic Diocese of Norwich, CT. After his graduate studies at Bl. John XXIII National Seminary in Weston, MA, he was a parish priest and taught Pastoral Scripture Studies at Sacred Heart University's Institute for Religious Education and Pastoral Studies in Bridgeport, CT. Along with his work as an award-winning feature writer for *U.S. Catholic* magazine, and a monthly columnist for *Today's Parish Minister,* he is author of *Between Sundays: Daily Gospel Reflections and Prayers* (2001), and is coauthor with Alice Camille, MDiv., of *The Forgiveness Book* (2008).

Elizabeth Brinkmann, R.S.C.J. (PhD Boston College) is chair of the Religious Studies and Philosophy Department at the College of New Rochelle in New Rochelle, New York. Dr. Brinkmann teaches and writes in the fields of sexual and biomedical ethics. Publications include articles in *Scripture Today* and *New Theology Review* as well as *Rhetoric and a Consistent Ethic of Life: Some Ethical Considerations* in a forthcoming volume of essays on the *Consistent Ethic of Life.*

Christopher Key Chapple (PhD Fordham) is the Navin and Pratima Doshi Professor of Indic and Comparative Theology at Loyola Marymount University in Los Angeles. A specialist in the religions of India, he has published twelve books, including *Karma and Creativity,* a co-translation of Patanjali's Yoga Sutra (2002), *Nonviolence to Animals, Earth* (1995), and several edited volumes on Religion and Ecology, including *Hinduism and Ecology and Jainism and Ecology* (2000). In 2002 he established the Yoga Studies program at LMU Extension's Center for Religion and Spirituality.

Charles Conniry Jr., PhD is Dean and Vice President of George Fox Evangelical Seminary, a graduate school of George Fox University. Academic background: BA, American Christian School of Religion; MDiv, Bethel Theological Seminary; Ph.D., Fuller Theological Seminary. Expertise and research interests include Christian Spiritual Discernment; American Religious History; Postmodern Philosophy; Postmodern Theology; Systematic Theology; and Praxis-based pedagogy.

Robert V. Doyle, MA is a doctoral candidate in Health Care Ethics (with a focus on Catholic Health Care) at Saint Louis University (St. Louis, MO). He recently received a Master's degree in Bioethics from Loyola Marymount University (Los

Angeles, CA) where he previously completed an MA in Theology, specializing in Christian Ethics. His Master's thesis, entitled *Framework for a Christian Common Good: Toward a Shared Ethic*, explored an ecumenical approach to the common good, culminating in universal health care access.

Mara Einstein (PhD New York University) is an Associate Professor of media studies at Queens College, as well as adjunct Associate Professor at the Stern School of Business at New York University. She has worked as an executive at NBC, MTV Networks, and at major advertising agencies. Her first book, *Media Diversity: Economics, Ownership and the FCC* (2004), was the cause for much debate when research from this work was used by the FCC as the basis for redefining the media ownership rules. She is the author, most recently, of *Brands of Faith: Marketing Religion in a Commercial Age* (Routledge, 2008).

Joel B. Green holds a PhD in New Testament Studies and has also done graduate work in neuroscience at the University of Kentucky. He has written extensively at the interface of theology and science, including his book, *Body, Soul, and Human Life* (2008). Green is Professor of New Testament Interpretation and Associate Dean for the Center for Advanced Theological Studies, Fuller Theological Seminary.

Ed Higgins (PhD Union Institute) is Professor of Writing/Literature at George Fox University in Newberg, Oregon. He is a poet, fiction writer, and essayist with a wide range of writing publications. He also is a part-time farmer, who draws much of his writing inspiration from his back-to-the-land experiences. His teaching specialties include fiction writing, science fiction, the contemporary novel, and values issues in literature.

Gerald Iversen served as the National Coordinator of Alternatives for Simple Living, 1995–2007 (SimpleLiving.org). A Minister of Music for 25 years, he is an Associate in Ministry in the Evangelical Lutheran Church in America (ELCA). He also served as a Development Director for Public Radio for 18 years. He holds masters' degrees in journalism and music, and two national music certifications.

Dwight J. Kimberly, M.S., is Associate Professor of Biology at George Fox University in Newberg, Oregon.

Nicholas J. Kockler, M.S., PhD, is Assistant Professor in the Bioethics Institute of Loyola Marymount University. He also serves as a clinical bioethics consultant for a Catholic health care organization in Los Angeles.

Candace Lev (AAS, BSN) is currently enrolled at Youngstown State University in Youngstown, Ohio, where she is pursuing a degree in Religious Studies.

Darnise C. Martin earned a PhD in cultural and historical studies from the Graduate Theological Union in Berkeley, California. She is currently Visiting Professor of African-American Studies at Loyola Marymount University, Los Angeles. She is the author of *Beyond Christianity: African Americans in a New Thought Church* (2005).

Ron Mock (JD Michigan) is Associate Professor of Political Science and Peace Studies at George Fox University in Newberg, Oregon, and serves as Director of the University Scholars Program and is Prelaw Advisor. Among his most recent works is: *Loving Without Giving In: Christian Responses to Terrorism and Tyranny* (2004), and he also collaborated with others to coauthor *When The Rain Returns: Toward Justice and Reconciliation in Israel and Palestine* (2005), a study highlighting Quaker responses to the Israeli-Palestinian conflict.

Lourdes E. Morales-Gudmundsson is Professor of Spanish Language and Literature at La Sierra University. Her doctorate from Brown University is in the area of religion and literature with a specialization in Golden Age Spanish literature. Her most recent book, *I FORGIVE YOU, BUT . . .* (2007), is available in English and Spanish.

T. Vail Palmer Jr. (PhD Chicago) is a recorded minister in Freedom Friends Church, Salem, Oregon. He has been clerk of the Center for Christian Studies at Reedwood Friends Church, Portland, Oregon. He has also been editor of *Quaker Religious Thought*, and Professor of Philosophy and Religion, and Chairman of the Department of Social and Behavioral Sciences, at Rio Grande College (in Ohio).

Deborah Pavelek (MA Loyola Marymount University) currently teaches Religious Studies at Blanchett Catholic High School in Salem, Oregon. Pavelek studied media and ministry and the theology of communication under Rose Paquette, FSP and Joanna Puntel, FSP. She has participated in National Film Retreats and City of Angels Film Festivals.

Stephen Potthof is Assistant Professor of Religion and Philosophy at Wilmington College in Wilmington, Ohio. His primary research interests include religion and ecology, indigenous traditions, and dream and visionary experience.

Randall Reed (PhD Chicago) is Assistant Professor of Religion at Appalachian State University in North Carolina. He teaches Religion and Social Theory and New Testament Studies. His latest book is *A Clash of Ideologies: Marxism, Liberation Theology and Apocalypticism in New Testament Studies* (2008).

Jonathan Rothchild (PhD Chicago) is Assistant Professor of Theological Studies at Loyola Marymount University in Los Angeles. Dr. Rothchild analyzes contemporary moral issues and social and legal structures through the lenses of Christian theology and ethics.

Stephen Sauer, S.J. (STD Catholic University) is Assistant Professor of Theological Studies at Loyola Marymount University. Fr. Sauer teaches in the areas of sacramental theology and liturgy, with special interests in the areas of lay ministerial preparation, and contemporary approaches to the celebration of, and discourse on the sacraments.

Elizabeth Shaw is a Political Science and Peace Studies student, and immigration activist, who has lived near the U.S.–Mexico border while growing up in Glendale, Arizona, and going to Loyola Marymount University in Los Angeles.

Elizabeth has worked in recent years with the Office of Peace and Justice Catholic Charities, No More Deaths, and the Arizona Interfaith Network.

Jeffrey S. Siker (PhD Princeton) is Professor of Theological Studies and Chair of the Department at Loyola Marymount University in Los Angeles. Dr. Siker teaches and publishes in the area of New Testament studies. He is the author of *Disinheriting the Jew: Abraham in Early Christian Controversy* (1991) and *Scripture and Ethics: Twentieth Century Portraits* (1996). He is also the editor of *Homosexuality in the Church: Both Sides of the Debate* (2006).

Phil Smith (PhD Oregon) specializes in Ethical Theory and Religious Studies. He is Professor of Philosophy and Head of the Department of Religion and Philosophy at George Fox University in Newberg, Oregon.

Tracy Sayuki Tiemeier (PhD Boston College) is Assistant Professor of Theological Studies at Loyola Marymount University in Los Angeles. Dr. Tiemeier's teaching and research interests include Hinduism, comparative theology, contemporary theological anthropologies and identity politics, Asian and Asian American theologies, feminist theologies, and post-colonial theory.

James J. Walter is the Austin and Ann O'Malley Professor of Bioethics and chair of the Bioethics Institute at Loyola Marymount University. He received his PhD in ethics from the Catholic University of Louvain in Belgium, and he has published widely in the field of bioethics.

Earl Zimmerman (PhD Catholic University) has been the Assistant Professor of Bible and Religion at Eastern Mennonite University, Harrisonburg, Virginia, and a Pastor at Shalom Mennonite Congregation. He recently published *Practicing the Politics of Jesus* (2007).

INDEX

ABC (Abstinence, Being, Condoms), 19–20

Abduh, Muhammad, 293

Abortion: aspects of, 1; bioethical issues on, 5–7; causes of, 8–9; court judgments pertaining to, 6–7; on demand, 3; effects of, 8–9; legalities of, history and, 2; political governing of, 7; purpose of, 1–2; societal factors and, 8–9; statistics of, current, 1. *See also* Birth control; Theological debate

Active *vs.* passive euthanasia, 142, 143

Acute rejection, 376

Addiction: alcoholism as a disease, treatment of, 11–14; economic motives of, influential, 14–15; organizations used for treatment of, 13; recovery from, 16; recovery industry, approach to treatment of, 10; religious views on, 10–11, 15–16; societal views on, 10–11; theological debate pertaining to, 13, 16

Ad Hoc Committee on Sexual Abuse, 105

Adventists, 240, 241

Advertising and religion, 324

Afghanistan, 402–3

Africa, 42, 249, 366

African Americans: death penalty and, 82; entrepreneurships of, 347; Fard Muhammad, role of, 343; Malcolm X, importance of, 341, 344–45; Million Man March, role of, 346; Muslims, 334–35; Muslims, role of, 341–42; nationalist movements for, 341–42; Nation of Islam (NOI), role of, 341–47; racism, forms of, 342; religion and civil disobedience,

100; rock music, 433–34; values of, 343–44

AIDS (Acquired Immune Deficiency Syndrome): birth control and, 69–70; causes of, 22–23; defined, 17; drugs, treatment and cost of, 18, 21; economic conditions related to, 23; history of, 17–18; organizations for treatment of, 19; prevention of, 23; religious concerns for, 17; societal conditions related to, 23. *See also* Human Immunodeficiency Virus (HIV)

Al-Afghani, 292–93

Al-Banna, Hasan, 294

Alcoholics Anonymous: alcoholism as a disease and, 11–14; concerns regarding, 13; controversies regarding, 12–13; founding of, 11; monitoring, role of, 13–14; religious organizations, commitment to, 15–16; Twelve Step program of, 11–12, 15–16

Alcoholism as a disease: addiction, treatment of, 11–14; Alcoholics Anonymous, 11–14; attitudes, changes in, 11–14; history of, 11; organizations for treatment of, 11; political advocacy pertaining to treatment of, 14; societal views on rising statistics of, 11–14; theological debate pertaining to, 11. *See also* Alcoholics Anonymous

Aliens: astrobiology, search for, 26–27; belief in, history of, 29; Christianity, ancient assumptions of sky and, 24, 29; conceptualization of, 28; cosmotheology, study of, 27, 29; habitable planets,